Modernizing VATs in Africa

Modernizing VATs in Africa

SIJBREN CNOSSEN
University of Pretoria &
CPB Netherlands Bureau for Economic Policy Analysis

OXFORD
UNIVERSITY PRESS

OXFORD
UNIVERSITY PRESS

Great Clarendon Street, Oxford, OX2 6DP,
United Kingdom

Oxford University Press is a department of the University of Oxford.
It furthers the University's objective of excellence in research, scholarship,
and education by publishing worldwide. Oxford is a registered trade mark of
Oxford University Press in the UK and in certain other countries

First Edition published in 2019

Published in the United States of America by Oxford University Press
198 Madison Avenue, New York, NY 10016, United States of America

British Library Cataloguing in Publication Data
Data available

Library of Congress Control Number: 2019934001

ISBN 978–0–19–884407–5

To my VAT students in the Master's Programme in Taxation of the African Tax Institute at the University of Pretoria

One [general lesson] is the political difficulty of making sensible changes to a VAT once it has been introduced: mistakes made at introduction are hard to undo.

(Keen, 2009)

We all now know that good VAT design makes good VAT administration easier and that bad design may make good administration almost impossible.

(Bird and Gendron, 2007)

Efficient regressive taxes (such as the VAT) when combined with generous well-targeted transfers can result in a net fiscal system that is equalizing.

(Lustig, 2017)

Contents

List of Figures

List of Tables

List of Boxes

1
Why VAT?

1.1 Introduction

In the past 30 years, 45 out of the 54 countries on the African continent[1] have introduced the value-added tax (hereinafter 'VAT')[2] as their main broad-based consumption tax. In doing so, they followed a worldwide trend that started in the late 1960s in the European Union (EU) and South America and spread from there across the rest of the world (Cnossen, 1998a; Ebrill et al., 2001).[3] Most African countries introduced a VAT around the turn of the century, but some have done so more recently. The DR Congo, the Seychelles, and Swaziland converted their sales taxes into a VAT in 2012. The Gambia followed their example in 2013, making it the latest member of the African VAT club. Ghana is the only African country that ever removed the VAT (two months after its introduction in 1995), only to reinstate it three years later (Terkper, 1996, 2000). Nine countries in Africa, one in six of all countries on the continent, do not (yet) have a VAT.

In theory, a well-designed VAT is the consumption tax of choice, because it is highly successful in freeing exports from tax and treating imports on a par with domestically produced goods and services through appropriate border tax adjustments (imports taxed, exports free of tax). This neutrality feature is important for the proper functioning of trade within regional economic development communities, which purport to abolish (implicit) discriminatory taxes on imports and subsidies on exports. All countries in Africa belong to one of eight regional economic communities on the continent, distinguished in this book, which attempt to facilitate trade among their members. More generally, the border tax adjustments under VAT are compatible with the tax provisions of the World Trade

[1] Not counting Western Sahara, which does not have an institutionalized tax system and whose sovereignty is disputed. The United Nations does not recognize Morocco's claim on the country or the self-proclaimed Sahrawi Arab Democratic Republic, although the latter is a member of the African Union.

[2] In some countries, the VAT is called goods and services tax (GST) but, as is well known, in principle the GST and VAT are identical taxes. In references, this book follows the particular country's usage, whether VAT or GST.

[3] The VAT was pioneered by Siemens (1920) in Germany who called it the 'improved turnover tax' (as reflected in its multistage nature) and Adams (1921) in the USA who referred to it as a tax on 'modified gross income' (in other words, gross profits, the difference between sales and purchases), but was improved by Lauré (1953, 1957), called '*le père de la TVA*' (*taxe à la valeur ajoutée*), in France. An early account of the history of the VAT can be found in Sullivan (1965). Recently, James (2015) provided a detailed account of the worldwide rise of the VAT. There is some confusion about the exact year of Siemens's proposal, but Pohmer (1983) and Terra and Kajus (2007) point towards 1919.

Organization (WTO), which seeks to replace protective import duties by general consumption taxes, such as the VAT, in an effort to promote regional and global trade (Ebrill, Stotsky, and Gropp, 1999).

In addition to being neutral with respect to foreign trade, a well-designed and well-administered VAT does not distort domestic production and distribution. Thus, under the VAT, it makes no difference to the tax liability how often a product is traded before it reaches the consumer, whether its value is added early rather than late in the production–distribution process, whether the product is manufactured with capital- or labour-intensive technology, or whether a taxable business is incorporated or not. Obviously, these features are important attributes of a 'good' consumption tax in economies that leave the optimal allocation of resources to the free play of market forces. Beyond that, the VAT is a productive, stable, and flexible source of government revenue. Since the VAT is collected on a current basis—say, monthly—its revenue-generating capacity is not negatively affected by inflation and the effect of rate changes on revenue is immediately visible.

This is the theory. In practice, a badly designed and/or badly administered VAT may turn into a highly non-neutral sales tax, possibly worse than the taxes it replaced. If refunds with respect to exports are not made or are not timely, the VAT becomes a tax on exporters, hampering investment. Similarly, if the VAT on imports cannot be credited forthwith against the VAT on domestic sales (if necessary, involving a refund if the VAT on imports exceeds the VAT on domestic supplies), the VAT becomes a tax on imports. More generally, a less than full and immediate tax credit with respect to inputs (including capital goods) turns the VAT into a cumulative turnover tax, which distorts consumer and producer choices and provides an incentive for the non-economic integration of business activities. Moreover, a VAT that effectively functions as a turnover tax tends to make the tax burden distribution more regressive, because the value of essential products, disproportionately consumed by the poor, is usually added early in the production–distribution process. Hence, the VAT on them is subject to more cascading (tax-on-tax effects) than the VAT on luxury goods and services.

1.2 VAT's Role in Africa's Tax Systems

Africa is often called the most promising continent of the twenty-first century. Living standards are expected to rise considerably in tandem with sustained economic growth.[4] But this is unlikely to come about without additional publicly financed investment in education, healthcare, public utilities, and transportation systems. Unfortunately, most government budgets are too small to make this

[4] In a cautious assessment, Rodrik (2014) expects moderate and steady growth of perhaps as much as 2% per capita. He believes that the traditional engines behind rapid growth—structural change and industrialization—still seem to be operating at less than full power.

possible. In about half of all countries on the continent, tax revenue as a percentage of GDP (called the tax ratio) is around 15 per cent or less, which is not enough to finance more human and economic development. Until recently, financial aid from developed countries could be used to finance public investment and shortfalls in current government budgets, but this source has largely dried up after the 2007–08 recession in the industrialized world.

This means that domestic tax revenue mobilization is called for if economic development is to proceed (also Bird and Gendron (2007) and International Monetary Fund (2017)). Whether or not tax ratios can be increased depends on each country's tax capacity—i.e. the tax revenue (expressed as a percentage of GDP) that can be raised in light of the country's economic and institutional environment. To the extent that a country is not fully realizing its tax capacity, its tax effort—i.e. the actual tax ratio as a fraction of tax capacity—is less than 1. The difference between 1 and the tax effort therefore indicates how much more a country can do to mobilize domestic tax revenue.

The tax capacities and tax efforts of several African (and other) countries have been calculated by Fenochietto and Pessino (2013), who use an econometric model to build a 'stochastic tax frontier' for panel data from 25 African (and 88 other) countries covering the period 1991–2012. Country-specific demographic, economic, and institutional characteristics that may change over time are taken into account. Table 1.1 shows the results for 25 African countries that have a VAT. Guesstimates have been added for the 20 countries not covered by Fenochietto and Pessino, derived on the basis of the same variables they use, as to whether each country's tax effort is likely to be low, medium, or high (see Cnossen (2015)).

In all, 17 out of 45 countries with a VAT can be classified as low-tax-effort countries, meaning that they collect two-thirds or less of the revenue that they can be expected to raise in view of their institutional and economic circumstances. In 20 other countries, the tax effort is labelled medium: the gap between tax effort and tax capacity is one-third to one-fifth of tax capacity. Eight countries exhibit a high tax effort.[5] Malawi, one of the poorest countries in Africa, with a per-capita income of US$1,100 in 2016 (purchasing power parity, PPP), has a high tax effort. Egypt, a middle-income country by African standards, with a per-capita income of US$11,100 in the same year, has a low tax effort.

The difference between the tax ratio and tax capacity represents the tax policy gap (exemptions and concessional rates), among other factors, rather than the compliance gap (inadequate enforcement and evasion), which is reflected in each country's proxies for the economic and institutional environment. This book focuses mainly on the policy gap of the VAT, which is often the most important source of tax revenue in African countries. As a revenue-raising instrument, the

[5] The high tax effort in Lesotho, Namibia, and Swaziland can partly be explained by the fact that the South African Revenue Service (SARS) collects the import and excise duties for these countries under the umbrella of the Southern African Customs Union (SACU).

Table 1.1 Africa: tax ratios, tax capacity, and tax effort in VAT countries

Country	Tax ratio (%)	Tax capacity (%)	Tax effort	Other countries whose tax effort is likely to be low/medium/high
Low tax effort (0.67 or lower)				
Guinea–Bissau	9.0	27.4	0.33	Central African Republic, Chad, DR Congo, Rwanda, Sierra Leone, Sudan
Egypt	16.7	35.9	0.46	
Algeria	16.8	36.1	0.47	
Cameroon	12.8	24.4	0.52	
Ghana	16.9	32.1	0.52	
Gambia	12.3	21.1	0.58	
Tanzania	15.3	26.0	0.59	
Madagascar	10.8	17.0	0.63	
Uganda	12.4	19.1	0.65	
Ethiopia	11.3	17.0	0.66	
Burkina Faso	14.1	21.0	0.67	
Medium tax effort (0.68–0.80)				
Congo	27.2	38.5	0.71	Benin, Botswana, Burundi, Cabo Verde, Côte d'Ivoire, Djibouti, Equatorial Guinea, Gabon, Mauritania, Mauritius
Niger	13.5	18.8	0.72	
South Africa	27.8	38.2	0.73	
Tunisia	25.5	34.6	0.74	
Senegal	19.4	26.0	0.75	
Kenya	20.7	27.1	0.76	
Mali	14.4	18.8	0.77	
Guinea	14.8	18.9	0.78	
Togo	15.9	20.1	0.79	
Morocco	24.3	30.4	0.80	
High tax effort (0.81 or higher)				
Mozambique	18.2	21.4	0.85	Lesotho, Seychelles, Swaziland, Zimbabwe
Namibia	25.3	27.8	0.91	
Malawi	23.3	23.8	0.98	
Zambia	16.6	17.0	0.98	

Note: Countries are ranked in ascending order of tax effort.

Source: Fenochietto and Pessino (2013, appendix 2) and the author's assessment based on the economic and institutional indicators used by Fenochietto and Pessino.

VAT is generally regarded as an easier tax handle and less detrimental to economic growth than the income tax.[6] VAT revenue enhancement should also make it possible to replace the loss of revenue from import duties, which have to be phased out if closer economic integration and outward orientation, which promote growth, are to be pursued in line with WTO guidelines.

In many African countries, the VAT does not live up to its revenue-raising potential. When introducing the VAT, most countries exempted or zero-rated a wide range of consumer goods, so much so that the so-called standard rate may

[6] Empirical evidence collected by Arnold et al. (2011), for instance, suggests that income taxes reduce the rate of economic growth more than consumption taxes do.

be labelled a luxury goods rate, because it is imposed on goods that are mostly consumed by higher-income groups.[7] What should be the 'actual' standard rate is in fact a set of varying effective rates on exempt consumer goods that differ depending upon the ratio of the tax on inputs, which are used to produce these goods, to price. These rates are capricious and indeterminate; their incidence cannot be determined and the tax on inputs may enter into the price of goods traded across borders.

The wide-ranging non-standard exemptions (so-called because they go beyond the standard exemptions found in the EU—which are quite comprehensive themselves) and zero rates on domestically consumed goods greatly erode the VAT base and hence revenue, and contribute little to a more equitable VAT burden distribution. These exemptions imply that many VATs can be characterized as a combination of import duties (since some two-thirds of most VATs is collected at borders) and excise taxes (since most of the remaining VAT is collected on excisable products).

1.3 Major VAT Policy Issues

This situation calls for reform, principally by proceeding from the notion that the VAT is primarily intended to raise revenue, predictably and efficiently. It produces revenue that grows as its base—consumption expenditures—expands with economic development. It differs from excise taxes in that it does not and should not change people's behaviour (relative prices should remain unchanged); it differs from the import duties in that it should not be used to support trade policy; and it differs from the income tax in that it cannot and should not be used to redistribute income or stimulate industry through investment incentives. To repeat, under VAT, the goal should be revenue, which can be used, of course, to finance programmes, such as education and basic healthcare, that benefit those who pay the VAT.[8]

The road towards a best-practice VAT calls for second-generation reforms of African VAT systems aimed at modernizing the tax by broadening the base. Current exemptions for most foodstuffs, public utilities, pharmaceutical products, building materials, agricultural and industrial inputs, and various other goods and services should be removed. Only unprocessed foodstuffs, restrictively defined, might be exempted, although this should not be presumed to be

[7] As is well known, if goods and services are exempted, registered businesses buying these goods or services cannot take credit for the VAT charged on their inputs, nor charge VAT on their sales. By contrast, zero-rating means that no VAT is charged on sales while input VAT is creditable (deductible) and refundable if the amount exceeds the tax on output. In various African countries, exempt goods and services are called exemptions without credit, and zero-rated goods and services are called exemptions with credit.

[8] Of course, this assumes that the revenue is indeed used to pursue these goals and not used for unproductive purposes. In many instances, budget expenditure controls and audits appear to fall short of minimum standards of probity, but this issue is not the topic of this book.

necessary in all cases. At the same time, transfer duty, registration duty, and stamp duty regimes should be re-examined with a view to abolition or incorporating them in the VAT system, because they resemble distortionary cascade types of turnover taxes, which the VAT seeks to replace. Generally, these regimes yield very little revenue, with the possible exception of transfer or registration duties on immovable property. Traditional excise goods—tobacco products, alcoholic beverages, petroleum products—should continue to be taxed for revenue and, above all, externality-correcting reasons. The case for retaining the excise taxes on goods considered as items of luxury consumption is weak, with the notable exception of passenger cars.

Although less urgent, a review of the VAT systems should also be used to take a hard look at 'standard' exemptions. Many government and quasi-governmental operations should be made taxable, if only to confront the users of government services with the full social cost of their production and to enhance the integrity and stability of the VAT. Further, immovable property transactions, except sales of used residential dwellings, can be made more fully taxable. The separate taxes on insurance and banking activities, found in several francophone countries, should be reviewed on account of their distortionary impact. Property and casualty insurance can be taxed under the VAT, as can fee-based banking services and gambling. To trim the tax roll of revenue-unproductive VAT payers, the registration threshold should be raised in some countries. The case for a presumptive turnover tax on small VAT-exempt business establishments is not strong.

Design changes should make it easier to administer the VAT. The abolition of exemptions for goods, services, and entities and, more generally, unnecessary design differentiations would reduce the weight and sway of legal opinions and increase the administrative resources available for monitoring compliance with the VAT. Revenue should benefit. Indeed, the VAT design reforms should go hand-in-hand with VAT administration reforms. Even without the design changes, it would be highly worthwhile to make an in-depth evaluation of VAT administrations in selected African countries to see whether the VAT on the statutes is actually the same VAT in practice, i.e. a tax on value added rather than on turnover (if no credit for the VAT on inputs is allowed), exports (because refunds of prior-stage tax are not forthcoming), or imports (again, because no credit is given for the VAT collected at the import stage). Changes in VAT design cannot achieve much if inefficient and wasteful, indeed sometimes counterproductive, administrative processes are left in place.

1.4 Organization of This Book

The book is organized as follows. Chapter 2 dwells briefly on the workings and the legal and economic nature of the VAT and enumerates the characteristics of a best-practice VAT, against which existing regimes are evaluated. Chapter 3 reviews other broad-based consumption taxes with which the VAT can be compared, especially the retail sales tax (RST). After these introductory chapters, Chapter 4 provides an overview of VATs in Africa, noting their broad characteristics and listing the general issues that arise. Logically, this is followed by Chapter 5, which highlights the shortcomings of the sales tax regimes in African countries that do not (yet) have a VAT and which can likely be resolved under a best-practice VAT.

Since the book is about mobilizing VAT revenues, Chapter 6 examines the revenue performance of the various regimes by calculating their collection efficiencies, which make a distinction between the policy gap (exemptions and reduced rates) and the compliance gap (evasion and lack of enforcement). Possible explanatory factors, such as the level of economic development, the VAT structure, and the effectiveness of the VAT administration, are reviewed.

Poor revenue performance can be attributed to, among other things, the many non-standard exemptions introduced to mitigate the (perceived) regressivity of the VAT. It is widely believed that lower-income groups actually pay more tax as a percentage of income than higher-income groups. Chapter 7 examines the validity of this claim regarding the exemption or zero-rating of food products and agricultural inputs on the basis of empirical evidence, mainly from South Africa. It also discusses the pros and cons of higher-than-standard rates or, alternatively, excise taxes on goods and services considered items of luxury consumption, in order to promote the progressivity of VAT regimes.

VATs have been introduced, among others, to reduce or eliminate the reliance on taxes on international trade. Most African countries have established regional economic communities to promote trade and investment between the participating member states. Chapter 8 reviews the various stages of economic integration that can be distinguished and discusses VAT (and excise tax) coordination in the presence and absence of border controls.

The analysis of the revenue performance of the African VATs and their actual burden distribution establishes the case for taking a closer look at the various tax base concessions, which can truly be called the Achilles heel of African VATs. Chapter 9 opens the discussion by drawing up a taxonomy of standard and non-standard exclusions, exemptions, and zero rates—highlighting the distortions caused by them and the administrative complexities to which they give rise. Broadly, it compares the treatment of various exemptions in the EU, which have also been adopted by most African countries, with their treatment under New Zealand's GST and South Africa's VAT. This is followed, in Chapter 10, by a detailed review and analysis of the manifold non-standard exemptions and zero rates found around the continent. This chapter also makes the case for the comprehensive inclusion of services in the VAT base. Appropriately, it describes the reforms that Kenya and Tanzania, and before them Benin and Senegal, have undertaken to do away with most non-standard exemptions in order to bring their VATs closer to a best-practice type of tax.

Subsequent chapters dig deeper into the treatment of difficult-to-tax sectors, including governments and their agencies, education and healthcare, immovable property, financial services, insurance, and gambling. These 'standard exemptions', as they are often called, are generally based on the EU's Common VAT Directive (2006) (previously called the Sixth VAT Directive). This Directive, originally issued in 1977 and not significantly changed since, does not meet the requirements of a modern best-practice type of VAT adopted by countries such as Australia, Canada, New Zealand, Singapore, and South Africa (along with the other members of the Southern African Customs Union (SACU): Botswana, Lesotho, Namibia, and Swaziland).

Chapter 11 on governments and activities in the public interest includes a discussion of the VAT treatment of public utilities and cultural goods. Chapter 12 on immovable property shows that the application of the VAT to newly created property is, in theory, equivalent to the VAT on rents and rental values generated during the lifetime of the property. The similarities and differences between the VAT and property transfer taxes are also reviewed. As shown in Chapter 13, the proper inclusion of financial services in the VAT base still eludes the grip of VAT experts. However, various substitute treatments found in South Africa and New Zealand, for instance, are worth considering. Chapter 14 shows that insurance can be included in the VAT base by taxing premiums and imputing a VAT credit to indemnifications. The equivalent applies to gambling, briefly discussed in Chapter 15.

Chapter 16 discusses VAT registration thresholds and the treatment of farmers. A high threshold is recommended to keep the number of taxable persons manageable. The VAT on exempt small businesses should be confined to the tax on their inputs. Additional, substitute assessment schemes are not favoured. Farmers are usually categorically excluded from the VAT for political reasons and because they do not keep adequate accounts. Circumstances permitting, they should be taxed subject to a (high) registration threshold. Farm inputs that have no alternative use outside the agricultural sector might be zero-rated to mitigate the effects of the VAT on the prices of unprocessed foodstuffs.

Tax administration is key to tax policy, particularly in developing countries. This book would not have been complete, therefore, without a discussion of basic administrative processes in Chapter 17. These processes comprise registration, filing, payment, collection, enforcement, and audit. The chapter concludes with a note on fraud, a major issue in African countries.

Chapter 18 concludes the book with a summary review of the findings and preferred choices on exclusions, exemptions, and zero rates discussed in the previous chapters. It contrasts the present situation in most African countries with a workable best-practice VAT. The ideal does not have to be attained overnight, but should not be lost sight of since it tends to indicate the type of reform measures, often second-best, that are in line with the ideal. Throughout, it should be kept in mind that VATs are revenue-generating taxes, as opposed to progressivity-enhancing taxes, such as the income and property taxes, or externality-correcting taxes in the form of excise taxes and environmental levies.

Basic information on the VAT regimes in African countries can be found in Appendix A on the VAT treatment of essential goods and services and in Appendix B on the VAT and excise tax treatment of luxury products. Further, Appendix C shows details of the sales tax and excise tax systems in African countries without a VAT. Appendix D provides background information by presenting some basic economic and institutional indicators for African countries with a VAT. Knowledge of all these details is essential in evaluating the VAT regimes and drawing up the comparative tables in the text. Although every effort has been made to collect the latest data and to verify their accuracy, no doubt some information is out-of-date or possibly incorrect. In many instances, moreover, the (non-)taxable status of a product or service had to be inferred from the fact that it was not mentioned in the legal provision or the schedule of the VAT act that lists the exemptions or the goods and services subject to a lower-than-standard or zero rate.

1.5 Acknowledgements

Best practice elsewhere has been the lodestar for the review. Various publications have analysed and described VAT practice around the world, some with particular reference to Africa. These publications, listed in Box 1.1, have been valuable sources of reference, not least because of the literature cited in them. This book differs from these publications in that it digs deeper into the details of VAT design on the African continent, which are relevant for the discussion of various policy issues.

The book proceeds from the premise that VATs (and other taxes) in Africa (and elsewhere), as works in progress, should be scrutinized continuously and improved as experience is gained and economic development proceeds. I am inspired by Richard Bird and Pierre-Pascal Gendron's motto that proper tax design makes good tax administration easier and by Nora Lustig's judgement that efficient VATs can result in a net fiscal system that is equalizing. At the same time, I am tempered by Michael Keen's reality check that mistakes made at introduction are hard to undo. With these well-grounded reasonings in mind, I hope that this book contributes to a growing awareness of the need for more neutral, simpler, and more revenue-productive VATs reformed in line with commonly agreed notions about a best-practice VAT, suitably adapted to the circumstances of each country. Recent regional conferences and workshops on VAT across the African continent indicate that the VAT is starting to receive the limelight it deserves.

Box 1.1 Selected publications on VAT

General

- **Liam Ebrill, Michael Keen, Jean-Paul Bodin, and Victoria Summers, *The Modern VAT*, International Monetary Fund, Washington D.C., 2001**

Written by a team of experts from the International Monetary Fund, this book examines the remarkable spread and current reach of the VAT, and draws lessons about the design and implementation of the innovative tax as experienced by different countries around the world. How efficient is it as a tax, is it fair, and is it suitable for all countries are among the questions raised in this highly informative and well-researched book that also looks at the likely future of the tax.

- **Richard M. Bird and Pierre-Pascal Gendron, *The VAT in Developing and Transitional Countries*, Cambridge University Press, Cambridge, UK, 2007**

VAT now dominates tax systems around the world. But should every country have a VAT? Is the current VAT always as good as it could be in economic, equity, and administrative terms? In developing and transitional countries, the answers to such questions are critical to stability, growth, and development. Although VAT is an important fiscal tool in most countries, it can often be better designed and almost always better administered. The key questions that must be answered in designing and implementing VAT are essentially the same in all countries. But different tax designs may best suit different countries facing different circumstances. This book reviews experiences with VATs around the world and assesses how the choice of particular design features may affect outcomes in particular contexts.

- **Alan Schenk, Victor Thuronyi, and Wei Cui, *Value Added Tax: A Comparative Approach*, 2nd edition, Cambridge University Press, Cambridge, UK, 2015**

This book integrates legal, economic, and administrative materials about the VAT. Its principal purpose is to provide comprehensive teaching tools—laws, cases, analytical exercises, and questions drawn from the experience of countries and organizations around the world. It also serves as a resource for tax practitioners and government officials who must grapple with issues under their VAT or their prospective VAT. The comparative presentation of this volume offers an analysis of the policy issues relating to the structure and base of the VAT, as well as materials on VAT avoidance and evasion and on China's VAT.

Africa

- **Richard Krever (ed.),** ***VAT in Africa*****, Pretoria University Law Press, Pretoria, South Africa, 2008**

Half a century after its introduction, the VAT has emerged as the world's most widely used consumption tax and a central component of public finance in Africa. Implementation in Africa has not been trouble-free, however, and in many instances the adoption of VAT has revealed the need for broader tax administration reform and modernization. At a technical level, too, issues have arisen as African economies have become more complex and more global, incorporating new forms of enterprises and commercial transactions, with cross-border trade in both tangible goods and intangible rights increasing daily. This collection of essays sheds light on these issues.

- **Michael Keen and Mario Mansour, 'Revenue Mobilisation in Sub-Saharan Africa: Challenges from Globalisation I—Trade Reform',** ***Development Policy Review*****, 28(5), 2010**

This article evaluates the nature and extent of, and possible responses to, one of the central challenges that globalization poses for revenue mobilization in sub-Saharan Africa—trade liberalization—against the background of a broad picture of revenue developments in the region between 1980 and 2005. Countries' experiences have varied, but the overall picture is one of non-resource revenues having been essentially stagnant. Within this, however, and with exceptions, reductions in trade tax revenue have been largely offset by increased revenue from domestic sources.

- **Sijbren Cnossen, 'Coordination of Indirect Taxes in the Southern African Development Community',** ***Tax Notes International*****, 21 March 2011**

The African Economic Community consists of several regional economic communities. The communities strive to become customs unions and subsequently common markets, drawing on the experience of the European Union. This essay outlines the criteria and stages of economic integration, with special reference to the Southern African Development Community (SADC). It discusses the various economic and institutional factors that have a bearing on tax coordination, particularly of import duties, VATs, and excise duties. As import duties are reduced, more intensive use of VATs has to replace forgone revenue. Further, excise taxes can be increased and better targeted to enhance social and market outcomes. The major lesson of this essay is that tax reform and tax coordination should go hand-in-hand.

Continued

Box 1.1 *Continued*

- **Mario Mansour and Grégoire Rota-Graziosi, 'Tax Coordination, Tax Competition, and Revenue Mobilization in the West African Economic and Monetary Union', Working Paper WP/13/163, Fiscal Affairs Department, International Monetary Fund, July 2013**

This paper reviews the current stage of the West African Economic and Monetary Union's tax coordination framework, against the main objectives of the WAEMU Treaty of 1994: reduce distortions to intra-community trade and mobilize domestic tax revenue. The process of tax coordination in the WAEMU is one of the most advanced in the world—*de jure* at least—but remains in many areas ineffective *de facto*. Nevertheless, the framework has, to some extent, succeeded in converging tax systems, particularly statutory rates, and may have contributed to improving revenue mobilization. Important lessons can be drawn from the WAEMU experience, particularly in terms of whether coordination should take the form of harmonization through a top-down approach, or a softer approach of sharing best practice and limiting certain types of tax competition.

- **Sijbren Cnossen, 'Mobilizing VAT Revenues in African Countries', *International Tax and Public Finance*, 22(6), 2015**

Several African countries have to increase their tax revenues to finance human and economic development. VATs are the preferred instrument for doing so, because they are less detrimental to growth than income taxes. To enable their use, VAT design has to be improved. Currently, many VATs are so riddled with exemptions and zero rates on domestic goods that they resemble extended excise tax systems, while the standard rate is mainly confined to luxury goods. Base-broadening would not only increase revenue but also reduce the economic distortions and administrative complexities of most VATs. Recently, Kenya has reformed its VAT, abolishing many non-standard exemptions for foodstuffs, utilities, and various other goods and services. The example deserves to be scrutinized.

Throughout a lifetime of involvement with VAT, I have benefitted greatly from discussions with and publications on VAT by Richard Bird, Lans Bovenberg, Michael Keen, Richard Krever, Mario Mansour, Charlie McLure, Ruud de Mooij, Marius van Oordt, Satya Poddar, and Stephen Smith. I continue to cherish their insights and friendship. I am greatly indebted to Pierre-Pascal Gendron for writing Chapter 17, a substantive contribution to this book. I have also benefitted from discussing VAT issues with him and Richard Krever when we taught various

VAT courses at the University of Pretoria. I am grateful for Leon Bettendorf's econometric analysis on understanding VAT performance in Chapter 6, and thank John Damstra for contributing the information on VAT C-efficiencies in African countries.

I wish to thank Riël Franzsen of the African Tax Institute at the University of Pretoria and Dan Witt of the International Tax and Investment Center for their encouragement and financial support throughout the writing of this book. Also, thanks are due to CPB Netherlands Bureau for Economic Policy Analysis for offering me a congenial environment in which to work on this book. Last but certainly not least, I am most grateful to Judith Payne for doing a superb job in copy-editing and managing the production of this book.

2
What Is VAT?

An appreciation of the economics of the VAT is helpful in understanding its legal and administrative design. Likewise, knowledge of the workings of the VAT is essential for evaluating its economic effects. This chapter starts, therefore, with a brief exposition on the workings of the VAT and its relationship to the profit and loss (P&L) account of a business. Subsequently, the nature of the VAT as a tax on transactions rather than activities and on consumption rather than value added per se is discussed, followed by some thoughts on its economic characteristics. Next, informed theory and feasibility considerations yield the contours of a best-practice VAT. As argued in the concluding section, VAT should be analysed in conjunction with excise taxes and import duties.[1]

2.1 Workings of the VAT

In this book, VAT is defined as a broad-based tax levied on sales of goods and services in all stages of production and distribution up to and including the retail stage, with systematic offsetting of the tax charged on goods and services purchased as inputs.[2] That is, while 'taxable persons' are required to charge tax on all their sales (output), they can also claim a deduction or credit for the tax charged on their purchases (inputs). As a result, only the accounting difference between sales and purchases, called value added, is taxed at any stage of production or distribution. Further, the VAT on sales and purchases is stated on tax invoices, which represent documentary evidence of the entitlement to a tax credit. Hence, the VAT is also called a credit-invoice tax. One taxable person's output VAT is another taxable person's creditable input VAT.

The workings of the VAT can be illustrated by reference to the stylized example in Table 2.1, which traces the manufacture and sale of the desk at which the draft of this book was written. Following the production and distribution chain, we start with the primary producer (P), who sells wood to the furniture manufacturer (M),

[1] The first four sections of this chapter draw on Cnossen (2011a).

[2] See also the definitions in Cnossen (1998a) and Ebrill et al. (2001, box 1.1). This book does not consider the gross product or net income variants of the VAT (see Shoup (1990)) as best-practice VATs because of their highly distortionary design features. They do not deserve to be called a tax (McLure and Bloomfield, 1987).

Table 2.1 Workings of the VAT

a. Basic transactions, excluding VAT (in US$)

Production–distribution chain	Purchases	Sales	Value added
Producer (P)	0	400	400
Manufacturer (M)	400	1,200	800
Wholesaler (W)	1,200	1,400	200
Retailer (R)	1,400	2,000	600
Consumer	2,000		
Total value added			2,000

b. VAT payments to suppliers and by buyers (10% tax; in US$)

Production–distribution chain	VAT paid to supplier	VAT paid by buyer	Net VAT
Producer	0	40	40
Manufacturer	40	120	80
Wholesaler	120	140	20
Retailer	140	200	60
Consumer	200		
Total VAT			200

c. Fractional collection of VAT paid by consumer (in US$)

Production–distribution chain	VAT paid to supplier	VAT paid to government
Consumer	200	
Retailer	140	60
Wholesaler	120	20
Manufacturer	40	80
Producer		40
Total VAT paid to government		**200**

who delivers the desk to the wholesaler (W), who distributes it to the retailer's furniture store (R), which in turn puts the desk for sale to the consumer. For simplicity, it is assumed that each stage purchases the whole output of the previous stage and that the primary producer has zero inputs.

In each stage, the value of the inputs increases by the value of labour (wages) and capital (business cash flow, to be defined in Section 2.4) applied in the production and distribution of the desk. Consequently, at the final stage—i.e. the retail stage—the sum of all the accounting differences between sales and purchases and, by the same token, the sum of all values added throughout the production–distribution process (in either case, US$2,000 in the example) both equal the consumer price, exclusive of tax.

The table highlights the VAT's workings by showing the transactions net of VAT (heading a), the VAT payments and VAT credits (heading b), and the collection of the total VAT paid by the consumer throughout the production–distribution chain (heading c). Generally, the VAT on all purchases made for the purposes of the business is immediately creditable against the tax on (unrelated) sales, or, if there are no sales, any excess credit is eligible for refund without delay.[3] Consequently, no net VAT is levied on transactions between taxable businesses and entities.

But if no net tax is due from registered businesses in relation to their own value added, how come each firm nevertheless remits some tax to the tax authorities? To understand this apparent paradox, the appropriate focus is to look upstream at financial flows rather than at the flow of goods and services downstream. The answer is then, as shown in the table under heading c, that the consumer pays the full tax which is collected, again in full, by the retailer, but which is remitted to the tax authorities by all registered businesses in proportion to their share in the total value added embodied in the final product. Any net tax remitted by upstream firms is simply paid to them by their successors in the production–distribution chain.[4] Incidentally, but importantly, this establishes that the VAT is a tax on consumption, not on value added as such.

In other words, the timing of tax collections under the VAT is the same as that under a retail sales tax in which the tax is collected at the time of sale to the consumer. The only plausible assumption that needs to be made for this equivalency to occur is that the average length of time for remitting tax and processing any net refunds is the same as the average length of time required for settling accounts receivable and payable (inclusive of VAT).[5] So, why not impose the tax at retail only? In essence, because retailers are less likely to default on the VAT invoiced to them by their suppliers than on the tax they would have had to pay in full to the tax authorities if, instead, an equivalent retail sales tax had been imposed.

This feature makes the VAT particularly robust from a tax collection point of view. It is reinforced by obliging sellers to state the VAT on invoices, which facilitates compliance control (cross-checking) and the correct and expeditious application of border tax adjustments, i.e. the zero-rating (also called 'exemption with credit')

[3] In legal terms (as stated unequivocally in article 11(3) of the European Union (EU)'s Second Directive on Value Added Tax (European Council, 1967)), a taxable business's right to a tax credit (and refund) arises *at the same time* that the supplier has to account for the tax: the date of both events is based on the same VAT invoice date. The 'refund without delay' is perhaps the most crucial feature of the VAT with which it stands or falls. Many African countries are notorious for failing to heed this essential requirement of a best-practice VAT, effectively turning their VATs into highly distortionary turnover taxes.

[4] Accordingly, the VAT does not, as Bird and Gendron (2007, p. 31) seem to believe, 'in effect "withhold" tax at each stage of the chain of production and distribution.'

[5] To be sure, cash-flow benefits (or costs) arise under the VAT (as well as a retail sales tax) if a taxable business's collection date (the date at which the tax is collected from customers before being handed over to the tax authorities) does not coincide with the remittance date (a date after the collection date but on or before the latest day designated for handing over the tax). This point and that about the timing of tax collections are made in Organization for Economic Cooperation and Development (1988). For an early treatment of cash-flow benefits and costs of the VAT, see Sandford et al. (1981). For more recent versions, see Hasseldine (2005) and Evans (2008).

of exports (the VAT shown on the exporters' purchase invoices is simply refunded) and the taxation of imports. In other words, the VAT leaves a clear audit trail, although this does not make the VAT self-enforcing. The invoice method also facilitates the calculation of the net tax liability: basically, the tax shown on all purchase invoices is simply summed and subtracted from the tax shown on all sales invoices.

2.2 VAT and the P&L Account

In understanding the VAT, it is useful to see how it relates to the accounts of a taxable person's business. As is well known, the profit and loss account is the central summary statement of a business firm's activities. Consider the stylized example in Table 2.2, which shows the P&L account of a trading firm (arranged to aid the understanding of the subsequent computations) as well as the items that enter into the VAT base and the corresponding gross and net tax liabilities.

The business sells goods and services that it produces by adding the value of the services of its labour and capital to its purchases from other firms. The left side of the table, under A, shows the firm's purchases of goods and services, including a piece of machinery acquired at US$100, which is depreciated over four years at US$25 per year. Also, opening and closing inventories are shown: US$200 has been added to inventories in the reporting period. The right side of the table, under B, shows the firm's sales of goods and services. Furthermore, C, factor rewards, gives details of the value added by the firm's labour and capital in the form of wages, depreciation, interest paid, and net profits earned. Also, the firm has some stocks and bonds on which it earns investment income, which is shown under D.

The VAT computations are shown in the top of the table under A and B. VAT is charged at a rate of 10 per cent on sales of goods and services for a total amount of US$190, and a credit of US$110 (10 per cent of US$1,100) is permitted for the VAT on purchases. Accordingly, the net VAT liability is US$80 (line F). This is equivalent to 10 per cent of the net VAT base of US$800, calculated as the difference between taxable sales of US$1,900 and taxed purchases of US$1,100. Note that factor rewards, C, and investment income, D, do not enter the computations.

Clearly, the entries for purchases in the conventional P&L account cannot be used directly to ascertain taxable value added. Although the P&L account and the VAT both record the transactions on an accrual basis, unlike commercial accounting usage the VAT is levied on a cash-flow basis of accounting.[6] Thus, no correction needs to be made for the change in the value of inventories, which must be made in the P&L account to match sales and purchases in the reporting

[6] Cash-flow accounting should not be confused with cash-basis accounting. In contrast to cash-basis accounting, cash-flow accounting is accrual-based: sales and purchases are recorded at the time the obligation to deliver or acquire them occurs.

Table 2.2 VAT and the P&L account
(in US$, excluding 10% VAT)

Costs	P&L account	VAT		Proceeds	P&L account	VAT	
		Base	Tax			Base	Tax
A. Purchases	**800**	**1,100**	**110**	**B. Sales**	**1,900**	**1,900**	**190**
Goods	950	950	95	Goods	1,600	1,600	160
Services	50	50	5	Services	300	300	30
Inventory—open: 150 close: 350	–200	-	-				
Machinery (depreciation—4 years)	-	100	10				
C. Factor rewards	**1,300**	-	-	**D. Investment income**	**200**	-	-
Wages	450	-	-	Dividends	125	-	-
Depreciation	25	-	-	Interest	75	-	-
Interest paid	35	-	-				
Net profits	790	-	-				
E. Totals (A + C; B + D)	**2,100**				**2,100**		
F. Value added and tax (B – A)		**800**	**80**				

period for commercial or business income purposes. Further, the cash-flow basis of accounting implies that the tax on the purchase of machinery is credited immediately against the VAT on sales rather than proportionately as the machine is written down.

Importantly, note that the VAT does not enter the P&L account; it is not a cost to business. Exceptionally, VAT would be included in the value of purchases shown in the P&L account if the business would be exempt, yet VAT had been levied on the inputs used in producing the purchases and become 'hidden' in its sales price. Of course, VAT may be an item on the balance sheet of the business as 'VAT payable' or 'VAT receivable'.

Following this brief introduction to the workings of the VAT and its place in the accounts of a business, it is time to have a look at its legal features and economic characteristics.

2.3 Legal Features of the VAT

Legally, the VAT is a tax on transactions. In Africa, as elsewhere, this is reflected in the imposition of tax on 'supplies of goods and services', meaning all economic activity, unless specifically exempted.[7] A supply of goods is defined as 'the transfer of the right to dispose of tangible property as owner', a civil law concept. Services, tangible as well as intangible, are defined in catch-all fashion as 'any transaction that does not constitute a supply of goods',[8] including 'obligations to refrain from an act or to tolerate an act or situation'. To be taxable, supplies of goods as well as services must be made against consideration, called the 'taxable value', which includes all forms of payment, broadly defined (including any inducement of supply), received by the supplier, in cash or in kind, whenever and however paid, regardless of who pays it. Gifts are not taxable, but non-business use of a supply—e.g. for personal or employee consumption—is taxable if provided free of charge or not at arm's length. Generally, this is achieved by denying the input tax credit for personal or living expenses, employee benefits, recreational equipment and facilities, and passenger vehicles, which even if used in the course of taxable activities are indistinguishable from goods and services bought by consumers.

As implied by this brief description of the charge to tax, legally the VAT is a tax on transactions by taxable persons against consideration undertaken in furthering economic activities. Lawyers would also maintain that the VAT is a tax on consumption expenditures rather than on, more broadly, consumption activities.

7 For excellent summary treatments of legal issues, see Williams (1996), Krever (2008a), and, at length, Schenk, Thuronyi, and Cui (2015).

8 As discussed below, some African VATs still enumerate the services that are subject to VAT, possibly missing out on newly introduced services.

Moreover, they assert that the VAT is a tax on current consumption—on all goods and services that leave the ring of taxable persons, regardless of whether they are consumed immediately or embody a stock of services that are consumed over the lifetime of the assets (e.g. residential housing, cars, household appliances, and furniture).

This contrasts with the view held by economists that, ideally, the VAT should tax all consumption activities, including self-produced items of consumption such as meals, because this would ensure equal treatment with other products bought in the marketplace. Lawyers would not consider the consumption of self-produced meals a taxable event, although they would tax, say, vegetables withdrawn from business stock for personal use by the greengrocer as a taxable self-supply on the argument that the vegetables are produced in a business context, not in a personal capacity. Accordingly, the greengrocer's home-grown carrots used for personal consumption (and not sold to customers) would not be subject to VAT. Economists would like to tax both events.

Economists also maintain that the VAT should be a tax on flows rather than stocks. Ideally, homeowners should be taxed periodically on the rental value of their properties, just as tenants should be taxed on the rent invoiced by the landlord. However, lawyers would argue that residential property should be taxed when the house is transferred from the taxable builder to the exempt owner-occupier. This follows from the legislator's view that owner-occupiers should not be registered for VAT purposes. Lawyers point out that the *in rem* nature of the VAT does not support the position that durable consumer goods should be treated differently from non-durable goods. As a transactions-based tax, VAT should be imposed when the title to durable consumer goods passes on to the exempt consumer.[9]

2.4 Economic Nature of the VAT

Apart from differences in the treatment of durable and non-durable goods, there are interesting economic differences and similarities between consumption, income, and payroll taxes. To understand this, note that the difference in the P&L account between sales and purchases equals the sum of wages and business cash flow. Business cash flow does not equal profits, but is the amount that remains after sales have been reduced by purchases and wages, where purchases include investment goods and additions to inventories. In Table 2.2, business cash flow

[9] As shown in Chapter 12, both views result in the same tax liability when the VAT on the value of newly created property is viewed, as it should be, as a tax on the present discounted value of the future dwelling services of the property. This implies, of course, that increases or decreases in the value of the dwelling services, reflected in changes in the value of the property, are not included in the tax base.

equals US$350, while net profits are US$790, a very different amount. The next chapter shows how business cash flow is computed.

In economic terms, business cash flow is the above-normal return to investment, which, in characteristic VAT fashion, remains if investments are dispensed immediately and deductions for interest are denied. To see this more clearly, consider the following simple equation showing the identity between the sources (wages and capital income) and the uses of income (consumption and saving) in a household budget or a country's national accounts for a closed economy and abstracting from government operations (Auerbach, 2008; Ebrill et al., 2001):

$$Y \equiv W + R \equiv C + S$$

and, as $S \equiv I$, it follows that

$$C \equiv Y - S \equiv W + R - I, \qquad (1)$$

in which Y is total income composed of labour income W and capital income R, C is consumption, and S is saving (which equals I, investment). R is the sum of the risk-free or normal return on capital (in other words, its opportunity cost), entrepreneurial rewards for risk-taking (which can also be considered as labour income), and economic rents. In short, R represents business profits, conventionally computed.

The opportunity cost of capital is also called the hurdle rate of return. At the margin, it equals the rate of return on a riskless project. Accordingly, it can be likened to the inflation-adjusted, risk-free world rate of interest. A business will go on investing up to the point at which the expected rate of return on the project just equals the discount rate, which is the opportunity cost of capital. Further, economic rents can be associated with, for instance, head starts, such as a favourable business location, a well-known trademark, a patent, or know-how concerning a new process or product. Economic rents can be taxed without influencing the investor's behaviour.

Each of the terms in identity (1) can serve as the base for a particular comprehensive, uniform-rate consumption tax. Basically, the retail sales tax has C as its base. It is paid by consumers to businesses selling at retail, who remit the tax to the government. Y – S represents the base for an individual consumption or expenditure tax that provides an allowance for saving. It resembles a tax on wage income that permits a deduction for pension contributions but taxes later pay-outs (including accumulated capital income), while the income net of the pension contribution is currently consumed. In practice, this wage income tax, which resembles a progressive individual consumption tax, is found in many countries.

The term W + R – I represents value added, which forms the base for the VAT. At business level, the term is equivalent to the difference between sales and purchases in the P&L account, but calculated on a cash-flow basis. In other words, investments (including inventories) are expensed immediately; the tax is fully creditable against the tax on sales, to use VAT terminology. This contrasts with the income tax's matching principle under which the cost of investments is expensed over their economic life; hence, the normal return on capital is taxed.

The taxation of business cash flow, R – I, distinguishes a consumption tax from a wage tax, which taxes W only. The two are equal if R – I is zero, which it is in a fully competitive market in which there are no economic rents to be earned. Further, investment, I, may be taken to represent the present value of services rendered by new business assets discounted at the normal rate of return on capital. Therefore, R – I represents the inframarginal return on old business assets. On the introduction or increase of a consumption tax, such as the VAT, this tax is capitalized in the form of a lower value of the old assets (in other words, it is a once-off wealth tax) suffered by the owners. For this reason, economists often refer to the VAT as a tax on wages plus old capital. The normal return on new capital, however, is not taxed. This distinguishes a consumption tax from an income tax, which taxes S (≡ I) twice by expensing new investments over their lifetime.

This discussion shows that the only difference between a consumption tax and an income tax concerns the tax treatment of the normal risk-free return on capital, which is exempt under a consumption tax but taxed under an income tax. It follows that a VAT can be converted into an income tax by disallowing an immediate credit for the tax on investment goods against the tax on sales, but permitting this credit to be spread over the economic life of investment goods.[10] By the same token, an income tax can be converted into a VAT by taxing wages plus business profits after permitting an immediate write-off for investment goods and clawing back any deduction for interest.[11]

Finally, what happens to the equivalencies in identity (1) in an open economy can best be illustrated by the balance-of-payments identity between current and capital account:

$$M - X \equiv E - I^f,$$

where M is imports, X is exports, E is net earnings from abroad, and I^f is net foreign investments (I^f is negative if inbound flows exceed outbound flows). By excluding exports from the base and including imports, a VAT now becomes equivalent to a tax on domestic and foreign labour income plus a tax on domestic and foreign capital income, net of new domestic and foreign investment.

[10] In the tax literature, this has been called an income type of VAT (Shoup, 1990), which is not considered a VAT in this book.

[11] For an interesting legal analysis showing the link between an income tax and a consumption tax, see Slemrod (1997), who also draws attention to the difference in the treatment of inventories and prepaid costs.

2.5 What Is a Best-Practice VAT?

On the basis of the legal and economic underpinnings discussed above, a best-practice VAT may be said to have the following characteristics:

- A best-practice VAT includes all goods and services in its base, unless specifically exempted on administrative grounds. This implies that the taxation of services is fully integrated with the taxation of goods. Admittedly, a VAT that enumerates a broad range of services that are taxable may not differ much from a VAT that taxes all services (and lists those that are exempted), but in practice enumeration involves delineation problems which a true VAT avoids. In this respect, the VAT in Guinea–Bissau, which enumerates the services that are liable to tax, is a borderline case.
- The VAT is a multistage transactions tax that covers all stages of production and distribution, including the retail stage. The VAT registration threshold (sometimes called the small-business exemption) is the criterion for determining whether or not a business firm is liable to VAT—not the stage at which the firm conducts its transactions, be it the manufacturing, wholesale, or retail stage.
- A best-practice VAT is levied at a single, uniform rate on all domestically supplied goods and services. Lower-than-standard rates are frowned upon since they are ill-targeted tools to relieve the VAT burden on lower-income groups or to achieve some other 'worthy' purpose. The income tax and the government's expenditure system are much better means to help the poor. If a lower-than-standard rate is levied on supplies considered essential goods and services, that rate should be set at a level that as a rule refunds do not arise.[12]
- The VAT eliminates cascading or cumulative tax effects[13] by granting taxable firms a full and immediate tax credit or deduction for the tax paid in respect of inputs (purchases) from other taxable firms, against their own VAT payable on sales (output). In principle, the right to a tax credit arises at the same time that the taxable supplier has to account for the VAT on sales. Accordingly, no good or service anywhere within the taxable production–distribution chain has VAT attached to it and inventories are held fully free of VAT. This neutrality feature implies that VAT does not interfere with market conditions, since relative prices between goods and services remain unaltered. In this respect, Nigeria's VAT, which prescribes that the tax on capital goods and services is not creditable against the VAT on output, is not a best-practice VAT.

[12] For a fuller account, see Cnossen (2004).

[13] These are the tax-on-tax effects that occur if the inputs and output of the same business are both taxed. Obviously, such effects create a strong incentive to integrate taxable activities of different businesses—in other words, they distort competitive conditions.

- Furthermore, the VAT is destination-based, because goods and services are taxed in the country of destination or consumption, not the country of origin or production. This means that exports should be zero-rated (which involves a credit or refund of prior-stage tax) in order to put exporters on the same tax footing in foreign markets as domestic suppliers in those markets. In practice, this criterion tends to be violated in many countries, because refunds are not forthcoming or not timely. Further, imports should be taxed on a par with domestically produced goods and services. Domestic purchasers of imported goods and services should receive an immediate credit (and refund, if necessary) for the equivalent VAT levied at the import stage.
- A best-practice VAT limits administrative and taxpayer discretion to a minimum. End-use exemptions—e.g. an exemption for tractors used by farmers—are frowned upon, as are exemptions for business inputs (including capital goods), products that are subject to another tax, or products bought by, say, government agencies. These exemptions undermine the integrity of the VAT system. Taxable suppliers should always charge VAT when they supply goods and services, regardless of the status of the purchaser. Again, many African VATs do not abide by this rule.
- The VAT is based on self-assessment. This requires that taxable persons file returns and pay VAT at their own initiative in accordance with their statutory obligations. It is important, therefore, that the VAT is easy to comply with and that it interferes as little as possible with the free functioning of business and trade. To make this possible, the VAT should be closely attuned to actual business transactions and accounting methods, which would keep the costs of complying with and enforcing the VAT as low as possible. Under a VAT based on self-assessment, the tax administration's task should be confined mainly to providing taxpayer education, monitoring late filers and late payers, and, particularly, auditing taxable persons' accounts.
- For administrative reasons, the VAT should exclude small businesses, which tend to have less reliable books of account, from registration. The definition of what 'small' constitutes depends on domestic industrial structures and market conditions, among others. Although a VAT is simple to comply with—basically requiring a spike on which sales invoices can be pinned and one to take purchase invoices—full compliance control requires a cash and bank book from which a balance sheet and P&L account can be drawn up, so that in-depth audits can be performed. Obviously, these accounts would be difficult for illiterate traders to maintain. Hence, these traders should be exempted, although an option to register should be provided for small traders who wish to claim credit for input VAT (and charge VAT to their customers). These considerations imply a much higher threshold than is prevalent in, say, the EU, where educational levels are high and VAT compliance and control can be ensured in conjunction with the business income tax.

2.6 VAT versus Excise Taxes and Import Duties

VATs must be distinguished from excise tax systems, which can be defined to encompass all selective taxes on tobacco products, alcoholic beverages, petroleum products, motor vehicles, pollutants, luxury items, and other goods and services selected for specific taxation—whether imported or produced domestically.[14] Unlike VATs, the economic function of excise taxes is to promote efficiency in resource allocation by internalizing the external (or social) cost of the production or consumption of the products on which they are imposed. In the absence of effective income and property taxes, moreover, excises on luxury goods, considered proxies for taxpaying capacity, may have a role to play in improving the progressivity of the tax system.

The basis of assessment for excise taxes is often some quantitative measure—e.g. volume, weight, or strength—to which a specific rate (an absolute monetary amount per quantity unit) is applied. Usually, excise taxes are levied at the manufacturer's stage, primarily because the basis of assessment and the higher rates require some form of physical control over production. This contrasts with VATs, which are imposed on actual transactions and prices throughout the entire production–distribution chain, and whose compliance is monitored through accounting controls.

Furthermore, VATs must be distinguished from duties on imports, which, generally, are levied at *ad valorem* rates (except imports of excisable goods). Similar to excisable goods, imports are subject to physical controls and goods are not released before duty has been paid or adequate surety provided. Taxpayer cooperation, essential for the adequate functioning of a VAT, generally is not required. In sharp contrast to the VAT too (but similar to excise taxes), collection arrears do not arise. In theory, import duties should not be used as a major revenue source, because of their non-neutral effects. In practice, however, import duties do fulfil this role if no other convenient tax handle is available.[15] In addition, a number of carefully designed supplementary import duties can be justified to provide (temporary) protection to domestic infant industries which the government wishes to encourage.

From a tax policy perspective, the protective function of the import duty should be given priority in order to create a level playing field with similar

[14] This definition of excise taxes goes beyond the usual Anglo-Saxon definition of excises as 'duties' imposed on the manufacture, sale, or consumption of certain domestically produced goods. For this reason, this book uses the term excise *taxes* rather than excise *duties*. The use of the term excise taxes is also meant to convey the notion that imported excisable products should be included in the domestic excise tax base. For an extensive treatment of excise taxes, see Cnossen (2005, 2006b).

[15] In the short run, a generally applied import duty would be equivalent in effect to a devaluation of the currency, because the price of foreign commodities increases. However, the reduced demand for imports would save on foreign exchange, which in turn would boost the value of the importing country's currency. In turn, the appreciation of the currency would reduce the domestic currency receipts of exporters. Consequently, an import duty in effect becomes a tax on exports.

domestically produced goods. This should be followed by the externality-correcting function of the excises to account for the external costs generated by the consumption or production of domestic as well as imported products. Lastly, the VAT should be imposed to ensure that relative prices stay the same, regardless of whether a product is imported or domestically produced and whether it is excisable or not. Technically, this means that at the import stage, excise taxes should be imposed on the import-duty-inclusive value of goods if levied at *ad valorem* rates and they should be added to that value if imposed at a specific rate. Since excises do not have a protective function (it is performed by the import duty), it is important that excisable imports are included in the domestic excise tax base and that the same rate applies to them. Furthermore, coordination with the VAT would be achieved by levying that tax on the excise-tax-inclusive value of excisable goods, while the VAT at the import stage should be levied on the value of imports plus import duties and excise taxes.[16]

[16] To illustrate, assume that for importation purposes the c.i.f. value of a litre of spirits is US$10, the import duty is 40%, the excise tax is US$6 per litre, and the VAT is 15%. Then the total tax of US$13 would consist of US$4 import duty, US$6 excise tax, and US$3 VAT.

3
Other Broad-Based Consumption Taxes

Following a sketch of the workings, nature, and design of a best-practice VAT, this chapter compares it with other, economically equivalent, broad-based consumption taxes, notably the retail sales tax. The P&L account in the previous chapter (Table 2.2) forms the basis for explaining how the tax liabilities under the various variants are computed. The accounting matrix is also used to note the similarities to and differences from a conventional business income tax ascertained on the basis of the matching principle. Subsequently, the practical differences between the taxes are discussed, as well as their prevalence around the world. A brief section on the major lessons from worldwide experience with VAT concludes.

3.1 How Can Consumption Be Taxed?

Much can be learned about the VAT by comparing it with other broad-based consumption taxes, which can be considered alternatives to a VAT. As shown in Table 2.1, the consumer price is always equal to the algebraic sum of all values added, is always equal to the sum of the differences between sales and purchases, and is always equal to the sum of wage payments and business cash flows. If this is kept in mind, it will readily be apparent that exactly the same total tax can be collected in either of two ways:

- in full under a retail sales tax; or
- fractionally throughout the production–distribution chain by confining the tax to the value added at each stage.

In turn, the fractional or multistage collection technique can be implemented:

- directly under the direct subtraction method by subtracting purchases from sales and applying the tax rate to the difference;
- indirectly under the indirect subtraction technique, called credit-invoice VAT, by crediting the tax on purchases against the tax on sales;
- directly by levying the tax on the components of value added, i.e. wages (payroll) and business cash flow; or
- directly by taxing labour income and capital income separately at the individual and business level, respectively.

Accordingly, the following consumption taxes can be distinguished, and are levied or proposed in the USA, in the EU, or in the tax literature:[1]

- a retail sales tax (RST) that is applied to sales of goods and services by registered businesses to consumers and unregistered entities;
- a credit-invoice method of VAT that taxes all sales by registered businesses but permits a credit (deduction) for the tax on purchases (including investment goods) from other registered businesses against the tax on sales;
- a direct subtraction method tax (also called business transfer tax (BTT) in the USA) that permits registered businesses to deduct purchases (including investment goods) from other registered businesses from sales and that taxes the difference between sales and purchases directly rather than indirectly as under the VAT;[2]
- an addition method tax that taxes aggregate wages as well as residual value added (business cash flow) by registered businesses as computed from the P&L account;
- a flat tax, much discussed in the US literature, that allows registered businesses to deduct wages from value added as calculated under the direct subtraction method, but that taxes these wages at the level of individual wage earners (permitting a basic exemption and hence effective progressivity). Residual value added is taxed at the business level at a single, uniform rate without an exemption—hence the name 'flat tax'; and
- a personal expenditure tax that taxes expenditures on goods and services at the level of the taxpaying individual by subtracting saving (including loan repayments and purchases of stocks, bonds, and non-residential real estate) from aggregate incomings (including loan receipts and proceeds from the sale of assets), both calculated on a cash-flow basis.

Table 3.1 illustrates the computations of the equivalent tax liabilities under the various consumption taxes in a stylized manner for the economic agents in a production–distribution chain, consisting of a primary producer, P, a manufacturer, M, a wholesaler, W, and a retailer, R—all making sales and purchases and adding value in the form of wages and business cash flow, as indicated. The table shows that under the basic assumption that the tax base and tax rate are identical, the total net tax collected under the retail sales tax (US$200, line B.1) equals the tax collected throughout the production–distribution process under the VAT (line C.3), which equals the tax under the direct subtraction method (line D.1), which

[1] For a discussion of different consumption taxes, see also McLure and Bloomfield (1987) and Schenk, Thuronyi, and Cui (2015).

[2] In this book, the acronym VAT is reserved for the credit-invoice method of consumption tax, although the direct subtraction method tax, the addition method tax, and the flat tax can also be considered variants of value-added taxation.

Table 3.1 Tax liabilities (T) under various forms of consumption tax levied at a rate of 10% (in US$)

Basic information/Kind of tax	P	M	W	R	T
A. **Transactions** (exclusive of tax)					
1. Sales	400	1,200	1,400	2,000	-
2. Purchases	0	400	1,200	1,400	-
3. Value added (A.1 – A.2)	400	800	200	600	-
a. Wages	(380)	(750)	(190)	(560)	-
b. Business cash flow	(20)	(50)	(10)	(40)	-
B. **Retail sales tax**					
1. Tax on retail sales (10% of A.1, R)	-	-	-	-	**200**
C. VAT					
1. Tax on sales (10% of A.1)	40	120	140	200	500
2. Tax on purchases (10% of A.2)	0	40	120	140	300
3. Net tax (C.1 – C.2)	40	80	20	60	**200**
D. **Direct subtraction method tax**					
1. Tax on sales minus purchases (10% of A.3)	40	80	20	60	**200**
E. **Addition method tax**					
1. Tax on aggregate wages (10% of A.3.a)	38	75	19	56	188
2. Tax on business cash flow (10% of A.3.b)	2	5	1	4	12
3. Total tax	40	80	20	60	**200**
F. **Flat tax**					
1. Tax on individual wages (10% of A.3.a)[a]	38	75	19	56	188
2. Tax on business cash flow (10% of A.3.b)	2	5	1	4	12
3. Total tax	40	80	20	60	**200**

[a] Ignoring the basic exemption applied at the individual level.

Source: Adapted from McLure (1989).

equals the tax under the addition method (line E.3), which, finally, equals the tax collected under the flat tax (line F.3).[3]

3.2 Accounting for Consumption Taxes

The figures in the P&L account (Table 2.2) can also be used to compute the tax liabilities of consumption taxes other than the VAT (with the exception of the

[3] The computation of the tax liability under the personal expenditure tax is not shown in Table 3.1 because its base is not derived from P&L accounts but from aggregate recordings of incomings and outgoings by individuals. Nevertheless, given the same base and rate, the tax liability under the personal expenditure tax should be the same as under the other consumption taxes. In the 1990s, the expenditure tax received much attention in the USA; see Seidman (1997).

personal expenditure tax) and, for comparison, the business income tax. For this purpose, the data in Table 2.2 are regrouped in Table 3.2. Cash-flow accounting is used for inventory and machine purchases, but the matching principle is applied in calculating the base and the tax liability of the conventional business income tax. The top of the table shows the tax base calculations, the bottom the computation of the tax liabilities.

The tax bases and tax liabilities can be calculated in a straightforward manner under the VAT, the direct subtraction method tax, and the flat tax, but not under the addition method tax. While wages are shown on a cash-flow basis, business cash flow must be ascertained by starting with taxable profits for business income tax purposes (US$790, line 13), subtracting investment income (US$200, line 11; this is not value added by the firm), the purchase of machinery (US$100, line 9), and the addition to inventory (US$200, line 8), and adding interest paid (US$35, line 7) and depreciation (US$25, line 6). Accordingly, business cash flow totals US$350, which is added to wages (US$450, line 4) to obtain taxable value added of US$800 (line 12).

These computations highlight the profound differences between an explicitly transactions-based (albeit accounts-controlled) tax, such as the VAT, and the accounts-based nature of the other variants. The net VAT liability can be computed straightforwardly as the difference between the total tax charged on sales minus the total tax invoiced on purchases. This is not the case, however, under the direct subtraction method tax, because there is no directly verifiable presumption that purchases have been subject to tax. Under the flat tax, too, the individualization of wage payments and the calculation of business cash flow require more accounting than is necessary under a transactions-based VAT. In particular, the ascertainment of the tax liability under the addition method tax has to be made on the basis of a P&L account. These differences are crucial if the tax is to be collected on a current basis—say, monthly. While the VAT can easily meet this requirement, the other accounts-based consumption taxes would have difficulties doing so.

The calculation of the retail sales tax is not shown in Table 3.2. It would be imposed on sales (US$1,900 in Table 3.2) at a rate of 10 per cent, so the tax liability would be US$190. This amount is the same as the sum of the net VAT liability in Table 3.2—US$80 (US$190 VAT on sales minus US$110 VAT on purchases)—and the VAT on purchases, US$110, which, under VAT, is paid by the firm to its suppliers, who remit this amount to the VAT administration in proportion to their own value added.

The calculations in Table 3.2, like the earlier accounting identities, establish that the four *in rem* consumption taxes and the flat tax are economically identical given the same base and rate. And, as noted above, this holds true for the personal expenditure tax, too.

Table 3.2 Accounting for tax under consumption taxes and business income taxes levied at a rate of 10% (in US$)

P&L account	Consumption taxes				Business income taxes	
	Tax credit method VAT	Direct subtraction method tax	Flat tax	Addition method tax	Conventional business income tax	Cash-flow business income tax
Tax bases						
1. Sales	1,900	1,900	1,900		1,900	1,900
2. Purchases	– 1,100	– 1,100	– 1,100		– 800	– 1,100
3. Value added/gross profits	= 800	= 800	= 800		= 1,100	= 800
4. Wages			– 450	+ 450	– 450	– 450
5. Rents/cash flow			= 350		= 650	= 350
6. Depreciation				+ 25	– 25	
7. Interest paid				+ 35	– 35	
8. Inventory change				– 200		
9. Purchase of machinery				– 100		
10. Operating profits				+ 590	= 590	
11. Investment income					+ 200	
12. Taxable value added	800	800	800	= 800		
13. Taxable profits/cash flow					= 790	350
Tax liabilities						
A. VAT	80					
a. VAT on sales (10% of 1)	190					
b. VAT on purchases (10% of 2)	– 110					
B. Direct subtraction method tax (10% of 3)		80				
C. Flat tax			80			
a. Tax on wages (10% of 4)			45			
b. Tax on rents (10% of 5)			35			
D. Addition method tax (10% of 12)				80		
E. Business income tax (10% of 13)					79	
F. Cash-flow business income tax (10% of 13)						35

For comparison purposes, Table 3.2 also shows the computation of the tax liabilities of two kinds of business income tax:

- a conventional business income tax, under which purchases are related to sales in the same reporting period (matching principle) and machinery is depreciated over a four-year period; and
- a cash-flow business income tax, which allows the immediate expensing of inventory additions and machinery, but which does not allow a deduction for interest.[4]

The application of the matching principle implies that a conventional business income tax includes the normal return on capital as well as economic rents—i.e. business cash flow (inframarginal profits)—in its base. By contrast, a cash-flow business income tax excludes the opportunity cost of capital from its base by allowing immediate expensing of investments and adding back interest. Not surprisingly, the base of a cash-flow business income tax is the same as the item 'economic rents' in the base of the flat tax, i.e. US$350. Accordingly, the return on marginal investments, the hurdle rate of return, is not affected by a consumption tax. Other things being equal, this should promote saving and investment compared with an income tax.

Finally, the calculation of the various consumption and business income tax liabilities from the P&L account indicates that all of these taxes are basically identical for tax compliance purposes. The VAT, like the business income tax, is an accounts-controlled tax. Accordingly, there is little difference between a VAT audit and a business income tax audit. This implies that these taxes should be administered by the same tax organization. VAT registration, return, and payment processing activities could be placed in a separate department, but VAT audits should be performed jointly with income tax audits. Also, tax enforcement procedures should be closely linked to similar procedures for income tax purposes.

3.3 Differences between Consumption Taxes

Although in theory all consumption taxes are economically equivalent, in practice various important differences arise between them. Design and feasibility constraints, and open economy aspects, have important implications for achieving basic, if sometimes conflicting, tax objectives, such as:

[4] It should be noted that the cash-flow variant is equivalent to a business income tax, conventionally computed, which permits a deduction from profits of the normal return on equity (equal to the inflation-adjusted world rate of interest) and which does not tax this return at shareholder level (nor the deductible interest on debt at debtholder level). This variant goes by the name of allowance for corporate equity or ACE (Institute for Fiscal Studies, 1991; Cnossen, 2018b).

- fairness in the tax burden distribution;
- neutrality with respect to producer and consumer choices;
- tax revenue allocation to the country of consumption (destination principle);
- minimization of administration and compliance costs; and
- restraining the ability of special interest groups to tinker with the tax base and rate, called political robustness.

Each of these implications is briefly reviewed below.

Fairness The retail sales tax, the VAT, the direct subtraction method tax, and the addition method tax are *in rem* taxes collected at the business level, without regard to the personal circumstances of individual consumers, who are assumed to bear the tax. In this context, fairness simply means that all goods and services should be taxed alike. The flat tax and, especially, the personal expenditure tax, on the other hand, are *in personam* taxes, primarily collected at the individual level and hence equipped to incorporate basic allowances and graduated rates in order to achieve vertical equity goals (including a progressive burden distribution). In fact, the personal expenditure tax, just like the income tax, can be levied fully in accordance with the ability-to-pay principle.

Neutrality If consumption taxes are not to interfere with producer and consumer choices, relative prices should remain the same after the imposition of the tax. This means that the base—all consumer goods and services—should be defined as comprehensively as possible and taxed at the same rate, while producer goods should not be taxed. As shown in real-world experience, this is possible under the VAT, but the retail sales tax has difficulty reaching services performed by small establishments (there is no tax on purchases that can be linked to the tax on sales) and in freeing dual-use goods (which can be used for exempt business as well as taxable personal purposes) from tax. Under the VAT, a tax credit will not be permitted unless the taxpayer proves to the satisfaction of the tax authorities that the dual-use goods have been applied for business purposes.[5]

There is no widespread experience with the design and administration of other *in rem* consumption taxes, but since they are accounts-based rather than transactions-based, in practice equal treatment of all goods and services may be more difficult to achieve than under the VAT.

Presumably, the flat tax and the personal expenditure tax should be judged primarily regarding their effects on the work–leisure choice and the intertemporal consumption choice. All consumption taxes are neutral regarding the choice between present and future consumption, but they discriminate in favour of

[5] This favours the VAT on the plausible assumption that a taxpayer is less likely to cheat the tax authorities under the VAT than his suppliers under the retail sales tax. Under the retail sales tax, moreover, a taxpayer has an incentive to treat his customers no less favourably (by refusing the exemption) than his competitor might do.

leisure, which cannot be taxed. By contrast, an income tax distorts both the work–leisure choice and the intertemporal consumption choice. However, since the base of the income tax is broader than the base of a consumption tax, the rate of an income tax can be set at a relatively lower level to yield the same amount of revenue. This lower rate should mitigate distortions, whose size tends to increase with the square of the tax rate. Accordingly, it is an empirical question whether an income tax or a consumption tax is, on balance, more distortionary.

Destination principle In an open economy, the revenue of the retail sales tax, the VAT, and the direct subtraction method tax is allocated to the country of consumption by applying appropriate border tax adjustments (BTAs). Exports are freed of tax, and imports are taxed on a par with domestically produced goods. In practice, the VAT is better equipped to apply correct BTAs than either the retail sales tax or the direct subtraction method tax, because the tax that has to be rebated is stated on purchase invoices, while any under- or over-taxation of imports is automatically corrected in domestic stages of production or distribution. Under the retail sales tax, the difficulty of freeing dual-use goods from tax means that the tax enters into export prices, while imports (whose price does not include any tax on dual-use goods) tend to be undertaxed compared with similar domestically produced goods. Under the direct subtraction method tax, furthermore, there is no presumptively correct documentary evidence (such as VAT invoices) of tax paid in previous stages of production and distribution, which hampers the application of unambiguous BTAs.[6]

In contrast, the addition method tax, the flat tax, and the personal expenditure tax would be levied on an origin basis (exports taxed, imports free of tax) or a source basis, to use income tax terminology. Generally, this means that the primary impact of the tax is on producers, because consumers can buy goods at world prices without tax. Producers would try to shift the tax forward to the consumer level, and would incur costs in doing so over and above the tax. In the economics literature, it has been proven that origin taxation is more likely to violate production efficiency than destination taxation (Diamond and Mirrlees, 1971).[7] The taxation of exports, moreover, would invite transfer pricing issues similar to those that bedevil the corporation tax under an arm's-length separate accounting system.

[6] Applying BTAs under a direct subtraction method tax might also invite objections from a country's trading partners, who would argue that it is not a tax on products per se but rather an accounts-based tax on value added comparable to the business income tax, and hence not eligible for export rebate under the rules of the World Trade Organization (WTO).

[7] See the lucid exposition in Crawford, Keen, and Smith (2010). These authors point out that under the equivalence theorem, it is asserted that it does not matter for trade and investment whether goods and services are taxed on a destination or an origin basis. Since imports are exchanged for exports, a tax on exports is equivalent to a tax on imports. In practice, however, the conditions for the equivalence theorem to hold are so restrictive that it is of little value for policy purposes.

Administration and compliance costs Compliance and tax administration costs should be largely the same under the VAT, the retail sales tax, and the direct subtraction method tax, but these costs would probably be greater under the flat tax and the personal expenditure tax, which are mainly collected at the level of individuals. Presumably, the retail sales tax, the direct subtraction method tax, and the addition method tax are more vulnerable to evasion than the VAT. Administratively, the retail level tends to be the weakest link in the production–distribution chain. The account-based nature of the direct subtraction method tax and the addition method tax also implies that the tax is not shown on invoices. Hence, there is less of an audit trail than under the VAT. Also, sellers and buyers do not have opposing interests in the amount of tax that is being charged, presumptively resulting in the same tax. The personal expenditure tax probably is the most complicated consumption tax, because it requires the registration and monitoring of wealth.

Political robustness Politically, the VAT is the most robust consumption tax, primarily because pre-retail firms do not benefit from exemptions that make it impossible for them to pass their suppliers' tax on to customers. By contrast, the subtraction method tax, the flat tax, and the personal expenditure tax, and to a lesser extent the retail sales tax, are vulnerable to erosion through political favouritism. Under the direct subtraction method tax, it would be tempting to exempt some 'worthy' product, sector, or activity. The flat tax and the personal expenditure tax would be susceptible to similar politically motivated concessions as arise under the individual income tax.

3.4 Preferred Choice: VAT or RST?

The two consumption taxes with which there has been much experience and which are probably 'most' feasible are the VAT and the RST. While the two are economically equivalent, there are important administrative differences that are worth mentioning (Cnossen, 1987, 2002, 2017b):

- VAT can afford a higher threshold (small-business exemption) than RST, because tax is imposed on sales to small exempt businesses, which is not creditable by them. Under RST, by contrast, no tax is collected from exempt businesses. In other words, the revenue lost on account of an equivalent threshold is smaller under VAT than under RST.
- Under most VATs, 80 per cent of the tax is collected from 20 per cent of registered businesses. Under an RST, the same amount of tax would have to be collected from perhaps three to four times as many businesses. Under VAT, the smaller number of large businesses, which have good books of account, is easier to audit than the larger number of small businesses under an RST, which often do not have reliable books of account.

- Under VAT, up to half of the tax may be collected at the import stage by customs; under RST, no tax is collected at customs (except on imports by individuals), but nearly all tax must be collected at retail.
- Under VAT, the whole production–distribution chain is involved in remitting the tax from the consumer to the government, not just the retail stage. Retailers are more likely to default on the tax that they owe to the government than on the tax that has been invoiced to them by their suppliers. This implies, among other things, that VAT can sustain a higher rate than RST.
- VAT may do a better job than RST regarding the tax treatment of dual-use goods, which can be used for business as well as private purposes (computers, furniture, carpeting, etc.). Under VAT, it is up to the business to prove to the satisfaction of the tax authorities that the goods are used for business purposes; under RST, business persons can show their exemption certificate relieving them from the obligation to pay tax, but subsequently use the goods for private purposes anyway. More generally, under a VAT sellers can be told that they always have to charge tax, regardless of the status of the buyer (business or consumer), whereas under RST the seller has to verify the stated purpose of the use of the goods by buyers who show an exemption certificate.
- Similar problems arise with consumption 'through the business'. VAT denies the tax credit for purchases of food products, beverages, employee fringe benefits, and personnel transportation, even if made for business purposes, say, to entertain clients. Likewise, 'reverse-charging' would have to ensure that consumption items bought free of tax are not diverted to personal use without payment of tax under RST. VAT may be better placed to tax these goods, because evading the tax requires taxpayers to fraudulently claim a tax credit. Reverse-charging, on the other hand, induces them simply to 'forget' that tax should have been self-assessed.
- VAT tends to be better at taxing services rendered directly to consumers to the extent that the provision of services involves the use of taxable goods. The tax on purchases can then be used in verifying the return of the services rendered.
- VAT is susceptible to the same kind of fraudulent practices as the income tax: understatement of sales, overstatement of purchases, consumption 'through the business', etc. However, this is also true of the RST, but the number of registered businesses that have to be monitored is larger than under VAT. The VAT, moreover, leaves a stronger paper trail than the RST (or the income tax), which has a 'preventive deterrence effect, leading to lower levels of evasion on transactions covered by the paper trail', which, globally, 'acts as a complement to the audit probability' (Pommeranz, 2015, p. 2566).
- A weak spot of the VAT—a serious one—is the necessity for refunds on exports, which are zero-rated. By contrast, refunds at export do not occur under RST, because retailers generally do not export or are forward integrated with the export stage—e.g. like Amazon.

On balance, the arguments in favour of VAT outweigh the arguments for RST (also see Bird and Gendron (2007)). The inherent operational drawback of the RST—not to be underestimated, particularly in Africa—is that the retail stage is the weakest link in the production–distribution process in terms of compliance and enforcement. On the other hand, the equally inherent administrative problem under the VAT, serious as well, is the need for refunds if the tax on purchases exceeds the tax on sales, which always occurs at the export stage where sales are zero-rated. Strong points in favour of the VAT are the involvement of large firms in the revenue collection process and the imposition at the import stage. While the VAT scores highly on neutrality and feasibility grounds, as an *in rem* tax it cannot be levied on an ability-to-pay basis (nor can the RST). But this should be acceptable if suitable adjustments to the income tax and social benefit schemes can be made or the expenditure side of the budget is used to finance pro-poor projects.

3.5 Prevalence of Consumption Taxes

Not surprisingly, the VAT is the most prevalent form of consumption tax in the world. Some 160 countries have adopted it, although in practice differences in design can be large. Viewed globally, the advance of the VAT is the most significant development in the field of taxation in the past 60 years (Cnossen, 1998a). The march of VAT started in the 1960s in the EU (where the introduction of the harmonized VAT is a non-negotiable condition for membership) and South America, and continued in the 1990s in Central and Eastern Europe and the countries that are now members of the Commonwealth of Independent States (CIS, the republics of the former Soviet Union). Australia is the latest industrialized country that has converted to VAT. In 2017, India introduced a dual VAT levied at the state level as well as the federal level. Saudi Arabia and the United Arab Emirates followed suit in 2018. The spread of the VAT owes much to the International Monetary Fund (IMF)'s Fiscal Affairs Department, where Michael Keen has been the intellectual driving force.

The retail sales tax is levied by 45 out of 50 US states and the District of Columbia (plus some 9,000 local governments), as well as by 3 out of 10 Canadian provinces.[8] The retail sales taxes in the USA are not as broad-based and neutral as most VATs are because they tend to exclude most services from the base and to widely tax investment goods. However, the distortions are tempered by the low rates. The Nordic countries and Switzerland also used to levy a retail sales tax, but these countries switched to the VAT because it is better equipped to free producer

[8] The federal government in Canada levies a VAT, called goods and services tax (GST), as does the province of Québec (called QST). The Atlantic provinces (New Brunswick, Newfoundland and Labrador, Nova Scotia, and Prince Edward Island) and Ontario have piggybacked the federal VAT in the form of surtaxes, called harmonized sales tax (HST). In addition to the federal GST, British Columbia, Manitoba, and Saskatchewan impose a provincial (retail) sales tax (PST). Oil-rich Alberta does not have an HST or PST. For a full treatment, see Bird and Gendron (2001).

goods of tax and easier to enforce. In Africa, Zimbabwe used to impose a retail sales tax but it switched to VAT in 2004.

Japan introduced a direct subtraction method tax in 1989.[9] In combination with an extraordinarily high threshold, it shields exempt small businesses from the effects of the tax on inputs, obviating the need for them to register in order to be able to pass the tax on to customers. The direct subtraction method tax used to be levied in Belarus, too, apparently with little success (Bird, 1995). Further, some member countries of the CIS used to impose a tax-credit type of VAT through producer stages, but taxed distributors on their margins. Although this does not seem to make much sense (the difference in function between producers and distributors can hardly be made relevant for tax purposes), the explanation should be sought in the way in which businesses were taxed under the old turnover tax (Summers and Sunley, 1995).

The flat tax has been proposed by Hall and Rabushka (1985, 1995). It has received much attention in the USA because its wage component resembles a progressive income tax through the application of a basic exemption.[10] As a result, it mitigates the regressivity of a consumption tax for lower-income groups. What the flat tax cannot do, of course, is make the tax burden distribution more progressive for higher-income groups by taxing capital income in full.

The addition method tax is used in some countries to tax the value added by financial institutions, which is difficult to compute under a credit-invoice VAT because the intermediation charge that should be taxed is embedded in the interest, premium, or return, which should not be taxed. Israel, Argentina, and France have experience with the addition method tax on banking. Italy administers a direct addition method tax, called regional production tax or IRAP (*imposta regionale sulle attività produttive*). It is not a destination-based VAT, however, because the tax is not refunded at export or levied at import (Cnossen, 2006a). In the USA, Michigan's 'single business tax' and New Hampshire's 'business enterprise tax' are addition-based kinds of VATs (Kenyon, 1996).

India and Sri Lanka used to levy a non-cash-flow type of personal expenditure tax in the 1950s, but abandoned it after a few years because the tax proved difficult to administer properly. Subsequently, the feasibility of the expenditure tax has greatly improved following the pioneering work of an able lawyer, William Andrews (1974), and in his wake the US Department of the Treasury (1977) and the Meade Committee (Meade, 1978). Andrews showed that annual taxable consumption expenditures can be computed on an aggregate cash-flow basis as the difference between incomings and saving rather than by having to add up all individual expenditures made during the tax year.

[9] For a description of the Japanese VAT, see Schenk, Thuronyi, and Cui (2015), who report that Japan is moving toward a credit-invoice VAT. An account of the history of the Japanese VAT can be found in Ishi (2001).

[10] For a cautious favourable assessment, see Gale (1998).

3.6 Lessons from Worldwide Experience with VAT

This chapter has shown that a discussion of various alternative consumption taxes sheds light on the nature of VAT. Economically, the VAT is equivalent to a retail sales tax even with respect to the timing of tax collections. VAT is the preferred form of consumption tax, however, because it is collected piecemeal throughout the production–distribution process, does not interfere with the forms and methods of doing business, unambiguously relieves exports of tax, is less vulnerable to evasion and avoidance, and is relatively easy to understand for the business community. By not taxing the normal return on capital, VAT does not affect the hurdle rate of return on investment.

With VAT, the eye should be on the ball, and the ball is revenue. As an *in rem* tax, VAT cannot be used to achieve vertical equity goals. Its main objective is to raise revenue as neutrally as possible. This requires the broadest possible base and a single rate. In this respect, the European VATs leave much to be desired (Cnossen, 2003). The EU pioneered the VAT and mistakenly tried to align its burden distribution as closely as possible to the old turnover taxes, although all member states had other more sophisticated instruments in place, such as income taxes and social benefit schemes, to adjust tax and expenditure patterns in line with the pre-tax situation.

With VAT, it is crucial to get it right from the start (Keen, 2009). Deviations from the undisputed requirements of a modern VAT are nearly impossible to undo once the tax has been introduced. Basically, the following lessons can be learned from the experience in new VAT countries, such as New Zealand, Singapore, and South Africa, and, to a lesser extent, Australia and Canada (which have unnecessarily muddled up the VAT rate structure):

- Limit exemptions to those dictated by strict administrative cost–benefit considerations. Exemptions violate the logic and functionality of the VAT. They distort input choices and harm exports. Accordingly, most health, education, cultural, financial, and insurance services and public bodies ideally should be brought into the VAT base. Europe and, in its wake, most African countries exempted these items, because it was considered 'not done' to tax (semi-)public bodies and in order to mimic the perceived burden distribution of the previous turnover taxes. This was a mistake, because exemptions cause over- or under-taxation, can become a tax on exports, penalize outsourcing and investment, and promote 'exemption creep'. Also, exemptions greatly increase administrative and compliance costs. Chapters 9 and 10 analyse the issues and repercussions more fully.
- Levy the VAT at a single rate and do not impose a zero rate on so-called basic necessities, such as groceries. As shown in Chapter 7, a zero rate on food is not a well-targeted instrument to alleviate the VAT burden on the poor. In absolute terms, the benefit of a zero rate accrues mainly to

middle- and higher-income consumers who buy more expensive varieties of food, eat out more often, and throw food away more easily. Consequently, the concessionary treatment of food tends to give twice as much relief to higher-income groups as to lower-income groups, an odd way of alleviating the plight of the poor. The zero rate should be confined to exports. Again, Europe started with highly differentiated rate structures (still found in the Maghreb countries, especially Morocco) to mimic the burden distribution of the old turnover taxes, a move that proved to be rather counterproductive.

- Provide a high threshold, discussed in Chapter 16, so that small businesses and farmers do not have to register and pay VAT, saving on administration and compliance costs. Compliance costs are disproportionately higher for smaller businesses than for larger ones. Of course, small entities would still pay VAT on inputs purchased from taxable businesses, implying that only part of the potential revenue would be forgone.[11] At the same time, optional registration should be provided for small businesses, so that they can pass the tax on inputs on to their customers, if desired. Perhaps there should be a minimum threshold, below which registration is not possible, to prevent very small businesses from cluttering up the VAT register.
- Target enforcement controls through selective risk-based audits in conjunction with the business income tax. In most African countries, fraud and evasion are probably dominated by shadow or informal economy fraud (as it is in the EU, but hugely so in Africa) and less by abuse of tax credits or contrived insolvency fraud, the domestic variant of carousel fraud.
- Provide for expeditious refunds of excess VAT credits, which should arise particularly at the export stage. The VAT administration has no right to keep the VAT paid on inputs by exporters and remitted to the VAT administration by their suppliers. As discussed in Chapter 8, the need for refunds on mineral exports, for instance, can be avoided by providing for a reverse-charge mechanism for imported capital goods. Other refund claims can be processed more quickly by distinguishing 'approved' exporters (eligible for refunds without much further ado) from first or 'non-approved' exporters, who should be subject to desk or field audit.

[11] Based on an earlier publication (Cnossen, 1994), Cnossen (2002) calculated that in the USA a $100,000 exemption would reduce the number of potential registrants (25 million at that time) to approximately 9 million (including 5 million voluntary registrants)—fewer than the number of registrants under a national retail sales tax. The exempt potential registrants would account for 2.6% of aggregate gross receipts. In other words, if their value added were one-third of gross receipts and the VAT rate were 10%, the revenue forgone would be less than 0.1% of gross receipts.

4
Overview of VATs in Africa

This chapter provides an overview of the countries in Africa that have a VAT, grouped by the particular regional economic community (REC) of which they are members. Salient features pertaining to the year of introduction, the predecessor sales tax, the range of non-standard exemptions,[1] the rate structures, and the coverage of the excises on luxury goods and services are noted and broadly discussed.

4.1 Regional Economic Communities

All African countries belong to one or more regional economic communities, which operate under the umbrella of the African Economic Community (AEC). The RECs pursue goals that are reminiscent of the early objectives of the EU. They purport to promote trade among members through the formation of free trade areas, customs unions, and common markets (and, further down the road, monetary unions and political federations). In terms of taxation, this involves the abolition of internal customs duties and the adoption of common external tariffs, but also the alignment of VATs (and excise taxes) to the extent that they interfere with the proper functioning of the RECs.

As shown in the legend of Figure 4.1, the AEC consists of eight pillars and four subgroups, which tend to be integrated somewhat more closely.[2] The (ambitious) goals of the AEC, agreed to in 1992, are a customs union by 2019 and a common market by 2023, followed by an economic and monetary union in 2028.[3] The Community of Sahel-Saharan States (CEN-SAD) is not shown in the figure. It has fallen behind schedule in implementing the integration stages of the Abuja Treaty and has been stagnant on stage two: eliminating tariff barriers and non-tariff barriers. Most of its members also belong to other RECs, in which

[1] Non-standard exemptions are exemptions other than the 'standard exemptions' of the EU's Common VAT Directive (2006). These exemptions are discussed in Chapters 9 and 10.

[2] See Chapter 8 for further details. African regional blocs not participating in the AEC (and not shown in Figure 4.1) are the Greater Arab Free Trade Area (GAFTA), the Economic Community of the Great Lakes Countries (CEPGL), the Indian Ocean Commission (IOC), the Liptako–Gourma Authority (LGA), and the Mano River Union (MRU).

[3] Presumably, these ambitious goals are superseded by the launch in Kigali on 21 March 2018 of the African Continental Free Trade Area (AfCFTA) by, more realistically, 2063 as soon as sufficient member countries have signed up to it; see Chapter 8.

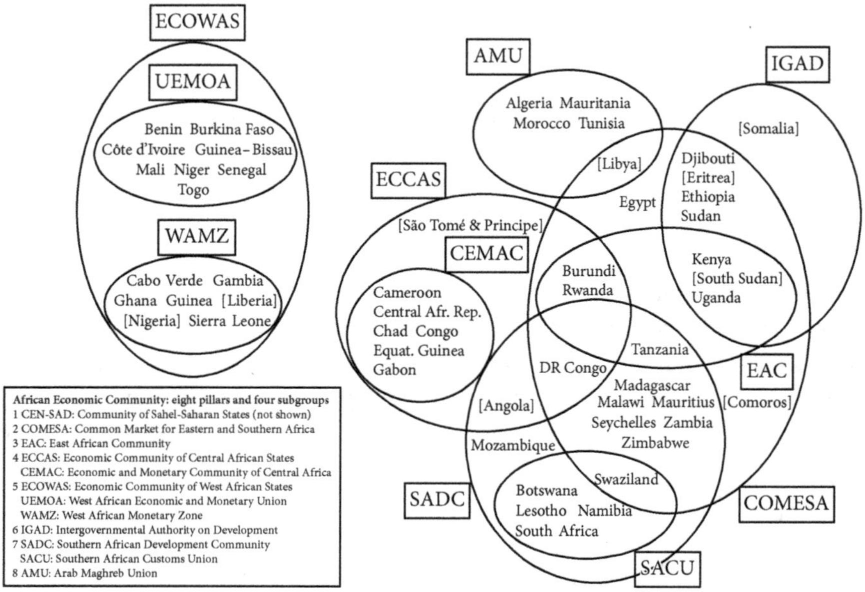

Figure 4.1 Africa: regional economic communities, 2018

Note: Square brackets indicate countries without a VAT.

Source: Adapted from Wikipedia (accessed March 2018).

they may play a more active role. Algeria and Mauritania do not participate in any of the pillars, although they are signatories to the AEC Treaty. Countries without a VAT have been placed between square brackets; their sales and excise tax systems are discussed in Chapter 5.

For the purposes of this book, the most relevant RECs (and their VATs) are the following:

- The Southern African Customs Union (SACU) is the most closely integrated REC of Africa. The VATs of Botswana, Lesotho, Namibia, and Swaziland are nearly identical, having been modelled after the VAT in South Africa, which in turn more or less resembles the broad-based New Zealand goods and services tax (GST). The South African Revenue Service (SARS) collects the excise taxes and import duties at import via South African ports for SACU member countries and distributes the proceeds among them.
- SACU is a subgroup of the Southern African Development Community (SADC). The VATs in eight other SADC countries in Figure 4.1 (Tanzania is also a member of SADC, but participates more fully in the EAC) are generally modelled after the anglo-, franco-, or lusophone VAT depending on which country provided the technical advice on the design of the VAT. Three member countries—DR Congo, the Seychelles, and Swaziland—introduced the VAT in 2012, leaving Angola as the only SADC member that does not (yet) have a VAT (see the next chapter).

- Six East African countries—Burundi, Kenya, Rwanda, South Sudan, Tanzania (which also belongs to SADC), and Uganda—form the East African Community (EAC). Except for South Sudan, all EAC member countries have a VAT and actively pursue VAT and excise tax coordination in their REC.
- A further six African countries belong to the Economic and Monetary Community of Central Africa (CEMAC, after its French name, *Communauté Économique et Monétaire de l'Afrique Centrale*). The VATs of these countries are largely identical and resemble the French version of the EU VAT.[4] CEMAC is a subgroup of the Economic Community of Central African States (ECCAS), which is not discussed further. ECCAS countries that do not belong to CEMAC are either a more active member of another REC (Angola, Burundi, DR Congo, Rwanda) or do not have a VAT (São Tomé & Principe).
- Eight countries belong to the West African Economic and Monetary Union (UEMOA, after its French name, *Union Économique et Monétaire Ouest Africaine*). Like CEMAC, the VATs of the UEMOA countries closely resemble the French VAT.
- UEMOA is a subgroup of the Economic Community of West African States (ECOWAS). As shown in Figure 4.1, the other ECOWAS countries launched their own West African Monetary Zone (WAMZ). Their VAT legislation is based on the British statute, except Guinea and Cabo Verde which have a franco- or lusophone type of VAT, respectively. Liberia and Nigeria do not yet have a VAT, strictly speaking. Liberia levies a manufacturers' tax of sorts and Nigeria a turnover tax. Admittedly, Nigeria calls its consumption tax a VAT, but it does not allow a credit for tax on capital goods and services, while refunds are provided through budgetary allocations, which, if exhausted, leave exporters and other taxpayers entitled to a refund stuck with the VAT on inputs.
- Four North African countries and Mauritania have joined hands in the Arab Maghreb Union (AMU). The AMU countries have closely followed the evolving practice of taxing consumption in France, starting with a production tax, adding a tax on services, and capping it with a consumption tax on luxury goods. These taxes have been merged into the VAT, but many vestiges of the old regimes are still discernible. Among the AMU countries, oil-rich Libya does not have a VAT.
- The Intergovernmental Authority on Development (IGAD) is little more than a talking group established for drought control and economic development in the Greater Horn of Africa. Among IGAD countries, Eritrea, Somalia, and South Sudan (which belongs to the EAC too) do not have a VAT.

[4] See Waerzeggers (2007) for a description of VATs in francophone African countries.

- The Common Market for Eastern and Southern Africa (COMESA), which overlaps with six other RECs, is not discussed separately, although it should be noted that in 2009 COMESA teamed up with ECOWAS and SADC to form the African Economic Community (AEC). Again, its member countries participate more fully in other, smaller, RECs.

Four RECs (SACU, EAC, CEMAC, UEMOA) can be considered more or less complete customs unions, which have abolished most intra-REC duties (but not necessarily non-tariff barriers) and adopted a common external tariff (with many exceptions). Further, there are three free trade areas (SADC, ECOWAS, COMESA) in which intra-REC duties have been abolished on many but not all products, while country-specific external tariffs are still being maintained. Finally, two RECs (AMU, IGAD) are 'not notified agreements' to the World Trade Organization.

The RECs actively discuss the alignment of their member countries' tax systems, including the VATs, in their quest to establish a common market. Although VAT harmonization has its advantages, it also tends to institutionalize existing shortcomings, as has happened in the EU with the promulgation of the Common VAT Directive in 1977. Experience has shown that the Directive is exceedingly difficult to adapt to new economic and institutional developments or best practices in other countries, since this requires the unanimous consent of all 28 member states.[5] Chapter 8 discusses the economic integration and tax coordination issues faced by African RECs more fully.

4.2 Broad Characteristics of VATs

Grouped by the REC to which they belong, Table 4.1 lists the VATs in Africa alongside their year of inception, the kind of sales tax levied previously, the extent of the non-standard exemptions (an important determinant of the VAT base and hence its revenue productivity), the VAT rate structures (lower, standard, and higher-than-standard rates), and the scope of the excise tax system, particularly the coverage of the excises on luxury goods, which serve a similar purpose to a higher-than-standard VAT rate.

Types of VAT

Broadly speaking, two kinds of VAT were introduced on the African continent. The SACU countries modelled their VAT, at the initiative of South Africa, on the

[5] For an assessment of the shortcomings of the EU VAT, see Cnossen (2003). For a dismal picture of the Dutch VAT reflecting the long shadow of the EU's Common Directive, see Bettendorf and Cnossen (2015).

Table 4.1 Africa: survey of VAT systems, 2018

RECs and countries	Year VAT introduced	Predecessor sales tax[a]	Non-standard VAT exemptions[b]	VAT rates			Luxury excises[d]
				Lower[c] (% and coverage)	Standard (%)	Higher (% and coverage)	
Southern African Development Community (SADC)							
SACU							
Botswana	2002	MST_{tc}	Few	0 (various)	12	-	Many
Lesotho	2001	MST_{tc}	Some	0 (various); 5 (few)	14	-	Many
Namibia	2000	MST_{tc}	Few	0 (many)	15	-	Many
South Africa	1991	MST_{tc}	Few	0 (various)	15	-	Many
Swaziland	2012	MST_{tc}	Some	0 (various)	14	25 (tobacco, alcohol)	Many
Other							
Congo, DR	2012	Turnover	Many	-	16	-	Various
Madagascar	1994	Turnover	Many	-	20	-	Many
Malawi	2005	Production	Many	0 (many)	16.5	-	Various
Mauritius	1998	Production	Various	0 (various)	15	-	Many
Mozambique	1999	Production	Various	0 (various); 7.2 (few)	17	-	Many
Seychelles	2012	Production	Many	0 (some)	15	-	Various
Zambia	1995	Production	Many	-	16	-	Some
Zimbabwe	2004	RST	Some	0 (various)	15	-	Some
East African Community (EAC)							
Burundi	2009	Turnover	Some	10 (food imports)	18	-	Various
Kenya	1990	MST_{sus}	Some	0 (few)	16	-	Various
Rwanda	2001	Production	Many	-	18	-	Some
Tanzania	1998	MST_{sus}	Many	-	18	-	Some
Uganda	1996	MST_{sus}	Many	0 (various)	18	-	Some

Continued

Table 4.1 *Continued*

RECs and countries	Year VAT introduced	Predecessor sales tax[a]	Non-standard VAT exemptions[b]	VAT rates			Luxury excises[d]
				Lower[c] (% and coverage)	Standard (%)	Higher (% and coverage)	
Economic and Monetary Community of Central Africa (CEMAC)							
Cameroon	1999	Production	Many	-	19.25	-	Many
Central African Rep.	2001	Turnover	Many	5 (few)	19	-	Many
Chad	2000	Turnover	Many	-	18	-	Many
Congo	1997	Production	Many	0 (wood); 5 (some)	18	-	Many
Equatorial Guinea	2005	Turnover	Many	6 (some)	15	-	Many
Gabon	1995	Production	Many	5 (cement); 10 (various)	18	-	Many
Economic Community of West African States (ECOWAS)							
UEMOA							
Benin	1980	Turnover	Various	-	18	-	Various
Burkina Faso	1993	Turnover	Various	-	18	-	Some
Côte d'Ivoire	1991	MST_{tc}	Various	9 (some)	18	21.31 (tobacco)	Some
Guinea-Bissau	1998	Production	Various	0 (medicines); 10 (many)	17	20	Various
Mali	1991	Production	Various	5 (few)	18	-	Some
Niger	1986	Production	Many	-	19	-	Some
Senegal	1980	Production	Various	10 (tourism)	18	-	Various
Togo	1995	Production	Various	-	18	-	Various

WAMZ							
Cabo Verde	2004	Turnover	Various	-	15	-	Many
Gambia	2013	MST_{sus}	Various	-	15	-	Some
Ghana	1998	MST_{sus}	Many	5 (real estate)	17.5	-	Some
Guinea	1996	MST_{sub}	Various	-	18	-	Many
Sierra Leone	2009	Production	Many	-	15	-	Some
Arab Maghreb Union (AMU)							
Algeria	1992	MST_{tc}	Some	9 (various)	19	-	Various
Mauritania	1995	MST_{sub}	Various	-	16	18 (fuel, telecom)	Some
Morocco	1986	MST_{tc}	Various	0, 7 (some); 10, 14 (various)	20	-	Some
Tunisia	1988	MST_{sub}	Various	7, 13 (various)	19	-	Various
Intergovernmental Authority on Development (IGAD) and Egypt							
Djibouti	2009	Production	Few	0 (some)	10	-	Some
Egypt	2016	Production	Various	5 (many)	14	22 (many)	Some
Ethiopia	2003	Production	Various	-	15	-	Many
Sudan	2000	Production	Various	-	17	30 (telecom)	Some

[a] The notations have the following meaning: MST = manufacturers' sales tax using the tax credit method (MST_{tc}), the suspension method (MST_{sus}), or the subtraction method (MST_{sub}) to eliminate potential cascading effects; Production = French-type production tax (basically an extended excise tax system); RST = retail sales tax; Turnover = cumulative (cascade) type of sales tax. See Box 4.1 for further details.

[b] Non-standard exemptions are all exemptions other than healthcare, welfare and social security work, education, non-profit organizations, cultural services, public postal and broadcasting services, insurance, financial services, gaming, immovable property (except if newly created), and 'out-of-scope' governments. The coverage of the non-standard exemptions is denoted by 'Few' (some enumerated basic foodstuffs and public transportation), 'Some' (more food items and one or two public utilities), 'Various' (most unprocessed foods, agricultural inputs, medical goods, newspapers, and more than two utilities), and 'Many' (all unprocessed foods, agricultural inputs, medical goods, two or more utilities, print, and fuel); details can be found in Table 10.1.

[c] The coverage of the lower rates is listed in ascending order as few, some, various, or many goods and services.

[d] The coverage of the luxury excises is listed in ascending order as some, various, or many goods and services.

Source: Appendices A and B.

New Zealand GST, which has very few exemptions and is essentially levied at a single rate (by contrast, SACU countries zero-rate a limited number of unprocessed foodstuffs and kerosene). As a result, the VATs in Southern Africa should be exceptionally revenue productive. Recently, Kenya has also moved closer to the New Zealand model.

The VATs in all other African countries are based on the EU's Common VAT Directive (2006), be it the anglo-, franco-, or lusophone version.[6] As is well known, the EU VAT has many more exemptions and differentiated rates than the New Zealand GST and, hence, tends to be more complicated. SADC member countries (outside SACU and with the exception of DR Congo, Madagascar, and Mozambique), the EAC countries (except Burundi and Rwanda), the WAMZ countries (except Cabo Verde and Guinea), and the members of IGAD based their VATs mainly on UK legislation. Like the UK, most of these countries apply a zero rate to various essential products, which is not permitted under the Common Directive.[7] Most other countries have followed in the footsteps of the French VAT, which is also levied in accordance with the EU's Directive but has a civil law flavour different from the UK VAT. Lastly, three countries—Cabo Verde, Guinea-Bissau, and Mozambique—have a Portuguese type of VAT, which again is based on the EU's Common Directive. Prima facie, the VATs appear to be more complicated as one moves from the South African to the French and Portuguese versions of the VAT.[8]

Year VAT Introduced

Most African countries introduced the VAT around the turn of the century (see Table 4.1), but some countries arrived much earlier on the VAT scene.[9] The year of introduction has some significance since it has been suggested that VATs (like wine) get better with age, presumably because VAT administrations and taxpayers gain experience the longer the tax has been around (Ebrill et al., 2001).

[6] Promulgated in 1977 as Council Directive 77/388/EEC of 17 May 1977 on the harmonization of the laws of the member states relating to turnover taxes, and subsequently codified and reissued (but not basically changed) as Council Directive 2006/112/EC of 28 November 2006 on the common system of value-added tax (OJ L 347, 11 Dec. 2006, pp. 1–118).

[7] Upon accession to the EU, the United Kingdom (and Ireland) obtained a derogation from this requirement. For a full legal commentary on the Common Directive, see Terra and Kajus (2015).

[8] An illustration of the complexity of the French VAT is the admonition in an early International Bureau of Fiscal Documentation loose-leaf edition of the European VATs that the rates should not be applied without consulting an expert. This telling advice may still be relevant in some North African countries.

[9] There may be some confusion about the exact date on which some countries introduced the VAT. Various African countries—for instance, Côte d'Ivoire—started with a manufacturers' sales tax using the tax-credit mechanism (essential to a VAT) to eliminate tax-on-tax or cascading effects. They called these taxes VAT from the beginning, although the wholesale and retail stages were included at a later date.

Predecessor Sales Taxes

The design and success of the VAT in various countries may have something to do with the form of the predecessor sales tax. For instance, countries with turnover taxes may have had fewer difficulties in taxing wholesale and retail traders, while countries with manufacturers' sales taxes with a tax-credit mechanism for eliminating cumulative effects may have had fewer problems in acquainting the business community with the properties of the VAT, as opposed to countries that used the suspension or subtraction method to avoid cumulative effects. Box 4.1 describes the various predecessor sales taxes listed in Table 4.1.[10] The inherent design flaws of these sales taxes distorted producer and consumer choices, and raised valuation problems and definitional complexities. These issues are discussed in the next chapter, which reviews the types of sales taxes found in African countries without VAT.

Non-Standard Exemptions

Another defining feature is the extent of the non-standard exemptions in various countries. As is well known, besides out-of-scope governments, 'standard' exemptions[11] include: healthcare, welfare and social security work, education, non-profit organizations, cultural services, public postal and broadcasting services, insurance, financial services, gaming, and immovable property (except if newly created).[12] In addition, however, most African countries exempt many non-standard items, such as basic foodstuffs, water, medicines and pharmaceutical products, newspapers and books, public transportation, feed, seed, fertilizer, agricultural implements, and handicrafts. In view of their prevalence, these exemptions might even be called 'standard' in the African context.

The exemptions, particularly when applied to tradable goods and services, distort domestic, regional, and international trade, because of the 'hidden' VAT on inputs for which no credit is provided. In Table 4.1, the extent of the exemptions

[10] It should be noted that many countries supplemented their previous manufacturers' and production taxes with a separate tax on designated services and often a low-rate turnover tax (as did France before it moved to a full-fledged VAT). Generally, the three taxes were merged into a VAT.

[11] The use of 'standard exemptions' in VAT jargon (see, for instance, Organization for Economic Cooperation and Development (2012)) is somewhat of a misnomer, since 'standard' denotes 'something established by authority, custom, or general consent as a model or example' (Merriam-Webster's International Dictionary). Surely, this does not apply to the VAT exemptions in the EU, which are anything but a model or example to emulate, although many countries have done so.

[12] Lately, various EU countries have begun to tax sports, cultural services, betting, lotteries, and gambling. Further, relatively new converts to the VAT, such as New Zealand, Canada, Australia, and South Africa, tax many if not most of the activities identified above as standard exemptions in the EU, with the exception of primary education, land, rents, rental values, financial services, and life insurance.

Box 4.1 Predecessor sales taxes in African countries with VAT

Turnover taxes: collected on sales at all or nearly all production and distribution stages without regard to the tax paid in previous stages; on account of their tax-on-tax or cumulative effects, these taxes are also referred to as cascade sales taxes.

Production taxes: collected on sales by producers to wholesalers, retailers, or other producers; transactions prior to the sale by the last producer are often partially exempted or taxed at reduced rates:

a. French-type production taxes: exempt domestically produced raw materials and intermediate goods, as well as imported goods that have not been further processed; and
b. other production taxes: exempt producer goods or apply reduced rates, while trading activities per se are excluded from the tax.

Manufacturers' sales taxes (MST): collected on sales by manufacturers to wholesalers or retailers, including occasional direct sales to consumers. While capital goods are usually exempted outright, various techniques are used to counter the cumulative effects of the taxation of raw materials and intermediate goods:

a. the suspension method (MST_{sus}): permits the tax-free purchase of inputs by traders and manufacturers registered for that purpose, tax being levied when products leave the 'ring' and are sold to unregistered persons;
b. the subtraction technique (MST_{sub}): allows for a deduction of taxable purchases from taxable sales; this can be done for:
   i. physically incorporated inputs only; or
   ii. on some other basis such as a deduction for inputs taxed at the same rate as the finished product;
c. the tax-credit principle (MST_{tc}): provides for a credit (deduction) for tax paid on purchases against tax payable on sales.

Retail sales taxes (RST): collected on sales by retailers to final consumers, including wholesalers or manufacturers selling occasionally to consumers. Producer goods are generally excluded by definition.

is denoted by 'few' (some enumerated basic foodstuffs and public transportation), 'some' (more food items and one or two public utilities), 'various' (most unprocessed foods, agricultural inputs, medical goods, newspapers, and more than two utilities), and 'many' (all unprocessed foods, agricultural inputs, medical goods, two or more public utilities, print, and fuel).

Rate Structures

The standard VAT rate ranges from 10 per cent in Djibouti to 20 per cent in Madagascar, Morocco, and Tunisia. The standard rate of most VATs is 15 per cent or higher, but in five countries the rate is lower than 15 per cent. As one would expect, the lower rates are found predominantly in Southern Africa, where VATs are particularly broad-based. The zero rate (other than on exports), mainly applied to some unprocessed foodstuffs, is generally confined to countries with Anglo-Saxon taxing traditions (as is well known, the UK and Ireland, as well as Australia and Canada, zero-rate various foodstuffs), but a zero rate is also found in the Congo for local wood sales. Other countries with French taxing traditions do not have a zero rate on domestically produced or consumed goods. As in France, they heed the *butoir* rule, which holds that rates should not be so low that, as a rule, a refund of prior-stage VAT becomes due. This greatly reduces the number of voluntary registrations and refunds, which have to be monitored carefully.

Various African countries with French taxing traditions, particularly Algeria, Morocco, and Tunisia, have lower-than-standard but positive VAT rates with a broad coverage. Very few countries have higher-than-standard rates and most countries that do confine this rate to one or two products. In many countries, however, the standard rate functions as a tax on luxury goods if the wide-ranging non-standard exemptions are taken into account. These exemptions give rise to widely varying effective VAT rates depending on the ratio of VAT on taxable inputs to the tax-exclusive consumer price. Morocco and Egypt have the most widely differentiated VAT rate structures. These countries did not use the introduction of the full VAT to streamline the multiple-rate structure of the previous sales tax regime.

Luxury Excises

Countries with Anglo-Saxon taxing traditions that are concerned about the regressive effect of the VAT on lower-income groups, and therefore zero-rate basic foodstuffs, also try to improve the progressivity of the tax system by imposing separate excises on a large number of luxury goods. Southern African countries and the Sudan are prime examples. This practice seems to be less prevalent in countries with French taxing traditions that exempt a large number of essential products from VAT. Further, various countries impose excises on revenue goods, such as coffee, tea, sugar, and soft drinks, which other countries incorporated into the VAT when that tax was introduced.

4.3 Issues to Be Explored

This brief review suggests a number of issues which will be discussed in subsequent chapters. If the VAT is mainly a revenue-raising instrument, how does it perform in African countries and what are the reasons behind its performance? To what extent should essential goods, disproportionately consumed by the poor, be favoured over other goods and services? If they are to be, what is the instrument of choice to mitigate the regressivity of the VAT: zero-rating essential goods, exempting them, or applying a lower-than-standard rate? Apparently, very few VAT countries have chosen to promote the progressivity of the VAT through higher-than-standard rates, but is there a case for trying to achieve this through separate excises on luxury goods and services? How extensive is the excise tax coverage and does this accord with equity and feasibility notions?

Further issues relate to the prevalence of non-standard exemptions, which form gaping holes in the VAT base, harm its integrity, and are costly to revenue. What have countries done to close the holes? The non-creditable or non-refundable VAT on inputs should also affect trade within and between RECs. If common markets are the near-term goal, how can border tax adjustments be made more transparent and expeditious? Is it feasible to embed the import duties into the VAT regime? And is there a case for streamlining the standard exemptions for public bodies and activities in the public interest, immovable property, financial services, insurance, and gambling? Finally, the size of the registration threshold is of great importance for the effective administration of the VAT.

5
Countries without VAT

Following the overview of countries with a VAT, this chapter surveys and evaluates the sales taxes of African countries that do not (yet) have a VAT and analyses the distortions, valuation problems, and definitional issues caused by these taxes.[1] Although VAT is not without problems either—in design but particularly in administration—it appears to emerge as a superior consumption tax to the regimes currently in force in the non-VAT countries, such as Angola, Liberia, and Nigeria.

5.1 Overview of Sales Taxes in Non-VAT Countries

Table 5.1 lists the essential particulars of the sales taxes in the nine African countries that do not (yet) have a VAT; Libya does not have any form of sales tax. Most countries impose a production sales tax, generally supplemented by a non-integrated tax on enumerated services. A production sales tax (see Box 4.1) is similar to a manufacturers' sales tax, but does not systematically eliminate the tax on raw materials and intermediate and capital goods, which are incorporated in output, through the use of the tax credit (deduction) or suspension (exemption) method. Both forms of sales tax do not include wholesale and retail margins in the taxable price, which results in capricious differences in effective tax rates at the consumer level. The unintegrated taxation of services causes similar uneven effects, while their less than comprehensive coverage may accentuate the regressive burden distribution of the tax (see Chapter 7).

As shown in Appendix C, the sales taxes in non-VAT African countries have as many non-standard exemptions as are found in VAT countries. Often, non-standard exemptions for unprocessed food products, for instance, follow from the definition of manufacturing which does not encompass agricultural production. Noteworthy are the highly differentiated rate structures in many non-VAT countries, which make these sales taxes akin to extended excise tax systems. It should further be noted that the higher rates that are applied to luxury goods fulfil the same function as the excises on these goods in VAT countries elsewhere on the continent.

Nigeria's sales tax is often called a VAT, but actually it is a multistage turnover tax, whose tax-on-tax or cumulative effects violate the criteria of a good consumption tax, so much so that it does not deserve to be called a tax (McLure and

[1] An earlier version of this chapter was published in Cnossen (2017a).

Table 5.1 Africa: sales taxes in non-VAT countries, 2018

Country	Type of sales tax	Anti-cascading method	Treatment of services	Rates	
				Standard	Other
Angola	Production tax	Exemption of raw materials and equipment used in industry	Taxation of wide range of services: water, energy, hotels, telecommunications, public auction sales, consultancy, rentals, admissions	10%	2%, 5%, 20%, 30% No separate excises
Comoros	Production tax	Exemption of imports by priority businesses	Taxation of limited number of services: water, electricity, private education, inter-island airfares, telecommunications, hotels, restaurants, banking, international airfares	10%, but 15% on imports and 25% on casinos	1%, 3%, 5% Few excises
Eritrea	Production tax	Refund of tax on raw materials Exemption of capital goods for agriculture, industry, and construction	Taxation of wide range of services	5%, but 10% on various services	3%, 12%, 15%
Liberia	Production tax	Exemption of raw materials and capital goods	Taxation of limited number of services: water, electricity, hotels, restaurants, travel agencies, telecommunications, professions, car repairs, sports, gambling	7%	10% Many *ad valorem* excises
Libya	None	-	-	-	-
Nigeria	Turnover tax	Credit for raw materials and intermediate goods, but not for capital goods and services	Taxation of wide range of enumerated services	5%	Selected excises
São Tomé & Principe	Production tax	Exemption for raw materials and equipment used in domestic industry	Taxation of wide range of services	2–20% Services: 5%	Many excises
Somalia	Production tax	None	Tax on hotel services	10%	5% Many excises
South Sudan	Production tax	None	Tax on hotel, restaurant, and bar services	18%, but lower rate for small businesses	Few excises

Source: Appendix C.

Bloomfield, 1987). Although the tax extends through to the retail stage, it does not comprehensively eliminate the tax on inputs and does not comprehensively include services in the tax base. The so-called VAT mitigates the cumulative effect to some extent by permitting a credit for the tax on raw materials and intermediate goods that are incorporated in final output, but no credit is provided for the VAT on services and capital goods. Accordingly, the tax causes many unintended and unnecessary distortions and complexities. Prominent among them is the strong incentive towards vertical integration of the production–distribution chain, which hampers specialization, the hallmark of economic progress. For these reasons, turnover taxes are not discussed further. The focus is primarily on the distortions, valuation problems, and definitional issues that arise under production taxes.

5.2 Distortions

Confining the sales tax to the production stage means that wholesale and retail margins are not included in the taxable price. This might not matter much if all trading margins represent the same proportion of the ex-factory value of goods. But, as is well known, distribution margins vary widely for different products. To illustrate, trading margins may range from as low as 20 per cent for bulk goods, such as rice, to as high as 150 per cent for luxury goods, such as jewellery. If a sales tax were to be levied at a uniform rate of 10 per cent, the difference in distribution margins means that, at the consumer level, rice would be taxed at an effective rate of 8.3 per cent, whereas the effective rate on jewellery would be only 4 per cent—less than half the rate on rice.

The example shows that under a consumption tax, as under other taxes, it is not the nominal or statutory rate that represents the tax burden on the ultimate consumer but rather the effective rate, i.e. the actual tax expressed as a percentage of the consumer price before tax. The example also makes clear that differences in distribution margins result in wholly arbitrary and capricious variations in effective rates of tax. Since trading margins are generally low on essential goods and high on luxury items, a production tax levied at a uniform rate discriminates in favour of luxury goods disproportionately consumed by higher-income individuals. Of course, higher tax rates on luxury products may correct for this effect. Thus, in the example, a rate of 21 per cent on the ex-factory price of jewellery would result in the same effective tax rate at the consumer level as the tax rate on rice. However, such corrections are highly arbitrary and create their own legal problems and avoidance practices.

A second major source of unequal treatment and lack of neutrality relates to the exclusion of most services from the base of a production tax. Since many services are rendered at the retail stage, they do not fit easily into the concept of production that is used to delineate taxable from non-taxable activities. But not taxing services means that the production tax discriminates against goods. Other things being equal, final customers will buy relatively more services, and thus more resources will be diverted to generating them than accords with allocative efficiency. Of course, the value of services rendered to producers, such as various professional services, would normally be included in the taxable price and therefore not escape tax. But services rendered to distributors and final consumers would not be taxed. Under a general consumption tax, such as VAT, these services would be included in the taxable base. Even if services are taxed fairly comprehensively, as appears to be the case in Angola, Eritrea, Nigeria, and São Tomé & Principe, their treatment is not integrated with the taxation of goods, which is likely to involve cascading if the services are rendered to taxable persons.

A third distortion under a production tax arises from the divergent treatment of domestically produced goods versus foreign-produced goods imported by non-registered traders. Since the taxable value of domestically produced goods is more likely to include various marketing expenses (e.g. advertising and warranties) than the taxable value of goods imported by unregistered wholesalers, retailers, and final consumers,[2] the tax on domestically produced goods will obviously be correspondingly higher. The law may try to correct for this by making the sale of imported goods by the importer in the domestic market a separate taxable event, but it is unlikely that this will achieve completely equal treatment.

Fourth, a production tax tends to discourage exports, because the tax on various dual producer/consumer goods, such as vehicles, office equipment, computers, containers, and similar items, bought by non-registered traders cannot be deducted or refunded. Accordingly, the tax paid by these traders enters into the cost of production and, other things being equal, would have to be borne by producers in violation of the destination principle.

The effects of a production tax in discouraging exports and encouraging imports should be taken seriously. As African economies become integrated more closely with the outside world, competition will increase and profit margins will narrow. In such a situation, it is important that the tax does not have to be paid out of the profits of exporters (on account of the tax on certain producer goods) or domestic producers (on account of the stage of imposition).

5.3 Valuation Problems

A vexatious problem under every production tax is ascertaining the correct value for tax. In a large and inevitably growing number of cases, a notional price must be established, because producers sell directly to retailers or even final consumers.

[2] Ignoring transportation costs of imported goods, which are likely to be small in most cases.

Under the previous Canadian sales tax imposed at the manufacturing stage, for instance, it was estimated that as much as half of all sales were made to retailers.[3] Since the price of such sales includes more distribution costs, the taxable value and hence the tax would be higher than on sales to wholesalers. This is considered unfair and sooner or later a production tax has to correct for the differential tax burden. Generally, the price charged to wholesalers, where the producer sells similar goods in the same quantities to wholesalers, might then be taken as the substitute taxable value for sales to retailers.

In a number of cases, however, the producer would not make representative sales to wholesalers. Therefore, artificial or notional values must be established by discounting the price charged to retailers or final consumers. Again in Canada, this phenomenon led to the practice of concluding numerous agreements between taxable businesses and sales tax authorities. Over time, these agreements involved extended arrangements with appropriate consultation and modification procedures, whereby a standard discount based on average mark-ups would be established for groups of businesses. Under Canada's manufacturers' sales tax, as many as one-third of all transactions were taxed on a notional basis.

Although discounts probably work in the right direction, they can never provide uniformity of treatment among businesses or industries, because of the diversity of distribution channels. A major drawback of the discount mechanism in Canada was that the rulings were complex, generally confidential (i.e. with the danger of bureaucratic favouritism), and not subject to review. On balance, little or no reduction of discrimination was achieved. Further, individual taxable persons might still have felt aggrieved by the discount approach, and had to be given the right to review and appeal. This increased operational costs.

Naturally, the imposition of a tax on the ex-factory price induces producers to shift their costs and profits forward to non-taxable stages in order to lower the taxable value and hence the tax. They can do this by establishing their own wholesale businesses to which they sell their products at a price of a little more than cost, or by arranging with independent wholesalers and retailers to take over marketing functions such as advertising, warranties, warehousing, transportation, and similar activities not involving production. In short, pre-retail sales taxes artificially discourage vertical integration of distribution activities and encourage backward integration of retail activities. In the past, some countries have responded to this phenomenon by deeming bogus wholesale businesses to be taxable producers. But this may involve considerable investigative and legal work, since such businesses would be difficult to uncover. Moreover, this method cannot correct for the loss of specialization and hence economic welfare that accompanies the effect on business organization.

[3] For an excellent account of the nearly overwhelming problems of the Canadian manufacturers' sales tax, which is akin to a production tax, see Gillis (1985).

Transportation (and insurance) charges present a special valuation problem. Neutrality demands that there should be no discrimination between the different ways or distances over which goods are transported. This means that all outward transportation costs (incurred from the producer's warehouse to the traders' doorsteps) should be included in the taxable value. On the other hand, simplicity may require that such costs should be excluded because they are often not known or identifiable; this would be the case if traders make their own arrangements for shipment.

5.4 Definitional Issues

A third set of problems that arises under a production tax has to do with the definition of production. Generally, production is defined as the bringing into existence of a different good from that out of which it is made. Normally, this definition extends to marginal producers who perform such operations as assembling, packing, repacking, and bottling. Thus, the tax cannot be avoided by physical producers selling in bulk to wholesalers, who would then break bulk and repackage the goods. Nevertheless, it is questionable whether even this broad definition will go uncontested over time. Other countries with pre-retail sales taxes have had very tightly worded definitions, yet court decisions on what constitutes production have been legion. A few examples, drawn from Williams and Guthleben (1990), may show what sales tax administrations have had to deal with.

Repairing goods would not normally be considered production. Elsewhere, courts have decided, however, that the retreading of tyres and the remodelling of worn fur garments, and, more generally, the rebuilding or reconditioning of used goods, should be considered production. Similarly, the framing of pictures and the act of taking flock out of an old mattress and putting it into a new mattress have been considered production activities. So have the treatment of exposed photographic or cinematographic film, the production of a computer program, and the copying or reproduction of visual images or sound. In a more extreme case, a court has ruled that the making of a wreath from individual flowers should be considered production.

In this connection, it should also be pointed out that most laws on production tax have no explicit provision for legal producers who do not actually produce things but who own or hold patents, copyrights, sales rights, or other proprietary rights to goods being manufactured. In cases where the value of goods is determined to a large extent by the value of the proprietary right (e.g. computers, medications, and cosmetics), the patent holders should be deemed to be producers if a large part of taxable value is the value of the right and therefore should not escape tax. Likewise, trustees, liquidators, executors, or other persons who continue the business of a producer in a fiduciary capacity should be deemed to be producers. If not, they would be able to liquidate the assets of the producer's business without paying tax.

5.5 Move to Wholesale Stage Not a Solution

Admittedly, the inclusion of wholesale margins in the taxable value—as used to be the case under the wholesale sales tax in Senegal, for instance—would result in a more even tax burden distribution, since the point of impact would be closer to the final consumer. Also, a wholesale sales tax tends to provide for more equal treatment of domestically produced goods vis-à-vis imports, because selling and promotion expenses incurred after importation are included in taxable value. But the problem of the valuation of fully manufactured imports by non-registered retailers or final consumers remains. In valuing such goods for tax purposes at the import stage, the domestic wholesale margin must, ideally, be taken into account—but adjustments, if any, would be arbitrary. Overall, the effect would not be very significant, moreover, because retail margins (which would not be included) are usually higher than wholesale margins. And it would still be difficult to include services in the taxable base and integrate their taxation with the taxation of goods.

Of course, a wholesale sales tax with a comprehensive tax deduction or suspension system would not be plagued to the same extent by discounting issues as a production tax, because producers selling directly to retailers can be assessed on actual price. Instead, however, a wholesale sales tax forms a strong inducement to backward integration by retailers who are encouraged to undertake warehousing, transportation, advertising, product specification, and other marketing activities whose value is not included in taxable value. An extreme form of backward integration is private branding whereby large department stores sell products under their own name. Under Australia's previous wholesale sales tax, uplifts were applied to correct for this, but they were an unpopular, arbitrary, and more troublesome device than the discounts prevalent under Canada's erstwhile manufacturers' sales tax. In Australia, it was estimated that approximately 90 per cent of all sales tax disputes arose from the difficulty of establishing the correct sales value. Whatever is done, a wholesale sales tax tends to discriminate against small retailers, who cannot provide for their own tax-free warehousing and transportation facilities.

On balance, definitional problems of what constitutes production might be eased somewhat under a wholesale sales tax (although by no means would they disappear). Instead, however, it would be necessary to delineate wholesale activities from retail activities performed by the same business. Where should the line be drawn on registration? In line with practice elsewhere, the criterion on registration might be put at the 50 per cent level—i.e. if half or more sales were made to retailers, then for tax purposes the trader would be classified as a wholesaler-retailer who would have to register and account for sales tax. Conversely, retailer-wholesalers making less than half of their sales to retailers (in other words, half or more to final users) would not be registered and consequently their whole inventory would be held on a tax-paid basis. This dividing line means that wholesaler-retailers would be discriminated against compared with ordinary wholesalers regarding sales made to final users (after all, their taxable value would be higher) and retailer-wholesalers would enjoy a tax advantage because the margin of their sales to ordinary retailers would not be included in the value for sales tax purposes.

In short, the marginal improvements that shifting the production tax to the wholesale stage would produce are not worth the effort. Countries such as Australia that have used a wholesale sales tax have found it severely wanting.

5.6 VAT Preferred

Clearly, whatever tinkering or patching up is done, pre-retail sales taxes cannot be made to achieve what should be the prime objective of a tax on consumption: the distribution of the tax burden in proportion to outlays on consumption. The exclusion of distribution margins and services results in wide variances in the pattern of effective tax rates across commodities. The unwieldy, confidential, and often discriminatory systems of discounts under a manufacturers' sales tax and the uplifts under a wholesale sales tax are breeding grounds for bureaucratic favouritism and constitute a misallocation of scarce administrative resources. As one astute observer has concluded, continued reliance on the erstwhile (Canadian) manufacturers' sales tax as a major source of revenue was comparable to the proverbial task of fashioning a silk purse from a sow's ear: it is not advisable even when possible (Gillis, 1985).

In sharp contrast, a VAT extending through the retail stage has none of the problems inherent to pre-retail sales taxes as operated in various African countries. First, there are no departures from neutrality, because in principle all distribution margins and services are or can be taxed and imports are automatically treated similarly to domestic supplies. Discounts or uplifts are unknown, production does not have to be defined, and traders do not have to carry tax-paid inventories (i.e. inventories that include the sales tax). Equally important, taxable values are invariably identical to actual prices. Any underpayment of tax due to non-arm's-length practices is automatically corrected in the next taxable stage, because the deduction for tax on inputs is correspondingly smaller. As a result, administrative discretion is reduced to a minimum. The implications of this are worth recalling: instead of focusing administrative talents on legal issues, more resources can be directed at compliance control, i.e. the audit of taxable persons' accounts.

But doesn't the production tax have some weighty administrative advantages over a full VAT because the number of producers is less than the number of all traders? Moreover, shouldn't producers be expected to have better records and hence a greater capacity for compliance with the VAT? Not necessarily so. The inclusion of deemed and legal producers would inevitably push the tax forward to the wholesale stage. Also, many distributors would want to be registered in order to be able to pass the tax on purchases on to their customers. More fundamentally, the business size/inadequate records issue suggests that the appropriate coverage of a VAT is not a stage problem, but rather a small-business problem. There is no reason why large and medium-sized wholesalers and retailers, such as supermarkets which may be assumed to keep adequate accounts, should not be registered. The appropriate treatment of small businesses is an issue that concerns all levels of production and distribution: producers, wholesalers, and retailers. In other words, the small-business issue is not solved by excluding the retail stage, but rather by designing a generous threshold applicable to all stages of production and distribution.

In summary, the best consumption tax is a VAT extending through the retail stage. The sole criterion for tax coverage should be the size of the business, regardless of the stage at which it is situated. Of course, this conclusion assumes that VATs are well designed and reasonably well administered. If not, it is possible that production taxes (or, rather, intermediate types of excise duty systems) are less distortionary and less susceptible to fraudulent practices than badly administered broad-based VATs. But while a VAT can be potentially well designed and administered, by definition production taxes will always be plagued by distortions, valuation problems, and definitional complexities. In short, a VAT can, but other sales taxes cannot, be improved.

6
Revenue Performance

There is general agreement that the main revenue-generating role in a system of taxes on goods and services should be assigned to a general, broad-based, neutral consumption tax, such as a VAT. Although excise taxes levied on widely consumed goods, such as tobacco, alcoholic drinks, and petroleum products, can be very productive of revenue, in essence their coverage is limited, while their externality-correcting function imposes limits on the amount of revenue that should be raised through them. The revenue-generating capacity of import duties is also limited, because domestically produced goods are not included in the base, while protective import duties should be reduced over time as the protected industries mature and are able to compete successfully with similar industries elsewhere.

6.1 Overall Revenue Performance

Table 6.1 presents the latest data on the tax ratios for all African countries with a VAT, as well as the contribution of the most important indirect taxes (VATs, excise taxes, trade taxes) to total tax revenue (defined to include social security contributions) and gross domestic product (GDP). The data broadly confirm the information shown in Table 1.1 for earlier years.[1] In most African countries, total tax revenue as a percentage of GDP is below the level that is needed to finance human and economic development. In more than one in three countries on the continent, the total tax ratio is around 15 per cent or less. In eight countries, it is even less than 10 per cent, and only seven countries, of which five are in the SACU region, collect more than 25 per cent of GDP in tax.

Jointly, VATs, excise taxes, and trade taxes (generally import duties) tend to account for nearly two-thirds of total tax revenue in low-income African countries, which reflects the ease with which the respective tax handles can be exploited at import and at the level of large domestic taxpayers.[2] This is obvious regarding import duties, but a well-known rule of thumb is also that 20 per cent

[1] The tax ratios for Algeria and Congo in Table 6.1 differ substantially from those calculated by Fenochietto and Pessino (2013) and shown in Table 1.1. Presumably, this reflects the treatment of oil revenues. Further, Table 6.1 shows notably higher tax ratios for the Gambia, Namibia, Niger, and Togo, and notably lower tax ratios for Egypt, Ethiopia, Kenya, Malawi, Morocco, Tanzania, and Tunisia.

[2] The seminal work on the role of tax handles in economic development is Musgrave (1969).

Table 6.1 Africa: revenue from VATs, excise taxes, and import duties, latest years

RECs and countries	Total tax as % of GDP	% of GDP				% of total tax revenue				Year of data
		Total indirect	VAT	Excise & other	Trade taxes	Total indirect	VAT	Excise & other	Trade taxes	
Southern African Development Community (SADC)										
SACU										
Botswana	25.8	14.7	3.9		10.8	57.0	15.1		41.9	2014
Lesotho	34.3	24.4	6.2		18.2	71.1	18.1		53.0	2017
Namibia	29.5	16.7	7.7		9.0	56.6	26.1		30.5	2016
South Africa	26.3	10.6	7.0	2.6	1.0	40.3	26.6	9.9	3.8	2016
Swaziland	29.0	23.4	4.2		19.2	80.7	14.5		66.2	2012
Other										
Congo, DR	7.2	5.0	2.4	0.1	2.5	69.4	33.3	1.4	34.7	2010
Madagascar	10.9	8.2	5.3	1.2	1.7	75.2	48.6	11.0	15.6	2016
Malawi	17.3	8.9	4.8	2.6	1.5	51.4	27.7	15.0	8.7	2017
Mauritius	18.1	13.6	8.0	5.3	0.3	75.1	44.2	29.3	1.6	2016
Mozambique	20.1	10.9	7.0	2.1	1.8	54.2	34.8	10.4	9.0	2016
Seychelles	31.6	20.0	10.6	7.5	1.9	63.3	33.5	23.7	6.0	2016
Zambia	14.9	6.6	3.7	2.0	0.9	44.3	24.8	13.4	6.0	2016
Zimbabwe	24.5	15.5	6.2	3.8	5.5	63.3	25.3	15.5	22.4	2012
East African Community (EAC)										
Burundi	12.9	9.2	5.0	2.9	1.3	71.3	38.8	22.4	10.1	2013
Kenya	16.3	8.2	4.1	2.5	1.6	50.3	25.2	15.3	9.8	2015
Rwanda	13.3	7.9	4.4	2.4	1.1	59.4	33.1	18.0	8.3	2017
Tanzania	12.1	7.7	3.4	3.0	1.3	63.6	28.1	24.8	10.7	2017
Uganda	12.9	8.5	4.1	2.9	1.5	65.9	31.8	22.5	11.6	2016

Continued

Table 6.1 *Continued*

RECs and countries	Total tax as % of GDP	% of GDP				% of total tax revenue				Year of data
		Total indirect	VAT	Excise & other	Trade taxes	Total indirect	VAT	Excise & other	Trade taxes	
Economic and Monetary Community of Central Africa (CEMAC)										
Cameroon	14.8	7.4	5.6		1.8	50.0	37.8	12.2		2015
Cent. Afr. Rep.	9.5	7.4	1.5	1.3	4.6	77.9	15.8	13.7	48.4	2012
Chad	7.8	..	..	..	..	..	..	..	..	2016
Congo	9.4	5.8	3.1	1.1	1.6	61.7	33.0	11.7	17.0	2012
Equat. Guinea	12.4	1.7	0.8	0.4	0.5	13.7	6.5	3.2	4.0	2015
Gabon	13.6	9.0	..	..	..	66.2	..	..	..	2015
Economic Community of West African States (ECOWAS)										
UEMOA										
Benin	15.5	12.3	6.9	1.1	4.3	79.4	44.5	7.1	27.7	2013
Burkina Faso	15.0	10.7	6.1	2.4	2.2	71.3	40.7	16.0	14.7	2016
Côte d'Ivoire	15.6	11.0	4.1	2.3	4.6	70.5	26.3	14.7	29.5	2016
Guinea–Bissau	8.5	..	..	..	..	..	..	..	..	2014
Mali	15.4	11.2	6.2	3.3	1.7	72.7	40.3	21.4	11.0	2016
Niger	16.0	..	..	..	..	..	..	..	..	2015
Senegal	20.5	14.1	7.6	3.8	2.7	68.8	37.1	18.5	13.2	2016
Togo	21.7	18.6	9.6	4.2	4.8	85.7	44.2	19.4	22.1	2016
WAMZ										
Cabo Verde	17.9	12.2	8.0	4.2		68.2	44.7	23.5		2012
Gambia	16.7	12.2	7.2		5.0	73.1	43.1		29.9	2016
Ghana	14.9	9.5	4.6	1.3	3.6	63.8	31.1	8.7	24.2	2011
Guinea	14.4	9.7	7.0		2.7	67.4	48.6		18.7	2015
Sierra Leone	8.6	4.6	2.0	1.3	1.3	53.5	23.3	15.1	15.1	2014

Arab Maghreb Union (AMU)										
Algeria	37.2	12.8	3.7	7.6	1.5	34.4	9.9	20.4	4.0	2016
Mauritania	18.7	..	..	..	..	..	..	..	..	2015
Morocco	21.4	13.2	8.9	3.4	0.9	61.7	41.6	15.9	4.2	2016
Tunisia	21.1	12.3	7.1	3.3	1.9	58.3	33.6	15.6	9.0	2012
Intergovernmental Authority on Development (IGAD) and Egypt										
Djibouti	20.1	11.4	..	..	..	56.7	..	..	..	2015
Egypt	12.5	7.1	3.4	2.8	0.9	56.8	27.2	22.4	7.2	2015
Ethiopia	8.8	6.5	1.9	0.4	4.2	73.9	21.6	4.5	47.7	2013
Sudan	5.3	4.8	3.4		1.4	90.6	64.2		26.4	2016

Source: IMF Government Finance Statistics, Budgetary Central Government (including social contributions), Yearbooks 2017 and 2016 (Zimbabwe only), accessed 9 May 2018, and IMF Staff reports for Cameroon, Chad, Djibouti, Gabon, Gambia, Guinea, Guinea–Bissau, Mauritania, and Sudan. Indirect taxes are defined as the sum of 'Taxes on goods & services', 'Taxes on international trade & transactions', and 'Other taxes n.e.c.'. Totals may not add because of rounding.

of VAT payers account for 80 per cent of VAT revenue, half of which tends to be collected at the import stage[3] and most of the remainder from producers of traditional excisable products. Much the same reasoning applies to the relatively prominent revenue position of excise taxes imposed on tobacco, alcohol, petroleum, and motor vehicles, which are generally produced in large manufacturing plants or imported (and often, incorrectly, booked as import duty revenue). The revenue importance of excise taxes varies rather widely. As examples, it is on average 21 per cent of total tax revenue (2.7 per cent of GDP) in EAC countries and some 16 per cent (2.8 per cent of GDP) in six UEMOA countries for which data are available. On a cross-country basis, excise taxes tend to become more important as the reliance on trade taxes declines.

As shown in Table 6.1, VATs make the most important contribution to revenue within the indirect tax revenue structures of African countries: close to 30 per cent of total tax revenue or 5.3 per cent of GDP.[4] This average, however, masks wide differences between countries. While VAT collections are merely 6.5 per cent of total tax revenue in Equatorial Guinea (0.8 per cent of GDP), Cabo Verde, a small island community, collects as much as 45 per cent (8 per cent of GDP) from this source. Out of 35 countries for which reasonably reliable data are available, 17 countries collect 5 per cent or more of GDP in the form of VAT. The VAT revenue ratio tends to be high in the SACU countries whose tax bases are among the broadest in Africa. Apart from the SACU region, other relatively important contributions should be put into the context of generally low overall tax ratios and the fact that, in many countries, up to half or more of the VAT is collected at import stages.

Clearly, VAT has taken over the revenue-generating role of import duties as the most important revenue raiser among taxes on goods and services (although customs controls still play a crucial role in collecting VAT on imported products). In many African countries, its contribution to GDP is more than twice as high as the contribution of import duties. By comparison, the share of import duties exceeds 5 per cent of GDP in only the Gambia and Zimbabwe. VATs, too, tend to be more revenue productive than the excise taxes. An explanation may be that in many countries, alcohol and tobacco products are subject to high import duties

[3] Ebrill et al. (2001, p. 50) report the following percentages for VAT on imports relative to VAT revenues for African countries: Benin (70), Burkina Faso (51), Cameroon (43), Gabon (51), Ghana (50), Guinea (62), Mauritania (66), Mauritius (60), Togo (68), Uganda (58), and Zambia (67). Although these figures are rather old, there is no reason to assume that the current data are very different. In a later report on Uganda, the International Monetary Fund (2005) concluded that, to a large extent, the VAT and the excise taxes are border taxes since approximately two-thirds of the combined revenue is collected on imported goods and the remainder on a few key domestic products that are produced by only 10–12 firms.

[4] Excluding countries, shown in Table 6.1, for which revenue data are not available or are incomplete or which have just introduced the VAT, so their revenue productivity is difficult to assess. The data of a few other countries may also be suspect, particularly if VAT (and excise duty) collections have not been properly separated out from import duty receipts.

Table 6.2 Selected African countries: revenue performance before and after VAT

Country	Year of VAT introduction	Revenue increase after VAT as % of GDP	VAT/GDP ratios		
			1998	2006	Latest year
Benin	1991	2.0	5.6	6.5	6.9
Burkina Faso	1993	0.9	4.0	4.4	6.1
Côte d'Ivoire*	1960	..	4.8	3.3	4.1
Gabon	1995	3.0	4.1	1.6	..
Ghana*	1998	..	3.8	5.6	4.6
Guinea	1996	1.0	2.5	3.7	..
Kenya	1990	0.8	5.5	5.6	4.1
Mozambique*	1999	..	2.7	5.2	7.0
Tanzania*	1998	..	3.2	4.4	3.4
Togo	1995	0.2	4.5	1.9	9.6
Uganda	1996	1.0	3.4	3.9	4.1
Zambia	1995	0.9	5.8	4.6	3.7

Source: Revenue increases and VAT/GDP ratios in 1998—Ebrill et al. (2001); VAT/GDP ratio in 2006—IMF Fiscal Affairs Department database; VAT/GDP ratio in latest year—Table 6.1.

(not shown as excise tax receipts), while it is difficult to tax locally produced substitutes (cigarettes and beer) not manufactured in large production units.

An interesting question, which Ebrill et al. (2001) have tried to answer, is whether, in terms of revenue, VATs have done better than their predecessor sales taxes (defined in Box 4.1 and listed in Table 4.1). Their findings for eight African countries that adopted the VAT in the 1990s are reported in the third column of Table 6.2 along with those for another four countries (marked with an asterisk, *). Although comparisons of this sort need to be interpreted with care, the authors conclude that the revenue gain—on average more than 1 per cent of GDP—realized in the first two or three years of VAT operation is impressive when compared with the revenue raised by the predecessor sales taxes in the matching period prior to the VAT. However, between 1998 and 2006, the VAT/GDP ratio deteriorated sharply in three of the eight countries reviewed by the authors; the same happened in Côte d'Ivoire. By comparison, VAT revenue gains over the same period were recorded in seven other countries. Finally, the latest data show a further revenue gain in the period since 2006 for six countries and a decline in VAT/GDP ratios in four countries (data for Gabon and Guinea are not available).[5] Perhaps countries have given in to political demands for exemptions or the VAT administration has deteriorated or perhaps exemptions have been withdrawn or the VAT administration improved. Whatever the case, VAT's revenue-generating role in African tax systems appears to be in need of review.

[5] VAT revenue gains in sub-Saharan countries are also reported by Ebeke, Mansour and Rota-Graziosi (2016), who compare VAT performance with two other tax reforms, i.e. large taxpayer units and semi-autonomous revenue agencies. The latter reform had a positive impact on revenue, too, but the former's impact was insignificant.

6.2 VAT Collection Efficiency

While VAT revenue shares and ratios are valuable indicators of the revenue performance of VATs, they do not explain differences in VAT performance. For this purpose, the tax literature—notably Ebrill et al. (2001) and Keen (2013)—has developed the concept of VAT collection efficiency (or VAT C-efficiency, for short), which can be related to the structural characteristics of the VAT (exemptions, reduced rates, thresholds) and various economic and social factors (including voluntary compliance and government effectiveness), as also reported by Aizenman and Jinjarak (2008), Fenochietto and Pessino (2013), and others. C-efficiencies measure a country's VAT performance as the ratio between the revenue actually collected and potential revenue found by applying the standard rate, τ, to final consumption expenditures (net of VAT) shown in national accounts.[6] In other words,

$$\text{VAT C-efficiency} = \frac{\text{Actual VAT revenue}}{\tau \times \text{Final consumption}}.$$

Accordingly, the VAT's C-efficiency indicates what percentage of final consumption expenditure is collected by each percentage point of the standard VAT rate. Obviously, C-efficiency has unit value for a uniform tax on all consumption expenditure. The difference between this unit value and the actual C-efficiency represents the VAT that is not collected on account of exemptions (net of the VAT on inputs), zero rates (other than on exports), and lower-than-standard rates, as well as shortcomings in VAT compliance and administration. The loss of VAT revenue attributable to exemptions and zero or lower-than-standard rates is called the policy gap, while the VAT's operational shortcomings are referred to as the compliance gap. To calculate these gaps, De Mooij and Keen (2015) have developed the following formula:[7]

$$\text{VAT C-efficiency} = (1 - \text{exemptions}) \times (1 - \text{lower rates}) \times (1 - \text{compliance gap}).$$

The formula focuses the attention of policymakers on deficiencies in VAT policy and administration. If VAT's C-efficiency is less than 1 and this is viewed as a potential concern, should compliance be improved or should the focus be on exemptions and lower rates that violate the logic and functionality of the VAT? Or should both aspects be the subject of further scrutiny? Although such an exercise

[6] Preferably, final consumption should be aggregated over households, governments, and non-profit organizations. For lack of data, however, the C-efficiencies in this chapter do not include government consumption expenditures in the denominator.

[7] For a further probing analysis of the concept, measurement, and pitfalls of C-efficiencies, see Keen (2013). For an analysis of the policy gap in advanced economies, see Ueda (2017). Also of substantial interest for African countries is the IMF Country Report on South Africa's VAT gap (International Monetary Fund, 2015), which describes and evaluates the different methodologies that can be used to determine the policy and compliance gaps.

would be highly worthwhile for the countries under review, unfortunately separate data for the policy and compliance gaps in African countries are not available.[8] The overall VAT C-efficiency is the only statistic that can be calculated.

Figure 6.1 shows the C-efficiencies in 2015 for most African countries with a VAT. The efficiencies range from a low of 0.07 in Guinea and Equatorial Guinea (endowed with much revenue from natural resources) to highs of 0.74 in Namibia and even 1.01 in the Seychelles, suggesting that all consumption is taxed at a uniform rate.[9] Further, in three-quarters of the countries, the C-efficiency is less than 0.50; in 19 countries, it is less than 0.35, and the average for all countries is 0.37. Not surprisingly, in view of their broad VAT bases, SACU and AMU countries stand out for their high C-efficiencies (comparable to those calculated for most European countries), while VATs in CEMAC and various UEMOA countries perform rather poorly.

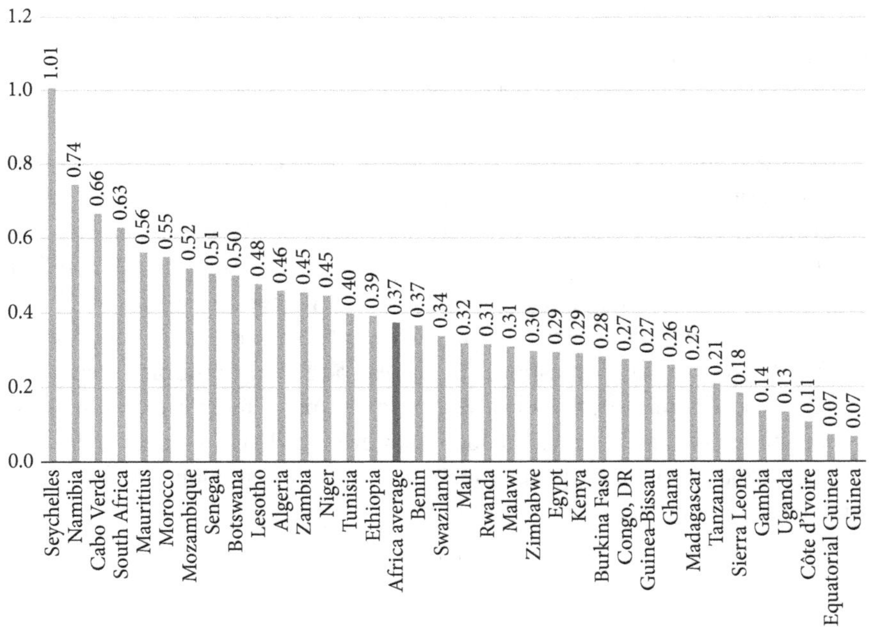

Figure 6.1 Africa: C-efficiencies, 2015

Source: International Monetary Fund, Fiscal Affairs Department.

[8] For EU countries, Keen (2013, p. 423) concludes that policy gaps (exemptions and rate differentiations) are in almost all cases far larger than compliance gaps, but this may not be the case in African countries.

[9] This is somewhat difficult to square with the information in Appendix A, which shows a range of non-standard exemptions on domestically consumed products for the Seychelles. Accordingly, other factors must be at work, including VAT payments by tourists without refund at export and overlapping VAT collection periods. Jenkins, Kuo, and Sun (2003) argue that this may be the case for Singapore, for which they calculated a C-efficiency greater than 1.

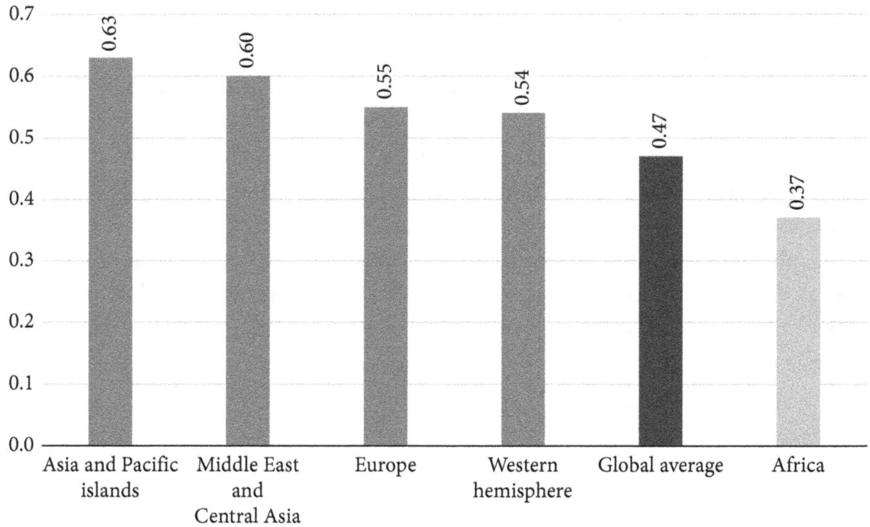

Figure 6.2 Regional C-efficiencies in the world, 2014
Source: International Monetary Fund, Fiscal Affairs Department.

VAT's revenue performance in Africa can also be compared with that in other regions in the world. As shown in Figure 6.2, VAT's C-efficiency in Africa (0.37) is, on average, distinctly lower than the global average (0.47). The C-efficiencies in other regions in the world, whether Asia and the Pacific (0.63), the Middle East and Central Asia (0.60), Europe (0.55), or the Western Hemisphere (0.54), on average exceed that in Africa. This may be attributable to economic factors (such as the degree of monetization), the share of agriculture (perforce exempted) in GDP, lack of administrative effectiveness, low taxpayer morale, or, more likely, a combination of these factors. No doubt, however, the low C-efficiencies should also be attributed to the tax policy gap, i.e. the myriad exemptions and zero rates on domestic products.

6.3 Understanding VAT Performance

Obviously, VAT performance depends on the statutory rules (rates, exemptions, and thresholds), the amount of final expenditure subject to tax, and the degree of compliance with the VAT. Given the difficulties in disentangling the interactions of these variables, Ebrill et al. (2001) focus instead on relating VAT yields both to characteristics of the VAT itself and to the economy at large.[10]

[10] Ebrill et al. (2001, table 4.2) report multivariate regressions, using a cross-section of (at most) 89 developed and developing countries. The dependent variable in their analysis is the (ln) ratio of VAT

Following their lead, this section attempts to relate VAT performance to various economic development factors, VAT structure characteristics, and operational aspects that may help in understanding VAT performance (in the lists below, a plus sign indicates an upward effect and a minus sign a downward effect). The data for these variables are shown in Tables 4.1, 6.1, and 16.1, Figure 6.1, and Appendix D.

Economic Development

- Per-capita income as a measure of the stage of economic development and perhaps administrative effectiveness (+).
- The share of agricultural value added in GDP, which generally measures the same thing as well as the size of the informal sector not subject to VAT (except with regard to taxable inputs perhaps) (–).
- The ratio of imports or trade (imports and exports, i.e. openness) to GDP, because imports are an easy tax handle to collect the VAT up front (+).

VAT Structure

- The standard rate (shown in Table 4.1), generally as a measure of compliance pressure (the higher the rate, the greater the incentive to evade the tax) (–).
- The age of the VAT, presumably because, over time, experience is gained in administering and complying with the VAT (+).
- The extent of the non-standard exemptions, which, like reduced rates,[11] depress VAT performance (–).
- The size of the threshold, which may reduce revenue because trading margins are not included in the VAT base, or which may have a salutary effect on VAT administration because a high threshold permits it to focus on large taxpayers (+/–).

revenue to private consumption. They find that this measure is positively related to the (ln) standard rate, openness, and the literacy rate. Further, Martinez-Vazquez and Bird (2011, table 6.3) explain efficiency measures, expressed in terms of both total consumption expenditures and GDP. The authors employ (unbalanced) panel data for 107 countries, covering the period 1990–2008. They find a significant positive effect of the (ln) population size and a negative effect of the share of agriculture in GDP, the share of urban population in total population, and the level of alcohol consumption. Tax morale has a negative effect on efficiency in developing countries but a positive effect in developed countries.

[11] Ebrill et al. (2001, fn. 20) also examine the influence of rate differentiation, measured as the difference between the highest and lowest statutory rates, but nominal VAT rate differentiation is the exception rather than the rule in African countries, while effective rate differentiation on account of the exemptions is difficult to measure.

Administration and Compliance

- The completion rate of primary schooling as a proxy for ease of taxpayer compliance; after all, the VAT purports to be a self-assessed tax (+).
- Ease of doing business, on the assumption that this includes the ease with which VAT obligations can be discharged (+).
- Government effectiveness as a measure of tax enforcement (+).
- Control of corruption, which, conversely, should measure the lack of enforcement (+).

Similar to Ebrill et al. (2001), Leon Bettendorf of CPB Netherlands Bureau for Economic Policy Analysis has done a regression analysis for 34 of the countries shown in Table 6.1.[12] His results are summarized in Table 6.3.

All effects have the expected sign. Of the variables representing economic development, a rise in per-capita gross national income (GNI) of 1 per cent increases C-efficiency by 0.12 percentage points. Since countries with higher incomes are characterized by smaller agricultural sectors (correlation equals −0.69), the share of agriculture in GDP has a negative effect on C-efficiency. As VAT is in practice largely imposed on imported goods, a significant positive relationship is found for the GDP share of imports and, similarly, for trade openness (equal to the sum of import and export shares in GDP).

Of the variables that represent VAT structure, only one has a significant coefficient. A rise in the standard rate by 1 percentage point is seen to decrease C-efficiency by 0.2 percentage points, presumably because evasion and, possibly, exemption creep increase. The other VAT structure variables are not significant, although efficiency is somewhat higher in (nine) countries that limit the number of non-standard exemptions (see Table 4.1). This result expands on the analyses of Ebrill et al. (2001) and Aizenman and Jinjarak (2008), whose data sets did not contain the extent of exemptions. The effect of the size of the threshold, often viewed as an important determinant of administrative efficacy, is rather small and insignificant. The age of the VAT is an insignificant contributing factor in contrast to Ebrill et al.'s finding. Among the variables on administration and compliance, efficiency benefits significantly from a high primary completion rate, an effective government, control of corruption, and a low administrative burden on the business sector.

It should be emphasized that the results are only suggestive of some correlations. Errors in the measurement of consumption data in countries with large subsistence sectors may skew the results, as may errors in the classification of revenues as

[12] Data problems implied that the following 11 countries had to be omitted from the analysis: Burundi, Cameroon, Central African Republic, Chad, Congo, Djibouti, Gabon, Guinea-Bissau, Mauritania, Sudan, and Togo. This implies the likelihood of selection bias, since insufficient data can be correlated with VAT performance.

Table 6.3 Africa: explaining C-efficiency (univariate regressions)

Variable	Coefficient	Adjusted R^2
Economic development		
ln(GNI per capita)	0.124***	0.387
Share of agriculture in GDP	-0.796***	0.291
Share of imports in GDP	0.693***	0.398
Openness	0.434***	0.454
VAT structure		
Standard rate	-2.473*	0.038
Dummy many exemptions	-0.052	-0.015
Dummy various exemptions	-0.035	-0.023
Dummy some exemptions	0.111	0.031
VAT threshold	0.001	0.009
VAT age	0.000	-0.031
Administration and compliance		
Primary completion rate	0.486**	0.195
Government effectiveness	0.223***	0.423
Control of corruption	0.201***	0.398
Ease of doing business	-0.002***	0.150

Note: Number of observations = 34, except for the share of agriculture (33) and the threshold (33).
*** $p < 0.01$, ** $p < 0.05$, * $p < 0.1$. Constant term included but not reported.

import duties instead of VAT or vice versa. Delays in VAT refunds at export, prevalent in many countries, could bias the results significantly, as could presumptive assessments in lieu of proper accounting for VAT on sales and purchases. In short, a myriad of large and small errors, intentionally or inadvertently, could influence the results.[13] It may well be, moreover, that econometric issues are more important than the measurement errors. Simultaneity (reverse causality) and endogeneity (statistical) bias are not addressed in the regressions and the results should therefore be interpreted with care.

Further, data on the compliance gap, reflecting the shortfall in VAT revenue measured as the amount that should be collected if the VAT law were fully adhered to and the amount that is actually collected, are not available. Generally, the compliance gap represents VAT evasion (unlike the income tax, avoidance is more difficult to conceive) through non-, under-, or over-reporting of tax on sales and purchases. Its mirror image is the inability of the VAT administration to monitor and enforce the obligations imposed on taxpayers by the VAT law. Data on the quality of the VAT administration are not available, but the effectiveness of

[13] For a wide-ranging discussion and analysis of these aspects, see Martinez-Vazquez and Bird (2011).

government,[14] of which the VAT administration is an integral part, should be a reasonable second-best proxy. If so, VAT administration leaves something to be desired in most countries.

The message is that although improvements in VAT design should make good VAT administration easier (Bird and Gendron, 2007), they should be accompanied by improvements in VAT administration, such as proper registration and, not to forget, deregistration, timely reporting and collection, effective examination and audit, and thorough investigation and prosecution, if called for. Alas, what is done is often very different from what reading the law suggests should be done, as Bird and Gendron (2007) note when citing Keen (2008), who pleads for a more systematic 'second-best' analysis of VAT.[15]

6.4 Can VATs Replace Trade Taxes?

Closer economic integration and greater outward orientation, which promote growth, would require the elimination of trade taxes and their replacement by domestic taxes, preferably broad-based consumption taxes such as VATs, but possibly also excise taxes. The case for replacing trade tax revenue by indirect tax revenue (and the many caveats to this benchmark result) for a small and competitive economy is set out in Keen and Ligthart (2001): gains in production efficiency are preserved by moving producer prices closer to world market prices, (slightly) lower consumer prices leave consumers better off, and government revenue is not reduced.[16] Whether this welfare-improving recipe has moved on to government policy menus is examined by Baunsgaard and Keen (2010) in an extensive and closely argued study based on panel data for 117 countries covering 32 years.

[14] Government effectiveness is defined as 'the quality of public services, the quality of the civil service and the degree of its independence from political pressures, the quality of policy formulation and implementation, and the creditability of the government's commitment to such policies' (Kaufmann, Kraay, and Mastruzzi, 2010).

[15] This is borne out by the author's own experience when he examined the VAT in a country that had adopted the tax in the early 1990s in replacement of a highly complex and distortionary set of turnover and excise taxes. Since its introduction, the VAT was praised for its simplicity and neutrality, as, allegedly, manifested in a broad base and single rate. The author found out, however, that 15 years after its introduction the VAT administration had simply continued with the imposition of the old turnover and excise taxes and that the VAT was just another addition to the existing jungle of complicated and distortionary levies on goods and services. For an equally sad tale, see Barlow and Snyder (1994) on Niger's VAT.

[16] In sharp contrast, however, as Keen and Ligthart (2005) prove, under imperfect competition examples are easily found in which revenue replacement unambiguously reduces domestic welfare. This is also the conclusion of Emran and Stiglitz (2005), who purport to show that replacement is welfare reducing in the presence of an informal sector since some final consumption cannot be reached through tariffs. For a rebuttal, however, see Baunsgaard and Keen (2010), who point out that VAT is in practice levied on imports and therefore functions as a tariff for wholly informal sectors. Keen (2008) made this point earlier, adding that the informal sector is also taxed through its VATable purchases from the formal sector. For a succinct review of the interaction between the VAT and the (in)formal sector, see Bird and Gendron (2007).

Specifically, the authors show that past replacement has been robust with regard to high- and, to a lesser degree, middle-income countries, but that the evidence for low-income countries is flimsy. The authors (p. 573) conclude that perhaps only 'something like one-sixth to one quarter of low income countries has succeeded in substantially replacing lost trade tax revenues'.[17]

Administratively, the replacement of trade taxes by VAT implies that a rather certain, physically controlled form of tax collection, at least for goods, is being replaced by a more uncertain, accounts-controlled form, largely based on voluntary compliance (although much VAT would continue to be 'pre-collected' at the import stage). The feasibility of revenue replacement, rather than its policy desirability, is of considerable interest, particularly since Baunsgaard and Keen (2010, p. 571) find 'no strong evidence that the simple presence of a VAT has aided revenue recovery'.[18]

Replacement feasibility is also dependent on the amount of revenue that should be raised. As Table 6.1 indicates, overall, replacement needs are quite significant, particularly in the rather highly integrated UEMOA REC and, more generally, ECOWAS. In terms of revenue, replacement seems to be manageable in the EAC, AMU, and SACU RECs should governments decide to reduce trade taxes.[19] Presumably, excise taxes can replace some of the forgone revenue, but the main replacement burden would fall on the VATs. How large that burden is would seem to depend on the replacement path. Little additional VAT revenue might be needed if the RECs adopt a high common tariff whose revenue is distributed to the member countries. This is the approach followed by SACU, for instance. Eliminating one tariff wall while leaving another wall intact does not make much sense, however, so another course of action would be to adopt a common tariff but at lower average rates than the previous country-specific tariffs,[20] and to make up for the revenue loss by increasing VAT yields.[21]

The analysis in this book appears to indicate that it is unlikely that African VATs in their current form are up to the task of generating much more revenue.

[17] Of further interest is Keen and Mansour's (2010) finding that non-resource revenues were essentially stagnant in sub-Saharan countries between 1980 and 2005, although reductions in trade revenue have generally been largely offset by increased revenue from domestic sources.

[18] Not surprisingly, therefore, Baunsgaard and Keen (2010, p. 568) caution 'that countries considering foregoing trade tax revenue as part of a process of trade liberalization would be well-advised to ask whether they can recover those revenues from other sources [even without relying on increased growth or other such effects]'. Baunsgaard and Keen's conclusion is supported by Ahlerup, Baskaran, and Bigsten (2015), who find that the presence of a VAT has no effect on total revenues either in the short or long run, a rather disheartening result.

[19] In the EAC, for instance, trade taxes account for around 10% of total tax revenue (1.4% of GDP).

[20] As pointed out by Ebrill, Stotsky, and Gropp (1999), in early stages trade liberalization may actually lead to an increase in trade tax revenue if prohibitively high tariffs, quotas, and exemptions are replaced by low(er) tariff rates.

[21] A third and probably preferable, but more difficult, path of action would be to eliminate most tariffs altogether under a most favoured nation (MFN) form of trade liberalization and to go for full VAT replacement: in other words, to adopt the Association of South East Asian Nations (ASEAN) way.

Replacement is not easy if VAT bases are too narrow and enforcement too shallow to put much trust in VAT's revenue-raising capacity.[22] The numerous concessions have generally been introduced to mitigate the tax burden on low-income households, whether effective or not, but they severely hamper the revenue performance of the VATs. Accordingly, they will have to be reviewed if revenue replacement is to have a chance and, more generally, if administrative simplification and tax neutrality are concerns. Bold VAT reform is needed, but first concerns about the VAT's incidence must be addressed.

[22] Arguably, this does not apply to the excise taxes, which are levied in a similar fashion to trade taxes, i.e. subject to physical control (although indigenous brews, cigarettes, and so on are difficult to tax and they compete with internationally traded products).

7
VAT Incidence and Rate Structure

By definition, the burden distribution of a broad-based VAT, measured against income, is regressive since the share of consumption in income falls as income rises, a phenomenon that is known as Engel's law (1857). In other words, a uniform tax on all goods and services weighs more heavily on lower than on higher incomes. This violates an important tax policy rule that holds that the after-tax income distribution should not be more unequal than the before-tax income distribution generated by the market. But in considering the regressivity issue, the burden distribution of other taxes, such as income and property taxes, which can be made progressive, should be taken into account.[1] Perhaps more importantly, the VAT's proceeds can finance expenditures on, for instance, education and healthcare, targeted to help the poor more than the rich.

In this spirit, this chapter examines the various ways in which African countries have dealt with the regressivity issue and looks at what seems to be the most appropriate approach.[2] Obviously, foodstuffs are the most important item in most household budgets. Therefore, this chapter starts by reviewing the ways in which African countries mitigate the VAT's regressivity, real or perceived, by providing concessionary treatment for foodstuffs. This is followed by a survey of the results of various overall VAT incidence studies, especially regarding South Africa. These results indicate that the incidence of most VATs is less regressive than is often thought. The discussion proceeds by highlighting the advantages and disadvantages in choosing the best instrument to mitigate the VAT's regressivity, if desired: taxing basic foodstuffs at a zero rate, taxing them at a lower rate, or exempting them.

Instead of mitigating regressivity, some progressivity may possibly be imparted to the VAT burden distribution by imposing higher-than-standard rates, or, equivalently, differentially higher excises, on luxury goods. The effect appears to be largely negligible. Apparently, little can be done to achieve some progressivity through the VAT. Further, the requirements for mitigating regressivity and promoting progressivity are discussed in some detail. In analysing these issues, the standard assumption is adopted that taxes on consumption reduce the disposable income of consumers proportionate to their expenditures on taxable

[1] Admittedly, this may also be problematic in developing countries. For arguments that the income tax does not add much to progressivity in the overall tax system of developing countries, see Bird and Zolt (2005).

[2] Parts of this chapter draw on Cnossen (2006b, ch. 6).

goods and services (Institute for Fiscal Studies, 2011; Organization for Economic Cooperation and Development/Korea Institute of Public Finance, 2014).[3]

7.1 The VAT Treatment of Foodstuffs

As shown in Appendix A, all African countries attempt to mitigate the regressivity of their VATs either by exempting essential goods and services disproportionately consumed by the poor or by applying a zero or reduced rate to them. The products that often receive favourable treatment (also in other countries with VAT) are the following:

- basic foodstuffs;
- water, electricity, kerosene;
- medicines, pharmaceutical products;
- newspapers, books;
- feed, seed, fertilizer, agricultural implements;
- public passenger transportation; and
- handicraft products.

The concessionary taxation of basic foodstuffs has the most important impact on mitigating the VAT's regressivity. Table 7.1 attempts to provide an overview of how African countries treat foodstuffs for VAT purposes at the producer level and, subsequently, when foodstuffs—unprocessed or processed—are traded before reaching the final consumer.

- As shown in Table 7.1, the agricultural sector (including forestry and fishery) can be taxed, subject to the threshold, or exempted outright. Most countries exempt agriculture, but the SACU countries tax the sector. In practice, the two approaches largely come to the same thing, particularly if exempt systems permit large farms or estates, as they generally do, to register for VAT[4] and if the threshold in taxing countries is fairly high, as it often is.[5]

[3] IHS (2010) has an extensive discussion of the theoretical and empirical literature on pass-through. Most studies note that, in some cases, the VAT may be less (or more) than fully passed on to consumers. This note of caution finds support in the analysis of Benedek et al. (2015). On the basis of a large data set providing disaggregated monthly data on prices and VAT rates for 17 eurozone countries over 1999–2013, the authors estimate that pass-through is less than full on average, and differs markedly across types of VAT changes. Pass-through is about 100% for changes in the standard rate, but merely around 30% for changes in reduced rates and essentially zero for reclassifications. Also, see Kosonen (2015) for a natural experiment on VAT pass-through.

[4] This is particularly important for large producers of cacao (Cameroon, Côte d'Ivoire, Ghana), tea (Kenya), coffee (Ethiopia, Uganda), tobacco (Malawi, Tanzania, Zambia, Zimbabwe), palm oil (Côte d'Ivoire, Ghana), and natural rubber (Côte d'Ivoire). These producers should generally be forward integrated to the export stage, while they incur no VAT on inputs if the VAT on imports is reverse-charged.

[5] As discussed in Chapter 16, this does not work well for (small) exempt farmers who incur VAT on inputs if the registration option is costly. The obvious solution is to zero-rate major farm inputs, such as fertilizer and pesticides, that have hardly any alternative use outside the agricultural sector.

Table 7.1 Africa: concessionary VAT treatment of agriculture, forestry, fishing, and traded foodstuffs, 2018

RECs and countries	Agriculture (** = unprocessed products)	Traded foodstuffs (not exhaustive)	
		Exemption	Zero or lower (L) rate (* = unless supplied as a meal)
Southern African Development Community (SADC)			
SACU			
Botswana	T	-	*Millet grain/meal, wheat grain, flour, sugar cobs, sorghum, maize meal Samp, brown bread, fresh milk, rice, vegetables, fruit
Lesotho	T	-	Beans, bread, lentils, maize, peas, sorghum, wheat, flour, samp, milk, eggs
Namibia	T	Unprocessed imports of fish, crustaceans, molluscs, and other aquatic invertebrates	*Mahango, maize, beans (except if canned or frozen), bread, cake flour, sunflower cooking oil, milk, sugar
South Africa	T	-	Brown bread, maize, samp, mealies, beans, lentils, rice, milk, eggs, cooking oil (except olive oil), canned pilchards, vegetables, fruit
Swaziland	T	-	Maize meal, samp, beans, brown bread, rice, milk, eggs, vegetable oil (except olive oil), fresh fruit, vegetables
Other			
Congo, DR	E	Bread, fish, flour, maize, wheat	-
Madagascar	E	Paddy, rice, corn	-
Malawi	E	Meat, fish, eggs, dairy products, natural honey, vegetables, fruits, nuts, cereals, malt, starch, infant milk, coffee, tea	Salt
Mauritius	**E	Bread, baby food, breakfast cereals, milk	Rice, wheat flour, sugar, dairy products, edible oil, margarine, live poultry
Mozambique	E	-	Bread, maize flour, wheat, rice, salt, sugar, infant milk powder, mackerel, edible oils, tomatoes

Continued

Table 7.1 *Continued*

RECs and countries	Agriculture (** = unprocessed products)	Traded foodstuffs (not exhaustive)	
		Exemption	Zero or lower (L) rate (* = unless supplied as a meal)
Seychelles	T	Rice, bread, meat, flour, edible oil, margarine, salt, sugar, milk powder, fish, infant food, lentils, vegetables, fruit	-
Zambia	**E	Animal and dairy products, fish, infant food	Bread, wheat, fresh vegetables, agricultural products predominantly sold in foreign markets
Zimbabwe	T	Mahewu, rice, eggs, margarine, lactose, vegetables, fruit	*Bread, mealie, maize, flour, cereals, dairy products, meat, eggs, cooking oil, infant food, salt, sugar, vegetables, fruit, potatoes
East African Community (EAC)			
Burundi	**E	**If sold by producer	L: imports of food and agricultural products
Kenya	**E	Maize	-
Rwanda	**E	Milk	-
Tanzania	**E	*Basic agricultural products: maize, wheat, cereals, meal flour, unprocessed meat, poultry, eggs, milk, fish, vegetables, fruits, nuts, coffee, tea	-
Uganda	**E	-	Cereals grown and milled in Uganda
Economic and Monetary Community of Central Africa (CEMAC)			
Cameroon	E	Bread, milk, fish	-
Central African Republic	**E	**If locally produced: bread, milk, meat, infant food, fruit, vegetables	L: imported milk, meat, sugar
Chad	**E	**If sold directly to consumers; bread, milk, poultry, meat	-
Congo	**E	**If of local origin; basic products	L: sugar, salt, tomatoes
Equatorial Guinea	**E	**If raw and sold directly to consumers	L: bread, rice, dairy products, meat, infant foods

Gabon	**E	**If of local origin; bread, flour, gluten, rice, dairy products, eggs, canned sardines, pilchards, pasta, sugar	L: sugar, chicken
Economic Community of West African States (ECOWAS)			
UEMOA			
Benin	**E	Milk	-
Burkina Faso	**E	**Also if frozen, including fish and meat	-
Côte d'Ivoire	**E	**If for domestic consumption	L: milk, pasta
Guinea–Bissau	E	Foodstuffs	L: cereals, rice, flour, bread, milk, agricultural products
Mali	**E	**If without their basic nature having been altered	-
Niger	E	Rice, flour, poultry meat, vegetable oil, fruit, vegetables	-
Senegal	**E	**If listed as basic necessities	-
Togo	E	-	-
WAMZ			
Cabo Verde	E	Meat, fish, eggs, milk, fruit, vegetables	-
Gambia	E	**If sold by producer; rice, bread, flour, sugar, meat, fish, salt, vegetables, cooking oil, infant food	-
Ghana	**E	**If in its raw state; rice, millet, maize, sorghum, cassava, yam, corn, plantains, butter, meat, salt	-
Guinea	E	Rice, flour, wheat, bread, palm oil, fish	-
Sierra Leone	**E	**Rice in its raw state; fish, birds, animals, edible fruits, nuts, vegetables	-
Arab Maghreb Union (AMU)			
Algeria	E	Bread, milk	L: basic foodstuffs, olive oil
Mauritania	E	Bread, meat, fish, vegetables, other basic foodstuffs	-

Continued

Table 7.1 *Continued*

RECs and countries	Agriculture (** = unprocessed products)	Traded foodstuffs (not exhaustive)	
		Exemption	Zero or lower (L) rate (* = unless supplied as a meal)
Morocco	E	Bread, cereals, milk, sugar, edible oil	L: canned sardines, milk powder, rice, pasta, salt, edible oil, tea, butter
Tunisia	E	Retail sales of milk, flour, edible oils, sugar, other foodstuffs	-
Intergovernmental Authority on Development (IGAD) and Egypt			
Djibouti	E	-	-
Egypt	E	Infant food, sugar, tea, coffee	L: processed potatoes, crackers, flour products, edible oils, tallow
Ethiopia	E	Injera, bread, grain, wheat, maize, sorghum, cereals, palm oil, milk	-
Sudan	**E	**If supplied in raw condition; meat, poultry, fish, dairy products, bread, locally produced flour	-

Note: The letters have the following meaning: T = taxed at the standard rate; E = exempt; Z = taxed at the zero rate; L = taxed at a lower-than-standard rate.

Source: Appendix A. Note that the agricultural sector is exempt or out-of-scope in most countries outside the SACU region, although the source materials may not disclose this explicitly.

- Most countries that exempt agriculture do so by exempting its products rather than the sector itself. This means that agricultural products are also exempted in subsequent taxable trading channels up to the consumer. To ensure that the exemption is restricted to agricultural products per se, most VATs add provisos that the products should be unprocessed (or, as some VATs say: 'in their raw state'—Equatorial Guinea, Ghana, Sierra Leone, Sudan; or 'without their basic nature having been altered'—Mali), of 'local origin' (Central African Republic, Congo, Gabon), 'sold by the producer' (Burundi, Gambia), or 'sold directly to consumers' (Chad, Equatorial Guinea). Some countries have broadened the exemption somewhat by saying that the exempt items should be 'listed as basic necessities' (Senegal) or be for 'local consumption' (Côte d'Ivoire).

- In addition to the exemption for unprocessed agricultural products, most countries explicitly exempt various basic processed foodstuffs, such as bread, rice, meat, dairy products, and cooking oil. Accordingly, the VAT on these products is limited to the VAT on the inputs into these foodstuffs if not also exempted. This should result in lower but most likely uneven effective tax burdens on these products.
- Nil or uniform VAT burdens are imposed on basic foodstuffs that are zero-rated or subject to a lower rate, respectively. SADC countries (except DR Congo and Madagascar) apply zero rates to basic foodstuffs. Most CEMAC countries, Algeria, Côte d'Ivoire, Egypt, Guinea–Bissau, and Morocco apply a lower rate instead. Some countries (Burundi, Central African Republic) use the VAT to discriminate against imported foodstuffs by applying a lower but positive rate to them while exempting local foodstuffs. Some CEMAC countries stipulate that the exemption applies only to agricultural products of local origin. This violates the division of the role each tax plays in the overall tax system, since import duties should be used for protectionist purposes, if at all.
- Various countries exempt infant food or apply a lower rate. This concession should favour higher-income groups since the income elasticity of infant food is likely to be higher than 1. A curious provision of Tunisia's VAT exempts retail sales of basic foodstuffs. The problems with this approach have been discussed in Chapter 5.

The general conclusion of this review is that most African countries exempt or zero-rate unprocessed agricultural products. In addition, they exempt or zero-rate a fairly large number of basic processed foodstuffs, unless supplied in restaurants. Processed foodstuffs, consumed on or off the premises, tend to be taxed. Outright exemption implies that the products still bear VAT on inputs, an issue to which we return in Chapter 16.[6] By contrast, most SADC countries zero-rate basic foodstuffs, while many other, mainly francophone, countries apply a lower rate. Below, the choice between using an exemption, zero rate, or lower rate in mitigating the VAT burden on lower-income groups is discussed in some detail, but first the overall VAT burden distribution in various countries is examined.

[6] In short, Table 16.4 shows that feed, seed, fertilizers, and pesticides are often exempted or zero-rated, but equipment and implements tend to be taxed more often. The VAT on inputs should wash out, of course, in countries that zero-rate basic foodstuffs, but not in countries that use exemptions to relieve foodstuffs of VAT. For this reason, some countries zero-rate fertilizers and pesticides. This would be more difficult for equipment and implements in view of their dual nature, i.e. their potential to be used for taxable as well as non-taxable activities.

7.2 VAT Burden Distribution in South Africa

The impact of the VAT on the poor and the rich is usually gauged from household budget surveys, which show detailed VAT-inclusive expenditures of individuals or families by income decile. The expenditure items can be grouped according to whether they are taxed, exempt, or not taxed. Next, for taxable expenditures, the VAT included in the individual expenditure items can be computed by dividing the amounts by 1 plus the (decimal) VAT rate and subtracting the result from tax-inclusive expenditures. For exempt expenditure items, an assumption has to be made regarding the VAT that has been paid in respect of the inputs of the exempt items and passed on to the consumer.

Subsequently, the VAT amounts calculated for each item of expenditure are aggregated by income decile and expressed as a percentage of income or consumption. On the assumption that the VAT is borne by consumers, changes in the ratio of VAT paid to income or consumption (excluding VAT) by individuals or households in different income deciles may then be taken to indicate the nature of its impact: a declining ratio across income deciles implies that the VAT is regressive, a rising ratio implies that it is progressive, and no change in the ratio means that the impact of the VAT is proportional.[7] Two main studies for South Africa—by the Katz Commission (1994) and the National Treasury (2011)—shed interesting light on the incidence issue.[8]

Katz Commission

Under the South African VAT, the zero rate applies to 19 basic foodstuffs and farming goods as well as kerosene (illuminating paraffin).[9] As documented in table 9.12 of Katz Commission (1994), expenditures of the very poor on the various zero-rated foodstuffs vary, but are largest for cereal products (7 per cent of household expenditure), vegetables (3.5 per cent), and milk and eggs (3 per cent). Expenditures on meat (8.6 per cent), which is taxed at the standard rate, are also an important item in the household basket of the very poor. On average, poor and low-income households spent more than 30 per cent of their income on food, against 10 per cent for high-income households.

[7] Although the arithmetic of this kind of impact analysis seems simple, there are usually conceptual and empirical difficulties in defining and measuring both the numerator (VAT paid) and the denominator (income or consumption) for various levels of income or consumption. For an early but still useful discussion of the issues, see McLure (1990).

[8] See also the study by Van Oordt (2016), who concludes that the South African VAT is regressive even when measured against consumption.

[9] The zero-rated food and farming items, listed in section 11(1)(j) of the VAT Act, are shown in Table 7.1. Originally, only brown bread and maize meal were zero-rated, but in 1992 and 1993, following extended public protests, various other essential foodstuffs were added to the zero-rate list.

The Katz Commission (1994) made a detailed investigation of the VAT burden distribution across income groups on the basis of household income and expenditure survey data for 1990 in metropolitan areas.[10] Also, the Commission examined the changes in the VAT's impact if there were no zero-rating and if, in addition to the current coverage of the zero rate, meat (widely consumed by the poor) were zero-rated. Furthermore, the Commission estimated the impact of a higher-than-standard rate of 25 per cent on luxury goods. Table 7.2 presents the results.

The following conclusions can be drawn from the findings of the Katz Commission:[11]

- The VAT is broadly proportional over most of the income range. Low-, middle-, and high-income households all spend some 7 per cent of their income on VAT. Some progressivity may be noted for very poor households and some regressivity for very high-income households.

Table 7.2 South Africa: VAT burden distribution by income group, 1994–95

	Very poor	Low income	Middle income	High income	Very high income
Average annual income (in 1990 prices; rand)	8,500	24,500	65,000	149,000	307,000
Number of households (thousands)	3,324	1,001	504	599	315
Total VAT (million rand)	2,430	1,720	2,320	6,080	5,060
VAT per household (rand)	731	1,719	4,607	10,151	16,068
Current zero-rating					
- VAT impact (%)	8.8	7.0	7.0	6.6	4.9
- relief per household (rand),[a]	115	218	337	477	671
VAT impact of alternatives (%)					
- meat zero-rated	7.6	6.1	6.2	6.1	4.5
- no zero-rating	10.6	8.4	7.9	7.2	5.3
- 25% rate on luxuries	8.8	7.1	7.0	6.6	4.9

[a] For 14 zero-rated goods.

Source: Katz Commission, 1994. Figures pertain to five out of nine income classes distinguished by the Central Statistical Service.

[10] The reference is to Central Statistical Service (1992). Subsequently, the Unit for Fiscal Analysis of the Department of Finance developed a VAT policy model using the data from the household expenditure survey. The analysis benefitted from the pioneering work of Fourie and Owen who developed a 'weighted equity gain' ranking for various products by dividing the percentage of the lowest-income budget spent on a particular product by the percentage of the highest-income budget spent on the same product. The ranking can be used to choose products for the zero-rate list as well as for a luxury-excise list. See Fourie and Owen (1993).

[11] For an analysis of the Katz Commission's findings, see Cnossen (2004). Attention should also be drawn to Botes (2001), who found that zero-rating actually made the South African VAT slightly more regressive than full taxation.

- In absolute amounts, zero-rating provides R115 relief for very poor households, against R671 for very high-income households. In monetary (rand) terms, therefore, the rich benefit six times as much from zero-rating as the very poor do. Only 30 per cent of the total benefit of zero-rating goes to the poorest households, who account for 60 per cent of the households covered in the table.
- The impact distribution would change little if meat were also zero-rated. The reduced impact, shown in table 9.12 of the report, can be almost entirely accounted for by the lower overall effective VAT rates across income groups.
- Similarly, the impact distribution would not change much if zero-rating were abolished—again after correcting for the effect of the lower standard rate under an equal-yield assumption.
- The impact of the suggested higher-than-standard rate on luxury products is negligible. By implication, this should also be the case for the current *ad valorem* excises. This issue is discussed further in Section 7.6.

To assess the impact of the current VAT, the absolute figures would obviously have to be adjusted for price changes since 1990, but it is not very likely that the percentage burden distribution of the VAT would have changed much since that year.

Broadly, the Katz Commission's findings were confirmed by Go et al. (2005), who used a computable general equilibrium model (CGE) to assess the VAT's burden distribution based on 2001 data. The authors found that the VAT in South Africa is mildly regressive, but also that the overall tax system is not.[12] They concluded further that the VAT is the most effective instrument for generating government revenue. Within this context, the conclusion of the Katz Commission (1994, p. 117) probably still holds: 'providing relief to the poor through exemptions and VAT zero-rating is likely to be both unsound tax policy and ineffective social policy'.

South African National Treasury

The findings of the Katz Commission (1994) and Go et al. (2005) find further support in a more recent thorough study by the National Treasury (2011) of South Africa. Instead of calculating the incidence of the VAT on foodstuffs and illuminating paraffin, this study computed: (a) the share of VAT savings accruing

[12] The regressivity of the South African VAT may have been further mitigated when the threshold was raised from R300,000 to R1 million in the 2008–09 Budget since many basic foodstuffs are traded through small exempt business outlets. Interestingly, Mugoya (1998) argues that the preferential treatment of foodstuffs in Tanzania does not make the country's VAT progressive, while it greatly erodes the VAT's revenue performance.

to different expenditure groups regarding goods and services that are currently zero-rated or exempt; and (b) the share of VAT paid by different expenditure groups in respect of various standard-rated goods and services for which a zero rate had been requested by interest groups. The results, shown in Table 7.3, leave little doubt that zero-rating is not the way to go. The results can be summarized as follows:

- With the exception of maize (meal), bread flour, and maize rice, the share of VAT savings attributable to zero-rated foodstuffs rises sharply as expenditure increases across expenditure groups.[13] Clearly, higher-expenditure groups benefit disproportionately from the zero rate on foodstuffs. This is also true for expenditures on cooking oil and paraffin (kerosene), which tend to be rather large expenditure items in most household budgets. The tax treatment of kerosene is of particular interest since its use generates negative externalities in the form of CO_2 emissions, which makes zero-rating difficult to justify.
- The same regressively distributed VAT benefit pattern is found for exempt public transport, regardless of the mode of transport. According to the National Treasury (2011, p. 150), the blanket exemption of public transport may even have increased the VAT's regressivity, as 'the more affluent using mainline passenger transport provided by luxury coach transport and touring operators also enjoy the benefits of the exemption'. Further (p. 170), 'uncertainty often exists regarding who must be the fare-paying person or whether an exempt transport service or a standard rated renting of a vehicle is involved'.
- Higher-expenditure groups also benefit disproportionately from the exemption for education. Beyond that, administrative complications arise when exempt institutes of higher learning are also engaged in taxable activities, such as research and the sale of books, whose taxation requires the apportionment of input tax. The National Treasury (2011, p. 170) opines that 'it is often not clear whether a certain service involves the supply of education or research, or whether a specific supply is "necessary for and subordinate and incidental to" the supply of educational services', and thus whether it qualifies for the exemption. Full taxation and increased targeted subsidies may be a better alternative.

Similar observations can be made regarding goods and services that are currently standard-rated but that might qualify as 'merit goods', such as water, electricity,

[13] Alderman and del Ninno (1999) confirm the logic of the zero rate on maize, which helps to improve nutrition in both urban and rural areas. The zero rate on bread has a similar impact on nutrient consumption, but a zero rate on meat is not justified in terms of equity or nutrition since it would favour non-poor urban households.

Table 7.3 South Africa: percentage of VAT savings or payments on various goods and services bought by different expenditure groups, 2006

Product	Expenditure groups and annual average expenditures within groups in 2000					Total
	Very low R5,314	Low R10,052	Middle R17,340	High R35,707	Very high R139,243	
A. Percentage of VAT savings accruing to different expenditure groups						
1. Zero-rated goods and services						
Corn, rice, grains, potatoes						
Maize	20.8	18.3	19.2	12.4	29.3	100.0
Maize meal	19.6	21.2	31.0	17.7	10.6	100.0
Bread flour	19.1	22.2	31.4	17.6	9.7	100.0
Rice	10.5	14.7	29.0	25.2	20.6	100.0
Maize rice	14.7	18.2	29.6	21.3	16.2	100.0
Brown bread	9.8	14.4	31.0	26.2	18.6	100.0
Potatoes	13.9	14.8	26.7	24.7	20.0	100.0
Dairy products						
Fresh milk	5.1	7.6	20.2	26.5	40.6	100.0
Sour milk	10.4	13.8	29.1	26.7	20.0	100.0
Milk powder	9.6	14.5	31.3	26.1	18.6	100.0
UHT milk	8.1	9.9	18.9	23.0	40.0	100.0
Eggs	7.9	11.5	26.6	26.0	28.0	100.0
Fruit and vegetables						
Tomatoes	10.9	13.7	27.3	24.6	23.6	100.0
Lettuce	0.7	1.6	6.9	21.1	69.6	100.0
Apples	0.3	3.0	9.5	24.1	63.1	100.0
Bananas	2.4	5.6	12.1	24.0	55.8	100.0
Oranges	1.0	2.0	10.2	28.3	58.5	100.0
Other						
Cooking oils	5.6	7.5	20.6	29.1	37.2	100.0
Paraffin (kerosene)	4.6	7.5	20.6	26.3	41.0	100.0
2. Exempt goods and services						
Public transport						
Buses	0.0	0.0	0.3	10.7	89.0	100.0
Trains	0.1	0.1	2.7	13.7	83.4	100.0
Metered cabs	0.2	0.1	2.5	9.8	87.5	100.0
Other	0.0	0.0	0.0	1.4	98.6	100.0
Education						
Pre-primary	0.4	1.0	5.2	17.6	75.8	100.0
Public	0.3	1.5	7.3	22.8	68.1	100.0
Private	0.0	0.0	0.1	5.1	94.8	100.0
Teacher training	0.3	1.2	3.6	9.6	85.2	100.0
Universities	0.9	3.3	11.5	27.4	56.9	100.0
B. Percentage of VAT paid by different expenditure groups on various goods and services that are standard-rated						
Public utilities						
Water	2.8	4.3	12.7	22.4	57.8	100.0
Electricity	1.1	2.5	10.8	25.3	60.3	100.0

Medicines						
With prescription	3.5	5.9	18.9	28.6	43.1	100.0
With prescription not covered by medical aid	0.0	0.1	1.2	9.6	89.1	100.0
Without prescription	3.3	8.3	23.1	31.2	34.2	100.0
Without prescription not covered by medical aid	0.2	0.2	1.4	8.3	89.9	100.0
Health services						
Flat fee	3.6	1.8	3.6	6.9	84.1	100.0
Not covered by medical aid	1.8	4.5	14.4	22.0	57.4	100.0
Doctors, dentists, etc.	1.5	2.5	8.8	15.6	71.5	100.0
Reading material						
Textbooks	0.1	1.0	8.8	25.3	64.8	100.0
Newspapers	1.7	3.6	11.7	24.6	58.3	100.0
Magazines	9.0	8.1	23.7	32.1	27.1	100.0
Books	6.3	8.6	19.9	24.5	40.7	100.0

Source: National Treasury, 2011, tables 31 and 32.

healthcare, books, journals, and cultural events, whose intrinsic value may be underestimated by consumers. Their purchase should therefore be stimulated by governments, the argument goes—e.g. by not levying VAT on them. But the National Treasury (2011) refutes this argument.

- Similar to foodstuffs, not taxing water and electricity would disproportionately benefit higher-expenditure groups, as shown in Table 7.3. As the National Treasury (2011, p. 150) observes, 'the affluent will merely pay less for the large volumes of [zero-rated] electricity or water used for luxuries such as using electricity for dishwashers, air conditioners, fridges and other electrical appliances and using [zero-rated] water to fill swimming-pools, for dishwashers, automatic washing machines, saunas and watering their gardens'. Further, a social exemption (tranche) for water and electricity, as found in various francophone countries, does 'not take into account the household structure of poorer families, where various generations, extended family and even friends are forced to stay under one roof. Their combined electricity consumption for basic use of appliances could equal or even exceed the use by an affluent couple, living in an up-market residence using luxury appliances'. Finally, the basic exemption can be abused—e.g. by installing two meters in what is essentially one dwelling.
- The same observation applies to the VAT benefit distribution if no (input) tax were levied on medicines and health services. The poor derive limited benefits from preferential VAT treatment, because most medical products are largely unaffordable or of a low priority to these groups and zero-rating would not save these people the VAT if they can access medical services and

medicines free through the public health system. Again, taxation and targeted subsidies, which are present practice in South Africa, do a better job in reducing distortions and administrative complexities whilst ensuring that the poor receive adequate medical care.

- Reading materials, too, are income-elastic items of consumption. Books, newspapers, and journals are mainly bought by the affluent. Currently, books and other printed or electronic media that are supplied as part of educational services and that are covered by school or tuition fees are exempt from VAT. Taxation and an increase in school subsidies would eliminate the distortion of input choice and prevent abuse of the exemption. It is often argued that the taxation of books amounts to a tax on knowledge, but, according to the National Treasury (2011), the relatively low book penetration in South Africa has its origins primarily in low levels of literacy and generally poor reading skills—in other words, in the failures of the education system.

In reviewing its arguments, the earlier Katz Commission (1994) estimated that the revenue forgone on account of zero-rating amounted to nearly 10 per cent of total VAT collections. In other words, the standard rate (12 per cent at that time) could be lowered by around 1.1 percentage points and raise the same amount of revenue if essential foodstuffs were taxed at the standard rate.[14] In a similar vein, the National Treasury (2011, p. 116) estimated that social grants could be increased by 11 per cent if zero-rating were abolished.

In practice, South Africa's high registration threshold of R1 million (equivalent to US$93,000) also has the effect of reducing the VAT burden on basic foodstuffs, because food products from small exempt farms traded through small exempt retail outlets do not enter the VAT base. Last but not least, zero-rating and exempting goods and services generate problems of definition and interpretation, create opportunities for evasion, and exacerbate administrative control problems. Interestingly, South Africa counters the administrative problems of refunds, which can be associated with the zero-rating of basic foodstuffs, by disallowing the registration of firms with taxable supplies of R50,000 (US$4,650) or less. Of course, this practice is at odds with the zero rate's objective.

7.3 Findings for Other Countries

The findings on the VAT's incidence in other countries are reviewed separately for developing countries and high-income countries.

[14] Here and elsewhere, it is assumed that changes in the VAT's rate or coverage do not involve behavioural changes.

Developing Countries

Bird and Gendron (2007) summarize the results of a number of VAT burden distribution studies in developing countries, many of which suggest mildly progressive results. The authors note that the VAT's impact depends on the design of the tax (rates, exemptions), the effectiveness of the VAT's administration, and the nature of local consumption patterns (e.g. the distribution of in-kind consumption).

In addition, of course, policymakers must consider the VAT's impact on economic efficiency and the utility of the corresponding government expenditures. Keeping this in mind, Sahn and Younger (1999) examine the progressivity of taxes and expenditures on health and education in eight African countries: Côte d'Ivoire, Ghana, Guinea, Madagascar, Mauritania, South Africa, Tanzania, and Uganda. They find that the burden distribution of the VAT in these countries is generally progressive.[15] Also, the benefits of social services are mostly progressive, but only primary schooling in South Africa is progressive on a per-capita basis. Individually, university education tends to be least progressive, to the point of being regressive in most countries. The benefits associated with hospital care are also less progressive than those of other health facilities.

On the tax side, similar results are found for a separate study on tax incidence in Madagascar (Younger et al., 1999). For Ethiopia, Muñoz and Cho (2003) note that the progressivity of the VAT comes mainly from the high ratio of in-kind transactions for poorer households, a share that is likely to decrease as the economy becomes more market oriented. In turn, this implies that over time the VAT is likely to become less progressive. On the expenditure side, however, the benefits of primary education accrue mostly to the rich. On the other hand, the poor benefit more from health expenditures.

Of interest, too, are the findings of Mansour (2015) for Morocco and Tunisia, two upper-middle-income countries in Africa. The author calculates the VAT forgone on account of exemptions and low rates and finds that the top quintile of the income distribution reaps about 40 per cent of VAT forgone in both countries, while the first quintile receives less than 10 per cent. These results suggest, as Mansour concludes, that more efficient policies can be designed whereby revenue from streamlining VAT exemptions and rate structures can be used, for instance, to increase support for the poor through conditional, albeit better-targeted, cash transfers.

Last but not least, using comparable fiscal incidence analysis, Lustig (2017) undertakes a sophisticated examination of the impact of fiscal policy on equality

[15] Further, excise taxes on petrol and diesel are highly progressive even when the indirect effects of petroleum taxes on users of transportation services are included. By contrast, taxes on kerosene are generally regressive. Mention should also be made of a study by the International Monetary Fund (2005), which used the national household survey and an input–output model of the Ugandan economy to assess the impact of the VAT and the excise taxes. It concluded that the impact of these taxes is roughly proportional to total spending, although slightly higher for the highest quintile of the income distribution. By itself, the VAT is mildly regressive, while the excise taxes are mildly progressive.

and poverty in 25 countries for around 2010 of which five countries are found in Africa. The African countries include two low-income countries (Ethiopia and Tanzania), two lower-middle-income countries (Ghana and Tunisia), and one upper-middle-income country (South Africa). For purposes of analysis, the author separates the 'cash' portion of the system (taxes, direct transfers, indirect subsidies) from the 'in-kind' portion (the monetized value of the use of government-provided education and health services).

Lustig (2017) concludes that while tax and expenditure (fiscal) policies unambiguously reduce income inequality in all African countries, that is not true for the cash portion of the ultra-poor in Ghana and Tanzania (net payers into the fiscal system with incomes of PPP US$0–1.25 per day) and the extreme poor in Ethiopia (with incomes of PPP US$1.25–2.50 per day). Consumption taxes on basic goods are the main culprits of the fiscally induced impoverishment. As regards the in-kind portion, health spending is pro-poor in all countries and so is primary school spending other than in Ethiopia. The incidence of secondary school spending is neutral across incomes, but government outlays on tertiary education tend to be regressive in various countries.

Since much of this chapter is about the VAT's incidence in South Africa, it appears worthwhile to quote the conclusions about the distributional impact of fiscal policy for that country that were reached by Inchauste et al. (2015):

> The results show that South Africa uses its fiscal instruments to significantly reduce market income inequality and poverty through a progressive tax system and highly progressive social spending. The rich in South Africa bear the brunt of taxes that we examined [personal income taxes, VAT, excise taxes on alcohol and tobacco, and the general fuel levy], and the government redirects these resources to the poorest in society to raise their incomes [through direct cash transfers, free basic services, and health and education spending]. . . . As a result, the fiscal system lifts some 3.6 million individuals out of poverty.

Higher-Income Countries

VAT impact studies of higher-income countries appear to confirm the conclusions of the Katz Commission (1994) and the South African National Treasury (2011).[16] In Ireland, for example, it was found that although the poor spend relatively more of their income on food than the rich, in absolute amounts the rich spend twice as much as the poor (Commission on Taxation, 1984). Rich people tend to buy more expensive varieties of food, eat out more often, and may throw food away more easily. Consequently, Ireland's zero-rating of food gives twice as much tax relief to high-income groups as to low-income groups—an odd way of alleviating

[16] For an early review, see Cnossen (1999b).

the plight of the poor. The OECD concludes that, although generally progressive, the low VAT rates on food in 15 member countries are poorly targeted and very costly.[17]

The same message is conveyed by (hypothetical) VAT impact studies for New Zealand and the United States. The New Zealand study indicates that merely 15 per cent of the benefit of a zero rate on food would go to households with the lowest 20 per cent of income (Australian Society of CPAs, 1998). In the same vein, calculations by the US Congressional Budget Office (1992) show that a zero rate on food would reduce the regressivity of a hypothetical VAT by only 18 per cent. Finally, a recent Dutch study concludes that for every €1 of VAT relief for lower-income groups, higher-income groups get €2 of relief (Bettendorf and Cnossen, 2015).[18]

In short, most studies provide evidence that zero rates (or exemptions) for foodstuffs hardly affect the VAT burden distribution in favour of low-income groups. A practical consideration is that in developing countries, most poor people buy their foodstuffs in local markets supplied directly from farms. In view of the high thresholds, it is unlikely that these foodstuffs would bear much VAT, except to the extent that farmers and distributors use taxable inputs (see also Martinez-Vazquez and Bird (2011)). More importantly perhaps, low-income households are best helped through compulsory health and education programmes. The revenue from taxing foodstuffs at the standard rate can be used to help finance these programmes.

While the application of the standard rate to all foodstuffs and other products currently singled out for favourable treatment would be the first-best solution, making that leap in one go may be difficult to accept in countries with limited capacity to mitigate the (perceived) VAT impact on the poor through other taxes and/or expenditure programmes. A second-best solution, therefore, would be to apply a reduced but positive rate to all food for human or animal consumption, as is done in many European countries and to some extent AMU countries. Finally, a third-best solution would be to combine the reduced or, preferably, standard rate with an exemption (rather than a zero rate) for a limited number of basic unprocessed foodstuffs, specifically enumerated in the law, as examined in the next section.

7.4 Zero Rate, Lower Rate, or Exemption?

The choice between a zero rate, a lower-than-standard but positive rate, and an exemption for basic foodstuffs mainly involves administrative and compliance

[17] Organization for Economic Cooperation and Development, 2014. Interestingly, the same study finds that the low VAT rates for social or cultural objectives exhibit regressive impacts. For OECD countries, see also Warren (2008).

[18] For similar conclusions, see Davis and Kay (1985), Crawford, Keen, and Smith (2010), and Godbout and St-Cerny (2011).

considerations rather than tax burden distribution issues. Zero and/or lower rates require registration and, possibly, refunds of prior-stage tax. The exemption approach eases these problems (if there are no other taxable supplies), but leaves an indeterminate amount of VAT paid on taxable inputs in output prices. The effect of the input tax on domestic prices can be nearly fully eliminated, however, by combining the exemption for basic foodstuffs with the zero-rating of major farm inputs, such as seed, feed, fertilizers, and pesticides, at the supplier level,[19] although this means that little or no tax would be paid by the agricultural sector and that the environmental impact of, for instance, fertilizers and pesticides would not be accounted for in the absence of an excise explicitly levied for that purpose.

By contrast, a zero rate (other than on exports) or lower VAT rate involves a significant increase in compliance costs for businesses, particularly small businesses. A firm that deals in products with different rates—e.g. a grocery that sells lower-rated milk along with standard-rated soft drinks and snack foods—should keep separate accounts for the different kinds of items. If the VAT on differentially rated products cannot be accounted for separately, the tax liability must be determined by applying presumptive methods (which, in turn, increases the difficulty of monitoring the taxpayer's compliance). Not surprisingly, in the UK, firms with multiple-rate output have double the compliance costs of firms taxed at a single rate (Hemming and Kay, 1981). Furthermore, there is substantial evidence that the increase in compliance costs is distributed regressively with respect to income: small businesses bear proportionately more of the burden than large ones (Sandford, Godwin, and Hardwick, 1989).[20]

In addition, zero-rating increases administrative costs. The number of voluntary registrants is likely to go up because they are anxious to obtain refunds of VAT. Refund returns must be monitored with particular care, even though no revenue is realized. Again in the UK, the number of VAT registrants increased by 13 per cent on account of the zero rate on essential products, which constitute nearly 40 per cent of the VAT base (Sandford, Godwin, and Hardwick, 1989).[21] Apart from wasting administrative resources, a zero/lower rate is likely to increase the chance of tax evasion. Empirical work indicates that by adding another VAT rate, the compliance rate is lowered by 7 percentage points (Agha and Haughton, 1996).

[19] As noted above, the zero-rating of agricultural equipment is more problematic, because of its dual-use nature. Incidentally, the less-than-full elimination of the input taxes means that exports of the exempt foodstuffs cannot be fully freed of tax and that imports cannot be taxed fully on a par with domestically produced goods. For this reason, the EU, for instance, does not permit its member states to exempt foodstuffs. But the less-than-complete border tax adjustments should be less of a concern for most African countries. Generally, large food-exporting firms would be integrated forward with the export stage and (elect to) be taxed.

[20] The authors show that, when size of business is measured by taxable turnover, the smallest businesses in the UK had compliance costs that were proportionately 20 times those of the largest businesses.

[21] But for the zero rate, these registrants would have been eligible for the small-business exemption. For an early review of studies on VAT compliance and administration costs, see Cnossen (1994); for a more recent analysis, see Barbone, Bird, and Vazquez-Caro (2012).

On balance, then, if the VAT on unprocessed foodstuffs is to be reduced but not in the form of a lower-than-standard rate, an exemption for a limited number of specified foodstuffs seems to be the preferred approach. As economic development proceeds, the exemptions should be replaced by a lower-than-standard rate, as applied in the EU and the AMU countries, or, even better, the standard rate as found in countries with truly modern VATs.

7.5 Higher Taxes on Luxury Goods

Household budget studies can also be used to examine the actual or desired tax burden on luxury goods. Luxury goods can be defined as goods whose income elasticity is greater than 1. This means that as income increases, expenditures on luxury goods increase faster than income increases. By taxing these goods differentially higher, VATs and excise taxes would impart some progressivity to the tax system.

On the basis of Appendix B, the following non-exhaustive list of products that are regarded as luxury goods in African countries, and hence eligible for higher taxes, can be composed:[22]

- salmon, caviar;
- toiletries, cosmetics, perfumes;
- jewellery, precious stones and metals;
- leather and fur products;
- watches, clocks;
- cameras, binoculars;
- radios, TVs, recorders, videos;
- motor vehicles;
- pleasure boats; and
- firearms, ammunition.

Generally, African countries do not use their VATs to tax the consumption of luxury products more heavily. The VATs in Côte d'Ivoire (21.31 per cent on tobacco products sold at wholesale to exempt retailers) and Swaziland (25 per cent on alcohol and tobacco products) have a higher-than-standard rate, but these rates are confined to one or two products or activities. Arguably, the higher tax impact could be better achieved by using the excise tax. This applies, too, to the higher rate of 18 per cent that Mauritania applies to fuel. Mauritania (18 per cent) and Sudan (30 per cent) also impose a higher rate on telecommunications. Egypt is the only country in Africa that imposes a higher-than-standard VAT rate, of

[22] More importantly, excise taxes—on smoking, drinking, gambling, polluting, energy consumption, and road use—can be imposed for externality-correcting or revenue-raising efficiency purposes. See Cnossen (2006b) for an analysis of the African scene and Cnossen (2010b) for an analysis of a developed country, Australia.

22 per cent, on a wide range of products regarded as luxuries. Guinea–Bissau appears to do so, too, at a rate of 20 per cent, but information on the extent of its coverage is not available.

As Table 7.4 indicates, various SADC and CEMAC countries make extended use of the excise system to tax luxury goods more heavily. Generally, all of the products shown above are included in the excise tax base. Further, a number of countries impose an excise on 'various' products, a description that, in general, covers the first three items in the list shown above. Many other countries tax 'some' or a 'few' luxury products, such as cosmetics and jewellery. Of course, countries that do not impose luxury excises may achieve the same purpose through the import duty system (in violation of its role).

Table 7.4 Africa: excise taxes on luxury goods and services, 2018

REC	Many	Various	Some
SADC, SACU	Botswana Lesotho Namibia South Africa Swaziland		
SADC, other	Madagascar Mauritius Mozambique	Congo, DR Malawi Seychelles	Zambia Zimbabwe
EAC		Burundi Kenya	Rwanda Tanzania Uganda
CEMAC	Cameroon Central African Republic Chad Congo Equatorial Guinea Gabon		
ECOWAS, UEMOA		Benin Guinea–Bissau Senegal Togo	Burkina Faso Côte d'Ivoire Mali Niger
ECOWAS, WAMZ	Cabo Verde Guinea		Gambia Ghana Sierra Leone
AMU		Algeria Tunisia	Mauritania Morocco
IGAD and Egypt	Ethiopia		Djibouti Egypt Sudan

Source: Table 4.1.

7.6 Are Excise Taxes on Luxury Goods Justified?

Again, the South African experience is instructive when evaluating the effectiveness of special excises in influencing the progressivity of the consumption tax system. As shown in Appendix B, South Africa imposes luxury excises on toiletries, photographic and sound equipment, TVs and radios, office machines, and various other items. Generally, the revenue collected from the excises on luxury goods, and hence the impact on the tax burden distribution, is small. According to the Katz Commission (1994), excise tax collections (inclusive of countervailing customs duties) on luxury products amount to approximately 7 per cent of total excise tax receipts and 1.4 per cent of VAT collections. Furthermore, the Commission investigated the impact of a hypothetical 25 per cent VAT rate on luxury goods,[23] which it found to be almost negligible. The Katz Commission (1994, p. 123) opined that 'the disadvantages of [differentially higher] multiple rates outweigh the possible redistributive gains available from this option'.

More generally, higher excises on luxury goods and services should be rejected for the following reasons:

- Experience elsewhere shows that the coverage of the usual luxury products (net of expenditures on traditional excise goods and motor vehicles) tends to be extremely narrow, hardly comprising more than 1–2 per cent of consumption expenditures. Consequently, the effect on progressivity or revenue is insignificant. Luxury excises on, for instance, jewellery, furs, perfumery, cosmetics, clocks, and watches are truly nuisance levies.
- Class-differentiated consumption patterns that are helpful in tax design for imparting progressivity may not exist for some luxury products (unlike basic foodstuffs). In South Africa, for instance, more than 60 per cent of the revenue from the *ad valorem* excises used to be collected on toiletries, although lower-income households tend to spend a larger share of their income on these items than higher-income households.
- Separate excises add to the costs of administration and compliance. The definitional refinements that are required to tax luxury items higher usually give rise to casuistic disputes on interpretation. Sound equipment is an example. Cheap items and spare parts are difficult to exempt and must therefore be taxed along with expensive items. The complexities of administering and complying with excises on luxury goods resemble those of manufacturers' sales taxes, discussed in Chapter 5.

[23] The goods selected for the 25% VAT rate were: garden furniture, food mixers and processors, dishwashers, tumble dryers, sewing machines, knitting machines, lawn trimmers, organs, TVs, decoders, video recorders, radios, gramophone records and tapes, computers and computer diskettes, aircraft, boats, sports equipment, power tools, and caravans.

- Many luxury products, such as jewellery and cameras, can easily be purchased abroad, particularly by higher-income groups. Subsequently, their importation could be concealed, would fall within the limits of the personal exemption, or would not be noticed at all.
- Finally, the income tax can better ensure progressivity than higher consumption tax rates can, because the former generally falls on households that buy luxury goods. In contrast, the income tax cannot take over the role of the exemption or zero rate for basic foodstuffs for the simple reason that it does not reach the very poor. Hence, the case for exempting basic foodstuffs is stronger than the case for imposing excises on luxury goods.

In short, a fairly strong case can be made for abolishing the excises on luxury products. They tend to be wasteful of the use of scarce administrative resources. Nonetheless, if it is decided to continue the taxation of luxury products at differentially higher rates, then, on impact grounds, higher-than-standard VAT rates are preferable to *ad valorem* excises levied at the manufacturing stage. The impact of VAT rates, which extends through to the retail stage, is more certain and distortions among taxable luxury products would be fewer because trading margins are included in taxable price. From an administrative point of view, however, the manufacturers' excises would seem to have the edge, because the number of taxable producers is fewer and a countervailing duty can be levied at the import stage. Enforcement would also be less problematic, although valuation problems might be greater.

Finally, excise taxes (or increased VAT rates) on tobacco and alcohol figure importantly in the burden distribution of consumption tax systems.[24] Usually, the tobacco excise is the most regressive of the traditional excises. Its impact is particularly harsh since the poorest households in developing countries spend on average 10 per cent of their expenditure on tobacco products (World Health Organization, undated). Some mitigation can be achieved if cottage-made cigarettes are excluded from excise tax coverage. The alcohol excise, on the other hand, is on average less regressive and may even be proportionate over large ranges of income. However, the income elasticity of beer (and hence the tax impact) is lower than that of wine and spirits. Artisanal brews, moreover, are often exempted or taxed at a (very) low rate, which should mitigate the impact of the beer excise (Bird and Wallace, 2010).

7.7 Evaluation of Rate and Base Differentiation

Before drawing final conclusions on the advisability of using rate and base differentiation to influence the impact of VATs and excise taxes on the overall tax burden distribution, it seems useful to list the requirements for doing so.

[24] For a full review of the excise taxes on tobacco, alcohol, petroleum products, and motor vehicles, see Cnossen (2005).

Requirements for Progressivity in Product Taxation

To begin with, the redistributive role of tax systems is inherently small: taxes can make the rich poorer but they cannot make the poor richer. Perforce, it is even smaller for *in rem* types of taxes, such as VATs and excise taxes. These taxes should only be used for redistributive purposes if there are limits on the capacity to administer comprehensive and progressive income taxes. This is often the case in developing countries. But even then a number of requirements must be met if tax rate and base differentiation is to be worthwhile.

- Necessities (luxuries) should be defined as products for which expenditures decline (rise) faster than income declines (rises), i.e. they should have an income elasticity of demand lower (higher) than unity (moreover, to limit substitution, own-price elasticities of demand should be low, i.e. below unity in absolute value).
- For the mitigation of regressivity (or promotion of progressivity) to be appreciable, consumption by lower- (higher-) income classes should be significant.
- It should be possible to break taxable goods and services down into subgroups, permitting the application of graduated rates that differ on the basis of the nature, quality, or price of taxable products, on the assumption that consumption patterns vary accordingly between poor and rich.
- Administrative feasibility requires precise definitions of taxable products in order to minimize the number of disputes and arbitrary assessments and to facilitate compliance.
- Finally, to increase the acceptability of the lower (higher) rates, a requirement might be that the consumption of the exempt or lower-rated products is widely regarded as a sign of poverty and, conversely, that the consumption of higher-taxed products is viewed as a sign of affluence.

Implications for VAT Exemptions and Lower-than-Standard Rates

In considering the implications of these requirements for mitigating the regressivity of consumption tax systems, it should first be pointed out that there is a principal difference between VATs and their predecessor pre-retail sales taxes. If consumption tax burden distribution issues are to be taken seriously, it is essential that manufacturers' sales taxes be transformed into VATs. This should have an appreciable positive effect since trading margins on goods are highest on luxury goods, while services have an income elasticity of demand that generally exceeds unity. Similarly, turnover taxes should be converted into VATs to eliminate inequitable and inefficient cascading effects.

Even in VAT countries, the case for a zero or lower rate on essential products is not strong. Income and property taxes and income-support measures are better suited than the VAT for bringing the overall tax impact distribution into line with society's notions of ability to pay and income redistribution. Taxing basic foodstuffs at the standard rate or a lower-than-standard rate would raise an amount of revenue far in excess of what would be needed to offset the regressive impact of the VAT on low-income households if properly targeted. Presumably, some of the regressive impact could be offset by increasing the basic exemption of the personal income tax, but this does not help the really poor, who are not subject to this tax. Accordingly, there is a residual case for exempting or applying a lower rate to foodstuffs and perhaps some other essential products. Class-differentiated consumption patterns would seem to facilitate this—probably more in practice than by design. It is likely that the effect would be most noticeable for rural families who purchase most of their foodstuffs from local small-scale producers whose output is either exempted or escapes taxation. The effect on poor urban families, who tend to buy more factory-made or processed goods, might be smaller.

If basic foodstuffs are to be treated favourably, however, exemption in conjunction with the zero-rating of various agricultural inputs would be preferable to zero-rating the foodstuffs themselves. In theory the effect might not seem as neat as under zero-rating, but in practice the result might well be similar. Administrative and compliance costs, however, would be much lower under the exemption approach. Exemption might also be more of a deterrent to political pressures to increase the number of favoured products. Incidentally, exemption is the route that most countries at a similar level of economic development to, say, the SACU countries, which zero-rate basic foodstuffs, have taken.

Implications for Promoting Progressivity

The case for promoting progressivity through consumption tax systems is weak, particularly under a VAT extending through the retail stage. Generally, the tax base for luxury goods is too small for the tax to have an appreciable effect. In fact, a strong case can be made for abolishing the *ad valorem* excises and against the introduction of higher-than-standard VAT rates on luxury products if contemplated. Most products subject to higher VAT rates or *ad valorem* excises do not meet the requirements for rate and base differentiation listed above.

However, the motoring field is a notable exception to this conclusion. The demand for passenger cars and passenger car fuels is usually highly income-elastic (although the demand for passenger car fuel tends to be price-inelastic—a good thing if revenue is not to suffer unduly), expenditures on them comprise a sizable part of household budgets, motor vehicles can easily be broken down into subgroups that would roughly correlate with purchasing patterns of high- and low-income groups, and related excise taxes are easy to administer and meet socially with a high degree of acceptance.[25]

In African countries, almost any form of differentially higher taxation of private motor vehicles may be expected to be an effective means of progressive taxation, as only high-income groups own them, but excises directly related to the value of the vehicle, if properly designed, are likely to have the most progressive incidence. The choice might then be between an excise tax on new motor vehicles with a bracketed *ad valorem* tax rising with the value of the vehicle, or an annual licence system with fees graduated in favour of cheaper and older vehicles. Licence fees would probably be better, as their administration is easier (the incentive to evade the tax is smaller than in the case of an equal-yield one-time levy) and, unlike an excise tax on new vehicles, increases in annual fees do not give rise to windfall profits on vehicles already on the road. In view of ownership patterns in developing countries, progressivity in excise taxation would also be imparted by higher taxes on petrol and diesel fuel.

7.8 The Heart of the Matter

To summarize, countries that zero-rate a limited number of foodstuffs may be advised to exempt them (but, importantly, not other products) to mitigate the VAT's regressive burden distribution. In this respect, the types of foodstuffs that receive favourable treatment in the SACU countries can serve as examples. Clearly, excises on luxury goods or higher-than-standard VAT rates to increase the progressivity of the tax system cannot be recommended. Efforts to achieve progressivity in the tax burden distribution of consumption taxes should probably be confined to the automotive field.

On balance, it is difficult for VAT to shed its regressive image, and recommendations that it should be as broad-based as possible (with concessions confined to sectors that are hard to reach administratively) and levied at a single rate do not make that image brighter. But in biting this bullet, it seems useful to draw attention to the work of Lustig (2017), a keen analyser of fiscal incidence, who concludes her survey, which includes five African countries, with the following advice:

> Efficient regressive taxes (such as the VAT) when combined with generous well-targeted transfers can result in a net fiscal system that is equalizing. Even more, because a net fiscal system with a regressive tax could be more equalizing than without it (Lambert's conundrum), policy recommendations—such as eliminating the regressive tax—based on piecemeal analysis could be flatly wrong.

[25] A system of properly designed road user charges, moreover, can do a good job in identifying consumer preferences and reducing excessive use of public facilities.

Accordingly, it is of crucial importance to focus on the combined effect of the tax and expenditure incidence. This is eloquently expressed by Galbraith (1984), referred to in Schenk, Thuronyi, and Cui (2015):

> The relation of the sales tax [VAT] to the problem of social balance is admirably direct. The community is affluent in privately produced goods. It is poor in public services. The obvious solution is to tax the former to provide the latter—by making private goods more expensive, public goods are made more abundant. Motion pictures, electronic entertainment and cigarettes are made more costly so that schools can be more handsomely supported. We pay more for soap, detergents and vacuum cleaners in order that we may have cleaner cities and less occasion to use them. We have more expensive cars and gasoline so that we may have more agreeable highways and streets on which to drive them. Food being relatively cheap, we tax in order to have better medical services and better health in which to enjoy it.

8
Economic Integration and Tax Coordination in Regional Economic Communities

As depicted in Figure 4.1, all African countries belong to a regional economic community (REC), and often to more than one. These countries are closely monitoring the remarkable combination of free politics and free economics achieved by the common market (now the single market) of the member states of the EU. Free trade and free competition raise the standards of living in participating member countries. In this setting, tax coordination should ensure that equal conditions for competitors are not distorted by discriminatory tax systems—a criterion that is referred to as tax neutrality. Import duties are the most obvious example of tax discrimination against out-of-state products, but VATs and excise duties can be used as trade barriers instead. At the same time, however, the participating countries should retain as much tax autonomy as possible in order to be able to pursue their own social and economic policy goals. Beyond that, operational costs (akin to a tax), imposed on taxpayers and tax administrations, should be minimized.

This chapter takes stock of the types of trade blocs that are found in Africa and the extent of economic and tax coordination in the various RECs.

8.1 Stages of Economic Integration and Tax Coordination

Various (cumulative) stages of economic integration and tax coordination can be distinguished as countries decide to join hands on the way to a common market.[1]

- Initially, in the context of a preferential trading area (PTA), regional tariff and non-tariff barriers to trade for selected products are reduced (but not abolished) among participating member countries.

[1] See Schiff and Winters (2003) for a survey of the empirical literature on trade agreements. It should be noted that departures by developing countries from the World Trade Organization (WTO) principle of non-discrimination (the most-favoured nation—MFN—clause) are sanctioned by the General Agreement on Tariffs and Trade's (GATT) article XXIV and the Enabling Clause, which relaxes the conditions, among others, by permitting developing countries to reduce tariffs on mutual trade in any way they wish.

- The extension of PTAs to most goods and services results in a free trade area (FTA) in which treaty countries agree to eliminate tariffs, quotas, and preferences on most (if not all) goods and services traded between them. Also, a common tariff nomenclature and harmonized valuation procedures are introduced. To avoid evasion through re-exportation, rules of origin are put in place under which the extent of local material inputs and value added are certified.
- The next step is the establishment of a common external tariff (CET). This form of economic integration can be called a customs union (CU). In a customs union, furthermore, efforts should be made to break down various non-tariff barriers[2] and eliminate the discriminatory aspects of internal indirect taxes. Naturally, a true customs union would also pursue a common trade policy.
- Subsequently, a customs union might evolve into a common market in which there would be complete free movement of goods, services, persons, and capital. Now, the coordination of the indirect taxes would be pursued at the supranational level under a broad, coherent mandate to foster free trade and free competition. Moreover, disputes regarding the meaning and implications of free trade and free competition would, in the last instance, be resolved before a common court of justice.
- As in the EU, the common market might be called an internal market, with the subsequent abolition of customs controls at internal borders and the elimination of technical barriers, such as health and safety regulations and product standards. Following this, work on eliminating the remaining non-tariff barriers and implementing an effective anti-trust policy would be pursued in what is called a single market.
- Finally, the introduction of a common currency would seal the establishment of a true economic and monetary union.

In considering the interaction between economic integration and tax coordination, Bird (1989) has pointed out that the two are related but separate dimensions of forming a common market. In practice, as shown by the experience in the USA and Switzerland, for instance, there need not be a single continuum

[2] The importance of the elimination of non-tariff barriers should not be underestimated. Non-tariff barriers include quotas, prohibitions, licensing schemes, export restraints, disparities in standards, different health and safety measures, and collusive government procurement policies, but also different customs procedures and documentation, poor application of the rules of origin, onerous import duty deposit schemes, administrative fees and charges, and clearance delays at ports of entry and border posts. The World Bank (2012) reports on various examples of non-tariff barriers, including simple but onerous ones, such as women carrying staple foods from DR Congo to Burundi, Rwanda, and Uganda having to pay off customs officers, and trucks provisioning supermarkets in Southern Africa having to file 1,600 documents and incurring US$20,000 annually to secure permits to distribute meat, milk, and plant-based foods. Also, most countries impose severe restrictions on the movement of accountancy, engineering, and legal services across borders.

between the economic and tax dimensions. In fact, economic union can exist quite separately without much tax (or political) integration. As Bird states provocatively (p. 150): 'Just as in federations, *identical* [emphasis added] tax systems may be neither necessary nor desirable in a common market in which member states have different policy objectives and different economic conditions.' Accordingly, the 'differential' approach instead of the 'equalization' approach seems most appropriate in principle. This dictum is also followed in this chapter.

8.2 Economic Policy Coordination

Table 8.1 lists the RECs that have been formed in Africa since 1975, listed in the approximate order of the extent of economic cooperation that is actually in place. The memberships can be ascertained by comparing the RECs with those shown in Figure 4.1.

Customs Unions

The following four, mostly incomplete, customs unions can be found in Africa:

- The Southern African Customs Union (SACU), established in 1920, has a common external tariff and a common excise tax schedule, but not a common trade policy. SACU is a supranational organization with a Council of Ministers (supported by a Customs Union Commission made up of senior SACU civil servants) as the highest decision-making authority. An independent ad hoc tribunal settles disputes regarding the interpretation and application of the agreement, which was last amended in 2002. SACU negotiates trade agreements with third countries and other free trade areas.[3] However, various quantitative restrictions remain, and, importantly, services, intellectual property rights, and the so-called Singapore issues (investment, competition policy, government procurement, and trade facilitation) are not covered by the agreement. SACU, which maintains a high level of protection against the rest of the world, has an agreed formula for distributing the import and excise duty revenues collected at external borders and domestically to the member countries.[4] Separate (customs) border posts have also been maintained.

[3] The SACU treaty can still be circumvented, for instance, by tariff preferences that South Africa applies to imports from the EU (under the free trade agreement), which apply *de facto* to all SACU members, and the imposition of extra excises on alcoholic beverages by Botswana and Lesotho, which are called 'levies' to distinguish them legally from excise duties, which fall under the SACU treaty.

[4] Customs duty revenue is distributed in proportion to intra-SACU import shares. Further, 85% of excise tax revenue is allocated to each member country on the basis of its share in SACU's combined GDP, while the remaining 15% is set aside for development purposes and distributed on the basis of deviations from the average combined GDP.

Table 8.1 Africa: regional economic communities (RECs), 2018

Name of trade bloc (for membership, see Figure 4.1)	Economic characteristics	Type of trade bloc	VAT coordination	Excise tax coordination
Southern African Customs Union (SACU)	Founding/recent treaty: 1920/2002 Population: 64.2 million GDP: US$328.0 billion Bloc exports: N/A	CU (CET); services not included	Similar statutes and structures, with zero rate on limited number of basic foodstuffs and agricultural inputs; limited number of non-standard exemptions; joint collection at the import stage by the South African Revenue Service (SARS).	Nearly identical excise tax systems, including a large number of luxury goods; joint collection at the import stage by SARS.
East African Community (EAC)	Founding/recent treaty: 1999/2000 Population: 168.0 million GDP: US$153.3 billion Bloc exports: 17.6%	CU (CET) and common customs procedures	Some similarity of statutes, with large number of non-standard exemptions for basic foodstuffs, pharmaceuticals, and agricultural inputs. Lower rate in Burundi and broad coverage of zero rate in Uganda. Coordination is actively pursued.	Few excises on luxury goods (except Burundi and Kenya), but on soft drinks and some other items. Coordination is pursued.
West African Economic and Monetary Union/ Union Économique et Monétaire Ouest Africaine (UEMOA)	Founding/recent treaty: 1994/2000 Population: 116.7 million GDP: US$98.5 billion Bloc exports: 14.5%	CU (CET) + CC	VAT legislation largely identical, with large number of non-standard exemptions for basic foodstuffs and agricultural inputs. No lower-than-standard rates except in Côte d'Ivoire and Guinea–Bissau.	Large number of excise taxes on luxury products, soft drinks, coffee, tea, and some other items.
Economic and Monetary Community of Central Africa/Communauté Économique et Monétaire d'Afrique Centrale (CEMAC)	Founding/recent treaty: 1994/2000 Population: 50.8 million GDP: US$76.3 billion Bloc exports: 0.8%	CU (no CET) + CC	VAT legislation largely identical, with large number of non-standard exemptions for basic foodstuffs, pharmaceuticals, and agricultural inputs. No zero rate, except for medical products in the Congo and Equatorial Guinea. Rate differentiation in Equatorial Guinea and Gabon.	Luxury excises on wide range of products. No coordination.

Southern African Development Community (SADC)	Founding/recent treaty: 1992/2000 Population: 277.7 million GDP: US$532.9 billion Bloc exports: 10.1%	FTA; harmonization of tax policies	Outside SACU: different VAT statutes, with large number of non-standard exemptions for food products, agricultural inputs, and public transportation. Agreed guidelines for VAT coordination.	Different excise tax systems, which include various luxury products and soft drinks in the base. Agreed guidelines for cooperation in excise taxes.
Economic Community of West African States (ECOWAS)	Founding/recent treaty: 1975/1993 Population: 357.8 million GDP: US$562.5 billion Bloc exports: 7.6%	FTA	French and British VAT legislation. No initiatives at coordination between UEMOA and WAMZ blocs.	No coordination.
Common Market for Eastern and Southern Africa (COMESA)	Founding/recent treaty: 1994/2000 Population: 572.0 million GDP: US$757.0 billion Bloc exports: 4.1%	FTA; progress in eliminating tariff and non-tariff barriers, single customs document	Different VAT statutes and structures. No initiatives for coordination.	Different excise tax systems. No coordination.
PM: West African Monetary Zone (WAMZ)	Founding treaty: 2000 Population: 241.1 million GDP: US$464.0 billion Bloc exports: N/A	NNA	VAT legislation similar (except in Guinea), with large number of non-standard exemptions for unprocessed food products and agricultural inputs, newspapers, and books. No attempt at coordination.	Excise taxes on some food products, soft drinks, and some luxury items. No coordination.
PM: Intergovernmental Authority on Development (IGAD)	Founding/recent treaty: 1986/1996 Population: 247.0 million GDP: US$500.8 billion Bloc exports: N/A	NNA, progress stalled	VAT legislation different, with highly graduated rates in Egypt. No higher-than-standard rates in Djibouti, Ethiopia, and Sudan (except telecoms). No coordination.	Extended excise tax system in Ethiopia. No coordination.

Continued

Table 8.1 *Continued*

Name of trade bloc (for membership, see Figure 4.1)	Economic characteristics	Type of trade bloc	VAT coordination	Excise tax coordination
PM: Arab Maghreb Union (AMU)/Union du Maghreb Arabe (UMA)	Founding/recent treaty: 1989/1994 Population: 154.9 million GDP: US$309.4 billion Bloc exports: 2.5%	NNA; agreements on trade and tariffs; not a member of the AEC	VAT legislation based on French model. Exemption of specified food products and various lower-than-standard rates. No coordination.	Limited number of excise taxes. No coordination.
PM: Economic Community of Central African States (ECCAS)	Population: 119.9 million GDP: US$215.2 billion Bloc exports: N/A	NNA, progress uncertain	No coordination with non-CEMAC countries.	No coordination.
PM: Community of Sahel-Saharan States/ Communauté des États Sahélo-Sahariens (CEN-SAD)	Founding treaty: 1998 Population: N/A GDP: N/A Bloc exports: N/A	NNA, progress stalled	No coordination.	No coordination.

Note: AEC = African Economic Community; CC = common currency; CET = common external tariff; CU = customs union; FTA = free trade agreement; NNA = not notified agreement to WTO (could be functionally equivalent to any of the other agreements); PM = pro memoria (not discussed further); PTA = preferential trading area. 'Bloc exports' are the sum of merchandise exports by members of a trade bloc to other members of the bloc. African regional blocs not participating in the AEC (and not listed in the table) are the Greater Arab Free Trade Area (GAFTA), the Economic Community of the Great Lakes Countries (CEPGL), the Indian Ocean Commission (IOC), the Liptako–Gourma Authority (LGA), and the Mano River Union (MRU).

Source: World Bank, 2016. For the (overlapping) memberships of the RECs, including non-VAT countries, see Figure 4.1. GDP data for Djibouti (COMESA, IGAD), Eritrea (COMESA, IGAD), Libya (AMU, COMESA), Somalia (IGAD), and South Sudan (COMESA, EAC, IGAD) are not available.

- The East African Community (EAC) purports to promote the free movement of goods, services, persons, and capital among its members in the context of a common market. It has a common external tariff and common customs procedures, but not a common trade policy. The right of free establishment has also been agreed to. Internal tariffs have mostly been abolished, but 58 important tariff lines have been classified as 'sensitive' and thereby excluded from the free trade list.[5] Article 83(2)(e) of the 1999 treaty obliges member countries to 'harmonize their tax policies with a view to removing tax distortions in order to bring about a more efficient allocation of resources within the Community'. The EAC has also made efforts to put the institutions in place that are indispensable for the proper functioning of economic cooperation. Specifically, an EAC Common Court of Justice has been established and has jurisdiction to hear and resolve disputes on the interpretation and application of the EAC treaty.
- The Economic and Monetary Union of West Africa (UEMOA, after its French name, *Union Économique et Monétaire Ouest Africaine*) does have a common external tariff and has made some headway in reducing tariffs vis-à-vis third countries, but still has to deal with many official and unofficial internal trade barriers, including differing rules of origin. Interestingly, UEMOA has an operational compensation fund from which pay-outs for tariff revenue losses can be made. Beyond that, UEMOA members have implemented macroeconomic convergence criteria with an effective surveillance mechanism, and initiated regional structural and sectoral policies that paved the way for a common currency, the CFA franc.
- An explicit objective of the Economic and Monetary Community of Central Africa (CEMAC, from its French name, *Communauté Économique et Monétaire d'Afrique Centrale*) is to promote economic integration, including the formation of a genuine common market. CEMAC does not have a common trade policy, however, although it uses a common currency, the CFA franc. CEMAC replaced quantitative import barriers by temporary surcharges (Gulde-Wolf, Tsangarides, and Martijn, 2006), but it has not yet been able to reach agreement on a common external tariff on imports from non-CEMAC countries. The countries share a common financial, regulatory, and legal structure, while capital can move freely within the region. CEMAC is part of the Economic Community of Central African States (ECCAS), which, in addition, has Angola, Burundi, DR Congo, Rwanda, and São Tomé & Principe as its members, but there is no economic policy coordination between these countries and CEMAC.

[5] The majority of the sensitive products are agricultural—milk and cream, wheat grain and flour, maize, rice, sugar, and palm oil—i.e. the main staples that constitute the consumption basket of most EAC households. Other sensitive products are selected textiles (including worn clothing), cigarettes and tobacco, cement, and some electrical products. The total level of protection of these products is the sum of the additional, often country-specific, duty and the applicable maximum common external tariff.

Free Trade Areas

In addition to the four customs unions, there are three free trade areas in Africa:

- The SACU area and 10 other countries form the Southern African Development Community (SADC),[6] with members as diverse as South Africa and Malawi or Angola. The strategic plan for the SADC, announced in 2004, sets out a time frame for the economic integration of the region. The measures adopted in 2005 included the creation of a free trade area by 2008, the establishment of a customs union in 2010, and the implementation of a common external tariff by 2015. None of these dates has been met. The need to maintain and enforce rules of origin, too, precludes the development of a full customs union.
- The Economic Community of West African States (ECOWAS) is composed of the UEMOA REC and the West African Monetary Zone (WAMZ), which attempts to establish a central bank and a single currency to rival UEMOA's CFA franc. How far the two ECOWAS subgroups will integrate is open to some doubt. UEMOA and WAMZ countries differ widely in terms of economic and social characteristics. Nonetheless, some vestiges of a customs union have been put in place with the adoption of a common external tariff in 2015.
- The Common Market for Eastern and Southern Africa (COMESA) is making some progress in eliminating internal tariff and non-tariff barriers and introducing a single customs document. In 2009, COMESA joined hands with ECOWAS and SADC to form the African Economic Community (AEC), which (ambitiously) purports to turn the continent into a customs union by 2019 and a common market by 2023, followed by an economic and monetary union in 2028. Recently, an attempt has been made to bolster this agreement with the launch of the African Continental Free Trade Area (AfCFTA) in Kigali on 21 March 2018.[7] The details of the accord are still to be agreed upon, however, including import tariff reductions (possibly to be made up by enhanced VAT collections) and non-tariff barriers.

Most other RECs are 'not notified agreements' to the World Trade Organization (WTO) (although this does not necessarily mean that they cannot be functionally equivalent to any of the 'notified' agreements). Progress in the Intergovernmental Authority on Development (IGAD), established for drought control and economic development, ECCAS, and the Community of Sahel-Saharan States (CEN-SAD)

[6] For a comprehensive review and evaluation of the extent of economic and tax coordination in SADC, see Cnossen (2011b); for an early analysis, see Khandewal (2004).

[7] AfCFTA is a flagship project of Agenda 2063, the African Union's long-term vision of an integrated, prosperous, and peaceful Africa. The 'single continental market for goods and services' would increase regional trade by a third and raise African GDP by 1% over time (*The Economist*, 24 March 2018).

is stalled or uncertain, while the Arab Maghreb Union (AMU) is plagued by traditional rivalries, particularly regarding the unresolved question of Western Sahara's sovereignty.

Evaluation

Economic cooperation in most RECs is largely voluntary in view of the absence of a strong executive authority and an authoritative court of justice that rules by exclusion on infringements of the treaties. This should not hinder intraregional trade much if free trade with the rest of the world is pursued concurrently, as is largely the case, for instance, in the Association of South East Asian Nations (ASEAN; Cnossen, 2013b). But, apparently, African countries wish to promote trade and investment within RECs and on the African continent, rather than in the world at large. The lack of regional economic integration so far is reflected in the low share of intraregional goods trade in total imports. In 2010, this share was merely 5 per cent in COMESA, 8 per cent in ECOWAS, and 10 per cent in UEMOA. By contrast, the share of intraregional goods trade in total imports was 20 per cent in ASEAN, 35 per cent in the countries of the North American Free Trade Agreement (NAFTA), and 60 per cent in the EU.[8]

The success and failure of African RECs have been analysed by, among others, Yang and Gupta (2005). The authors produce data that show that the RECs have had only a small positive though uneven effect on intra-African trade. Since the turn of the century, RECs do not yet seem to have had a significant impact on Africa's export performance in world markets, while competitiveness may have declined.[9] Most African countries still have very restrictive trade regimes with high tariffs, a large number of often specific and seemingly arbitrary exemptions, and a significant degree of tariff escalation. The RECs' small markets, administrative capacity constraints, low product complementarity, and high transaction costs owing to inadequate transport, information, and communications infrastructures are all obstacles to the expansion of intraregional trade. The authors also suggest that most-favoured nation (MFN) liberalization is probably more conducive for growth and trade than fostering intraregional trade and investment.

Yang and Gupta (2005) point out that potential revenue losses have been a key obstacle to broader trade liberalization. Consequently, intraregional tariff reductions (and the removal of non-tariff barriers) have made only limited progress

[8] For these figures, see World Bank (2012). Relative bloc exports are another measure of the degree of regional economic integration. The sum of merchandise exports by member countries to other members is close to 20% in the EAC and 15% in UEMOA, but exports hardly exceed 10% in SADC, while bloc exports of other RECs are insignificant.

[9] The authors point out that the ultimate criterion for judging the welfare effect of RECs is whether consumer gains outweigh the loss of government revenue and production. They opine that this may not have been the case in SADC.

and usually none regarding widely consumed sensitive commodities. Further, individual country tariffs vis-à-vis third countries have been maintained. In fact, external trade barriers remain relatively high—the simple average of applied MFN tariffs is higher in Africa than in other developing regions of the world. These obstacles to trade liberalization can only be brought down by the replacement of trade taxes by domestic taxes, notably VATs and excise taxes.

8.3 Tax Coordination

Various tax questions arise as RECs integrate their economic policies more closely. Should VAT and excise tax bases and rates be harmonized? And should border controls be maintained to apply border tax adjustments for the VATs and excise taxes or should these controls be abolished in favour of some other destination- or even origin-based system of treating goods and services that enter into intraregional trade? Clearly, base harmonization is not desirable if, as has happened in the EU, harmonization institutionalizes existing shortcomings. And rate harmonization is undesirable if countries are to retain as much tax autonomy as possible.

Table 8.1 shows the extent of VAT coordination and excise tax approximation in the various RECs. Fairly close coordination has been achieved in SACU, UEMOA, CEMAC, and, to a lesser extent, in the EAC. In most other countries, however, membership of an economic community does not appear to have made much difference to the design and implementation of the VAT and excise tax regime.

VAT Cooperation and Coordination

VAT cooperation is necessary in a REC if an equal playing field is to be created. Coordination is required if member countries decide to do away with border controls.

Neutrality of intra-REC trade

It is doubtful whether most current VATs in Africa sufficiently satisfy the requirements of the neutrality criterion regarding goods and services entering intra-REC trade. Although perfection need not be the goal (the best is often the enemy of the good), intractable problems arise regarding the treatment of the non-standard exemptions currently applied to a large number of goods and services. Most countries exempt unprocessed foodstuffs, medicines and medical equipment, printed matter, and agricultural inputs. If exempt, an indeterminate amount of VAT enters into intra-REC export prices (because the seller cannot obtain a refund for the tax incurred on the inputs to the products), violating the neutrality criterion.

Thus, tax neutrality regarding intraregional trade emerges as another reason why bold VAT policy reform is necessary. VAT reforms do not imply, however, that the various RECs should go as far as the EU in aligning the bases and rate structures of their VATs. The important thing is that ambiguity is removed with respect to border tax adjustments, particularly VAT refunds of prior-stage tax on exports. Presumably, for the time being, border controls will remain in place, providing an up-front collection point for the various VATs. An incidental, if welcome, side effect would be that the import VAT effectively serves as a 'withholding' device for businesses that are not registered (the informal sector) or do not fully declare their sales (Keen, 2008).

Administrative reform is also called for. Reportedly, refunds on intra-REC exports of VAT paid in previous stages of production and distribution are not made expeditiously.[10] Accordingly, exporters incur an interest charge—akin to an extra tax!—which violates the tax neutrality criterion. Similarly, VAT on imports levied at intra-REC borders may not be creditable against the domestic VAT liability until they are resold. Again, therefore, importers incur an interest charge to the extent that they have to advance the VAT before they can take credit for it in the return they have to file when the goods are sold on. The import VAT turns into a real import duty if the VAT on domestic supplies is lower and a refund is not provided. The late export refunds and import VAT credits warrant close scrutiny if trade within RECs is to be conducted on a level playing field.

An important step toward VAT cooperation has been made by SADC through the issue of guidelines along with a commentary (Southern African Development Community, 2016a). The (non-binding) guidelines start with a commitment of member countries to gradually abolish import duties in pursuance of WTO requirements, and recoup the revenue forgone through a broad-based VAT.[11] The guidelines also state a preference for excise taxes instead of higher-than-standard VAT rates on luxury goods and services; a lower VAT rate is not contemplated. Further, the guidelines foresee agreement on minimum rates and the harmonization of the coverage of exemptions and zero rates on domestically traded goods and services. Exchange of information and mutual assistance in countering fraud are also envisaged.

Abolition of border controls

An issue that is much debated in the SADC and to some extent the EAC is how goods and services should be taxed if border controls are abolished. Should the destination principle (imports taxed, exports freed from tax) be maintained or should it be replaced by the origin principle (exports taxed, imports not taxed)? Some have taken the view that goods and services should be taxed in the country

[10] See Harrison and Krelove (2005) for an analysis of VAT refunds and Ernst & Young (2017) for a practical guide.

[11] For a general treatment, see Organization for Economic Cooperation and Development (2017).

of production (origin) rather than the country of consumption (destination), because this would obviate the need for customs posts.[12] There is now a professional consensus, however, that the destination principle is to be preferred. The origin principle, being imposed on producers, distorts trade more than the destination principle, whose incidence is on consumers.[13] Further, it has been pointed out that the origin principle is incapable of proper administration. Exports would have to be valued for tax purposes (to ensure that all domestic value added were taxed) and a notional tax credit would have to be attached to imports (to ensure that imports were not implicitly taxed at the first inland stage under a tax-credit type of VAT). These 'new' border tax adjustments could turn an origin-based VAT into an administrative nightmare and require the reimposition of border controls.

On closer examination, moreover, it appears that the destination principle does not require border controls but can be administered through books of account, obviating the need for physical border controls. The principle can be applied in either of two ways: under the deferred payment scheme (also referred to as reverse-charging) or a tax-credit clearing system.[14]

Under the deferred payment scheme, customs clearing methods are set aside by incorporating the compensatory import tax in the domestic ambit of the VAT. In fact, the tax-credit mechanism of the VAT is relied upon to ensure that the first taxable person in the importing country implicitly accounts for the compensatory tax, since there is no offsetting credit. Alternatively, but with the same result, the deferred payment system can apply the reverse-charging mechanism usually applicable to imported services or goods. In that case, the recipients of the goods have to account for the VAT (and provide themselves a credit for the tax at the same time, so no net VAT would be due). Furthermore, eligibility for the export rebate (zero-rating of exports) can be proved on the basis of documentary evidence (bills of lading, payments from abroad, and so on) rather than through physical clearance at the border. Consequently, exporters do not have to show a certificate or affidavit signed by the customs authorities (as proof that the goods have left the country) to qualify for a refund of the VAT. The deferred payment system could be implemented in the SACU region.

Under the tax-credit clearing system, exports would be taxed by the exporting country, while importers in the importing country would be permitted to take a credit for the tax invoiced by exporters. But to restore the destination principle,

[12] For instance, see Glenday and Hollinrake (2005). In the early economics literature, the origin principle was also preferred for the European Union to be able to eliminate border controls and, it was thought, border tax adjustments.

[13] In other words, the destination principle provides production efficiency, while the origin principle furthers exchange efficiency. See Lockwood, de Meza, and Myles (1994).

[14] The tax-credit clearing system was first suggested by Cnossen (1983). Subsequently, it was adopted by the European Commission as the definitive regime for VAT coordination, but the member states still cling to the deferred payment system. The system sparked a lively debate, particularly after Keen and Smith's (1996) proposal for such a system. For other contributions, see Bird and Gendron (2000), Keen (2000), Keen and Smith (2000), and McLure (2000). For a review of the debate and a note of caution, see also Cnossen (2010a).

the exporting country's tax administration would pay the gross tax collected from exporters to the importing country's tax administration, which permitted the credit for the VAT charged by exporters. Under a clearing-house arrangement, only net balances would be payable by countries that are net exporters. Under this approach, as well as under the deferred payment scheme (and a liberalized conventional import exemption system), cross-border consumer purchases would be taxed on an origin basis. As in the EU, special rules could be put in place for mail-order businesses, motor vehicles, pleasure boats, and purchases abroad by exempt entities to ensure that the purchases are always taxed in the country of destination. Interestingly, a form of tax-credit clearance is being operated between South Africa, on the one hand, and Lesotho (see Agreement (2015)) and Swaziland, on the other.

Excise Tax Approximation

According to Appendix B, excise tax systems within most RECs differ as widely as VATs. Excise tax approximation (and administrative cooperation) may be more urgent than VAT coordination, because most excisable products combine high values (on account of the high excises) with small volumes, which implies that illicit trade can be highly lucrative and easily conducted. This suggests that a distinction should be made between highly taxed traditional excisable goods, such as alcohol, tobacco, and petroleum products, and moderately taxed non-traditional goods, such as sugar, soft drinks, coffee, and tea. Accordingly, the following approach, followed in the EU, can be recommended:

- First and foremost, excise taxes should be the same regardless of whether the excisable product is domestically produced or imported. As the EU experience shows, excise taxes can interfere with the functioning of a common market if they are imposed on imported products that are not produced domestically (although the imports do compete with similar domestic products) or if they are imposed at high *ad valorem* rates that favour the use of cheap domestic materials over expensive imported materials. Examples of these practices can be found in Appendix B.
- Within RECs, agreement is desirable regarding common definitions for the various bases of assessment of the excise taxes on alcohol, tobacco, and petroleum products. Agreement is also desirable on subjecting these products to specific rates, which, as a minimum, reflect the external costs of their use or consumption. Border tax adjustments for the traditional excisable goods could remain in place; if they were abolished, some form of in-bond transportation system would have to be devised for the REC.
- REC member countries would remain free to impose excises on other goods and services, but they would not be allowed to impose border tax adjustments

for them. Accordingly, cross-border trade in them would be permitted. This would not have consequences for taxes on, for instance, entertainment-related activities since they are inherently destination-based. Further, excise taxes on tea, coffee, sugar, and soft drinks could be integrated in the VAT. For important items of luxury consumption, such as cars and pleasure boats, the excise taxes could be linked to the country of registration, permitting the imposition of differentially higher taxes. Excise taxes on other luxury goods should probably be abolished.

As in the case of VAT, the Southern African Development Community (2016b) has issued (non-binding) guidelines for excise tax cooperation between member countries. According to the guideline, excise taxes should also be considered when creating the 'fiscal space' for the substitution of import duties by other indirect taxes. The guidelines call for the harmonization of the excise taxes on tobacco, alcoholic beverages, and petroleum products. *Ad valorem* excises are recommended for luxury goods and services in lieu of a higher-than-standard VAT rate. Cooperation in combating cross-border smuggling is called for.

Actual Tax Harmonization: The UEMOA Example

Mansour and Rota-Graziosi (2013), on which this subsection draws, reviewed the current state of the UEMOA's tax coordination framework against the main objectives of the 1994 founding treaty, which were to reduce tax-induced distortions of intra-REC trade and to mobilize domestic tax revenue. Rate- and base-setting for the indirect taxes has been pursued in the form of regional directives issued by the UEMOA Commission, following approval by the Council of Ministers. Further, the treaty mandates the convergence of the tax revenue to GDP ratio to at least 17 per cent and the approximation of the tax revenue structures. Under the *transition fiscal*, the member countries must adopt tax and tariff policies that, over time, enable them to shift their revenue structure from trade to domestic taxes. This far-reaching form of tax harmonization led a 2002 IMF survey[15] to conclude that UEMOA should be considered 'the furthest along the path toward integration' among the African REC subgroups, including SACU and CEMAC.

As Mansour and Rota-Graziosi (2013) observe, however, this advanced *de jure* process of tax coordination is not confirmed by the ineffective *de facto* situation. Although a customs union with a common external tariff is in place, the share of intra-REC trade in total UEMOA trade has not increased (although total trade has increased, primarily due to the devaluation of the CFA franc). Non-tariff barriers—administrative delays, roadblocks, etc.—provide member countries

[15] Quoted in US Department of State (2002).

with opportunities to protect their own markets (Goretti and Weisfeld, 2008). Along with poor transportation, these non-tariff barriers continue to hinder intra-REC trade.

As is the case in the EU, the common UEMOA VAT directive lists the mandatory exemptions, which, in addition to the EU's exemptions, include raw foodstuffs, social tranches for household consumption of water and electricity, natural gas, printed matter, and real-estate sales if subject to registration duties. Interestingly, agricultural supplies can be treated as out-of-scope of VAT. The directive also prescribes rules for the calculation of taxable transactions, lower and upper bounds for the registration threshold (separately for goods and services), a standard rate of between 15 and 20 per cent, and a lower rate of between 5 and 10 per cent for specified foodstuffs, agricultural equipment, computers, solar energy equipment, and tourism-related services. A tax credit or refund of the VAT on inputs that enter into exports can only be claimed if and to the extent that the supplies are also taxable in the domestic market. Along with other features, Mansour and Rota-Graziosi (2013) opine that the VAT directive today has moved further away from a modern VAT. As in the EU (Cnossen, 2003), the UEMOA's common VAT directive has 'harmonized' the shortcomings of the existing VATs, making it much more difficult to reform them since each member country's approval is required.

The UEMOA's excise tax directive mandates *ad valorem* taxes on alcoholic beverages and tobacco products, which fail to account for external costs and effectively protect domestic production if import substitutes command higher prices. The tax-exclusive rates—50 per cent maximum for alcoholic beverages and 45 per cent for tobacco products, very low by international standards—do not accord with externality-correcting and revenue-raising efficiency considerations. The optional excises that are permitted on coffee, cola, and marble may serve as export taxes or, in the case of flour and edible oils, favour local products. Finally, the petroleum excise tax directive does little to harmonize rates; its main purpose was to eliminate subsidies.

In sum, the tax coordination framework may unintendedly contribute to the fragmentation of policymaking at the national level, particularly since member countries can (and do) enact special tax regimes outside their tax laws proper (as some SACU countries have done, too). The opportunity to do so is made possible in the absence of credible regional institutions that can call member countries to task and undertake effective surveillance. The REC's Court of Justice has never been called upon to rule on infringements of the treaty. Instead, directives have been changed to enable non-compliant countries to become compliant.

Mansour and Rota-Graziosi (2013) conclude their pertinent analysis with an important lesson. After observing that the future of the UEMOA's tax coordination framework is somewhat in doubt, they point out that deeper harmonization can only be achieved through stronger political commitment, and the delegation of authority and resources to regional institutions to effectively monitor compliance and impose sanctions, as happens in the EU. Although consistent with the 1994 treaty, this may be too hard to achieve. If so, the current lack of commitments should probably be taken as given and a more flexible approach adopted based on best practices, information sharing, and self-enforcing commitments. Less ambitious in legal terms, this approach may improve the effectiveness of tax coordination in line with the objectives of integration while safeguarding each country's tax autonomy.

8.4 Creating Common Markets with Tax Diversity

It may seem like forcing an open door, but *common* markets are successful only if they truly function as common *markets*, i.e. if resources are allocated on the basis of equal conditions for competitors. These conditions may be distorted by discriminatory VAT and excise tax systems between and within member countries. Import duties are protectionist by definition, but VATs and excise taxes may also discriminate against foreign products. Moreover, VATs and excise taxes may exhibit cumulative effects that distort consumer and producer choices at home and abroad. The major lesson of this chapter, therefore, is that tax reform and tax coordination should go hand-in-hand.

The Road Ahead

The road ahead for African RECs is long.

- Customs duties, as well as quantitative restrictions and measures having equivalent effect, must go. The obvious starting point is the abolition of intra-REC import and export duties and the establishment of a common external tariff. As in the EU, the concept 'customs duties' should be broadly interpreted. Also, an examination of the new tricks of the trade—i.e. different product, health, safety, and environmental standards (non-tariff barriers) that impede the entry of products—should be initiated. Strong and impartial institutions, such as a common court of justice, are needed to ensure that no unfair and non-neutral obstacles remain.
- External neutrality cannot be attained without internal neutrality. Most VATs exhibit cumulative, distortionary effects that spill over to other countries. Neutrality can be improved by broadening the tax base and by providing a full and immediate credit and refund for the tax on inputs to exports. Services should be taxed comprehensively and the number of exemptions and zero rates reduced. Common definitions and procedures should help the coordination process. Also, various turnover-tax-type stamp duties should be abolished.

- Under VAT, administrative efforts should be concentrated on the expeditious handling of requests for refunds. One way to reduce refunds under VAT is to expand the scope of the reverse-charge mechanism at import for capital goods (making the inland purchaser liable for the VAT at import but permitting him to take a credit for the same VAT at the same time). Further, comprehensive audits should be performed in conjunction with the business income tax to separate certified (trustworthy) filers from non-certified filers (first filers, businesses without a good tax record, etc.). Obviously, false refund claims cannot be filed without a VAT registration number, indicating the need to (re)canvass businesses, weeding out those that are not compliant and hence cannot claim refunds. This should be shored up by requiring VAT registrants (which are generally large) to appoint a representative from a reputable accounting firm to handle their VAT dealings with the tax authorities. Finally, filing periods of longer than a month should be replaced by one-month filing periods, as is done in most VAT countries. As a result, less tax would be at stake at any one time.
- Excise tax systems should also be reformed. Obvious forms of discrimination, such as higher rates on imported products, should be abolished forthwith. More broadly, the goal should be to eliminate various indeterminate (cumulative) effects that are inconsistent with the functioning of a common market. This means that the excise tax base should be confined to the traditional excise goods, motor vehicles, and environmental taxes. *Ad valorem* rates should be converted into specific, inflation-adjusted rates that account for the external costs of (abusive) consumption. Separate excises on items of luxury consumption are preferred to higher-than-standard rates of VAT, although the case for either approach is weak.

Overall, the objective in modernizing VAT and excise taxes should be to move away from selective, excise-type methods of taxation, which are inherently distortionary (unless confined to the internalization of external costs) and involve difficult definitional and valuation issues, to comprehensive VAT methods that include all goods and services in the base, take actual sales values as the basis for tax computation, and are fully controlled through books of account rather than being measured physically.

How Much Tax Coordination?

A common market is created by and for the member countries, not the member countries for the common market. In this light, the crucial question regarding tax coordination is not, it appears, how the various taxes can be equalized as soon as possible, but how much tax diversity can be permitted without interfering with the establishment of a common market. Tax diversity takes account of differences in preferences for one tax over another in the various member countries, which reflect differences in economic and social structures, different perceptions on the role of taxation, differences in the acceptability and feasibility of various taxes, and, perhaps more fundamentally, differences in preferences for public sector size among the member countries.

The EU has probably gone further with indirect tax coordination than would seem required for the formation of a single internal market or justifiable in light of the situation in countries with federal systems of taxation. Surely, closely aligned rate structures, as seems to be the thinking in the East African Community, are not necessary for the VAT. Generally, spillover effects do not occur for imported products that are sold through taxable trading channels, because the tax-credit mechanism of the VAT ensures that every product in each member state is always taxed at the rate that is levied at the retail stage in that state, regardless of the exporting member state's VAT rate. Even cross-border retail sales would be limited as long as border controls are maintained (and tax is levied by the customs authorities).

The problem with product tax coordination is how to keep the ultimate goal attuned to changing realities. As shown by the EU experience, initially firm commitments to do away with all forms of product tax discrimination are called for if the goal of a true common market is to be attained. Probably, such commitments, and the institutions executing them, have to be stronger than required for the coordination of product taxes levied by subordinate levels of government in a federal country, where political integration has preceded economic integration. Precisely because the political base for tax coordination is rather weak in a common market (basically, the process is reversible), its institutions have to be relentless in pursuing the abolition of all forms of tax discrimination if the market is to become established. African countries, however, have hardly started on the way to a common market. They should probably be advised, therefore, to pursue more product tax coordination than may be necessary in the end if that end is to be achieved.

9
Exemptions and Exclusions
The Achilles Heel of VAT

For political or administrative reasons, all VATs exempt or exclude specified goods, services, activities, entities, or sectors, but most African VATs go much further down this road than accords with VAT's functionality and logic. The difference between exemptions and exclusions is largely semantic. In both instances, activities, entities, and sectors that are exempted or excluded do not pay VAT on output but do incur VAT on taxable inputs. But, in contrast to exempt entities, excluded entities cannot opt to register for VAT, charge tax, and pass their input VAT on to customers. Exemptions and exclusions have in common that they erode the VAT base to the detriment of revenue, distort production and consumption choices, and considerably complicate the VAT's application. Exemptions and exclusions are truly the Achilles heel of the VAT.

As a general introduction to the issues and practices, this chapter lists the types of exemptions and exclusions found under the VATs in Africa, notes the economic distortions and administrative problems caused by them, and outlines the solutions that have been found by countries with a best-practice VAT. Subsequent chapters deal in greater detail with specific exemptions and exclusions.

9.1 Kinds of Exemptions and Exclusions

Exemptions and exclusions are of the standard and non-standard kind. Standard exemptions and exclusions are those found in OECD countries, more specifically those laid down in the EU's Common VAT Directive (2006). They have been widely adopted by African countries that have relied on expertise from EU member states in designing their VATs, and most have done so. As will be seen, the connotation 'standard' does not mean that the exemptions and exclusions accord with best practice.[1] The arguments in support of the exemptions and exclusions are not necessarily correct; taxation is often feasible. Non-standard exemptions and exclusions for, say, basic foodstuffs, agricultural and industrial inputs, and various services are not found in the EU's VAT legislation but are a typical African

[1] As noted above, the use of 'standard exemptions' in EU VAT jargon is somewhat of a misnomer, but the terminology is used here to facilitate discussion. See also the terminology and analysis in De la Feria and Krever (2013).

phenomenon. They are especially detrimental to revenue, as is evident from the tax expenditure budgets that various African countries are publishing annually.

Standard Exemptions and Exclusions

Following the EU's Common Directive, most African countries exclude or exempt governments, activities in the public interest, services that are difficult to tax conceptually, and, for administrative reasons, small businesses and the agricultural sector. The following breakdown can be made:

- 'Out-of-scope supplies' (also called excluded or non-taxable activities), which are assumed not to enter the VAT's ambit. Examples are governments and their agencies. The exclusions are rationalized on the (questionable) argument that there is no consideration involved in rendering the activities or that administrative considerations preclude the taxation of these activities.[2] Further, the taxation of governments has traditionally, albeit incorrectly, been considered redundant, because the recipient of the VAT would also be its payer.
- Activities in the public interest' as referred to in the EU's Common Directive, for services (often called 'merit goods') whose consumption should not be constrained by the imposition of VAT. Even if it would be feasible to individualize the service, measure the benefit, and charge the full cost, it is deemed socially not desirable to do so. Examples are healthcare, education, and social services.
- 'Conceptually difficult-to-tax activities', such as rental values (and rents), sales of residential property, financial services, insurance, and gambling. These exempt activities are also found in the EU's Common Directive and have been adopted by most African countries. Again, it will be seen that the arguments in support of the exemptions are not necessarily correct and that, to a large extent, taxation is feasible.
- 'Administratively difficult-to-tax sectors', such as small businesses and agriculture, the turnover of which does not exceed a specified amount or is difficult to ascertain. These sectors are freed from the obligation to register, file returns, and pay VAT. In both cases, there is usually an option to register and pay tax for entities that would be harmed by being left out of the VAT base.

[2] In addition to out-of-scope suppliers, there are some out-of-scope supplies that are not taxable. Examples are the absence of a direct and immediate link between the supply and the consideration received in respect of the supply, supplies of inaction, supplies at large, involuntary supplies, and the characterization of some dealings in financial securities as non-taxable investment activities. See De la Feria and Krever (2013). Out-of-scope supplies are not discussed further.

Non-Standard Exemptions and Exclusions

'Non-standard exemptions' (including zero rates), which are not found or are found to a lesser extent in countries with a best-practice VAT, are the following:

- basic foodstuffs and medical supplies, in order to mitigate the VAT burden on lower-income groups;
- for similar reasons, passenger transportation and public utilities, as well as petroleum products (which, it is argued, are already subject to excise duty), particularly kerosene;
- newspapers and printed materials, considered merit goods whose consumption should not be constrained by the VAT;
- agricultural inputs to eliminate VAT on inputs to foodstuffs that may be passed on into consumer prices or has to be borne by the producers of the foodstuffs;
- industrial machinery and equipment to mitigate refund problems (the VAT on machinery would be washed out anyway for registered businesses, so no net revenue is at stake);
- for similar reasons, extraterritorial exemptions for activities in industrial free zones, which are treated as foreign jurisdictions for VAT purposes, and exemptions of imports for foreign aid projects; and
- services not enumerated in the law as being taxable for reasons that are not entirely clear.

Best-practice treatment of all of these exemptions and exclusions is briefly discussed below; subsequent chapters provide more detail. But first attention is drawn to the economic distortions and administrative complexities of exemptions and exclusions.

9.2 Economic Distortions and Administrative Complications

Exemptions and exclusions distort consumer and producer choices, discriminate against exports, favour imports, greatly increase administrative complexity, and promote tax avoidance. The most important effects are the following.[3]

First, because the VAT on taxable purchases cannot be credited (washed out), exempt entities tend to substitute these purchases by lower-taxed or non-taxable goods and services, which they would not buy if the goods and services were taxable. In other words, the exemption distorts input choices. The input choice

[3] See Ebrill et al. (2001), from which this discussion has benefitted.

distortion is especially onerous in the case of investment goods. Whereas the VAT on purchases of intermediate goods and services that are essential inputs for the exempt entity's output is difficult to avoid, the VAT on investment goods purchases can be reduced by buying second-hand equipment and machinery or postponing their acquisition. In other words, the exemption is a disincentive to proper and timely investment.

To the extent that the VAT on purchases cannot be passed on, it reduces the rewards of the factors involved in producing the supply. If a business-to-consumer (B2C) supply is exempt (in other words, treated favourably relative to fully taxed goods and services), then consumers will buy more of the exempt supply than they would in the absence of the exemption, and the producer will produce more of the exempt supply. If the exemption is of the intermediate business-to-business (B2B) type, then the sale price will be higher (cascading) or the net reward of the production factors lower on account of the non-creditable VAT. In most cases, both effects are likely to occur and they would not necessarily be confined to the exempt supply but could work their way through the entire production–distribution chain. The effects tend to be capricious and indeterminate regarding final prices and rewards of production factors.

Second, and analogous to the distortion of input choices, exempt entities will try to avoid the tax on the labour element included in the price of taxable purchases by performing in-house various activities that would normally be outsourced.[4] Administrative activities, IT, cleaning, catering, and safety-provision services are examples of this form of uneconomical integration. The do-it-yourself effect will be greater for high-taxed supplies for which low-taxed inputs are used. Further, taxable firms should be less inclined to conduct research through, say, hospitals and universities, because these exempt entities cannot pass on the VAT on their taxable inputs.

Third, international trade will be distorted. As discussed in Chapter 8, the VAT follows the destination principle, i.e. prior-stage VAT is refunded at export and imports are included in the tax base. As a result, relative prices are unaffected; in other words, the VAT does not hinder the competitive position of domestic firms in international markets. Exemptions of financial and insurance services, for instance, violate the destination principle, because exporting firms using the services do not get a refund for the VAT on the inputs of financial industries, which increases their export prices or reduces the rewards of the factors producing the exports. Further, firms will tend to import exempt services if these are not subject to tax abroad or if the VAT is refunded at export by foreign VAT administrations.[5]

[4] The VAT provisions in most EU countries include a tax avoidance clause designed to ensure that such in-house services, if excessive, do not escape tax. However, no member state has made use of this clause.

[5] In the EU, the VAT of exempt financial services supplied to other member states is not refunded, but firms are eligible for refunds on exports to third countries. This forms an artificial incentive for exempt entities to sell their exports to other member states through third countries.

Fourth, exemptions will invite tax avoidance. Lobby groups will push for extending exemptions to suppliers and customers of exempt entities. Although the reach of these lobby groups is probably limited in the EU (but not in African countries) because the exemptions have been harmonized, nevertheless the lobbyists can still argue for favourable interpretations and applications that expand the effective scope of the exemptions. Exemptions also form an incentive to avoid the VAT—e.g. by converting the (exempt) lease of immovable property into an agreement for the (taxable) storage of goods, so that the VAT-liable purchaser can credit the input tax against the VAT on his own sales. Finally, the correct attribution of the VAT on inputs to taxable and exempt supplies, when required, forms a potential bone of contention between exempt entities that make taxable supplies too and VAT administrations. An example is the provision of taxable accounting and advisory services by exempt banks.

Last but certainly not least, leaving so-called 'non-commercial' activities of governments out of scope should distort competition because governments can offer their goods and services at a lower VAT-inclusive price than private suppliers of similar goods and services. The EU's Common VAT Directive (2006, annex I) mentions a number of goods and services that should always be taxed, but various services that can be equally well performed by the private sector remain out of scope. Municipal rubbish collection is often cited as an example.

It should be noted that the distortions and complexities of exemptions at intermediate stages of production and distribution are arguably worse than those with regard to exemptions of, say, unprocessed foodstuffs sold directly to consumers by exempt (small) farmers (which may have to be exempted on administrative and political grounds). This is because the exemptions at intermediate stages are likely to involve more non-creditable input VAT. The stage at which the exemptions are imposed also determines the effect on revenue. Exempting B2C supplies that are rendered directly to consumers (e.g. unprocessed foodstuffs) reduces revenue. However, exemptions of intermediate B2B supplies (e.g. financial services) might increase revenue due to the cascading (tax-on-tax) effect of the non-creditable VAT paid on purchases by the exempt entity, which is included in the price of the supplies that the entity provides and that are used towards making taxable supplies.

In sum, revenue erosion, cascading, self-supply bias, disincentive to invest, and administrative complexity are the issues that have to be confronted in dealing with exemptions and exclusions.

9.3 Dealing with Exemptions and Exclusions: An Overview

As a summary of the analyses in succeeding chapters, it seems useful to present a brief overview of the effects of the distortions and complexities of the various exemptions and exclusions and the ways in which countries have tackled the issues. For this purpose, Table 9.1 sums up the situation in African countries

Table 9.1 Most common practices of VAT exemptions and exclusions in Africa and the European Union, New Zealand, and South Africa

Description	African countries (other than SACU) and the European Union	New Zealand	South Africa
Legislation	VAT legislation and EU Council Directive 2006/112/EC of 28 November 2006	Goods and Services Tax Act 1985	Value-Added Tax Act 1991
Non-standard exemptions (Chapter 10)			
1. Unprocessed foodstuffs, medical supplies, print, kerosene	Exempt or zero-rated, but taxable in EU	Taxable	Taxable, but zero rate on 19 basic foodstuffs and kerosene
2. Agricultural inputs	Exempt, but taxable in EU	Taxable	Taxable
3. Industrial machinery and equipment	Exempt, but taxable in EU	Taxable	Taxable
4. Non-enumerated services	Exempt, but taxable in EU	Taxable	Taxable
5. Goods and services for industrial free zones	Exempt, but taxable in EU	No free zones	No free zones
Out-of-scope supplies (Chapter 11)			
1. Government authorities and other bodies governed by public law	Exempt, unless significant distortions of competition arise and except in respect of annex I activities[a]	Taxable	Exempt
Public-interest activities (Chapter 11)			
1. Hospital, medical, and dental care, including related professional services; transport of sick or injured persons	Exempt if governed by public law	Taxable	Exempt if governed by public law
2. Education and vocational (re)training, sport or physical education, private tuition	Exempt if governed by public law	Taxable, except primary education	Exempt if governed by public law
3. Welfare and social security work, old people's homes, protection of children and young persons	Exempt	Taxable	Exempt
4. Non-profit organizations	Exempt if no distortion of competition	Zero-rated	Exempt if no distortion of competition
5. Religious or philosophical institutions	Exempt	Exempt	Exempt

6. Cultural services by public bodies	Exempt if governed by public law	Taxable	Taxable
7. Public radio and television services	Exempt, except advertisements	Taxable	Taxable
8. Public postal services	Exempt	Taxable	Taxable
Conceptually difficult-to-tax activities (Chapters 12–15)			
1. Buildings, land	Exempt, unless newly created	Taxable, except used dwellings	Taxable, except land and used dwellings
2. Leasing or letting of immovable property	Exempt but optional taxation permitted[a]	Taxable, except used dwellings	Taxable, except used dwellings
3. Financial services, including credit transactions and banking services	Exempt (except debt collection) but optional taxation permitted	Exempt; zero rate on B2B transactions	Taxable, except if margin-based
4. Insurance and reinsurance	Exempt	Taxable, except life insurance	Taxable, unless long-term
5. Management of investment funds	Exempt	Taxable	Taxable
6. Brokerage services	Exempt	Taxable	Taxable
7. Betting, lotteries, gambling	Exempt	Taxable	Taxable
Administratively difficult-to-tax sectors (Chapter 16)			
1. Small businesses threshold	See Table 16.1; EU: €5,000	NZ$60,000	R1,000,000
US$ equivalent	See Table 16.1; EU: US$6,000	US$42,000	US$76,000
2. Agriculture, forestry, fishery	Exempt	Taxable	Taxable

[a] Annex I lists the following activities that are always taxable: water, gas, electricity, thermal energy; transport of goods and passengers, port and airport services, travel agents; telecommunication services; warehousing; organization of trade fairs and exhibitions; running of staff shops and canteens; commercial radio and television broadcasts.

[b] But always taxable: hotels, holiday camps, parking spaces, letting of permanently installed equipment and machinery, hire of safes.

Source: VAT legislation.

(other than the SACU countries), which tend to follow the EU's Common Directive, under New Zealand's GST, which is the most modern in the world, and under South Africa's VAT, which occupies an intermediate position and which appears to be the most suitable alternative for adoption by African countries. But in modernizing African VATs, it would seem useful to keep in mind the contours of the ultimate best-practice VAT, i.e. New Zealand's GST.

Non-Standard Exemptions

Apart from the economic distortions and administrative complexities that they cause, non-standard exemptions are especially detrimental to revenue. They greatly erode the base and harm the integrity of the VAT. The argument that exempting basic foodstuffs and medical supplies benefits the poor is true, but misleading to the extent that well-to-do households benefit at least twice as much in absolute terms from the exemption or zero-rating as poor households do. As pointed out in Chapter 7, the income tax and social benefit systems, if available, are far better instruments to alleviate the plight of the poor, and so are targeted government expenditures on basic education and healthcare. Particularly, zero-rating rather than exempting basic foodstuffs greatly complicates VAT's operation for taxpayers as well as tax administrations.

Much the same reasoning applies to the exemption or zero-rating of passenger transportation and other public utilities. The role of various taxes in the overall tax system is being confused if petroleum products are exempted because they are already subject to an excise. The excise should be imposed to internalize external costs, the VAT to leave relative prices unaffected. Further, printed materials tend to be income-elastic items of consumption, a reason to tax them. The exemption of agricultural and industrial inputs violates the integrity of the VAT as a tax on all inputs, which can subsequently be credited against the VAT on output.[6] This is particularly relevant if these producer goods are bought by or sold on to exempt businesses or entities, which otherwise would not pay any VAT (or other tax, for that matter). Similar considerations apply in the case of extraterritorial exemptions for activities in industrial free zones. Finally, enumerating services that are taxable is not as comprehensive a charge to tax as taxing all activities that are not goods, the most common formulation.

For all of these reasons, most countries with a best-practice VAT do not have non-standard exemptions but follow South Africa's and New Zealand's treatment, as shown in Table 9.1. Chapter 10 takes stock of the non-standard exemptions in African countries, provides reasons for abolishing them, and draws attention to the experience in Benin, Kenya, Senegal, and Tanzania, which have done so for most exemptions. Chapter 10 also dwells on the exemptions for agricultural and industrial machinery and equipment and the less-than-comprehensive coverage of services.

Out-of-Scope Supplies

Governments and their agencies are often considered out of the VAT's scope, but obviously to the extent that they purchase goods and services from taxable

[6] This describes the ideal situation. Chapters 10 and 16 will argue that the exemption or zero-rating of some of these items is not entirely without merit if refunds of VAT on inputs are not made or are slow in being made.

persons, they are subject to the same distortions as exempt entities—disincentives to outsource and invest, difficulties in allocating the VAT on inputs between taxable and exempt supplies, and competitive distortions vis-à-vis the private sector. The solutions that countries have introduced to deal with the self-supply bias and the disincentive to invest are to refund the tax on inputs of the out-of-scope entities, either partially (various EU member states) or sometimes fully (Canada), or to subject the entities to VAT (Australia and New Zealand).[7] Refunds or rebates solve the self-supply bias but not the competitive distortions, because governments can supply on a non-tax basis but private sector entities have to charge the full VAT to their customers. Chapter 11 goes into considerable detail on how governments and activities in the public interest are treated under the EU VAT and in most African countries and what best-practice VAT countries are doing.

Activities in the Public Interest

The exemptions for healthcare, education, and social services figure prominently in the exemption schedules of VAT legislations in African countries. The revenue forgone—but, emphatically, not the welfare costs of the distortions and complexities—is a less serious issue than in the case of non-standard exemptions. If healthcare, education, and social services were taxed, presumably the outlays on these activities would have to be increased to keep the level of physical output constant. In other words, budget subsidies would have to be increased, which indeed looks like a pay-out and claw-back arrangement, particularly if the taxable services are supplied against administered prices.

It is often argued that health and educational services and, more generally, social and cultural services generate (possibly) positive internal and external effects, which justify the exemption. Presumably, the same argument can be extended to exempt sociocultural institutions, cooperative arrangements, and sporting organizations. But even if the merit-good argument is acknowledged, full taxation (inclusive of subsidies, if any) in combination with increased subsidies could leave the total net amount of the (VAT-inclusive) charge for the service (previously exempted) unaffected without, however, distorting the exempt entity's input choices and outsourcing policies and without discriminating against similar taxable services provided by the private sector (which should then also be subsidized). Best-practice VATs therefore tax most of these services (albeit sometimes at a zero rate), which make an important contribution to GDP. Again, Chapter 11 dwells in detail on the issues.

[7] Non-profit organizations are the only entities under New Zealand's GST that are not taxed; in fact, they are zero-rated.

Conceptually Difficult to Tax: Immovable Property

Obviously, it would not be possible, administratively or politically, to tax the rental value and the sale of owner-occupied dwellings. For this reason, the EU VAT exempts immovable property but taxes new buildings as a proxy for the VAT on the services that the buildings will render over their lifetime. Registered owners or lessors of non-residential buildings can opt for full taxation on a current basis. By contrast, New Zealand and South Africa tax the sale and leasing of non-residential buildings, which provides for a fuller inclusion of immovable property in the VAT base, because future increases in values will also be taxed. This and the EU approach are analysed more fully in Chapter 12.

Conceptually Difficult to Tax: Financial Services, Insurance, and Gambling

Perhaps even more important is the rather generous exemption of financial services, for which the value of intermediation services, embedded in interest rates, returns, or rewards, cannot be attributed to customers on a transaction-by-transaction basis, which is necessary if the VAT is to be passed on to VAT-liable businesses. For this reason, financial services are exempted from VAT in nearly all countries (or, exceptionally, their value added is taxed as the sum of wages and business cash flow).

But the exemption is much less generous in countries with a best-practice VAT than in the EU and most African countries. Thus, the exempt services of brokers and agents, the administration of investment funds, and explicit fee-based charges for banking services are all taxed in India, New Zealand, Singapore, and South Africa. Another approach, found in Australia but also New Zealand and Singapore, is to apply a zero rate to B2B margin-based banking services (to avoid cascading) and to exempt B2C margin-based banking services (to charge some VAT, if not the full amount). Currently, a combination of both approaches is considered best practice, although the literature has developed more neutral but at the same time more complicated solutions. Chapter 13 discusses the issues in more detail.

Best-practice VATs have pioneered solutions for the taxation of insurance and gambling, as discussed in Chapters 14 and 15 respectively.

Administratively Difficult to Tax

In most African countries, the agricultural and small business sectors would be difficult to tax for administrative and political reasons. Hence, they are exempted, as is the case in most EU member states. Best-practice countries do tax the agricultural sector, however, subject to a threshold for exemption and optional registration. Chapter 16 discusses the issues and practices.

Industrial Free Zones

This overview of non-standard exemptions would not be complete without a reference to VAT concessions granted through investment codes in connection with industrial free zones, tax holidays, or individualized tax rulings. These exemptions can be called extraterritorial because the businesses that are entitled to them are treated as if they are outside the country's jurisdiction. To all intents and purposes, shipments of goods to these businesses are considered exports and are, hence, zero-rated. Although much less publicized, the concessions can be quantitatively important. The numerous difficulties that can be associated with these concessionary regimes include difficulties in monitoring the objectives, lack of periodic evaluation, fraudulent use, and, above all, loss of revenue.

Foreign Aid Projects

Finally, it is worth drawing attention to the treatment of consumer goods, including durables, that are used or consumed in connection with foreign aid projects funded by donor countries. Current practice is to exempt goods and services financed by aid but consumed domestically. This is an area where VAT exemption makes little sense since the contracting parties and the taxable goods can clearly be identified and VAT collected at customs. The exemption creates at least three problems. First, it distorts consumption choice and creates administrative difficulties. Second, the approach forgoes revenues that are badly needed, while the ability to pay of project participants (e.g. foreign personnel in the field) is not in doubt. Finally, the practice hinders the functioning of the VAT, if, say, a car owned by an aid worker is sold on to a local consumer (Chambas, 2005). On the other hand, it has been argued that foreign aid budgets do not typically include funds to pay for foreign taxes, including host-country VAT. One solution to this problem for host countries that operate a VAT is to draft a provision that allows VAT paid on projects to be credited (and refunded if called for) as input VAT in the donor country.

10
Non-Standard Exemptions and Zero Rates

As indicated in the previous chapter, non-standard exemptions and zero rates are most costly in terms of revenue forgone. The logic and functionality of the numerous gaps in the VAT base should be reviewed and evaluated, if the VATs in Africa are to live up to their role as the major revenue-raising instrument in the fiscal policy kit. For this purpose, Tables 10.1 and 10.2 provide a bird's-eye view of the major exemptions and zero and lower rates summarized in Appendix A. Specifically, Table 10.1 lists the non-standard exemptions of unprocessed foodstuffs, agricultural inputs, medical supplies, utilities, print, fuel, and some other goods and services on a country-by-country basis. For each item, some indication is provided about the reach of each exemption. Table 10.2 does the same for the zero or positive but reduced rates on the same items.

Although there is some overlap, this chapter discusses the exemptions and zero/lower rates under three headings: consumer items (where most revenue is lost), producer goods (the tax on which should be creditable or refundable), and services (which should be taxed comprehensively). The chapter concludes with an overview of the VAT reforms in four countries—Benin, Kenya, Senegal, and Tanzania—that have eliminated most, if not all, non-standard exemptions and zero rates, a move that other African countries may wish to consider too.

10.1 Consumer Items

Tables 10.1 and 10.2 indicate that unprocessed foodstuffs are widely exempted, zero-rated, or taxed at a lower rate. Although unprocessed foodstuffs generally means products in their raw or natural state, drying, threshing, cooling, freezing, or slaughtering is generally assumed not to alter that condition. In addition, unprocessed foodstuffs are defined to include bread and milk.

Broadly, francophone countries tend to exempt basic foodstuffs, while anglophone countries have a preference for zero-rating them. Interestingly, latecomers to the VAT—e.g. Gambia, Ghana, the Seychelles, and Sierra Leone—exempt rather than zero-rate basic foodstuffs. Various CEMAC, UEMOA, and AMU countries, following in France's footsteps, levy a lower rate on unprocessed foodstuffs. Chapter 7 has pointed out that zero-rating is not a well-targeted tool to mitigate

Table 10.1 Africa: non-standard VAT exemptions, 2018: main items[a]

RECs and countries	Unprocessed foodstuffs	Agricultural inputs	Medical supplies	Utilities	Print	Fuel	Examples of other items
Southern African Development Community (SADC)							
SACU							
Botswana			√	√			
Lesotho				√			Low-income housing
Namibia				√			
South Africa				√			
Swaziland				√*			Gambling
Other							
Congo, DR	√	√*	√*	√	√		Admissions, supplies for extractive industries, artist work
Madagascar	√	√*	√*	√	√*	√	Fabrics, solar panels
Malawi	√	√	√*	√	√	√*	Coffee, tea, raw materials, gambling
Mauritius	√*	√	√*	√	√		Admissions, gambling, artist work
Mozambique	√	√*	√	√	√		Gambling, waste removal, artist work
Seychelles	√		√	√*	√		
Zambia	√*	√	√	√	√	√	Transport, gambling
Zimbabwe	√			√		√*	Tourism
East African Community (EAC)							
Burundi	√*		√*	√*			
Kenya	√*	√*	√	√			Specified plant and machinery
Rwanda	√*	√*	√*	√	√	√	Tourism, machinery, raw materials
Tanzania	√*	√*	√	√	√	√*	Gambling, tourism, solar equipment
Uganda	√*		√*	√		√*	Gambling

Continued

Table 10.1 *Continued*

RECs and countries	Unprocessed foodstuffs	Agricultural inputs	Medical supplies	Utilities	Print	Fuel	Examples of other items
Economic and Monetary Community of Central Africa (CEMAC)							
Cameroon	√	√*	√	√*	√		Woodworking, energy-saving equipment
Central Afr. Rep.	√		√*	√*	√		
Chad	√	√	√	√*	√		Building materials, admissions, cotton machinery
Congo	√	√*	√	√*	√	√*	Oil production, culture, artist work
Equat. Guinea	√	√*	√		√		Cultural services, imported capital equipment, mining
Gabon	√	√*	√	√	√		Low-rent housing, inputs for extractive industries
Economic Community of West African States (ECOWAS)							
UEMOA							
Benin	√*	√*	√	√*	√		Computers, artist work
Burkina Faso	√*		√	√	√		Social housing, solar energy equipment, IT materials
Côte d'Ivoire	√*	√		√	√	√*	Low-cost housing, tourism
Guinea–Bissau	√*						Independent professional services
Mali	√*	√*	√				Artist work
Niger	√*	√*	√	√*	√		Cultural services
Senegal	√		√	√*	√*		Artist work
Togo	√*			√		√*	Entertainment

WAMZ							
Cabo Verde	√-	√	√	√			Culture, artist work, garbage removal
Gambia	√*	√*	√	√			
Ghana	√*	√*	√	√*	√	√*	Industrial and mining machinery
Guinea	√		√	√	√		Second-hand goods
Sierra Leone	√	√*	√	√	√	√*	Industrial and mining machinery
Arab Maghreb Union (AMU)							
Algeria	√-		√		√		Machinery and equipment for new firms
Mauritania	√				√		
Morocco	√-				√		Social housing, driving schools
Tunisia	√ (retail)				√		Tourism, industrial inputs, solar water heaters
Intergovernmental Authority on Development (IGAD) and Egypt							
Djibouti					√		Cultural services
Egypt	√-		√	√		√	Advertising
Ethiopia	√-	√	√*	√*	√*	√	Workshops for the disabled, government imports
Sudan	√*	√	√				

[a] The symbols (√) have the following meaning:
- unprocessed foodstuffs: √- = limited number of enumerated items; √ = large number of items; √* = all unprocessed foodstuffs.
- agricultural inputs: √ = feed, seed, fertilizer; √* = in addition, machinery and implements.
- medical supplies: √ = medicines, pharmaceutical products; √* = in addition, medical equipment.
- utilities (water, electricity, natural gas, postal services, telecommunications, public transportation): √ = one or two items; √* = more than two items.
- print: √ = newspapers, books, periodicals; √* = most published materials, printing machinery.
- fuel: √ = kerosene; √* = all petroleum products.

Note: Standard exemptions are not shown, because they are found in all countries without a modern VAT. Standard exemptions include healthcare, education, social and cultural services, immovable property (except if newly created), financial services and insurance, postal and broadcasting services, gambling, and 'out-of-scope' governments. See Organization for Economic Cooperation and Development (2012).

Source: Appendix A. Blanks indicate that a provision for an exemption could not be found in the source material, not necessarily that an exemption does not exist.

Table 10.2 Africa: non-standard zero or lower rates, 2018: main items[a]

RECs and countries	Unprocessed foodstuffs	Agricultural inputs	Medical supplies	Utilities	Print	Fuel	Examples of other items
Southern African Development Community (SADC)							
SACU							
Botswana	√⁻	√*		√		√*	
Lesotho	√⁻	√		√ (5)		√	Commercial transportation
Namibia	√⁻		√	√*		√*	Land and buildings
South Africa	√⁻	√				√*	Housing subsidies, municipal property rates
Swaziland	√⁻	√	√		√	√*	
Other							
Congo, DR							
Madagascar							
Malawi		√*	√	√			Building materials, machinery, trucks, tourist goods
Mauritius	√	√	√	√	√	√	Irrigation
Mozambique	√			√			Bicycles; public works (7.2)
Seychelles							Travel agents, tour operators
Zambia	√	√*	√		√		Tourism, energy-saving appliances
Zimbabwe	√	√*	√	√			Building bricks, electronic cash registers
East African Community (EAC)							
Burundi	√ (10)						
Kenya			√	√			
Rwanda							Minerals sold in domestic market

Tanzania							
Uganda	$\surd^{-}$	√	√		√		
Economic and Monetary Community of Central Africa (CEMAC)							
Cameroon							
Central Afr. Rep.	$\surd^{-}$ (5)						
Chad							
Congo	$\surd^{-}$ (5)					$\surd^{*}$ (5)	Local wood; cement (5)
Equat. Guinea	$\surd^{-}$ (6)						
Gabon	$\surd^{-}$ (10)			√			Cement (5), computers (10)
Economic Community of West African States (ECOWAS)							
UEMOA							
Benin							
Burkina Faso							
Côte d'Ivoire	$\surd^{-}$ (9)					$\surd^{*}$ (9)	Solar energy equipment (9)
Guinea–Bissau	$\surd^{*}$ (10)		√		√ (10)		Consulting (10)
Mali							Computers, solar energy equipment (5)
Niger							
Senegal							Tourism (10)
Togo							
WAMZ							
Cabo Verde							
Gambia							

Continued

Table 10.2 *Continued*

RECs and countries	Unprocessed foodstuffs	Agricultural inputs	Medical supplies	Utilities	Print	Fuel	Examples of other items
Ghana							Real-estate agent sales (5)
Guinea							
Sierra Leone							
Arab Maghreb Union (AMU)							
Algeria	√⁻ (9)	√ (9)	√ (9)	√ (9)		√* (9)	Computers, construction, handicraft (9)
Mauritania							
Morocco	√ (7/10/14)	√*	√ (7)	√ (14)	√ (7)		Social housing; hotels/restaurants, professions (10)
Tunisia		√ (7)	√ (7)	√ (7)	√ (13)		Hotels/restaurants and tourism professions (13)
Intergovernmental Authority on Development (IGAD) and Egypt							
Djibouti							Imported construction goods
Egypt	√⁻ (5)	√ (5)				√* (5)	Air-conditioned transport, construction, professions (5)
Ethiopia							
Sudan							

[a] Numbers in parentheses indicate the reduced rate. The symbols (√) should be interpreted as follows:
- unprocessed foodstuffs: √⁻ = limited number of enumerated items; √ = large number of items; √* = all unprocessed foodstuffs.
- agricultural inputs: √ = feed, seed, fertilizer; √* = in addition, machinery and implements.
- medical supplies: √ = medicines, pharmaceutical products.
- utilities (water, electricity, natural gas, postal services, telecommunications, public transportation): √ = one or two items; √* = more than two items.
- print: √ = newspapers, books, periodicals.
- fuel: √ = kerosene; √* = all petroleum products.

Source: Appendix A.

the regressivity of the VAT. For revenue purposes, it makes a difference, of course, whether the reach of the concession is limited, broad, or encompasses all unprocessed foodstuffs. Country practices differ rather widely.

Like unprocessed foodstuffs, medical supplies (medicines, pharmaceutical products) are also widely exempted, zero-rated, or taxed at a lower rate (e.g. in the AMU countries and Egypt). Exemption appears to dominate zero-rating, which is largely confined to the SADC countries. Quite often, the concessionary treatment extends to medical equipment or all medical supplies. Based on the South African experience, Chapter 7 surmises that the concession does not necessarily benefit lower-income groups, particularly if they are not charged for the cost of medical treatment or do not have access to medical facilities.

The treatment of public utilities (water, electricity, natural gas, postal services, telecommunications, public transportation) is of particular interest if the various VATs are to become the revenue-raising instruments they are intended to be. Clearly, public utilities are not universally taxed. SADC countries often zero-rate some utilities, while AMU countries tend to tax them at a lower rate. Water and electricity are often exempted, but some countries apply a zero or reduced rate. Various countries provide a basic, volume type of exemption (social tranche) for water and electricity, a concession that must be difficult to monitor properly. Postal services and public passenger transportation tend to be exempted across the continent, although the benefit for the poor is questionable, as Chapter 7 indicates. Chapter 11 discusses the taxation of public utilities in greater detail along with the treatment of various cultural services.

Newspapers and periodicals are widely exempted and sometimes even zero-rated (after all, they must spread the good news about the VAT). Under some VATs, the concession extends to school books, most printed materials, or even printing machinery. The favourable treatment of school books does not make much sense if education is subsidized. In Tanzania, the exemption for print includes children's colouring and drawing books and examination question papers and answer booklets. Abuse of the concession by misclassifying higher-taxed items as exempt items is just around the corner.

Perhaps the exemption or zero rate for fuel is the most difficult to rationalize. Understandably, kerosene receives favourable treatment in many countries, although this practice is at odds with the objective that fossil fuels should be taxed differentially higher on account of their contribution to global warming. The exemption or zero-rating of petrol and diesel fuel is more difficult to understand because it favours well-to-do car owners (the VAT on industrial use of fuel is washed out anyway). The argument that exemption or zero-rating is indicated because the products are already subject to excise does not hold. Excises are meant to internalize external costs and therefore should be included in the VAT base along with production and distribution costs, while VATs are intended to leave relative prices unaffected and therefore should apply as widely as possible.

Applying the excise as well as the VAT is not a form of double taxation. Finally, nothing can be said in favour of zero-rating or exempting building materials, admissions to organized cultural events, and gambling, and little for the concessionary treatment of tourism.[1]

The conclusion of this brief overview is that the non-standard exemptions and zero rates on domestically consumed goods and services turn many VATs into what may be called extended excise tax systems. After all, in practice, it may not make much difference whether goods are specifically enumerated as being taxable (the excise tax approach) or whether a large number of specifically enumerated goods are exempted or zero-rated (the African VAT approach). Economically, the non-standard exemptions give rise to indeterminate variations in effective VAT rates depending on the ratio of VAT on taxable inputs to tax-exclusive consumer prices, while the zero rates greatly complicate the VAT administration. Last but not least, the exemption or zero-rating of many products disproportionately consumed by the poor effectively turns the standard rate into a tax on luxury goods and services.

VAT base-broadening, necessary to augment revenue and pave the way for the replacement of trade taxes, may have to proceed in steps. The most immediate goal should probably be to tax items that can hardly be called 'essential', such as fuel, utilities, construction, tourism, pharmaceuticals, and entertainment, but it would also be desirable to exempt or zero-rate far fewer foodstuffs than is currently done in many countries. For this to succeed, it should be made clear that the favourable treatment of foodstuffs does little if anything to mitigate the VAT burden of low-income households and that governments have better instruments at their disposal to alleviate their plight.

10.2 Producer Goods

Important exempted or zero-rated items are agricultural inputs and, not shown in Tables 10.1 and 10.2, industrial machinery and equipment. Nearly all VATs in Africa provide concessionary treatment for these items in one form or another, sometimes subject to limitations, sometimes not. Malawi's VAT is a particularly striking example of the zero-rating of nearly all agricultural and industrial investment goods. Table 10.3 shows the details. In addition, insecticides and pesticides, as well as tractors and heavy-goods-carrying vehicles, are exempted along with petroleum products.

Admittedly, zero-rating or exempting feed, seed, fertilizers, insecticides, pesticides, and agricultural equipment ensures that little non-creditable input VAT

[1] But for arguments to treat tourism leniently, see Ebrill et al. (2001, p. 73). Tax competition is often cited as a reason for this treatment. The reduced rate on tourism in Senegal, for instance, was justified as a means of attracting tourists who might spend their holiday on the Canary Islands or Cape Verde if the standard VAT rate were applied.

Table 10.3 Malawi: zero-rated investment goods

- Agricultural, horticultural, and forestry machinery for soil preparation or cultivation; lawn or sportsground rollers
- Other agricultural, horticultural, forestry, poultry-keeping, or bee-keeping machinery, including germination plant fitted with mechanical or thermal equipment
- Other machinery, including that for cleaning, sorting, or grading seed, grain, or dried leguminous vegetables; machinery making pulp or paper; printing machinery (excluding certain automatic data processing machines) and machinery for type founding or typesetting; sewing, stitching, and weaving machines (looms)
- Machinery (excluding household or laundry-type washing machines) for washing, cleaning, wringing, drying, ironing, pressing, bleaching, dyeing, dressing, finishing, coating, or impregnating textile yarns, fabrics, etc.
- Converters, ladles, ingot moulds, and casting machines, of a kind used in metallurgy or in metal foundries
- Machines for boring, drilling, milling, threading, or tapping by removing metal, other than lathes
- Machine tools for working stone, ceramics, concrete, asbestos-cement, or like mineral materials or for cold-working glass
- Machinery for working rubber or plastics or for the manufacture of products from these materials
- Machinery used in manufacturing and construction
- Motor vehicles for the transport of goods of a gross weight of 3 tons and over
- Most categories of trailers or semi-trailers, and other vehicles not mechanically propelled with a gross weight exceeding 10 tons
- Imported specialist equipment for use in the fishing industry
- Imported capital equipment, other than road vehicles, for the electricity, telecommunications, water utility, mining, and dairy industries
- Building materials for construction of factories and adjoining warehouses
- Fishing equipment

Source: Malawi Value Added Tax Act provisions, downloaded from IBFD online services.

enters into the price of agricultural products when marketed by exempt farmers and subsequently sold through exempt or taxable distribution channels. If taxed, it would be possible to wash out the input VAT by allowing taxable purchasers of farm produce a presumptive VAT credit approximately equal to the input VAT borne by exempt farmers (Cnossen, 2018a). This rough-and-ready approach is used in many EU member states that exempt the agricultural sector. Alternatively, major inputs can be zero-rated, which is a better-targeted and easier-to-administer form of relief, except for dual-use goods, such as various agricultural implements and tractors, which can also be used for taxable purposes. A major drawback is that exempt farmers then end up hardly paying any tax at all. For this reason, Keen (2008) argues that agricultural inputs should be taxed as a way to secure some revenue from the sector, which tends not to be subject to any other tax at all. The issues are discussed more fully in Chapter 16.

The zero-rating or exemption of industrial machinery and equipment infringes on the integrity of the VAT. Suppliers can no longer be told to always charge VAT since a registered purchaser can take credit for the tax anyway. Zero-rated or exempted (imported) machinery sold to an exempt user implies that the user pays no VAT. While this may be defensible for agricultural products, it is difficult to justify for industrial products if the VAT charge-and-credit philosophy is not to break down completely. Zero-rating or exempting inputs from VAT implies that taxable value added is pushed down the production–distribution chain. In other words, fewer upstream registered traders and producers are involved in collecting the VAT from the final consumer—the VAT's main advantage over an RST. VAT administrations, moreover, should not be in the business of defining capital goods but of monitoring compliance by checking returns and payments and by auditing taxpayer accounts.

Exemption or zero-rating has the advantage, of course, that refund problems do not arise in the case of businesses that would otherwise be in excess credit situations, because they start up operations, are seasonal, or export their output. Taxation without a full credit or delays in refunding input VAT is tantamount to a tax on investment. This is an important argument in favour of not taxing investment goods, since the refund issue, particularly at export, appears to bedevil nearly all African VATs. If most machinery is imported, as appears to be the case in Malawi, an alternative to zero-rating or exemption would be to apply a reverse charge at import, which would not involve cash-flow problems either. The difference with zero-rating or exemption is that reverse-charging tends to be linked to registered purchasers whereas zero-rating or exemption is product-specific. This implies that reverse-charged inputs will be taxed if sold beyond the reverse-charge point whereas zero-rated or exempt inputs will retain their tax-free status. This should not make much difference if the inputs are sold to registered businesses since no net VAT would be collected anyway. However, VAT would be collected if the inputs are sold to exempt entities.

10.3 Services

In charging VAT, many African countries specifically enumerate services that are included in the base, particularly countries that previously taxed specified services in conjunction with a manufacturers' or production tax. By way of example, the VAT of Guinea–Bissau specifically lists as taxable: hotels and restaurants, telecommunications, transportation and storage of goods, and the leasing and letting of movable property. The implication is that services not listed as taxable do not attract VAT. Even if, in other countries, a catch-all clause is included in the legislation, the definition of services is still relevant if the threshold for registration is lower for services than for goods. Further, the distinction may be important for rules of supply that differ between goods and services. By contrast, best-practice VATs minimize differences in the treatment of goods and services by defining services as all performances that do not involve goods and by providing a single uniform threshold.

Why Services Should Be Taxed Comprehensively

The case for the comprehensive inclusion of services in the VAT base can be made on equity, economic efficiency, and feasibility grounds (Kay and Davis, 1990). As regards equity, empirical evidence indicates that the overall income elasticity for services is higher than that for goods. In other words, expenditures on services rise faster than income rises. This means that a uniform-rate VAT applied to services as well as to goods would mitigate its overall regressive impact.

The efficiency case for taxing services rests on three arguments. First, given the amount of revenue that has to be raised, omitting various services from the VAT base means that the rate has to be higher on goods. This increases the excess burden of the VAT by the square of the rate increase. Second, as economic development proceeds, productivity gains are likely to be larger in the industrial sector than in the services sector. It would certainly not be good policy, therefore, to tax the economic gains in the industrial sector higher than is necessary. Third, most services—transportation, storage, professional services, communication—are used for personal as well as business purposes. Businesses providing these services will purchase taxable inputs. Taxing intermediate services means that the tax on inputs can be passed on to the ultimate consumer and does not become a distortionary element in the tax system.

VAT has greatly increased the feasibility of taxing services (and goods) that have extensive mixed use. The reason is that a full VAT is in little need of conditional exemptions by reference to the use that is made of the services or the status of the purchaser, whether a producer or a consumer. As a producer, the purchaser can take a credit for the tax, but the seller does not have to know. In other words, the VAT does not have to make a distinction between producer and consumer services. Further, taxing services increases the potential for cross-checking compliance. It has been said that this feature has less relevance for services because most value is added at the place of production. However, the value added by purchased inputs as a percentage of total output, although diverging widely across service sectors, still averages between 30 and 40 per cent in many countries. Therefore, the potential for cross-checking is by no means negligible. The low capital–labour ratio, however, does imply a large number of small establishments in the services sector, limiting the feasibility of taxing all of them.

Two approaches can be adopted in extending the taxation of services. Under the selective approach, as currently used in various African countries, taxable services are individually enumerated in the law, the implication being that services not named are not taxable. On the other hand, under the comprehensive approach, all services, in principle, would be taxable except those specifically designated as being exempted, such as the standard exemptions.[2] In order to qualify for the exempt status, however, the institutions providing the exempt services must be operated on a non-profit basis by an essentially volunteer management and the services must be rendered against administered prices and not distort competition vis-à-vis the commercial sector. The 'standard exemptions' extend to fundraising activities carried on by the institutions providing the services.

Review of Individual Services

In view of the taxation of services by enumeration in various African countries, this subsection discusses individual services and the next subsection indicates that a comprehensive charge to tax is to be preferred.

Laundry, dry-cleaning, and dyeing services, as well as various personal care services provided by hairdressers, beauty shops, etc.

A strong case can be made for taxing these services, and most countries—even if they tax services selectively—do so. Generally, the income elasticity of these services is high and record-keeping by the taxable businesses should be good. Small, single-person establishments would fall under the small-business exemption. In Africa, some personal care services are provided to tourists. Therefore, unless the supply would be curtailed because of the tax—not very likely—part of the tax would not be borne by residents. Administratively, the exclusion of laundry and dry-cleaning services would involve delineation problems when performed by hotels. If the hotels are taxed but ancillary services are not, total turnover (and input tax credits) must be split between taxable and exempt turnover, which complicates compliance and audit.

Hotels, restaurants, and similar establishments providing food, drink, and shelter

Two issues arise in considering the taxation of hotel and restaurant services under the VAT. The first issue relates to accommodation, which must be considered in conjunction with the (exempt) treatment of rental and owner-occupied housing. The second issue concerns the treatment of food and drink supplied by hotels and restaurants. Here, the comparison is with possibly preferentially taxed food and drink bought in shops and consumed at home.

[2] In the EU, the tendency is to restrict the standard exemptions, particularly of cultural services, postal services, and public radio and television broadcasts. More and more, the view is being adopted that these services constitute activities that compete with other forms of taxable entertainment, telecommunications, private letter or parcel carriers, and newspapers and periodicals. Exemption raises the cost of the services for business (the tax on inputs to the exempt service cannot be passed on) and lowers the cost to consumers. This is hard to square with the philosophy of the VAT.

Hotel accommodation is usually taxed, even in countries with a partial VAT and where no distinction is made between accommodation provided to tourists or to residents. (The exemption of hotel accommodation for residents is difficult to rationalize or to monitor properly.) Definitional issues arise in distinguishing hotels from boarding houses, homes for the aged, etc. Some countries provide an end-use exemption for the latter forms of accommodation, but the best rule is probably a straightforward time-period exemption stating that accommodation provided for a stretch of time in excess of, say, one month or six weeks is exempt.

Food and drink are invariably taxed when supplied by hotels and restaurants, the small-business exemption being used to leave small establishments outside the VAT's coverage. If taxed at the same rate as hotel accommodation, the bill does not have to be separated into higher- and lower-taxed portions, preventing tax avoidance. Sometimes, five-star hotels and restaurants are taxed at a higher-than-standard rate, but such classifications unnecessarily complicate tax administration.

Amusement and entertainment services, such as theatre performances, amusement parks, circuses, bowling alleys, night clubs, and discotheques

Whereas hotels and restaurants take care of the body, amusement and entertainment services tend to the mind. A good VAT does not make a distinction between the two kinds of services, but taxes both. Since most of these services are rendered in combination with food and drink, taxation at the same rate eases compliance and administration. If it is considered desirable to tax some forms of entertainment differentially higher, additional but separate excises should be imposed on them.

Supply of electricity and gas

Sometimes the argument is made that the supply of electricity and gas should not be taxed, because the services are rendered at administered prices by publicly owned utilities whose surplus income, if any, usually has to be transferred to the government budget anyway. But this argument is wrong. Although the effects of the VAT can be exactly replicated by manipulating the price of electricity or gas, a differentiated price structure would have to be devised. Thus, ideally, the tax on inputs should be passed on to consumers, but not to producers, who would be able to credit the tax if electricity or gas were taxable. Moreover, the tax on inputs would vary between gas-, oil-, and coal-fired utilities. Inclusion in the VAT base would provide for a more even-handed treatment and enable business customers to take a credit for tax.

Furthermore, there is a presumption that public utilities would be more forthcoming in remitting the VAT that they have charged their clients (and which they cannot rationalize as funds generated by themselves) to the treasury than in transferring their surplus income, which would usually be ascertained long after the close of the fiscal year. Last, but not least, the income elasticity of electricity and gas is high. In other words, taxation would make the tax burden distribution of a uniform-rate VAT less regressive.

Telecommunication services, such as telephone calls, cable, telex, and facsimile services

The arguments that have been made with respect to the taxation of the supply of electricity and gas apply in equal measure to telecommunication services. In fact, the progressivity argument is even stronger. Moreover, often various telecommunication services are provided by private companies.

Public transportation of passengers

The public utility arguments do not have the same force when it comes to the taxation of public transportation of passengers by governments. There need not be concern about the passing on of input tax, nor would a tax on passenger transportation contribute to progressivity in the tax burden distribution (in fact, the opposite may be true). To be sure, public transportation is an alternative to private transportation (owner-driven cars, privately operated vans, taxis), but usually prices do not reflect cost and hence public transportation is not meant to be a competitive alternative. Since public transportation is usually provided by local authorities, its taxation might be a sensitive issue. On balance, exemption is recommended. The exemption should extend to taxis, whose receipts cannot be audited properly (instead, their licence fee should be raised).

Transportation of goods and storage

The transportation of goods is quite a different matter, as indicated by the difficulties its exemption raises under, say, production taxes (see Chapter 5). Freight should always be taxed, whether provided by private businesses (trucks, boats) or by public authorities (trains). Of course, the storage of goods should also be taxed. Even in countries that tax services selectively, these items are almost invariably included in the base.

The problem with freight is not so much conceptual as practical. African countries tend to have large numbers of owner-operated truckers. Presumably, small-business transport would also be a readily available substitute. In either case, receipts would be difficult to monitor effectively. An alternative would be to impose a flat-rate tax on owner-operated truckers based on the tonnage of the vehicle(s) and the area they operate in. The same might apply to freight transport by boat.

Leasing and letting of movable property, such as cars, boats, computers, and other equipment

The dictum that goods can be supplied in the form of services is readily apparent when leasing and letting are considered. If these activities are not included in the base, producers might set up leasing companies and rent their products out to customers. If services were not taxed, no tax would be due because ownership of the goods would not have been transferred. This might not matter much in the case of leased capital equipment used in the production process of other registered firms, because there would be no corresponding tax credit. But it would matter when (durable) consumer goods are made available for hire (or when dual-purpose equipment is let that can be used for consumer as well as producer purposes). Clearly, leasing and letting of movable property should be taxed. In all instances, taxation of the entire charge (amortization, interest, administrative fee) is a must.

Leasing and letting of immovable property, such as buildings and apartments

Ideally, the rental of buildings, houses, apartments, and other kinds of immovable property should also be liable to VAT. This would be discriminatory, however, if owner-occupiers were not taxed on the rent that can be imputed to their property. The administrative implications of taxing rents and imputed rental values are mind-boggling. Hence, alternative treatment is recommended in Chapter 12.

Repair and maintenance services provided by repair shops and garages for movable goods (business equipment and household appliances, cars, boats, etc.)

The borderline between real production, which consists of bringing into existence a different article from that out of which it is made, and all kinds of ancillary or related activities is tenuous. The same applies to the distinction between the sale of a good and its maintenance. If only the sale is taxed, the market would react by selling cheaper goods, which would be more often in need of repair. Administratively, much can be said for the inclusion of repair and maintenance services. If these services are not taxed, shops selling goods as well as rendering repair services to them would be tempted to lower the taxable price on the invoice accompanying the sale of a good and to increase the invoice indicating its repair (real or imaginary).

Repair and maintenance of immovable property

There is a strong case for taxing all services to immovable property, as argued above for movable property.

Engineering and architectural work; designing and decorating buildings

In countries with a selective approach, these services are often listed as being taxable. They should be treated in a similar manner to repair and maintenance of movable and immovable property, i.e. taxed in full.

Publicity, advertising, marketing, and various administrative services, including data processing, printing, etc.

The marketing of a product is as important as the product itself, and the value added by advertising for it is indistinguishable from the value added inside the factory. There is no reason to treat one activity differently from the other. The discussion of production taxes in Chapter 5 shows that it is highly important to include marketing activities in the base if distortions are to be avoided. Also, luxury products, for instance, owe much of their value to the skill with which they are marketed, including the design and printing of wrappers, etc. These are all persuasive arguments for including these activities in the VAT base.

Legal services, accountancy, consulting, and other similar professional services

What applies to marketing activities applies also to professional services. Economically, it is important that the tax on inputs, if any, to these services is passed on. Professional services rendered to consumers should certainly be taxed, and the professions should have no difficulties in complying with the requirements of the VAT. It may be argued that the taxation of some professional services—e.g. those provided by lawyers—interferes with the attainment of justice by making it more expensive. For this reason, some countries exempt legal services relating to family affairs. Generally, the exemption is narrowly interpreted.

Transfer and exploitation of copyrights, patents, trademarks, and other proprietary rights

As noted above, goods can be sold as services (and the other way around). Also, as Chapter 5 points out, it is important that patent holders are deemed to be taxable producers, because much of the value of goods may be determined by the value of the proprietary right. A general clause should cover these situations. Incidentally, it is important to define the term 'delivery' so as to include hire purchases, finance leases, situations in which materials are made available (but ownership retained), etc. A broad definition closes off various tax avoidance routes.

Preferred Solution

The discussion of the pros and cons of the taxation of individual services indicates that services are indistinguishable from goods. No satisfactory borderline can (or should) be drawn between goods and services on philosophical, economic, or legal grounds. Both kinds of commodities satisfy consumer wants. Often, services are readily substitutable for goods and vice versa. Compliance and administration are greatly eased if both are taxed at the same rate and subject to the same threshold. The much-preferred approach, therefore, is to tax services comprehensively rather than selectively. Taxing services comprehensively, like taxing all goods, obviates the need for fine legal distinctions that add to administrative complexity, keep numerous people busy, but generate no revenue. Services should only be exempted if there are weighty social considerations (healthcare, education, social services) or decisive administrative reasons (banking, rents and rental values). The bottom line is that a VAT functions best if all goods and services are taxed equally and if, subject to the small-business exemption, all persons selling such goods or services are liable to VAT.

10.4 African Countries that Have Led the Way in VAT Modernization

The need to improve VAT performance in order to increase revenue calls for a bold round of base-broadening reform in many African countries. Even countries whose performance is better than average can still improve the quality of their VATs through base-broadening. Fortunately, some countries have already led the way by revamping their VAT legislation and other countries are in the process of doing so, not an easy task since it has been observed that mistakes made at introduction are hard to undo (Keen, 2009). Generally, there is much to be learned from the SACU countries, which have had a broad-based, neutral VAT, inspired by the New Zealand example, from the beginning, although they complicate their VATs with a zero rate on various basic foodstuffs.

Below, four countries are singled out for reforming their deficient VATs. Benin and Senegal revisited their original VAT as early as 1991; Kenya followed suit in 2013 and Tanzania in 2015. Benin and Senegal replaced their multi-rate, exemption-ridden VATs, levied at the manufacturing stage, by a broad-based, single-rate VAT in 1991 (ignoring Senegal's lower rate on tourism).[3] Until 2013, Kenya had a very narrow-based VAT with numerous exemptions and a zero rate on agricultural inputs, medical goods, print, petroleum products, and various other goods and services, as well as a lower-than-standard rate on electricity. Its base-broadening reform in 2013 was initially emulated by its neighbour, Tanzania, but much of it was subsequently reversed.

Details of the reformed VATs in these countries are shown in Table 10.4. Basically, all four countries retained all standard exemptions (not shown in the table) for healthcare, education, social and financial services, gambling, and public broadcasting. Commendably, Kenya limits the application of some of the standard exemptions—e.g. education by prescribing that the exemption 'shall not apply in respect of business or user training and other consultancy services designed to improve work practices and efficiency of an organization'. Further, stage plays and cultural performances are only exempted if conducted by educational institutions. Interestingly, following the South African example, Tanzania now taxes fee-based financial services, and property and casualty insurance. Unlike in South Africa, however, gambling retains its exempt status.

[3] See Ebrill et al. (2001, p. 70), who note that the UEMOA Council of Ministers adopted a directive agreeing on a single-rate VAT (in the 15–20% range) with limited exemptions (provided in a list by the UEMOA Commission) to be adopted by member countries by 2002. But contrast this *de jure* picture with the *de facto* situation described by Mansour and Rota-Graziosi (2013)—see Chapter 8.

Table 10.4 Benin, Senegal, Kenya, and Tanzania: VAT reform

Items	Benin	Senegal	Kenya	Tanzania
Introduction/Reform	1980/1991	1980/1991	1990/2013	1998/2015/2018
C-efficiency, 2015	0.37	0.51	0.29	0.21
Threshold (US$)	50 million (95,000)	50 million (95,000)	5 million (50,000)	100 million (44,000)
Zero rate				
Unprocessed foods			Maize, flour, bread, milk, cream	
Processed foods			None	
Agricultural inputs			Pesticides	
Medicines			Specified medicaments and pharmaceuticals	
Exemptions				
Unprocessed foods	Bread, maize, milk, potatoes, peas, beans, millet, sorghum, cereals (except rice), vegetables, fruits, tubers, horticultural products, fish offal	Unprocessed foodstuffs and basic necessities determined by the Minister of Finance; agriculture, livestock, fisheries	Wheat or meslin flour, maize flour, rice, soya beans, groundnuts, meat, fish, unprocessed milk, eggs, vegetables, fruits, cereals, green tea, copra, live animals	Food, basic agricultural products and livestock supplies for human consumption (unless provided by restaurants and hotels) Oil and cotton cake, maize, wheat and rice bran Live animals
Processed foods	Food especially made for infants		Bread, milk and food specially prepared for infants, employer-operated canteens and cafeterias	Food

Agricultural inputs	Feed, seed, cocoa beans, machinery and equipment for agriculture, animal husbandry, and fisheries, products for livestock breeding, poultry, and aquaculture; inputs for small businesses processing and storing agricultural products, phytosanitary instruments	Seed, feed	Feed, seed, fertilizer, plant and machinery, tractors; agricultural, veterinary, and horticultural services; tea and coffee brokerage services	Animal feed, fertilizers, pesticides, veterinary supplies, all sorts of implements, tractors for agricultural use, fishing gear and vessels, bee-keeping and dairy equipment
Medicines, equipment for the disabled	Medicines, vitamins, antibiotics, vaccines, medicaments for therapeutic and prophylactic purposes, dressings, selected medical articles and instruments, invalid carriages, dental work	Vitamins, hormones, antibiotics, vaccines, penicillin, medicaments and pharmaceutical products, various medical instruments and equipment, dental work, invalid carriages	Syringes, antibiotics, vaccines, penicillin and other medicaments for therapeutic or prophylactic use, dressings, dental cements, first-aid boxes, sanitary towels, contraceptives Equipment for the handicapped, including specially designed motor vehicles (once every four years) Burial and cremation services	Approved medicines, drugs, and pharmaceutical products (excluding food supplements or vitamins, but including packaging materials) Sanitary pads Medical equipment and appliances Articles for people with special needs, including spectacles Funeral services
Water, electricity, gas	Social tranche (basic exemption), gas	Social tranche (basic exemption)	Water supplied by government (unless bottled), LPG, biogas	Water (unless bottled or canned), sewerage
Public transportation	Public passenger transportation	Public passenger transportation; phone devices not subject to excise tax	Public passenger transportation	Passenger transportation, except taxi cabs, rental cars, boats, air charters

Continued

Table 10.4 *Continued*

Items	Benin	Senegal	Kenya	Tanzania
Print	Newspapers and periodicals (other than advertisements), books, postal and fiscal stamps, artist work	Newspapers and periodicals (other than advertisements), books, postal and fiscal stamps, authors' original work		Books, newspapers, magazines, maps, except items for children and examinations
Petroleum products				Jet fuel, kerosene, petrol, diesel, bitumen, LPG, importation of equipment
Investment goods	Equipment for service stations and fuel tanks, computer equipment	Fishing boats, aircraft, supplies for use in mineral and oil prospecting and exploration	Solar equipment, construction materials for power-generating plants; supplies for use in geothermal, oil, or mining prospecting or exploration; aircraft	Wind generators, solar thermals, equipment for mining and drilling, firefighting equipment

Source: Author's compilation from country legislation: Benin—Code Général des Impôts du Benin, Version 2012 (issued by Raymond Mbadiffo Kouamo), article 224 and annexe 1; Senegal—Code Général des Impôts, 27 December 2012, article 361; Kenya—Value Added Tax Act No. 35 of 2013 (revised edition 2017), First Schedule; Tanzania—The Value Added Tax Act, 2014, Special Bill Supplement No. 3, 12 May 2014, Jedwali, as amended by Finance Act 2018.

The most notable feature of the VAT reforms in Kenya and Tanzania is the abolition of the zero rate on most foodstuffs and various other goods, and its replacement by an exemption of specifically enumerated foodstuffs, features that are also found in the VATs of Benin and Senegal. Presumably, monitoring and enforcing the application of the zero rate drew valuable administrative resources away from more lucrative revenue-generating VAT audit activities. The zero rate, as discussed above, did little more than an exemption of agricultural and fishing products would do in terms of mitigating the VAT burden on lower-income households. Exceptionally, Kenya retained a zero rate for maize, flour, bread, milk, and cream. It will be interesting to see whether the country can withstand the pressure of producers of other basic foodstuffs clamouring for a zero rate on their products. Further, Kenya now exempts rather than zero-rates agricultural inputs, except pesticides which continue to be zero-rated.

Medicines are exempted in all four countries, but generally only if sold for therapeutic or prophylactic use, which appears to exclude over-the-counter pharmaceutical products. Again, Tanzania burdens its VAT administration by requiring it to monitor the end-use exemption of packaging goods for pharmaceutical products. In Kenya, the social tranche (a basic exemption in kilowatt-hour terms) for electricity consumption was abolished, whereas Benin and Senegal have kept it. Kenya is the only one of the four countries to abolish the exemption for newspapers and books, while all four retain the exemption for passenger transportation. As noted in Chapter 7, South Africa's National Treasury (2011) tends to frown upon these exemptions.

All four countries retained the exemption for specified (imported) capital goods, although a better alternative would have been to apply a reverse charge at the import stage so that some tax would be paid by non-registered firms. Kenya is phasing out its exemption for petroleum products but Tanzania is keeping it. Full taxation and adjustment of the excises (so that the total tax burden does not change) would be a better alternative.

Most of these changes are improvements over the previous situation. The broader VAT bases and the elimination of special rates should make it easier to administer and comply with the tax. Interestingly, the VATs of Benin and Senegal seem to be more comprehensive than their counterparts in Kenya and Tanzania. Not surprisingly, they are also more productive of revenue. Senegal's C-efficiency stands at 0.51 and Benin's at 0.37 (the average for Africa), compared with 0.29 and 0.21 for Kenya and Tanzania, respectively. Perhaps the C-efficiencies of the EAC member countries will improve as the reforms take hold, or perhaps the reforms were not bold enough. Unfortunately, Tanzania revoked many aspects of its well-conceived VAT reform, generally reverting to the pre-reform situation.

11

Governments and Activities in the Public Interest

From the beginning (i.e. the 1960s), governments and activities in the public interest, collectively referred to as public bodies, were not taxed under the VAT in the EU. Going back to the philosophy of the seventeenth-century Sun King Louis XIV, this was considered not the done thing in France, the country that invented the VAT. Governments extracted monies from the public, not from themselves. Doing so, moreover, was perceived as a pay-out and claw-back arrangement, which did not yield any net revenue. This approach finds few supporters these days. Nevertheless, the EU's position on considering governments out of the VAT's scope has been adopted by nearly all African countries. This is also the case with what are called 'activities in the public interest', such as hospitals and schools, which are governed by public law, and various non-profit organizations and charities if their activities are not likely to cause distortion of competition.

Following a digression on the nature of supplies provided by public bodies, this chapter discusses the EU legacy, illustrated by the African experience. As is well known, the EU's out-of-scope approach is bedevilled by distortions arising from the self-supply bias, the investment disincentive, and, somewhat more remotely, unfair competition vis-à-vis the private sector. As discussed next, outside Africa, countries with VAT have addressed these issues differently. Various EU countries and Canada, for example, have designed input tax refund mechanisms to eliminate the self-supply bias and the investment disincentive. Still other countries, such as New Zealand, tax governments and activities in the public interest in full and have thus come to terms with the unfair competition issue, too. A concluding section summarizes the characteristics and effects of the various approaches and attempts to formulate a recommendation for African countries.

11.1 Nature of Supplies by Public Bodies

Public bodies perform a wide range of activities which involve the provision of both public and private goods and services, regulatory and redistribution activities. In contrast with private sector supplies, the activities tend to be financed through a variety of means which include charges, user fees, taxes, subsidies, grants, and funds from borrowing, often without a direct link between the supplies and the means of financing. Supplies, moreover, tend to be made for nil, nominal, or break-even consideration.

Based on the EU's Common VAT Directive (2006), Table 11.1 gives a flavour of the types of public bodies that are of interest for the discussion. Characteristically, public bodies are 'governed by public law' and are 'non-profit organizations', and their activities do not give rise to 'distortion of competition', legal phraseology that is briefly discussed below. Economically, four broad categories of public body activities can be distinguished.[1]

Table 11.1 Types of public bodies

Governments	Activities in the public interest
States, regional and local government authorities governed by public law	Hospital and medical care by bodies governed by public law Medical and paramedical professions Human organs, blood, and milk; transport for sick or injured
Government departments, ministries	Dentists and dental technicians Welfare and social security work
Regulatory bodies Redistribution agencies	Protection of children and young persons by bodies governed by public law
Government enterprises	School or university education, vocational training, or retraining governed by public law
	Private tuition by teachers covering school and university education
	Religious or philosophical institutions providing healthcare, social security work, protection, or education
	Political, trade union, religious, patriotic, philosophical, philanthropic, or civic non-profit organizations if not likely to cause distortion of competition
	Sport or physical education by non-profit organizations
	Cultural services by bodies governed by public law
	Fundraising activities by non-profit organizations
	Public postal services other than passenger transport and telecommunication services
	Public radio and broadcasting services

Source: Author's compilation based on articles 13 and 132 of the EU's Common VAT Directive (2006).

[1] This expands on the seminal article on the treatment of public sector bodies in the EU by Aujean, Jenkins, and Poddar (1999).

- *Redistribution of income and wealth in the form of taxes, social benefits, subsidies, and grants*, which do not constitute consumption nor add value to a country's output. But the redistributing bodies do incur administrative costs, which involve value added. They are also faced with VAT on taxable inputs, which distorts input choices, broadly defined.
- *Provision of pure public goods and services*, such as defence, public administration, law, and order, which are non-rivalrous (consumption by one person does not reduce the amount available for others) and non-excludable (non-paying consumers cannot be prevented from accessing them) in consumption, and for which it is not possible to charge a specific price. Again, however, the VAT on inputs is an issue.
- *Provision of quasi-public goods and services*, which are either not completely non-rivalrous (e.g. by being subject to congestion) or not completely excludable, such as healthcare, education, libraries, museums, preventive medicine, and sewage disposal. Although it is possible to charge a price for quasi-public goods and services, overriding social or distributional reasons usually stand in the way of doing so. In the EU and Africa, quasi-public goods and services are labelled activities in the public interest; elsewhere, they are often associated with non-profit organizations and charities.[2]
- *Provision of other goods and services that are similar to goods and services supplied by the private sector which are sold at market prices*. Examples are electricity, gas, water, postal services, radio and television broadcasting, and telecommunications. Generally, these services are supplied against a fee, charge, or price to which the VAT can be applied, but at the same time their provision may involve subsidies, grants, or loans from governments.

The exemption from VAT of these four categories of activities gives rise to self-supply bias and an investment disincentive on account of the VAT on inputs. Generally, refunding VAT on inputs would eliminate the input choice distortions in the case of administrative costs incurred in redistributing income and wealth and in providing pure public goods. There is no unfair competition to worry about because private supplies simply do not exist. Fully refunding the VAT on inputs, however, does not eliminate the unfair competition issue in the case of quasi-public goods and services or goods and services that are similar to private supplies. In fact, input VAT refunds could aggravate the distortion because the price difference vis-à-vis private sector supplies subject to VAT tends to become larger. Not surprisingly, these last two categories of activities are responsible for virtually all of the issues and problems that arise in the application of VAT to

[2] Particularly by Gendron (2013), who refers to *p*ublic bodies, *n*on-profit organizations, and *c*harities as the PNC sector. This book follows the usage of the EU's Common VAT Directive (2006), reflected in the legislation of most African countries.

governments and public-interest activities. As will be seen, they can only be fully solved through full taxation.

An important argument in the EU for leaving public bodies out of the VAT's scope has been the perceived absence of a consideration comparable to a market price. Governments and public-interest organizations provide their services partially or fully free of charge, the argument goes, so there is no taxable value to which the rate can be applied. But under best-practice VATs, it is contended that the supplies or 'sales' of public bodies include not only fees and charges but also grants and subsidies and, in the case of local governments, proceeds from local taxes. If grants and subsidies go untaxed, public sector bodies are able to supply goods and services at lower prices than the private sector. Against their tax on 'sales', VAT-liable public bodies should, of course, be able to credit the VAT on inputs. An incidental if welcome side effect of full taxation is that it increases the accountability and transparency of government and public-interest operations.

11.2 EU-African Legacy

Under the EU's Common VAT Directive (2006), the tax applies to the supply of goods and services for consideration by taxable persons within the territory of a member state. In principle, therefore, all activities of economic agents, including public bodies, are within the scope of the VAT. However, article 13(1) states that:

> States, regional and local government authorities and other bodies governed by public law shall not be regarded as taxable persons in respect of the activities or transactions in which they engage as public authorities, even where they collect dues, fees, contributions or payments in connection with those activities or transactions.

This exception to the main rule is also found in most African VAT laws that are based on the Common Directive. In other words, governments and other public bodies governed by public law are not taxable persons: their transactions fall outside the scope of VAT. The main implication of non-taxability is that, unlike exempt entities, bodies engaging in non-taxable transactions cannot opt for registration and taxation enabling them to recover their input VAT.

However, there are three important provisos to this basic EU-African VAT rule, which can all be found in article 13 of the Common Directive and in African VAT legislation.

- First, public bodies are still regarded as taxable persons if their treatment as non-taxable persons leads to significant distortions of competition (distortion clause).
- Second, public bodies are always regarded as taxable persons for activities listed in annex I of the Common Directive—activities that in the main can

be associated with public utilities for the provision of water, electricity, gas, telecommunications, transportation, broadcasting, etc.—unless the activities are carried out on such a small scale as to be negligible (non-negligible clause).

- Third, member states may treat specified activities in the public interest engaged in by bodies governed by public law as activities in which these bodies engage as public authorities (exempt activities clause; see Table 11.1).

Figure 11.1 recapitulates the possible treatment of supplies by public bodies in the EU and African countries whose VAT is based on the Common Directive.

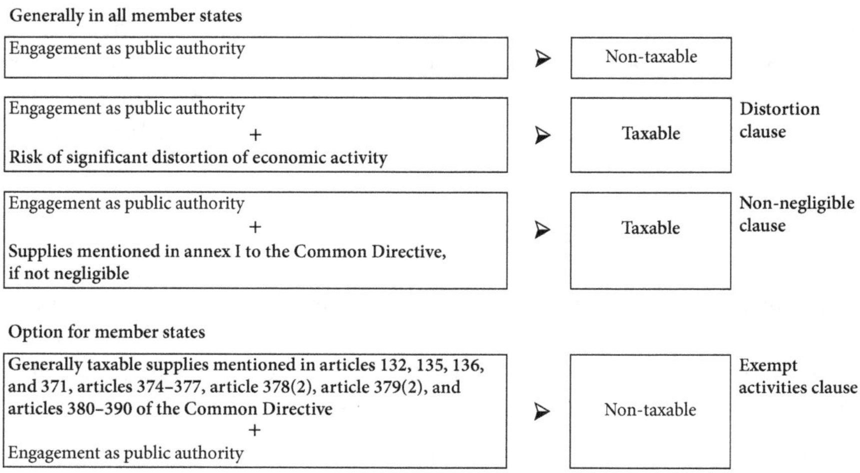

Figure 11.1 EU VAT treatment of supplies by public bodies
Source: KPMG AG reproduced by Copenhagen Economics (2013).

To summarize, VAT authorities have to answer the following questions in order to determine whether or not the activity public bodies engage in is liable to VAT (Copenhagen Economics, 2013):

- Is the activity an 'economic activity' for the purposes of VAT (see article 9 of the Common Directive)?
- Is the activity engaged in by the public body acting as such, i.e. as public authority?
- Would there be significant distortions of competition if the public body were treated as a non-taxable person?
- Is the activity listed in annex I of the Common Directive or a similar schedule in African VAT legislations?
- Is the activity covered by an exemption from VAT (and, if so, is the activity out-of-scope)?
- Are the revenues received for the activity directly linked to its supply?

Clearly, this schematic treatment of public bodies in the EU raises more questions than it answers, as the following brief discussion of the various concepts that are used shows.[3]

- *Governed by public law?* The European Court of Justice (2000) has ruled that the body governed by public law must itself be part of the public administration. A public notary, even if exercising the powers of a public authority, can never be a body governed by public law. Further, private law companies do not qualify for the exemption, even if fully owned by the government.
- *Acting as public authority?* According to the European Court of Justice (1990, 1991), the main criterion for 'acting as public authority' is the legal regime applicable to the public body under national law as determined through the member state's court system.
- *Significant distortion of competition?* The European Court of Justice (2008) has ruled that the scope of this clause covers not only actual competition but also potential competition if the possibility of a private operator entering the market is not hypothetical. Further, the clause should be interpreted narrowly—a distortion of competition is considered significant if it is more than negligible.
- *Non-negligible?* Public utilities and various other activities listed in annex I are presumptively engaging in taxable activities, but member states are free to decide that annex I activities carried out on a negligible scale nevertheless are taxable (European Court of Justice, 1989).
- *Activities in the public interest?* Exemptions for entities providing healthcare, education, social services, and public broadcasting in essence are non-taxable (out-of-scope) activities without the right to opt for registration and taxation. The European Court of Justice (2009) has ruled that the application of the exempt clause requires member states to make an express legal provision to that effect.

This complex treatment of public bodies goes a long way in robbing the VAT of its inherent simplicity. Not surprisingly, Aujean (2010b, p. 514), an astute observer and long-time participant in the EU VAT debate, has labelled the VAT treatment of public bodies 'complex, inefficient, costly, and legally uncertain'. The treatment is complex as evidenced by the criteria mentioned above, which are subject to widely different interpretations, particularly since they are to a large extent dependent on specific national laws. The treatment is inefficient because its application gives rise to the self-supply bias and the cascading effects discussed in Chapter 9. It is costly because many lawyers and accountants have to apply their sophisticated

[3] This discussion draws on Copenhagen Economics (2013).

skills to the application of the exemptions. And for much the same reasons, it is legally uncertain, the more so since the overlap between what is public and private differs from one member state to another member state and also changes over time. Finally, not mentioned by Aujean, the exemption of activities in the public interest by public bodies is not always matched by an exemption for similar activities by the private sector—a blatant form of discrimination.

In the same vein, another able tax lawyer, De la Feria (2009), has documented the highly complex web of conditions, derogations, movements into and out of scope of VAT, and transitions between 'exempt' situations, 'taxable' situations, and 'non-taxable because out-of-scope situations'. She has attempted to lay this down in a flow chart, which shows that it is almost impossible to establish and apply a single and consistent VAT treatment to all public sector bodies. She opines that the Common Directive is becoming more out of step with economic realities as time passes. The EU treatment, moreover, entails very significant compliance and administrative costs, as well as frequent and costly litigation.

11.3 African Situation

The situation in Africa strongly resembles that of the EU, where most VATs came from. Nearly all African VATs exempt governments and activities in the public interest with reference to the same criteria as found in the EU's Common VAT Directive (2006). But the approach in the SACU countries is somewhat different and perhaps simpler. Further, public utilities deserve separate treatment since they make an important contribution to revenue. By contrast, the VAT on cultural goods and services may not raise much revenue, but their scope is often extended to include related goods and services that should be taxed.

SACU Countries

In line with the EU approach, most African VATs consider healthcare, education, social welfare, and various societal organizations and associations to be non-taxable rather than exempt. Further, government entities are considered out-of-scope if their activities are governed by public law, are carried out under public authority, and do not cause significant distortions of competition or, put differently, are 'non-commercial'.

The uncertainty regarding the treatment of public bodies is minimized under the South African VAT (also found in other SACU countries), which, like the EU, considers governments and their agencies as the final consumer of goods and services if they use the inputs to provide goods or services on a non-commercial basis (South African Revenue Service, 2017). Accordingly, as in the EU, supplies by public bodies do not attract VAT and any VAT on inputs is a cost to them. Uncertainty about the classification 'public body' is removed, however, by reference to the Public Finance Management Act (PFMA), which lists all public bodies in South Africa, for determining whether an entity should be regarded as an exempt public authority. Even then though, subject to a business test, a public body can still be regarded as carrying on an 'enterprise', the supplies of which attract VAT. This would require an apportionment of input VAT between exempt and taxable enterprise supplies.

Similar to Canada, the South African Minister of Finance has the authority to designate activities by public entities (as well as welfare organizations and public–private partnerships) as enterprise activities for supplies in competition with private sector supplies. For instance, public utilities owned by (subordinate) governments fall within the definition of enterprise. They have to register for VAT purposes and, interestingly, are deemed to supply a taxable service for grants or subsidies received from public authorities, which are taxed at the standard rate. The use of the enterprise concept bypasses the difficulty of determining whether or not supplies are made in actual or potential competition with the private sector.

The SACU approach eliminates many of the uncertainties around the VAT status of public authorities. In other countries, enough uncertainties with respect to concepts such as 'public law' and 'public authority' remain to keep the VAT administration and the courts busy. Also, there is no mandatory taxation of public utilities and other 'annex I'-type activities. Whereas healthcare and education are to a large extent state-sponsored activities (so taxation would not add much to revenue if subsidies would have to be increased to make up for the tax), public utility and cultural services are important chunks of the VAT base and therefore deserve to be scrutinized in some detail.

Public Sector Utilities

Public utility services are given special attention in the EU's Common VAT Directive (2006), which prescribes mandatory inclusion in the VAT base. Also, VAT-liable customers of the utilities would presumably want to recover the input tax incurred by the public utilities, which can only be done if they are taxable, regardless of their form or the law under which they are supplied. The goods and services listed in annex I to the Common Directive include: telecommunications; the supply of water, gas, electricity, and thermal energy; the transport of goods; passenger transport; warehousing; commercial broadcasting; and some other goods and services.[4]

[4] Obviously, a drawback of this kind of enumeration is that it fails to stay in tune with changing realities, such as innovations in the variety and delivery of services.

In African countries, the most important activities of public sector utilities, often organized in the form of state enterprises, include the supply of water, electricity, passenger transport, postal services, telecommunications, and radio and television broadcasts. Table 11.2 indicates the VAT treatment of these supplies (often determined by inference).

Surveying the field, water is taxed in 29 countries, including one (Morocco) that taxes it at a lower rate. Several countries exempt or zero-rate 'social portions' (*tranches sociales* in francophone Africa) of water: i.e. a first block of water (in m^3 or monetary amount) consumed by (normally) a household in a prescribed period is exempt or zero-rated. The basic social exemption for water is mostly found in francophone Africa. In fact, the common VAT directives in UEMOA and CEMAC prescribe it for all member countries. Further, Botswana zero-rates a social tranche of water, while Kenya, Mauritius, Namibia, and the Seychelles zero-rate water altogether.

Electricity is taxable in about three-quarters of the VAT countries in Africa. This group includes three countries (Lesotho, Morocco, Tunisia) where electricity is taxable at a lower-than-standard rate. Four SADC countries apply a zero rate to electricity. Seven countries exempt and tax electricity at the same time using a system of social tranches whereby the first x kilowatt-hours (or monetary amount) is exempt or zero-rated and all kilowatt-hours (or monetary amount) over the exemption are taxable. Again, in UEMOA and CEMAC countries, the social tranche is compulsory. Other countries that use this social tranches model include Ghana, Madagascar, and the Seychelles.

The negative revenue impact of the zero rates, exemptions, and tranches can be quite significant. Contrary to what is generally believed, the benefit of concessionary treatment probably accrues disproportionately to higher-income groups (especially in the poorest countries with low access to water and electricity), as discussed in Chapter 7 with respect to South Africa. If so, the policy is regressive, particularly since households that are not poor tend to have private access to water and electricity. The revenue forgone could be used to enhance access to water and electricity for households that really need these services.

Passenger transportation, explicitly indicated as taxable in annex I of the EU's Common VAT Directive (2006), tends to be exempt in countries with anglophone VAT systems but taxable in most francophone countries. In Mauritius, public passenger transport is exempt while passenger transportation by air or sea is zero-rated. Morocco and Tunisia apply a lower rate to public passenger transportation. Postal services are widely exempt (often as indicated by an exemption for postal stamps, reflecting the 'sales' of postal offices), although they should be taxed because they compete with taxable private letter or parcel carriers. Telecommunication services are taxable in almost all countries listed in Table 11.2. Exceptionally, Lesotho applies a lower rate, Namibia zero-rates them, and Algeria has a lower rate for subscriptions to internet providers. Private sector radio and TV broadcasts are taxable in all countries except Egypt, which exempts them.

Table 11.2 Africa: VAT treatment of public utilities by public or private sector entities, 2018

RECs and countries	Water	Electricity	Passenger transport	Postal services	Telecommunications	Radio and TV broadcasts
Southern African Development Community (SADC)						
SACU						
Botswana	Z/T	T	E	T	T	T
Lesotho	E	L	E	E	L	T
Namibia	Z	Z	E	T	Z	T
South Africa	T	T	E	T	T	T
Swaziland	E	E	E	E	T	T
Other						
Congo, DR	T	T	T	E	T	T
Madagascar	E/T	E/T	T	E	T	T
Malawi	T	T	E	E	T	T
Mauritius	Z	Z	E/Z	E	T	T
Mozambique	T	T	T	E	T	T
Seychelles	E	E	E	E	T	T
Zambia	E	T	E	T	T	T
Zimbabwe	E	Z	E	T	T	T
East African Community (EAC)						
Burundi	E	E	E	E	T	T
Kenya	Z	T	E	T	T	T
Rwanda	E	T	E	T	T	T
Tanzania	E	T	E	T	T	T
Uganda	T	T	E	E	T	T

Continued

Table 11.2 *Continued*

RECs and countries	Water	Electricity	Passenger transport	Postal services	Telecommunications	Radio and TV broadcasts
Economic and Monetary Community of Central Africa (CEMAC)						
Cameroon	E/T	E/T	T	E	T	T
Central African Rep.	E/T	E/T	T	E	T	T
Chad	E/T	E	T	E	T	T
Congo	E/T	E/T	T	E	T	T
Equatorial Guinea	T	T	T	T	T	T
Gabon	T	T	T	E	T	T
Economic Community of West African States (ECOWAS)						
UEMOA						
Benin	T	T	E	E	T	T
Burkina Faso	T	T	T	T	T	T
Côte d'Ivoire	T	T	T	T	T	T
Guinea–Bissau	T	T	T	T	T	T
Mali	T	T	T	T	T	T
Niger	E	E	E	E	T	T
Senegal	E/T	E/T	T	T	T	T
Togo	T	T	E	T	T	T
WAMZ						
Cabo Verde	T	T	T	E	T	T
Gambia	E	E	E	T	T	T
Ghana	E	E/T	E	E	T	T
Guinea	T	T	T	E	T	T
Sierra Leone	E	T	E	T	T	T

Arab Maghreb Union (AMU)						
Algeria	T	T	T	T	L/T	T
Mauritania	T	T	T	T	T	T
Morocco	L	L	L	T	T	T
Tunisia	T	L	L	T	T	T
Intergovernmental Authority on Development (IGAD) and Egypt						
Djibouti	T	T	T	T	T	T
Egypt	T	E	T	T	T	E
Ethiopia	E	E	E	E	T	T
Sudan	T	T	T	T	T	T

Note: The taxable or exempt status of public utility supplies in some countries has been determined by inference: i.e. if not mentioned in the source materials, the status has been deemed to be taxable. Letters have the following meaning: T = taxed at the standard rate; E = exempt; L = taxed at a lower-than-standard rate; Z = taxed at the zero rate.

Source: Appendix A.

This broad survey indicates that many countries could collect substantial additional revenues from a fuller taxation of public utility services, especially water, electricity, passenger transport, and postal services. Of course, good arguments can be brought to the fore to provide concessionary treatment for these services, but if more revenue is to be secured, public utilities should be taxable. In many countries, public utility services are provided through state-owned enterprises. Accordingly, the prices of their products and services are very likely to be administered prices. For that reason, there seems to be little reason to use the VAT to raise revenue for general purposes through public utilities. It may be thought that, after all, the surplus income of the public utilities, if any, will be transferred to the government budget anyway.

This argument is wrong, as pointed out in Chapter 10. Although the effects of the VAT can be exactly replicated by manipulating the price of the products, inclusion in the VAT base provides for more even-handed treatment and enables business customers to obtain credit for VAT paid on purchases of services. Further, there may be a presumption that government-owned enterprises will be more forthcoming in remitting the VAT that they have charged their clients (and which they cannot rationalize as funds generated by themselves) to the treasury than in transferring their surplus income, which is usually ascertained some time after the close of the fiscal year. This process is less transparent than what a well-functioning broad-based VAT achieves.

Cultural Goods and Services

Cultural goods and services are another area where the VAT treatment differs across the African continent. Table 11.3 summarizes the treatments, subdivided as: newspapers and books; artists and authors; entertainment; sports; and gambling. To be sure, cultural and sporting services supplied by non-profit organizations and amateur clubs are considered as activities in the public interest and hence exempted in nearly all countries. Table 11.3 therefore indicates the VAT treatment of these services if provided by private sector entities that are not organized as (exempt) non-profit organizations.

Newspapers and books are for the most part exempt, except in the SACU countries, where they are taxable. Swaziland taxes printed matter but applies a zero rate to school books. Mauritius zero-rates all printed matter. In the EAC and ECOWAS RECs, some countries appear to tax newspapers and books at the standard rate. Ghana exempts locally printed newspapers and books but taxes imported printed materials. Other than Egypt and Sudan, which seem to tax newspapers and books, the remaining countries simply exempt them. This concessionary treatment again reflects the old European attitude towards newspapers,

Table 11.3 Africa: VAT treatment of various cultural goods and services supplied by private sector entities other than non-profit organizations, 2018

RECs and countries	Newspapers, books	Artists, authors	Entertainment	Sports	Gambling
Southern African Development Community (SADC)					
SACU					
Botswana	T	T	T	T	T
Lesotho	T	T	T	E/T	T
Namibia	T	T	T	T	T
South Africa	T	T	T	T	T
Swaziland	Z/T	T	T	T	E
Other					
Congo, DR	E	E	E	E	E
Madagascar	E	E	T	E/T	T
Malawi	E	E	T	T	E
Mauritius	Z	Z	E	T	E
Mozambique	E	E	E/T	T	E
Seychelles	E	T	T	T	T
Zambia	E	T	T	T	E
Zimbabwe	T	T	T	T	T
East African Community (EAC)					
Burundi	T	T	T	T	T
Kenya	T	T	T	T	E
Rwanda	E	T	T	T	E
Tanzania	E	T	T	T	E
Uganda	T	T	T	T	E
Economic and Monetary Community of Central Africa (CEMAC)					
Cameroon	E	E	T	T	T
Central Afr. Rep.	E	E	T	T	T
Chad	E	E/T	E	E/T	E
Congo	E	E/T	E	E/T	T
Equat. Guinea	E	T	E	E	T
Gabon	E	E/T	T	T	T
Economic Community of West African States (ECOWAS)					
UEMOA					
Benin	E	E	T	T	T
Burkina Faso	E	E	T	T	T
Côte d'Ivoire	E	T	T	T	T
Guinea-Bissau	T	T	T	T	T
Mali	T	E	T	T	T
Niger	E	T	T	T	T
Senegal	E	E	T	T	T
Togo	T	T	T	T	T
WAMZ					
Cabo Verde	T	E	E	E	T
Gambia	T	T	T	T	T

Continued

Table 11.3 *Continued*

RECs and countries	Newspapers, books	Artists, authors	Entertainment	Sports	Gambling
Ghana	E/Z	E	T	T	T
Guinea	E	E	T	T	T
Sierra Leone	E	T	T	T	E
Arab Maghreb Union (AMU)					
Algeria	E	T	L	E	T
Mauritania	E	T	T	T	T
Morocco	E	E	E/T	T	T
Tunisia	E	L	L	T	T
Intergovernmental Authority on Development (IGAD) and Egypt					
Djibouti	E	E	E	E	E
Egypt	T	T	T	T	E
Ethiopia	E	T	T	T	T
Sudan	T	T	T	T	T

Note: In some countries, the taxable or exempt status of public utility supplies has been determined by inference: i.e. if not mentioned in the source materials, the status has been deemed to be taxable. Letters have the following meaning: T = taxed at the standard rate; E = exempt; L = taxed at a lower-than-standard rate; Z = taxed at the zero rate.

Source: Appendix A.

although radio and television broadcasting (taxable if privately supplied) probably dominates newspapers in reaching the poor.

Works by artists and authors are taxable in all SACU VAT countries as well as in three IGAD countries. Outside those regions, such works are also taxable in some 20 countries dispersed across the other regions. Mauritius zero-rates them. The remaining countries simply exempt artists and authors, whose turnover would probably fall below the threshold anyway. Most often entertainment, including cultural services, in its various forms is taxable at the standard rate. Algeria, however, taxes it at the lower rate. In Morocco, entertainment is exempt if it consists of documentaries, educational films, and certain artistic shows, but otherwise it is taxable. Mozambique exempts cultural guides. Entertainment is exempt in eight countries, all in francophone Africa except Mauritius. Sport-related activities, not carried on by non-profit organizations and amateur clubs, appear to be taxable in most countries. Gambling is discussed in Chapter 15.

To recapitulate, newspapers and books tend to be exempted, followed by works of artists and authors, entertainment, and sports. The fact that all of these goods and services are exempt in some countries is somewhat surprising since the consumption of many of the items tends to be income elastic; the rich benefit more from the exemption than the poor. This is more obvious in the case of books and works by artists and authors, but perhaps less so in the case of sports, newspapers, and gambling. On the whole, the income elasticity of consumption of cultural goods and services makes it difficult to justify exemptions on distributional grounds. It is also difficult to justify the exemption on externality grounds. The best practice is therefore to tax such goods and services fully.

11.4 Refund Systems in Europe and Canada

Various EU member states attempt to neutralize the self-supply bias and investment distortions caused by the exemption of public bodies by refunding the VAT on inputs for selected activities performed by these bodies. Canada does this rather comprehensively. The refund systems may be of interest to African countries.

European Union

Various EU member states have established refund systems, called VAT compensation schemes, to compensate public bodies for the input VAT paid to make exempt or non-taxable supplies.[5] The refund systems tend to be run outside the VAT framework and may be funded out of general revenues or by the public bodies themselves. Further, they may be confined to public bodies or include private entities, too, such as charities and physicians. They may be restricted to non-taxable activities or include exempt activities as well. As it should, the Netherlands also provides refunds for the VAT incurred in other EU member states, but its example is not followed elsewhere. In contrast to the Canadian model, the application of EU refunds is not universal and is far less uniform and certain in the systems that do exist, as pointed out below.

Table 11.4 lists the member states that provide refunds to certain sectors that would otherwise be stuck with the VAT on inputs. The sectors include public administration (municipalities, departments, provinces, or Länder), healthcare, education, cultural services, postal services, waste and sewage disposal, and public broadcasting. Five member states reimburse municipalities for the VAT incurred on inputs. Denmark, Finland, and Sweden do so nearly in full, but the cost is financed by reducing the grants to the beneficiaries (Denmark) or by reducing the corporation tax revenue to which the municipalities are entitled (Finland). Interestingly, in the UK, the refund applies, among others, to VAT on taxable activities that are outsourced, a particularly effective way of eliminating the self-supply bias.

[5] See Henkow (2013) for a description and discussion of the VAT compensation schemes in Denmark, Finland, France, the Netherlands, Norway, Portugal, Sweden, and the UK.

Table 11.4 EU member states: activities eligible for VAT refunds

Member states	Public administration	Healthcare	Education	Cultural services	Postal services	Waste and sewage disposal	Broadcasting
Austria	No	Yes	No	No	No	No	No
Denmark	Yes	Yes	No	No	No	No	No
Finland	Yes	Yes	Yes	No	No	No	No
France	No	No	No	No	No	No	No
Netherlands	Yes	No	No	No	No	Yes	Yes
Portugal	No	No	No	No	No	No	No
Sweden	Yes	No	No	No	No	No	No
UK	Yes	Yes	Yes	Yes	No	Yes	Yes

Source: Copenhagen Economics, 2013, p. 105.

In Austria, unlike other member states, the health sector is nearly fully covered by the refund scheme. Hospitals, physicians, dentists, nursing homes, retirement homes, and social security entities are all entitled to a refund of VAT paid on inputs.[6] The coverage of the schemes in Denmark, Finland, and the UK is more limited. Educational institutions are rarely refunded for the VAT on their inputs, perhaps because there is less VAT to be refunded or because the value added consists mainly of labour services, although this would not be true with respect to technical training and research. The same applies to cultural services supplied by public bodies. Public postal services are not eligible for refunds in any of the refund-scheme countries, most of which have privatized postal activities. Waste and sewage disposal, traditionally a municipal activity, is eligible for compensation in the Netherlands and the UK, as is public broadcasting.[7]

The VAT literature opines that the various national refund schemes in the EU, in their current form, do not fully solve the self-supply bias and the investment disincentive. In fact, selective compensation causes new distortions—e.g. because the price difference (inclusive of VAT) vis-à-vis activities that can also be performed by the private sector becomes even larger.[8] Further, the schemes do not apply to hidden VAT in services provided to public bodies by exempt entities, except in Denmark. Reportedly, the nature of the accounting systems of public bodies (not registered for VAT purposes) often makes it difficult to track the amount of non-deductible VAT for compensation purposes. Apparently, the situation calls for deeper reforms (Aujean, 2010a), possibly the introduction of comprehensive refund schemes as in Canada.

Canadian Solution

In Canada, six out of ten provinces have harmonized their GST, appropriately called harmonized sales tax (HST), with the federal GST.[9] The HSTs are collected by Revenue Canada, the federal tax collection agency. Broadly, supplies to and by the federal, provincial, and municipal governments and their agencies are treated as follows:

- Supplies by the federal government and its agencies are exempt, while their inputs are taxed.
- Supplies by provincial governments (and territories) and their agencies are exempt but supplies *to* provincial governments and their agencies are

[6] The Austrian treatment of the health sector resembles that of Australia, which zero-rates healthcare under its VAT.

[7] VAT compensation schemes have recently reappeared in EU discussions and research activity, more recently under the heading of partial exemption. See De la Feria (2010).

[8] See, for example, Wassenaar and Gradus (2004), who review and evaluate the compensation mechanisms in Denmark, Finland, the Netherlands, Norway, Sweden, and the UK.

[9] The discussion in this subsection draws on Gendron (2013).

zero-rated, except for provinces which, like the federal government, have agreed to pay GST on their supplies to simplify the GST's administration for vendors.

- Supplies by municipalities and their agencies (including universities, schools, and hospitals) are exempt, while the GST on inputs is partially or fully refunded.[10] The status as a municipality, which is broadly defined to include, for instance, volunteer fire organizations and privately-run water, sewerage, or drainage systems, has to be acknowledged by Canada Revenue.
- Supplies by all governments in competition with the private sector are taxable if in excess of CAD 50,000 per annum.[11] This applies, for instance, to provincial public sector enterprises (Crown corporations), such as the large electricity suppliers, which are treated like any other business that is taxable for GST purposes.

In this system, public bodies that make a combination of taxable and exempt supplies must allocate GST/HST on inputs to taxable and exempt activities. They are entitled to input tax credits for GST/HST paid on the portion of purchases allocated to taxable supplies, just like any other business. They are also entitled to a Public Body Service (PBS) rebate of the GST/HST paid on the portion of purchases allocated to exempt supplies.[12] Reportedly, in situations where taxable supplies (eligible for full input VAT credit), exempt supplies (eligible for a partial or full input tax refund), or non-taxable supplies (no VAT credit or refund) are made by a PBS, segregating purchases, tracking tax, and allocating GST/HST to such transactions is still complicated when compared with fully taxable transactions (Gendron, 2013).

Table 11.5 shows the input VAT rebate factors for various types of PBS bodies. Rebates are funded out of general government revenues.

Even though the effects of the Canadian refund system are more transparent and comprehensive than those of the European refund and exemption systems, it still exhibits a number of drawbacks. It distorts consumer choice between zero-rated and taxable goods, and violates economic neutrality because some private goods are zero-rated if supplied by the MUSH sector but fully taxable if supplied

[10] Interestingly, the original rationale for doing so was not based on concerns about the self-supply bias or investment disincentives. Rather, the institutions, unlike the provincial governments, were subject to the tax on their inputs under the predecessor manufacturers' sales tax. For this reason, the federal government decided to provide a partial refund of taxes on inputs purchased by the municipalities, universities, schools, and hospitals (MUSH) sector in order to keep these bodies in more or less the same relative tax position. Although the refunds varied by type of provincial body, on average they amounted to roughly two-thirds of input taxes paid by the sector (Gendron, 2013).

[11] Although all governments are subject to GST (and HST, if applicable) on taxable supplies, all departments, branches, corporations, and agencies are registered as one entity and hence supplies within any government (broadly defined) are not taxable. In addition, certain supplies are specifically exempted, including most registration, information provision, and licensing activity as well as homemaker services provided in residences, waste disposal, and law enforcement and fire protection.

[12] A gross revenue threshold of CAD 250,000 also applies to charities and public institutions, which limits the number of refund applications.

Table 11.5 Canada: rebate factors for federal GST, 2013

Type of organization	%
Municipality	100
University or public college[a]	67
School authority	68
Hospital authority, facility operator, or external supplier	83[b]
Charity or public institution	50
Qualifying non-profit organization	50

[a] Includes affiliated colleges or research institutes.
[b] Healthcare rebate applies to charities, non-profit organizations and public institutions that render services similar to those usually rendered by hospitals.
Source: Gendron, 2013.

by the private sector. Further, it introduces additional complexity in the GST system by requiring rules to define and delineate zero-rated supplies (versus taxable and exempt supplies), and to monitor their application. It may also trigger 'zero-rating creep', i.e. additional demands for extending the zero-rated treatment to goods and services outside the MUSH sector. These problems can only be solved under full taxation, as found in New Zealand and Australia.

11.5 Full Taxation in New Zealand and Australia

The base of New Zealand's GST is the broadest in operation today. The treatment of public sector bodies plays an important role in explaining this fact. As in the case of Australia, New Zealand's GST distinguishes itself from other VATs around the world by obliging public bodies to register for GST purposes. Their supplies are taxable if they are not exempt.[13] The taxable value of supplies is calculated on the basis of the appropriations by the parliament and the rates, fees, levies, and other charges paid by the public. Subject to a threshold of NZD 60,000, this also applies to the supplies of activities in the public interest carried out by non-profit organizations, unless they supply donated goods, in which case they are exempt.

Accordingly, under New Zealand's GST, supplies by health organizations, educational institutions, cultural organizations, social assistance agencies, child welfare groups, postal services, and public broadcasting companies, exempt in the EU, are all taxable. According to Aujean, Jenkins, and Poddar (1999), this has 'permitted there a dramatic simplification of VAT rules as they apply to public bodies'. The effect on revenue, moreover, would be nil to the extent that the charge for the activities and their financing are determined by public bodies.

[13] The number of exemptions is very limited, comprising residential rents and sales of residential premises, financial services that cannot be zero-rated (see Chapter 13), and supplies by a non-profit body of donated goods and services.

This simple and neutral treatment effectively eliminates the numerous non-neutralities encountered when public body supplies are exempt while similar private sector supplies are taxable. The reduction in complexity is also considerable, since public bodies, public authorities, and tax exemptions do not have to be defined, although there are still some conceptual difficulties with pure public goods, such as defence and fire protection. Beyond that, some difficulties arise in determining the 'sales' of public bodies. Some (e.g. Gendron, 2013) contend that grants should only be included in sales if they are directly linked to the supply. But it requires only a third-rate VAT lawyer to turn a product grant (a specified amount per, say, ticket sold) into a budget subsidy (not linked to the number of tickets sold).[14] So, best practice would be to include grants in full, as South Africa does. Presumably, the proceeds of borrowing should also be included in the taxable base if not made at arm's length.

The Australian GST is similar to the New Zealand GST, except that it allows for more zero-rating and exemptions. Zero-rated are food, water and sewage, health services, cars for use by disabled people, childcare, education, and skill training. Public bodies can opt for GST registration even though their supplies do not exceed the threshold. In the absence of a consideration, the supply of government services has no GST consequences. Unlike New Zealand, expenditure budgets approved by parliament are not viewed as consideration for the supply of the services rendered by the public body. Generally, non-profit organizations are taxable. Grants and sponsorships (but not pure gifts) attract GST if the supply is carried on in return for the funding.

As in New Zealand, the full taxation of public bodies removes the self-supply bias, the investment disincentive, and the competitive distortion. It does not do so, however, for government activities that are left out of the scope of GST.

11.6 What Is Best Practice for African Countries?

Following a summary evaluation of the discussion of the VAT treatment of public bodies in this chapter, this section attempts to formulate a best-practice approach that may be suitable for most African countries.

What Is Best Practice?

Table 11.6 summarizes the previous discussion on the treatment of the activities of public sector bodies: (a) under exemption in the EU and Africa; (b) under

[14] Copenhagen Economics (2013) rightly notes that public bodies could avoid the VAT under full taxation by transforming product subsidies (taxable under the EU's Common VAT Directive) into budget subsidies (not taxable). Therefore, budget subsidies, even if not directly linked to the supply, should also be included in the taxable base, which is what best-practice VATs do.

Table 11.6 Comparative VAT treatment of supplies and inputs of public bodies

Characteristics and types of distortions	Exemption	Exemption with selected refunds (compensation)	Exemption with (nearly) full refunds	Full taxation
Where applied	Africa and EU	Some EU member states	Canada	New Zealand, Australia
Treatment characteristics				
Supplies (output)	Not taxed	Not taxed	Not taxed	Taxed
Consideration (taxable value)	Not an issue	Not an issue	Not an issue	Should include fees, charges, subsidies, grants, and budgetary allocations
Inputs (tax credits)	Not available	Only available for designated activities	Available for municipalities, universities, schools, and hospitals	Fully available
Distortions				
Self-supply bias	Strong	Only solved for selected activities	Generally solved	Fully solved
Investment disincentive	Strong	Only solved for selected activities	Generally solved	Not an issue
Distortion of competition	Strong	Enhanced	Enhanced	Not an issue
Complexity				
Legal refinements	Extreme	Hardly improvement over exemption	Manageable	Minimized
VAT apportionment if required	Necessary for exempt activities	Necessary for exempt activities to which compensation scheme does not apply	Necessary for exempt activities to which compensation scheme does not apply	Not necessary
Exemption or refund creep	Strong	Moderate	Moderate	Not an issue

Source: Author's compilation.

exemption with refunds for input VAT in respect of selected activities in various EU member states; (c) under exemption with nearly full refunds for the MUSH sector in Canada; and (d) under full taxation as in New Zealand and Australia.

Characteristically, the supplies of public sector bodies are not taxed under any of the exemption approaches. The determination of the consideration should then not be an issue, but may still be needed to apportion input VAT if the exempt entities perform taxable as well as exempt or non-taxable activities. Alternatively, some physical distribution key is needed for allocating input VAT. If supplies of public sector bodies are fully taxed, the consideration should be comprehensively defined to include fees, charges, subsidies, grants, and approved budgetary allocations. Accordingly, credits for VAT on inputs would be fully available, in contrast to exemption-with-refund approaches where they would be restricted to designated activities or sectors. Distortions and complexities take on extreme forms under the exemption approach in the EU and Africa and are only partially solved if a selective refund system applies. While refund schemes address the self-supply bias and the investment disincentive, only full taxation solves the unfair competition problem.

The taxation of as many supplies by public bodies as possible promotes simplicity, accountability, transparency, and the workings of the VAT. Delineation issues regarding taxable versus non-taxable activities become redundant and the VAT chain remains intact through to the consumer level. Distortions of input and outsourcing choices are reduced and so are administrative costs because the VAT on taxable purchases does not have to be allocated between taxable and exempt supplies. Although public bodies do not pursue profit maximization, cost minimization is their aim and this goal is promoted by applying the VAT as widely as possible.

Copenhagen Economics (2013) has calculated the efficiency gain that could be reaped in the EU if government activities and exempt supplies were taxed (with credit for the VAT on intermediate goods and fixed assets). It analysed the effects of six core services—cultural activities, education, healthcare, waste disposal, postal services, and radio and television broadcasts—which jointly contribute 14.2 per cent of GDP in the EU-27 (not including Croatia). The efficiency gain of fully taxing these services, which is what New Zealand does, would be 0.34 per cent of the EU-27's GDP, while the alternative of refunding input taxes would produce a gain of merely 0.02 per cent. Full taxation should have a significant positive effect on medium-sized and small businesses, which account for almost the whole of business services in these sectors.

Not surprisingly, Copenhagen Economics (2013, p. 12) concludes: 'we recommend to look towards a full taxation solution', the more so since the expanding interrelationships between public and private activities make it increasingly difficult to say whether or not a government acts as government and whether or not competition is distorted. Many government activities can be performed equally well by the private sector. And even if this is not the case, the exemption of public bodies still generates distortions of input and outsourcing choices, which harm competition too.[15]

What Should African Countries Do?

Having followed in the EU's footsteps, the VAT treatment of public bodies in most African countries is likely to be extraordinarily and unnecessarily complex, highly inefficient, and most likely inequitable, while the arguments that have been advanced to justify the exemption of the vast majority of the goods and services delivered by the sector are weak. While developed countries would do well to consider seriously the full taxation of the public sector, this conclusion should not be extended to African countries that do not have well-developed and sophisticated tax administrations. One of the reasons is that such a reform would require important (and most likely prior) reforms on the expenditure side of the budget.

Depending on the circumstances, however, more limited but still substantial reforms should be undertaken. Paramount among the reforms is a thorough review of the non-standard exemptions and zero rates, discussed in Chapters 9 and 10, which are highly detrimental to revenue and which should have a higher priority than streamlining the VAT's application to public sector bodies and activities in the public interest. Having said this, various activities in the public interest and cultural services could be taxed more fully—e.g. admissions to museums, parks, and nature reserves; sale of licences and permits; waste disposal; rentals of public facilities for conferences, concerts, and similar events. Given that health and education are politically sensitive areas in many developing countries, it probably makes sense to maintain the exemption for supplies in these sectors. Beyond that, a strong case can be made for taxing the public utility services more fully in various countries.

[15] The (unnecessarily) complicated legal and procedural rules and the complex jurisprudence around the VAT treatment of public bodies in the EU are analysed by De la Feria (2009).

12
Immovable Property

In most African countries, housing services—in the form of rents and rental values of owner-occupied property—comprise a sizable part of consumption expenditures as computed for national accounts purposes. Clearly, housing is too large a sector to ignore in the design and operation of a broad-based, properly functioning VAT. Since residential housing is often an income-elastic item of consumption, exemption of this sector would be regressive with respect to income; in other words, the rich would benefit more than the poor.

This chapter examines the VAT treatment of immovable property in Africa.[1] It starts by setting out how immovable property should be taxed under a pure and a best-practice VAT. This is followed by a review of the actual treatment of immovable property in Africa, including the VAT's interaction with transfer taxes and stamp duties. Possible directions for reform are considered, before a recapitulation of policy proposals concludes.

12.1 How Should Immovable Property Be Taxed?

How should immovable property be taxed under a cash-flow, tax-credit type of VAT? And what concessions have to be made to a pure VAT to make it workable, i.e. to turn it into a best-practice VAT?

Treatment under a Pure VAT

The dictum that VAT should be imposed on the widest possible range of goods and services that are used or consumed by businesses and individuals applies also to immovable property. All transactions in property—land and buildings, residential or commercial, privately or publicly owned or leased—should be included in the VAT base and taxed at the standard rate. This rate should apply to the construction, repair and maintenance, sale, lease, or owner-occupancy of new and

[1] This chapter draws on Cnossen (2011c). For a description and analysis of the VAT treatment of immovable property in Australia, Canada, Germany, Japan, Mexico, and the UK, see Van Brederode (2010). Millar (2010) provides an interesting analysis of the VAT treatment in the Antipodean countries.

used property. The VAT's tax-credit mechanism should be relied upon to ensure that the VAT sticks only to consumer or end use of the services provided by immovable property, not to business use.

To understand the correct treatment of immovable property, it is instructive to view land and buildings as stocks that can be used for consumption or production purposes. If property, such as a factory building, is used for production purposes, the services that it generates should not be subject to VAT. Normally, the value of these services will be incorporated in the price of production that, if a sale were involved, would be subject to VAT. Moreover, any VAT paid at the time of the purchase of the building should be creditable against the VAT chargeable on the products made and sold by the factory. If there is no VAT on sales, simply because there are no sales, a refund would be due.

Ideally, the same treatment should be accorded immovable property that generates housing services. The ideal solution would be to register all persons, natural as well as legal, who own or buy residential immovable property, for VAT purposes. By purchasing a dwelling, these persons would become producers (called taxable persons under typical VAT legislation) of housing services. In their role as producers, they would subsequently sell the housing services to consumers. These consumers could be lessees who buy the services for consideration—that is, a rental charge—but it is also possible that the producers would put the dwelling at their own disposal. In other words, as owner-occupiers (landlords), they would 'sell' the housing services to themselves in their role as occupier-consumers (tenants).

The VAT consequences of these events are obvious. The taxable person who buys a bundle of housing services in the form of a dwelling pays VAT on the purchase price but, at the same time, is entitled to a VAT credit (and refund, if due) for the same amount. If he sells the housing services to a lessee, he would have to charge VAT on the amount of the rental. The lessee, being a non-taxable consumer, would not be able to pass the VAT on; he would be stuck with it just like consumers of other services and goods. Similarly, in his role as owner-occupier, the producer of housing services would 'charge' VAT on these services, whose value equals the rental value of the dwelling, rendered to himself as consumer. Like the lessor, he would have to remit that VAT (net of any VAT on inputs, such as repair and maintenance services) to the VAT authorities. And just like the lessee, he would be stuck with the VAT on the rental value of his dwelling.

The treatment of land would not differ from the treatment of buildings. If land generates production services, as in agriculture, it should be treated in the same manner as the factory above. If it is a producer good that generates consumption services because it is used for camping or hunting purposes, for example, then the same reasoning holds as given above in respect of housing services. Feasibility considerations may dictate other solutions, but it seems incorrect to say that land should be left out of the base because it is not a consumer good. The issue is whether land generates (on balance, untaxed) production services or (in principle, taxed) consumption services.[2]

In sum, under a pure VAT, residential property would always be a producer good.[3] Sales, rentals, and rental values would be taxable and a credit would be available for the VAT on purchases. The rationale for taxing rental values under a pure VAT runs parallel to that of an income tax. Rather than earning a return on his house in the rental market, on which he would be taxed, the owner-occupier offers the return to himself as investor, which should be included in his income tax assessment. Taxing the return under the income tax as well as the VAT is not a form of double taxation, just as the application of the VAT to the consumption of a market-earned rental charge, on which income tax has been paid, is not considered double taxation. The application of both taxes arises because owner-occupied houses are an investment as well as a consumption good.

A Second-Best Approach

The registration for VAT purposes of all owner-occupiers and the computation of all rental values would present formidable administrative (and political) difficulties, which are not considered surmountable in practice. But if rental values cannot be taxed, the taxation of rental charges would appear to favour owner-occupiers over lessees.[4] In addition, the taxation of rental charges only would involve the registration of many small landlords, and complications would arise from changes in the status of dwellings from owner-occupation to rental use and vice versa.

As a second-best approach, therefore, all countries with a VAT exempt rental values and nearly all countries exempt rental charges as well. Instead, these countries tax new residential construction and sales of new housing. But since the purchase price of a house may be taken to represent the present discounted value of its future services, by extension the VAT on the purchase price may be considered a good proxy for the discounted value of the VAT that should have been levied on the flow of housing services. Thus, owners and lessors of dwellings

[2] It is quite another matter that land is not a produced input—that its supply is fixed (except perhaps in Holland), so that taxing landownership is taxing an economic rent. Accordingly, the tax would be capitalized in the value of the land without any effect on economic activity. But this feature calls for a separate land or land value tax, not a VAT. Under a VAT, the tax on land would be washed out if the land is used for taxable activities by taxable persons, but not if used or owned by non-taxable persons.

[3] Consequently, it does not seem useful to view immovable residential property as a *combination* of a consumption good and an investment good; in fact, it is both, as discussed later. For an exposition of the 'combination' view, see Conrad and Grozav (2008).

[4] In this respect, the treatment of immovable property differs from the treatment of other consumer durables, such as cars, which are taxed in full if purchased by a consumer (just like newly built residential property), but whose lease by a taxable person is also taxed (unlike housing rentals).

Table 12.1 Equivalence of taxation and exemption of rents and rental values
Assumptions: acquisition price of building = US$2,000; straight-line depreciation (40 years) = 2½% per year; rate of return = discount rate = 10%; VAT rate = 20%

	Year 0	Year 1	Year 2	Years 3–38	Year 39	Year 40
A. VAT on rents and rental values (illustrative amounts in US$)						
VAT on building	400					
Input tax credit	-400					
Rents or rental values		250	245	....	60	55
VAT on rents or rental values		50	49	....	12	11
Total VAT	0	50	49	....	12	11
Present value of VAT	400					
B. No VAT on rents and rental values (illustrative amounts in US$)						
VAT on building	400	-	-			
Input tax credit	0	-	-			
Rents or rental values		250	245	....	60	55
VAT on rents or rental values		0	0	....	0	0
Total VAT	400	0	0	....	0	0
Present value of VAT	400					

are indirectly subject to VAT on the consumption of housing services by themselves or by lessees.[5]

The equivalence between a VAT on rents and rental values and the 'prepayment' of the same amount of tax through a VAT on the value of newly constructed (non-)residential premises, as well as the subsequent exemption of rents or rental values, is illustrated in Table 12.1. Working our way through the example, the value of the newly constructed dwelling is (for ease of calculation) supposed to be US$2,000, which attracts VAT at 20 per cent for an amount of US$400, invoiced to the purchaser and payable by the seller to the authorities. However, since the buyer is subject to VAT on the rent that the dwelling fetches or the rental value if he 'lets' the dwelling to himself, he is eligible for a tax credit of the same amount. Accordingly, his net VAT liability at the time of purchase in year 0 is nil.

Furthermore, in year 1, the rent or rental value can be calculated as the sum of the depreciation in that year (US$50) plus the return on the investment (10 per cent of US$2,000), for a total of US$250. Similarly, in year 2, the return is US$50 plus 10 per cent of the remaining investment of US$1,950, for a total of US$245, and so on for the remainder of the life of the building. As shown, in years 39 and 40

[5] For a discussion of the equivalence notion, see Poddar (2010).

(when the building is fully written down), the rents or rental values can be calculated at US$60 and US$55, respectively. The VAT collected on these rents or rental values in years 1 and 2 is US$50 and US$49, respectively, and US$12 and US$11 in years 39 and 40. The present value of the sum of these VATs on all rents or rental values equals US$400, the same amount of VAT that was charged on the sale of the dwelling but that was washed out through the tax-credit mechanism.

The calculation is much simpler when the dwelling is taxed but rents or rental values are exempt. In that case, VAT is charged on the sale of the dwelling (charged to the buyer, but invoiced by the seller), while rents or rental values are not subject to VAT. The amount of VAT remitted to the authorities is US$400, exactly the same as the present value of the VAT that would have been collected in years 1 through 40 on the taxable rent or rental value.

Prima facie, this is a neat result that indicates that the exemption of lessees (and landlords) and owner-occupiers does not favour housing services over the consumption of other goods and services. Of course, the equivalence between the VAT on newly constructed immovable property and a hypothetical VAT on the present discounted value of all future rental charges does not hold in the face of changing property values and, by extension, the changing value of the housing services provided by the property.[6] In addition, changes in VAT rates put the equivalence into doubt.[7] Nevertheless, the equivalence idea debunks the notion that residential property is not taxed under the VAT. Like other durable consumer goods, it is taxed on a prepayment basis.

Two approaches can be used to put the equivalence notion into practice: the 'exemption method' and the 'tax method'. They are discussed below.

12.2 Exemption Method versus Tax Method

Under the 'exemption method', prescribed in the EU's Common VAT Directive (2006), the sale, lease, and use of immovable property (residential and non-residential) are, in principle, exempt, but newly constructed buildings, as well as alterations and maintenance of the existing building stock, are taxable without credit for tax. The exemption method needs a definition of specified non-residential use, such as hotel accommodation, boarding houses, camping facilities, and parking space—all of which should be taxable. Furthermore, since the business use and sale of existing non-residential immovable property are also exempt, an opportunity

[6] Implicitly, it is assumed that the rate of return (also the discount rate) does not change over the lifetime of the immovable property. Obviously, this is not a realistic assumption. Property values rise and decline, with implications for the level of rents and rental values and, by extension, the VAT that, in theory, should be payable on the current use of building services. This issue is discussed further below.

[7] Some people might also consider the taxation of rental values alien to a transactions tax, such as the VAT, which taxes actual expenditures rather than presumptive consumption.

for optional registration and payment of VAT is desirable to avoid potential discrimination and cascading of tax.[8]

Under the 'tax method', adopted by the SACU member countries, the sale and lease of all immovable property are, in principle, taxable, but residential rents (and rental values) are exempt (or outside the scope of the VAT), as is the sale of previously occupied residential property (unless sold by a taxable person). This implies that the construction, sale, lease, alteration, and maintenance of all non-residential buildings are taxable. Sales of existing buildings are also taxable, unless such buildings constitute residential property. The tax method requires a definition of residential use (but not of specified non-residential use, unless taxed differentially lower or higher), but an option to register and pay VAT for commercial purposes is not neccessary.

Both methods must address the VAT implications of the supply of land, which is traded even less often than buildings are and is used more often for productive purposes in exempt sectors. The EU's Common Directive exempts all land, except building sites. In the EU, as in Africa, the VAT treatment of land is closely tied in with the treatment of the agricultural sector. If agricultural activities are exempt, as is widely the case, it seems to make sense to exempt land as well. If not, the case for including land in the VAT base is strong.

Elsewhere, Australia, Canada, and New Zealand did not wish to tax land at the inception of their VATs since this would constitute a one-off wealth tax on landowners. New Zealand, and initially South Africa too, achieve this by taxing land as a second-hand good. Persons registered for VAT are allowed a notional tax credit in respect of land bought from non-registered persons against the VAT on the sale. This effectively shelters such land from taxation, except on the increase in value. Australia only taxes the margin by allowing a deduction for the acquisition price of the land. Canada taxes the sale of all land, except land held for personal use. Land acquired by a non-registered person remains exempt, as is the resale of used residential property. Land held for personal use becomes taxable when sold to a registered person.

12.3 Taxation of Immovable Property in Africa

Generally, the tax method for the VAT treatment of immovable property (taxing all transactions, except the lease and sale of used residential property) is found in the SACU countries and some other SADC countries. Most other African VATs have adopted the exemption approach of the EU's Common Directive on VAT (exempting all transactions, except the sale of newly built property). In SACU

[8] For an early analysis of the EU approach, see Vermeulen, Schellmann, and Amand (2005).

countries, too, only agricultural land is exempted, whereas elsewhere all land is exempted, except building sites.

Table 12.2 summarizes the situation in individual African countries. To facilitate the exposition, it seems useful to distinguish construction activities from the lease and sale of commercial property (the lease and sale of used residential property are invariably exempted, and hence not shown). In nearly all countries, property transfer taxes, including stamp duties, which are imposed on gross selling prices, interact with the VAT and often replace it. Accordingly, an exemption for VAT could well mean that a non-creditable transfer duty applies in full. The transfer duty rates are also shown in the table.

As indicated by Table 12.2, construction activities are nearly always subject to VAT. In terms of revenue, this is mainly relevant for residential construction and with regard to exempt sectors, since the tax on commercial construction is washed out through the credit system. Exceptionally, Namibia, following the UK example, zero-rates the immovable property sector in its entirety. Morocco applies a zero rate to the supply of social housing, which is exempted in various other countries, including Burkina Faso, Gabon, and Lesotho. Still other countries, such as Algeria and Egypt, apply a reduced rate; Ghana does so with regard to sales by real-estate developers.

Construction activities involve the supply of building materials, the supply of repairs and maintenance, and the construction of new buildings. VAT treatment differs somewhat across sub-activities and countries. Nearly all countries tax building materials at the standard rate, but they are zero-rated in Djibouti (if imported), Lesotho (if used for commercial buildings), Malawi (if used for factories and warehouses), Namibia, and Zimbabwe (for building bricks). This should not affect revenue, but may violate the VAT's integrity. Interestingly, Chad protects the local industry by exempting locally produced building materials. Generally, the treatment of repairs and maintenance follows that of building materials.

The taxation of the lease and sale of commercial (i.e. non-residential) immovable property is heavily concentrated in SADC and EAC countries, followed by the IGAD countries. With the apparent exception of Benin and Burkina Faso, all CEMAC and UEMOA countries exempt these transactions. The VAT treatment of immovable property sales is closely related to the application of a transfer or registration duty on them, as shown in the last column of Table 12.2.[9] Clearly, rates vary greatly, ranging from 0 per cent on some transfers in South Africa to 15 per cent on various transfers in Cameroon, Central African Republic, Guinea, Mali, and Senegal. Sometimes, rates are differentiated depending on the value of the property or its location.

[9] In francophone African countries, the transfer duty is referred to as registration duty. Generally, the difference is one of name only, and so is the difference with the stamp duty which is levied on the sales price agreed to between the parties to the transaction or on the fair market value of the property.

Table 12.2 Africa: VAT treatment of immovable property, 2018

RECs and countries	Construction			Commercial property		Transfer duty (%)[a]
	Building materials	Repairs and maintenance	Newly created	Lease	Sale	
Southern African Development Community (SADC)						
SACU						
Botswana	T	T	T	T	T	5
Lesotho	Z/T	T	E/T	E	T	3/4
Namibia	Z	Z	Z	Z	Z	12
South Africa	T	T	T	T	T	0–12
Swaziland	T	T	T	T	T	2–6
Other						
Congo, DR	T	T	T	E	E	6
Madagascar	T	T	T	E	E	6
Malawi	Z/T	T	T	T	T	1.5
Mauritius	T	T	T	T	T	5/10
Mozambique	T	T	T	E	E	2/10 (+0.2)
Seychelles	T	E/T	E/T	T	T	5
Zambia	T	T	T	E	E	5
Zimbabwe	Z/T	T	T	T	T	1–4
East African Community (EAC)						
Burundi	T	T	T	E	E	3
Kenya	T	T	T	T	T	4/2
Rwanda	T	T	T	T	T	-
Tanzania	T	T	T	T	T	1
Uganda	T	T	T	T	T	..

Continued

Table 12.2 *Continued*

RECs and countries	Construction			Commercial property		Transfer duty (%)[a]
	Building materials	Repairs and maintenance	Newly created	Lease	Sale	
Economic and Monetary Community of Central Africa (CEMAC)						
Cameroon	T	T	T	E	E	5, 10, 15
Central Afr. Rep.	T	T	T	E	E	6, 7.5, 12, 15
Chad	E/T	T	T	E	E	3, 5, 10, 12.5
Congo	T	T	T	E	E	3, 10
Equatorial Guinea	T	T	T	E	E	3, 5, 10, 12.5
Gabon	T	T	T	E	E	6 (+2)
Economic Community of West African States (ECOWAS)						
UEMOA						
Benin	T	T	T	T	T	8
Burkina Faso	E/T	T	T	T	E	8
Côte d'Ivoire	E/T	E/T	E/T	E	E	7/7.5
Guinea-Bissau	T	T	T	E	E	5
Mali	T	T	T	E	E	15/7
Niger	T	T	T	E	E	5 (+3.5)
Senegal	T	T	T	E	E	15 (+0.8)
Togo	T	T	T	E	E	9
WAMZ						
Cabo Verde	T	T	T	E	E	1.5
Gambia	T	T	T	T	T	..
Ghana	T	T	T	E	E	0.25, 0.5, 1
Guinea	T	T	T	E	E	2, 5, 10, 15
Sierra Leone	T	T	T	E	E	Specific

Arab Maghreb Union (AMU)						
Algeria	L	L	L	E	E	5
Mauritania	T	T	T	E	E	1
Morocco	T	T	E/T	E	E	6
Tunisia	T	T	T	E	E	5 (+2/4)
Intergovernmental Authority on Development (IGAD) and Egypt						
Djibouti	Z/T	T	T	E	E	7/10
Egypt	L	L	L	T	T	2.5
Ethiopia	T	T	T	T	T	2
Sudan	T	T	T	T	T	-

[a] Including substitute *ad valorem* stamp duty.

Note: Letters have the following meaning: T = taxed at the standard rate; E = exempt; L = taxed at the lower rate; Z = taxed at the zero rate. In the last column, '-' means no transfer duty and '..' means information not available. The VAT interacts with the transfer duty on buildings and land, so a VAT exemption does not imply that no tax is levied.

Source: Appendix A. Some information may be incomplete or out of date.

Many countries waive the VAT if the transfer duty applies. The VAT legislation in the CEMAC countries does so explicitly. Viewed on their own, transfer taxes (and stamp duties on official documents related to transactions in immovable property) exhibit the same capricious effects as a cascading turnover tax: their burden increases the more often the property is sold. Also, the duties cause lock-in effects, since people will hold on to their property longer than they would in the absence of the duties; in other words, residential mobility suffers. Further, there is an element of double taxation if VAT as well as transfer duty applies—for instance, in the case of a newly built dwelling (subject to VAT) that is subsequently sold by its owner (subject to transfer duty). The discussion that follows explicitly addresses the interaction between VAT and transfer and other duties involving immovable property.

12.4 Directions for Reform

A review of the VAT treatment of immovable property in African countries should be used to move it closer to best practice. A more fundamental reform, which has been under consideration in South Africa, would replace the distortionary transfer taxes and stamp duties by a surrogate VAT on increases in the value of exempt properties realized upon their sale (Cnossen and Badenhorst, 2008).

Moving Closer to Best Practice

Important among the measures that would move the existing treatment of immovable property closer to best practice is the widest possible application of the standard rate to building land, construction, social housing, renovation, and repair. Lower-than-standard or zero rates distort consumer choices and tend to be ill-targeted measures to help the poor, promote property ownership, or boost employment in the construction sector. For example, the benefit of reduced rates on the renovation and repair of existing buildings may leak away and increase tax evasion. Similarly, a reduced or zero rate for new social housing that is partially or wholly financed by government can be replicated by an adjustment of the subsidy, which would block a potential avenue for tax evasion.

Although all best-practice VATs have capital goods schemes which adjust the VAT incorporated in the price of exempt property when bought for taxable purposes, the adjustment periods tend to be rather short (e.g. 10 years) in most countries. The shorter the adjustment period, the more tempting it becomes for exempt entities to establish a taxable business that buys the property and rents it out to an exempt entity. The business would credit the VAT on the purchase of the property against the VAT on the taxable rental charges, and would transfer the property VAT-free to the exempt entity after the prescribed adjustment period expires. An extension of the adjustment periods would forestall this form of tax avoidance.

Finally, there is much to be said for the adoption of the tax method (taxing all immovable property except the lease and sale of used residential property), which seems superior to the exemption approach (exempting all immovable property except if newly built) on the philosophy that exceptions to the first-best VAT treatment of immovable property should be formulated restrictively. The tax method does this by including changes in non-residential property values in the VAT base (if the property is used for taxable purposes), while the exemption method does not do so if no use is made of the registration option.[10] Since the reach of the tax method is greater than the reach of the exemption method, it results in more even-handed and neutral treatment.[11] Non-SACU countries should perhaps consider adopting the tax method.

Neither the tax method nor the exemption approach includes increases in the value of exempt property in the VAT base, although this would be desirable on neutrality grounds. The issue is particularly important regarding used residential property, but under either the tax method or the exemption approach it would also be relevant for used non-residential property sold by exempt entities to other exempt entities.

Margin Scheme and Transfer Duty

Apart from the revenue they raise—an important consideration but not at any cost—the only possible rationale for levying transfer, registration, or stamp duties on immovable property transactions between non-taxable persons is that they resemble a poorly designed surrogate VAT on the increase in rents and rental values associated with increases in property values. But if this is the rationale, the base of the transfer duty should be redefined as the difference between the selling price and the purchase price (or some proxy if information on the purchase price is not available) of immovable property traded between non-taxable persons. This difference (or margin), which reflects the present value of the increase in anticipated future building services, should be included in the VAT base and taxed at the standard rate, at the level of either the seller or the buyer of the property through a reverse charge. Essentially all transactions in immovable property

[10] Note that both methods would have the same effect if all registered persons opted for taxation of non-residential property under the exemption approach.

[11] Administratively, however, the tax method is more likely to involve contentious issues about splitting property into residential and non-residential use (e.g. a lawyer having an office at his home), which would occur less often under the exemption method. However, in most countries, the income tax rules can be used to solve the problem. This is done in Canada, for instance; see Alarie and Gendron (2011).

between non-taxable persons should be subject to the reformed transfer duty, including those by or between governments and non-profit organizations. Also, the increase in value should be taxed if immovable property passes on to heirs and legatees; after all, title passes on too.

The proposed margin scheme for transactions in exempt immovable property could be incorporated in the VAT (and the transfer duty abolished), or it might continue to be called transfer duty while retaining the tax collection procedures (for exempt persons, such as individuals and non-registered entities) currently on the transfer duty statutes. Since the new transfer duty should be levied in close cooperation with the immovable property registrar's office, retention of the transfer duty mechanism for assessing and collecting the new tax is probably to be preferred.

The exact design of the new transfer duty in an individual country would depend on the nature of the existing transfer, registration, or stamp duty regime, but some common issues can be identified. The most important issue would be to ascertain the acquisition value of properties in order to compute the taxable margin. Most properties would have been bought many years ago, possibly even before the introduction of the VAT. Subjecting the value increases of these properties to the new duty might be viewed as a form of expropriation and would ignore the impact of the alternative taxes levied previously. The issue is akin to the taxation of land upon the introduction of the GST in Australia and New Zealand, and the solution might be similar: do not tax the full value (increase) when the property is sold by exempt persons to taxable persons but only the presumptively determined margin (and subsequent increases in value).

The new transfer duty should be refunded if the property is sold below its acquisition value. The future value of the housing services embodied in the property has declined and so has the value of future consumption. The refund would be calculated on the difference between the selling price and the (presumptive) acquisition price, but only if VAT has been paid at the time of construction. In practice, the refund issue is unlikely to arise because, as a cash-flow tax, the VAT is based on nominal, not real, values of properties actually sold. Further, much can be said for a credit against the new transfer duty for any VAT paid on major renovations that have increased the value of the property. Currently, these renovations are taxed twice, under the VAT as well as the transfer duty. On feasibility grounds, a minimum would have to be prescribed for the size of renovations (expressed, for instance, in terms of the property's value), while the eligibility for the credit should be limited to a specified period immediately preceding the sale.

The redesigned transfer duty resembles a capital gains tax, but it is not one despite appearances. The difference is that taxable capital gains represent an *ex post* adjustment for past accruals of income. Ideally, income tax should be imposed as the gain accrues rather than upon realization. Accordingly, it would be appropriate to levy tax on the interest over the period during which the gain accrued. By contrast, the VAT on the increase in value added should be considered an *ex ante* tax on the discounted present value of anticipated future housing services. Interest or indexing arrangements would therefore seem inappropriate. True, the owner-occupier who sells his house has benefitted from not having had to pay more VAT after he bought the dwelling, but this fortuitous result is inherent to a cash-flow consumption tax under which the VAT on durable consumer goods is prepaid rather than imposed as the services of the durable goods are consumed. Moreover, the owner would not have received a credit for the VAT paid on repair services, which maintain the value of the property. Some imperfection has to be accepted here in the interest of feasibility.

The proposed margin scheme is found in some countries and has also been discussed in the literature. New Zealand and Australia, for instance, apply the scheme to land or increases in business property values and have done so since the introduction of the VAT. Ebrill et al. (2001) have argued that the value increase should be included in the VAT base, but do not consider this practicable for owner-occupied property. Others favour the taxation of value increases of exempt immovable property, but want to apply the scheme in full, going back to before the introduction of the VAT (Poddar, 2010).

Finally, a detailed margin scheme has been proposed for housing in South Africa in lieu of the transfer duty (Cnossen and Badenhorst, 2008). VAT would be levied on the difference between the selling price and the purchase price (presumptively determined) of exempt properties, net of, ideally, the cost of subsequent renovations, which are capitalized in the value of the property (and on which VAT has been paid). The VAT on the margin would replace the distortionary transfer and stamp duties. In the meantime, South Africa has abolished stamp duties—a major improvement—but the transfer duty is still being levied if VAT is not charged.

12.5 Recapitulation of Policy Proposals

If the tax method and the margin scheme were adopted, the present and proposed application of VAT to transactions in immovable property could be summarized for most African countries as follows:

- As at present, sales of immovable property between taxable persons are considered 'normal transactions', i.e. VAT is imposed by the seller and a tax credit is available to the buyer.
- Currently, sales of immovable property by taxable persons to non-taxable persons also attract VAT (which is included in the sale price) in the normal way, although the purchaser, not being a taxable person, cannot take credit for the VAT.

- Sales of immovable property by non-taxable persons to taxable persons attract VAT under the capital goods scheme, which entitles the buyer to a notional VAT credit if he opts for taxation or is subject to the tax method.
- Sales of immovable property by non-taxable persons to other non-taxable persons should be made subject to a reformed transfer duty—i.e. a surrogate VAT—on the increase (or decrease) in the value of the property.

These transactions would all be subject to VAT (or transfer duty) and no other transactions taxes would apply, but the new approach would not preclude the (annual) taxation of the ownership or use of immovable property (on benefit-received grounds) or, for that matter, the imposition of net wealth taxes, estate duties, and gift taxes.

13
Financial Services

13.1 VAT's 'Last Frontier'

The appropriate treatment of financial services is the single most important design issue that remains to be solved under the VAT. While conceptual and feasibility issues regarding public sector bodies and immovable property have been solved (albeit not always implemented), conventional wisdom holds that margin-based financial services, as opposed to fee-based services, cannot be included in the VAT base calculated on the tax credit method, because the intermediation charge which should be taxed cannot be separated from the pure interest rate, premium, or rate of return which should not be taxed. For this reason, most countries with a VAT exempt financial services entirely, whether margin-based or fee-based.[1]

The exemption of financial services means that financial institutions incur VAT on their inputs, but cannot charge VAT on their output of financial services. As a result, individual consumers (and other end users) of such services face effective tax rates that differ from statutory rates, distorting their choice vis-à-vis fully taxed goods and services. Generally, their consumption of financial services would be undertaxed. What is probably worse, the input VAT incurred by financial institutions cannot be passed on to VAT-registered business users of financial services, which are unable therefore to take credit for it against their VAT on sales. This means that they tend to be overtaxed. Clearly, this state of affairs is unsatisfactory. In many countries, the finance industry contributes nearly 10 per cent to GDP, which is too large an activity to be ignored under a broadly-based VAT. Faced with this situation, various attempts have been made, in practice and in the tax literature, to limit the reach of the exemption and/or to mitigate its cascading effects.

This chapter reviews the issues and the options. To begin with, financial services are defined. This is followed by a brief review of the selective taxes, not

[1] In the early 2000s, there was a short but intense debate about the fundamental question of whether financial services should be in the VAT base, at least conceptually. Grubert and Mackie (2000) and Jack (2000) argued that they should not be taxed. In response, however, Auerbach and Gordon (2002) showed persuasively that financial services facilitated the purchase of goods and services and that the VAT would leave relative consumer prices unchanged if and only if the financial services were subject to tax, with credit being given for VAT on inputs. Accordingly, the prevailing view that has emerged in the last five years—when arguments to the contrary ceased to appear—is that such services should form part of a broad-based consumption tax. For a recent review of the arguments, see Grubert and Krever (2013).

based on value added, that some African countries impose on financial services. These taxes exhibit cumulative effects that violate the neutrality criterion of a broad-based consumption tax, such as the VAT. Subsequently, it is explained in some detail why it is so difficult, conceptually, to include margin-based financial services in the base of a tax-credit VAT. Their inevitable exemption follows the early (and present) practice in the EU, also adopted by most African countries, whose main features are then described.

To limit the effects of the rather broad EU type of exemption, two kinds of modifications have been adopted. First, the reach of the full exemption has been narrowed down by taxing fee-based financial services, which means that more input tax is creditable by business users of financial services and that consumers are more fully taxed. Second, the cascading effects of the exemption have been mitigated by zero-rating the provision of financial services to registered businesses, providing for partial input VAT recovery, or by permitting financial services providers to opt for taxation. Further, financial services can be taxed under the accounts-based subtraction or addition methods of ascertaining value added, to which some countries have resorted. Finally, an ingenious cash-flow method of taxing financial services and a reverse-charging approach have been developed in the tax literature—more fundamental modifications, which are also briefly reviewed. The chapter concludes by drawing some lessons from the analysis which may be useful for African countries that wish to review the treatment of financial services under their VAT.

13.2 Categories of Financial Services

Financial services include a broad range of services rendered by financial institutions, such as banks and brokerage and insurance companies. What is often (and loosely) called 'financial services' really refers to financial intermediation services. These services usually fall into one of the five categories, as set out by Poddar (2003), in Table 13.1. The first four categories are the subject of discussion in this chapter. Insurance is dealt with in the next chapter, where it is shown that property and casualty insurance can be included in the base of a tax-credit VAT, be it in a somewhat roundabout way, and that life insurance can be taxed, if desired, under the addition method of calculating VAT.

In addition to the distinction by type of service, Poddar (2003) distinguishes financial services by type of provider, by economic function, by the form of service provided, and by the nature of the consideration. The distinction by type of provider—e.g. between commercial and saving banks—is only workable if a particular activity is regulated and assigned to a financial institution of a particular type. Deregulation and disintermediation have made this distinction largely superfluous. More useful, particularly for analytical purposes, is the distinction

Table 13.1 Main categories of financial services

1. **Deposits, borrowing, and lending**
   a. Banking operations
   b. Credit card operations
2. **Purchase, sale, and issuance of financial securities**
   a. Bonds, shares, options, guarantees, and foreign currencies
   b. Gold and precious metals
3. **Brokerage and other agent services**
   a. Buying and selling of financial securities
   b. Underwriting and other transactions where agents act as principals
4. **Advisory, management, and data-processing services**
   a. Asset management and investment advice
   b. Administrative and information services, incidental or supplementary to financial services
   c. Other
5. **Insurance**
   a. Property and casualty
   b. Life and health

Source: Poddar, 2003.

by economic function. Thus, financial institutions intermediate between borrowers and lenders, pool savings and risks, provide liquidity, transact clearing services, create and make markets, and perform agency services.

Economically, risk pooling is one of the important functions of financial institutions. Indeed, in Canada, the presence of financial risk is used as an important determinant for distinguishing exempt financial services from taxable non-financial services. Risk also features in distinguishing principals from agents in transacting financial services. Principals enter into financial contracts under their own name and at their own risk. Agents, on the other hand, act on behalf of principals, who continue to bear the risk for the transaction. Often, both roles are performed by the same person or institution. An investment broker, for instance, may act as an agent for his clients, but may also engage in financial transactions as a principal, i.e. on his own behalf.

The distinction between principals and agents is also relevant for the nature of the consideration. Generally, agents will work for an explicit fee or commission, which is relatively easy to tax under a VAT. The remuneration for principals, on the other hand, comes in the form of a financial margin, which represents a consideration for a bundle of transactions. In the case of banks, for instance, the margin will represent the payment of interest, a risk premium, and an intermediation service. Of these elements, only the consideration for intermediation services should be taxable, but it is generally impossible to separate it from the interest and the risk premium. The fact that many financial service activities are remunerated by margins turns out to be critical for the applicability of VAT. The multiplicity of the services also suggests difficult definitional and delineation problems in determining the proper treatment.

13.3 How Are Financial Services Taxed in African Countries?

Before discussing the VAT treatment of financial services, it may be instructive to review current practices in African countries. While all countries on the continent exempt financial services under their VAT, various countries, particularly those with a francophone taxing background, impose separate taxes on a variety of financial activities.[2]

Table 13.2 provides details of taxes on banking activities in eight francophone African countries for which data could be found. The activities that are taxed are quite diverse. The Congo imposes a low-rate tax on money transfers, but most countries tax the fees, commissions, or charges related to financial activities, as would the VAT. Mali and Togo appear to tax net revenue or gross profits of banks, an accounts- rather than transactions-based approach. Côte d'Ivoire differentiates the tax rate by the size of the enterprise and Guinea by the period for which the loan is taken out, and Mali and Senegal apply a lower rate to export-related transactions. In Guinea, Mali, Senegal, and Togo, the tax on banking activities is deductible in ascertaining corporate profits, which should mitigate its distortionary impact. Loans to governments, interbank transactions, and services by leasing companies tend to be exempted.

Although this review is rather sketchy, a few observations can be made. Judged overall, taxes on banking activities apply rather unevenly within as well as between countries. No doubt, too, definitional problems abound, exacerbated by rate differences and exemptions. Nearly all charges are in the nature of turnover taxes: suppliers cannot recover tax embodied in inputs and customers cannot take credit for tax on purchases of financial services. The size of the distortions caused by these types of taxes increases with the square of the tax rate, which may be as high as 17 per cent. As discussed below, it is far preferable to apply VAT on fees and commissions and let financial institutions claim credit for the VAT on inputs apportioned to taxable activities. But first a more fundamental analysis and broader discussion of the issues and options are in order.

13.4 Difficulties in Taxing Financial Services under the VAT

To better understand the issues and options for bringing financial activities into the VAT base, it is useful to dwell briefly on the role of financial institutions.

[2] In addition, most African countries (francophone, anglophone, or lusophone) impose anachronistic stamp duties on a large number of financial instruments and documents, but these are not discussed here.

Table 13.2 Taxes on banking activities in francophone African countries, 2018

Country	Tax base	Exemptions	Rates
Central African Republic	Commissions from international transactions of banks and other agents		10%
Congo	Money transfers (gross amount)	Diplomatic personnel, scholarship payments, loans for specified investment programmes	1%
Côte d'Ivoire	Bank charges (fees, commissions, rents)	Services by leasing companies, interbank charges, interest and bank charges on loans for low-cost housing and small farmers	10%, but 5% for small and medium-sized enterprises
Guinea	Financial activities (interest, commissions)	Transactions not specifically linked to the money trade, interbank transactions, financial consultations, accountants' fees, leasing and other transactions subject to VAT	13%, but 5% on loans for more than one year; deductible for corporate income tax purposes
Mali	Revenue from financial transactions	Leasing agreements	17%, but 15% for export financing; deductible for corporate income tax purposes
Mauritania	Interest, commission, other forms of compensation	Premiums for cash discount operations and loans by foreign banks, interest on interbank loans and loans from specific financial institutions or to the state, profits from foreign exchange transactions	14%
Senegal	Banking activities (interest, fees, commissions)	Residential mortgage loans, loans to businesses in Industrial Free Zones	17%, but 7% on export-related transactions; deductible for corporate income tax purposes
Togo	Financial activities (gross profits)	Purely financial transactions, exchange operations	10%; deductible for corporate income tax purposes

Source: International Bureau of Fiscal Documentation (2018) and IMF Tax Summaries in Staff Reports of various years. Some information may be out of date or incomplete.

Financial institutions facilitate the flow of funds from savers and lenders to investors and borrowers, and vice versa. For instance, banks, to which this discussion is confined, bring together depositors and borrowers with different preferences regarding the location, timing, and duration of financial transactions. Banks 'buy' the use of money from depositors against a charge, called interest. They mix this money with the funds received from other depositors and 'sell' it to borrowers against a higher charge, also called interest.

Obviously, it would not be appropriate to tax the full amounts of these transactions. The principal amounts should not be taxed since they are merely transfers of funds and do not represent consumption. Also, the pure rate of interest and the risk premium should not be taxed since they are the depositor's reward for postponing consumption and the bank's reward for bearing the lending risk, respectively—i.e. they are forms of income, not consumption. Only the intermediation charge—i.e. the spread between the interest charged to borrowers and the interest paid to depositors—represents the cost of the intermediation services provided by banks. This cost consists of cheque services, risk pooling, the provision of scale economies, and other such services (Henderson, 1988).

The fundamental problem is that the intermediation charge is embedded in the interest rate and is hence unknown with respect to margin-based financial services. In essence, depositors receive a rate of interest that is lower than the pure rate of interest and borrowers pay a higher rate of interest than the pure rate of time discount. The inability to separate the intermediation charge from the pure rate of interest makes it difficult to tax the charge without also taxing the interest.[3] By taxing the net interest, neutrality would be achieved in transactions between registered VAT payers, because the tax on the pure rate of interest and the risk premium charged by the bank would be cancelled out by the tax credit at the registered business level.[4]

The same cannot be said for transactions between banks and households. The problem is not that all households with a bank account would have to be registered for VAT purposes. This can be circumvented by requiring banks to collect and remit the tax owing by depositors under some kind of reverse-charge mechanism (Hoffman, Poddar, and Whalley, 1987). The banks would then issue themselves an invoice for the VAT on the net interest and treat this as a creditable input tax. However, this approach drives a wedge between the pure rate of interest received by the depositor and the pure rate of interest paid by the borrower. The intertemporal distortion can be avoided by permitting banks to calculate a notional input

[3] Of course, there is also the problem of allocating the intermediation charge between the depositor and the borrower.

[4] At one time, Argentina taxed gross interest on most loans under its VAT, at about half the standard rate. Not only does this overstate value added, but, in the absence of a tax-credit feature, it also resulted in cascading effects for business users of financial services. Actually, the tax had little, if anything, to do with the VAT, but was intended to curb borrowing in order to reduce inflation. Consistent with the macroeconomic policy objective, interest on deposits was exempt. See Schenk and Zee (2004).

tax credit for interest paid. But this would move us back to square one. Instead of having to calculate the VAT on an indistinguishable intermediation charge, the bank would have to calculate the tax on the pure rate of interest—which is equally indistinguishable from the net interest.

A way out of the dilemma would be to zero-rate the provision of financial services. Under this approach, banks would register for VAT purposes and be reimbursed for the tax incurred on inputs.[5] This would solve the cascading effect with respect to the business sector, but would be a form of 'overkill' with respect to financial services provided to consumers, which should be taxed in full. While it might be defensible to zero-rate services relating to saving, it would clearly be inappropriate not to tax services related to consumer loans and cheque accounts. Moreover, banks also provide a variety of other services relating to, say, financial advice, real estate, and travel, which should be taxed in any case.

All the problems associated with exemptions (see Chapter 9) apply in the case of financial services: distortion of input choice, self-supply bias, cascading, discrimination against exports and in favour of imports, and administrative and compliance difficulties regarding the allocation of input VAT between exempt and taxable transactions. As noted by Gendron (2008), these complications are likely to be large because a typical supply of financial services may bundle various types of supply, each with its own margin, and it may be nigh impossible to unbundle those services and price them appropriately for VAT purposes. Further, financial services may embody some services that are exempt and some that are taxable. For instance, taxable ancillary services (e.g. accounting and tax advice, or data processing) must be delineated from exempt core services and the input tax apportioned accordingly. Also, the data that would be needed to carve out intermediation charges in typical margin transactions are generally unavailable because financial institutions are unwilling to reveal such charges, for competition reasons.

In conclusion, it is difficult to extract the intermediation element from a typical margin transaction in a way that is consistent with the application of an invoice tax-credit VAT levied on a transaction-by-transaction basis. The blanket exemption of financial services in place in many countries sidesteps the problem by exempting not only margin services but also fee-based services that could be taxed. The conventional analysis of the exemption suggests that the resulting partial taxation of financial services (using inputs as the tax base) undertaxes final consumers and overtaxes businesses relative to the true consumption base. Before discussing a number of alternatives to the blanket exemption of financial services, the EU's approach, on which most current practices in Africa are based, is examined in some detail.

[5] Québec, a Canadian province that used to have its own VAT distinct from the federal GST, used to zero-rate financial services, but its approach fell short of pure zero-rating since a compensatory tax was imposed on payroll and assets, and input VAT credits on purchases of certain business inputs were denied.

13.5 The EU's Exemption Approach

In view of the difficulties discussed above, most countries in Africa with a VAT exempt financial services. In doing so, these countries generally follow the distinction that the EU's Common VAT Directive (2006, article 135(1)(b)–(g)) makes between 'core' services and 'secondary' services. The exempt core services include transactions in money, stocks, and other securities, the operation of current and deposit accounts, lending money and advancing credit, and the management of special investment funds. Importantly, related intermediary services are also exempt, as well as, in some cases, management services linked to the financial activity. The taxable secondary services, for which an explicit charge is made, include financial advice, debt collection, the rental of safe-deposit boxes, and the keeping of securities. Most countries zero-rate financial services supplied to third countries. So does the EU, but not with regard to financial transactions between member states (article 169).

Definitions

In sketching the issues and outlining the options, it seems useful to dwell briefly on the definition of financial services that are exempted under the EU's Common Directive and which can also be found in most African VAT legislations.[6] In addition, some recent developments in the EU are discussed—all to illustrate the minefield of complexities around the VAT treatment of financial services.

> **Coins and bank notes**, defined as '*transactions, including negotiation, concerning currency, bank notes and coins used as legal tender, with the exception of collectors' items, that is to say, gold, silver or other metal coins or bank notes which are not normally used as legal tender or coins of numismatic interest*'.

This provision has not given rise to much litigation in the EU. Theoretically, the exemption should probably be considered an anomaly, because by definition the transfer of money cannot be considered consumption. In the EU, the minting of coins and the printing of money are either exempt because the activities are performed by government as such, or are zero-rated (UK). Generally, transactions in gold are subject to VAT, except in transactions with the member state's central bank or the European Central Bank, in which cases the zero rate applies.

[6] For a useful succinct discussion of the financial services exemption in the EU, with many references to the European Court of Justice's case law, see Henkow (2008, ch. 4). Henkow notes that the rationale for the exemption appears to rest on pragmatic considerations (defining the taxable amount) and the (dubious) argument that taxation would increase the cost of consumer credit and interfere with the workings of the capital market. The fact that financial services were exempt (i.e. input taxed) under the turnover taxes preceding the VAT was also taken into account.

Sales of collectors' items by taxable persons are subject to the standard VAT rate applied to the difference between the sale price and the purchase price. Taxation of the full price of these 'used' goods might cause unwarranted cumulation of tax and divert the trade to private channels. The Common Directive harmonizes the treatment of collectors' items and other used goods in the EU by prescribing the application of the standard rate to the gross margin without a credit for input tax. Further, exports of used goods are not zero-rated and imports are not taxed.

> **Payment activities**, defined as '*transactions, including negotiation, concerning deposit and current accounts, payments, transfers, debts, cheques and other negotiable instruments, but excluding debt collection*'.

This exemption covers all services related to the opening and closing of financial accounts, postings to such accounts, the preparation and issue of financial statements and documents, etc. Courts have ruled that the provision should be interpreted restrictively. The installation of automatic payment facilities, for instance, would be subject to the regular VAT. Gift and value coupons that entitle the holder to a payment in money or a discount upon the purchase of specified goods, such as books or CDs, are taxable at the time of issue.

Activities related to debt collection (usually against a fee or percentage of the amount owed) are not exempt. In all member states, debt collection is interpreted as the performance of an indivisible sequence of activities to ensure the payment of an outstanding debt and not as the mere receipt of money or cheques. Factoring (a type of debtor finance in which a business sells its accounts receivable to a third party at a discount) used to be excluded from the exemption along with debt collection, but has been deleted from the text. Genuine factoring involves the taking over of the payment risk from the person who originally issued the invoice. The transfer of the debt is then exempt, as are the subsequent collection activities of the factorer. Non-genuine factoring occurs when the original creditor retains the payment risk. In the event, the collection and administrative activities on behalf of the creditor are taxable as debt collection.

Somewhat different positions have also been taken with respect to the treatment of 'plastic money'—notably, credit cards. Generally, services supplied to cardholders are considered exempt payment activities or the exempt granting of credit. The fee charged by credit card organizations to traders, however, is taxable. Various attempts to label the transactions as a form of (genuine) factoring, which would be exempt, foundered in the British courts.[7]

> **Credit transactions**, defined as '*the granting and the negotiation of credit and the management of credit by the person granting it*' and '*the negotiation of or any dealings in credit guarantees or any other security for money and the management of credit guarantees by the person who is granting the credit*'.

[7] For an interesting exposé of the VAT treatment of credit card services, see Grubert and Krever (2013).

The term 'credit' is broadly interpreted. It covers loans, but also extensions of payment credits (suppliers' credits) and payments in advance (customers' credit). Normally, VAT is due when goods and services are supplied. Thus VAT is due immediately on supplies under a hire-purchase contract or an instalment sale, but the tax applies to the price exclusive of interest, if shown separately (except in France, where the interest is taxable if the credit transaction is linked to the taxable supply[8]). The treatment of financial leases is similar to that of hire purchases, but operational leases, which are considered a continuous rental service, are taxable on the amount of the periodic 'rental' payment. Discounts for advance payments or for payments in cash are not taxable. In all member states, the exemption for credit activities comprises not only interest, but also the costs incidental to the conclusion and prolongation of the credit. The tax on inputs of these activities is therefore not creditable. This applies also to any dealings in credit guarantees or any other security for money.

> **Securities**, defined as '*transactions, including negotiation but not management or safekeeping, in shares, interests in companies or associations, debentures and other securities, but excluding documents establishing title to goods, and the rights or securities referred to in Article 15(2)* [rights or interests in immovable property which may be regarded as tangible property]' and '*management of special investment funds as defined by Member States*'.

The exemption, which is to be interpreted restrictively, does not comprise financial advice, market research, or similar activities that are not directly related to dealings in securities. The management and safekeeping of securities are taxable in the EU, analogous to the rental of safe-deposit boxes. In contrast, the management of special investment funds is exempt (although estate planning advice is taxable). The rationale for this exemption is unclear. Perhaps the objective is to provide equal treatment vis-à-vis securities or money deposits held by individuals. To add to the complexity, mutual fund management is taxable, as is portfolio management with buy/sell discretion to the investor, but not non-discretionary management.

Evaluation

This summary conveys that it is not easy to define the scope of the exemption for financial services. The supply of financial services per se brings in its train various complementary or component services, such as legal, accounting, and tax advice, which, if supplied independently, are taxable. Segregating these taxable elements

[8] Thus, in France, these transactions are treated on a par with payment credits involving an interest charge extended by retailers and manufacturers when goods are sold to consumers. In contrast to the interest charged by banks, the interest charged by retailers and manufacturers and included in the selling price is subject to VAT.

from pure financial transactions is difficult, to put it mildly. If the complementary services are also exempted, financial institutions would be induced to provide them 'in-house' rather than purchasing them from specialized traders, which would give rise to a non-creditable input VAT. Equal treatment between financial institutions and between such institutions and specialized traders is difficult to achieve in practice.

Another complication is the apportionment of the input tax between taxable supplies (including zero-rated exports and supplies related to exports) and exempt supplies. In the EU, financial institutions can use a variety of methods for apportionment purposes, including the turnover basis, the direct attribution rule, and other bases, such as floor area or computer time. A *de minimis* rule below which no recognition of exempt use is required is also allowed. The turnover basis is the most widely used apportionment basis. It divides the tax on inputs into deductible and non-deductible amounts in the same proportion as taxable (including zero-rated) and exempt supplies bear to total turnover. Usually, the apportionment is based on the previous year's turnover, with an annual year-end reconciliation.

Perhaps surprisingly, the exemption of financial services causes few complaints in the EU. One reason may be that some member states permit financial institutions to use the gross margin, i.e. the difference between lending revenues and borrowing costs, instead of total lending revenues as the denominator in the apportionment formula. This 'bankers' method' significantly increases the amount of deductible tax.[9] Another way to manipulate the turnover method is to artificially increase the level of taxable supplies by transacting a small number of high-value zero-rated transactions, such as in gold (Organization for Economic Cooperation and Development, 1988). This situation should diminish the appetite for reform among business users of financial services. As Huizinga (2002, p. 516) concludes, 'tax administrations currently provide banks with almost full VAT input credits—against the spirit of the exemption system'.[10]

European Commission's 2007 'Three Pillars' Proposal

The European Commission (2007a, 2007b, 2007c) presented two legislative proposals in 2007 to amend the EU VAT treatment of financial services and insurance. The objective of the proposals was twofold: first, to enhance the

[9] At the request of the European Commission (2007a), PricewaterhouseCoopers (2006) studied 22 financial services providers and found that between 0% and 74% of VAT on inputs was recovered, depending, among others, on the location of the provider and the nature of the customer base. The average recovery rate was 20.7%. Also, De la Feria and Lockwood (2010) have estimated that the irrecoverable VAT is 0.5% of total tax revenue or less in France, Germany, Italy, the Netherlands, and Spain, and 0.86% in the UK, which has a very large financial sector.

[10] Buettner and Erbe (2014) estimate that repealing the German exemption for financial services would increase revenue by some €1.7 billion or 1.3% of VAT revenue and yield a modest welfare gain of about €1 billion or 0.04% of GDP.

functioning of capital markets; and second, to improve the competitiveness of European financial institutions on the international stage. The objectives were intended to be met through the following so-called 'three pillars':

- *Pillar* 1—clarification of the rules governing the exemption for financial supplies, in particular the redefinition of financial services that are subject to exemption. New forms of financial products and new supply structures have made the field increasingly complex, making it extremely difficult to determine whether a particular service is exempt or taxable (De la Feria, 2007). Clarification would be achieved by amending the interpretative guidelines and issuing separate, ancillary lists of exempt and taxable services.
- *Pillar* 2—clarification of the legislative framework of cost-sharing groups engaging in financial and insurance services by allowing economic operators to pool investments and redistribute the cost of these investments to members of the group without being subject to VAT. An incidental, if welcome, effect of cost sharing is that it would remove the self-supply bias that would arise if individual members of the group continued to manage their own affairs. However, it has been pointed out by De la Feria and Lockwood (2010) that this may only be true for small financial operators, which already tend to make use of outsourcing opportunities.
- *Pillar* 3—introduction of a compulsory option to tax, i.e. compulsory for member states to allow taxation but optional for financial institutions to opt in for taxation.[11] The European Commission (2008) has suggested that the option should apply to B2B as well as B2C transactions, be available on a transaction-by-transaction basis, and not be subject to time limits. In their commentary on the Commission's proposal, De la Feria and Lockwood (2010, p. 185) opine that, 'if firms do not or cannot coordinate their behaviour, opting to tax is profitable for the firm if and only if a transaction is B2B, i.e. a sale to a taxable person who can reclaim the VAT'.

De la Feria and Lockwood (2010, p. 171) conclude that the first and second pillars 'would give rise to considerable interpretative and qualification problems, resulting in as much complexity and legal uncertainty as the current [exempt] regime'. Pillars 1 and 3 have been used elsewhere before.[12] For instance, Canada has slowly implemented Pillar 1 over time and this has barely made a dent in the extent of the exemption. Pillar 3 has been tried in its purely optional version without any EU-wide standard (see Section 13.7). Pillar 2 has been tried in other VAT contexts in Australia and in transfer pricing contexts, in the form of cost-sharing arrangements. Such groups are never simple to administer, however, and it is hard

[11] Currently, article 137(a) of the Common Directive allows taxable persons a right to opt for taxation in respect of financial transactions, except insurance transactions.

[12] The information in this paragraph has been communicated to me by Pierre-Pascal Gendron.

to see how they could contribute to enhancing the functioning of capital markets. One may assume that sophisticated financial institutions would have taken advantage of such methods on their own to reduce costs. Presumably, all three pillars taken together will do little to mitigate in any significant way the adverse impacts of the blanket exemption of financial services in the EU.

In short, not being able to tax financial transactions properly under a tax-credit VAT violates the neutrality criterion and involves a degree of administrative and taxpayer discretion that should be alien to a good tax. Business use of financial services is overtaxed and individual consumer use undertaxed. Since higher-income people tend to consume more financial services than lower-income people, the distribution of the benefit of the exemption tends to be regressive with respect to income. Not surprisingly, as discussed in the next two sections, efforts have been made to tax financial services more fully on a value-added basis by narrowing the application of the exemption or by mitigating its cascading effects.[13]

In discussing various modifications or alternatives to the tax credit method, the criteria that should be heeded in evaluating them are the following (Poddar, 2003):

- the taxable base of financial services should be confined to or approximate the value of the intermediation service; inclusion of the pure rate of interest and the risk premium violates the basic tenet of a consumption tax;
- taxing financial services more fully than under the exemption system should not lead to an increase in cascading; VAT-registered users of taxable financial services should not be burdened by the tax;
- this having been said, a broader coverage of financial services is desirable, because the exemption itself is a source of economic distortions and discrimination; and
- new approaches should not involve undue increases in compliance and administration costs, including behavioural changes and tax avoidance activities.

13.6 Taxing What Can Be Taxed

One obvious way to narrow the exemption approach entails the full taxation of all agency services remunerated by fees and commissions, while restricting the exemption to margin services performed by principals. According to Poddar (2003) due to disintermediation and the unbundling of prices for financial products and services, fees and commissions have come to account for as much as 70–80 per cent of financial institutions' total revenues. If so, taxing all fees and commissions

[13] For an early, pioneering analysis of the various alternatives, see Bakker and Chronican (1985); for another early examination, see Edgar (2001); and for a comparison between the EU and the Australian approach, see De la Feria and Walpole (2009).

would substantially narrow the scope of the exemption for financial services. Currently, Australia and Singapore tax agency services and restrict the exemption to transactions performed by principals.[14] In Singapore, for instance, taxable services include brokerage for executive transactions for the sale of securities on behalf of customers, brokerage for life or general (non-life) insurance, general insurance premiums, and merchant banks' fees for corporate restructuring.

It is instructive to consider what some African countries have done recently in this regard. South Africa has taken a practical approach to the problem by subjecting all fee-based financial services to VAT. Examples of services thus captured include: currency exchange transactions; transactions involving cheques, letters of credit, or debt, equity, or participatory securities; and some credit transactions. Botswana and Namibia appear to have followed the South African approach in taxing fee-based financial services. In 2011, the government of Malawi indicated its intention to make some financial services fees taxable under VAT, but refrained from following this up with actual legislation. Under its reformed 2015 VAT Act, Tanzania exempts financial services supplied free of charge, by implication taxing fee-based services. An evaluation of its experience is not yet in.

In 2013, Ghana started charging VAT on supplies of a broad range of fee-based services. Table 13.3 shows the list of taxable financial services issued by the Ghana Revenue Authority. Unfortunately, the measure led to so much confusion and misunderstanding that the imposition was suspended in 2017. Reportedly, the government could have worked more closely with institutions in the financial sector to develop the list of taxable (as well as exempt and zero-rated) services rendered by banks. The same collaborative process should yield a standardized method to apportion VAT credits—required by the existence of mixed supplies consisting of taxable fee-based services and exempt margin-based services.

An old criticism of the South African method and similar variants in use in Australia and Singapore, never substantiated by convincing evidence, is that financial institutions may respond to the introduction of the application of VAT to fees by converting fee- and commission-based services into services remunerated by margins. In fact, there are usually good economic reasons for remunerating different services differently, so it is not clear that changing the VAT treatment would change the fee structure. Competitive conditions in output markets often place hard constraints on institutions' ability to effect such conversions. Registered businesses, moreover, may push for fee-based financial services in order to be able to obtain a credit for the VAT on the financial institution's taxable inputs. In short, it appears that the South African method is a good starting point to begin taxing financial services more fully.[15] At the same time, cascading effects can be reduced by an option permitting financial institutions to extend the VAT to

[14] For accounts of the Australian and Singaporean situations, see Jenkins and Khadka (1998).
[15] See Gendron (2016), on whose work this paragraph draws.

Table 13.3 Ghana: VAT on financial services fees, commissions, and similar charges

1.	Current accounts (foreign/local)—corporate bodies only
2.	Bank drafts (payment orders)
3.	Stopped cheques
4.	Returned cheques
5.	Commission on turnover (corporate bodies only)
6.	Overdraft processing or renewal fees
7.	Revolving acceptance fees
8.	Arrangement fees for facilities
9.	Statements and certificates of balance
10.	Clearing charges
11.	Cheques for collection
12.	Standing orders
13.	Telephone banking
14.	Safe custody
15.	Chequebooks: sale of cheque leaflets, replacement of lost chequebooks
16.	Debit cards and credit cards
17.	Revolving credits
18.	Collateral management
19.	Transfer of documents to other banks
20.	Guarantees/bonds/tender/performance
21.	Requests for forex drafts
22.	Outward transfers: SWIFT/telex, draft/money orders—customer
23.	Traveller's cheques, drafts
24.	Cheque lodgements (for corporate bodies and third parties only)
25.	Evacuation fees (cash-in-transit)
26.	Unpaid standing orders
27.	Closure of accounts
28.	Remote banking services: online banking, e-statements, e-clients, phone banking, SMS banking, mobile banking (monthly subscriptions, financial transaction fees)
29.	Lending fees: commitment fees (arrangement fees, processing fees, facility fees), processing fees, property valuation fees (open market value), guarantee commission, bid security, bank credit letters (letters of intent), mobilization guarantees, retention guarantees, performance bonds (default or restructured)
30.	Other loans, excluding salary advances: arrangement fees, new loans, top-ups, early settlement fees
31.	Letters of credit (imports): establishment commission (arrangement fees, presentations under letter-of-credit drawings), amendments (increase in amount, extension of period, discrepancy)
32.	Documentary bills for collection (imports): handling charges—customers, negotiation commission (advice of fate, bills deleted, protest), payment commission (holding charges), prior approval—customers with own resources (telex/cable charges, swap charges) and customers allocated funds from banks (exchange, telex/cable charges)

Source: Energybank, final list of taxable financial services issued by the Ghana Revenue Authority (online).

margin services as well either by providing for partial input VAT recovery or by zero-rating B2B margin services as New Zealand does.[16] Revenue may suffer somewhat, but, unlike the cascading effect of exemption, a compensatory rate increase would not be distortionary.

13.7 Mitigating Cascading Effects

Taxing fee-based financial services taxes consumer use more fully and permits business users a tax credit for the VAT invoiced by banks, which should mitigate the cascading effects of the financial services exemption. Cascading is also mitigated by providing for full or partial recovery of the input VAT incurred by banks (similar to the input VAT recovery for the MUSH sector in Canada) with respect to B2B financial services or by providing an option to tax.

Full or Partial Recovery of Input VAT

Cascading is addressed head-on under the New Zealand GST, which zero-rates supplies of financial services mainly to non-financial businesses, subject to the requirement (for individual businesses or related groups of businesses) that the proportion of taxable supplies made by the recipient of financial services (or the group of which the recipient is a member), measured on a 12-month period basis, equals or exceeds three-quarters of the recipient's total supplies for the same period (Pallot, 2011). The recipient's status is determined on the basis of customer-specific information or as agreed to by the Commissioner of Inland Revenue. The rebatable GST of the financial services provider is determined on the basis of common apportionment rules, notably the turnover method.[17] Margin-based supplies of financial services that meet the criterion for zero-rating are valued on a net basis, and fee-based services on a gross basis. A look-through provision ensures that the input GST of a financial services provider is also zero-rated if the services are rendered to another provider who, in turn, makes supplies to registered businesses that are eligible to purchase zero-rated financial services.

In Singapore, financial services are taxable if they are provided in return for a brokerage fee, commission, or similar form of compensation, while most core financial services are exempt (Jenkins and Khadka, 1998). However, financial institutions can claim input VAT credits using two methods. The 'special method'

[16] See Poddar (2003), who provides a positive evaluation of the taxation approach to explicit financial fees and commissions.

[17] The usual services are included but the following are not treated as financial services: debt collection, fire and general insurance, investment and other financial advisory services, leasing of equipment, and sales ledger and accounting services.

requires segregation of financial services eligible for the zero rate from total services provided to all customers, similar to the New Zealand approach. The 'fixed input tax recovery method' relies on input VAT recovery rates that depend on the type of financial institution and reflect the mix of their business and non-business customers. The purpose of the method is to prevent cascading (and preserve the price competitiveness of the financial institutions). However, this method undertaxes financial services provided to consumers even more than pure exemption would do.

Australia's GST also includes financial agency and brokerage services in the base. The exemption for financial services is restricted to transactions performed by principals. To mitigate cascading of the GST with regard to financial services provided to non-financial entities, Australia allows a credit equivalent to 75 per cent of the GST paid on a defined list of inputs acquired to make exempt financial supplies. Ostensibly, the credit's purpose is to mitigate the self-supply bias, but it does not address the problem of cascading or international competitiveness. Further, Poddar and Kalita (2010) question the efficiency of the approach, noting that the definition of input services eligible for the 75 per cent credit is not simple, is somewhat arbitrary, and will likely require constant review as patterns of outsourcing evolve.

Option to Tax

A little-known (and little-appreciated) clause in article 13C of the EU's Common VAT Directive (2006) permits EU member states to give financial institutions the option of being taxed in respect of financial services (the clause is referred to as the optional option) (Dixon, 1991). [18,19] Six member states—Austria, Belgium, Estonia, France, Germany, and Lithuania—have incorporated the option in their VAT legislation. The option should appeal to financial institutions that deal mostly with registered business customers that can claim credit for VAT paid on inputs. The German and French optional options deserve to be explored in some detail.

Germany has had the financial services option ever since it introduced the VAT in 1968. The option can be exercised with respect to all financial services listed in article 13B(d) of the Common Directive, except the management of special investment funds. Since the prevention of cascading was the primary motive for its introduction, the option can only be used for financial services supplied to taxable entities. In other words, financial services supplied to non-taxable entities, including private individuals, are treated as being exempt. Cascading is not prevented to the extent that taxable businesses use taxable financial services supplied

[18] This subsection draws heavily on Cnossen (1999a).

[19] For a succinct recent discussion of the option to tax, see Nathoeni and Braakman (2010).

to them for exempt activities. In effect, cascading would be more serious than in the exempt situation. For this reason, in 1980, the *Gesamptoption* (meaning that the option, if exercised, applies to all services, except if supplied to non-taxable entities) was replaced by an option applicable on a transaction-by-transaction basis.

Few conditions are attached to the exercise of the option. Both supplier and customer must be registered VAT payers, and financial institutions must account separately for taxable transactions and the input tax attributable thereto. In conformity with the Common Directive, financial services exported to third countries are zero-rated. Initially, the option was used mainly by small new banks (with large amounts of input tax). Presently, large banks also use the option, particularly for large transactions. Apparently, for small transactions, the costs of having to account separately for the tax are greater than the amount of the remaining input tax.

France restricts the option to specified financial services and institutions (as was the case under legislation predating the VAT). Financial services that are covered include activities relating to credit transactions (but not the interest), legal means of payment, the management of bank accounts, trade in securities, the management of investment funds, and factoring. The option is not available for transactions between banks (apparently to prevent the shifting of input credits). Two categories of persons are eligible for the option. The first category comprises credit institutions, stock exchanges, *changeurs*, *compteurs*, and *remisiers*. The second category comprises persons primarily engaged in the rendition of financial services (more than half of turnover). The option, if used, used to be irrevocable (except for the second category of eligible persons) and applied to all financial transactions, including those supplied to private individuals. In 2005, however, legislation was introduced that made the option revocable, which provided financial institutions more flexibility in choosing the most profitable option (Pons, 2006). Although precise data are not available, the option is apparently widely used. Possibly, its use is stimulated by the *taxe sur les salaires*, which is levied on the payroll of financial institutions, discussed in the next section.

Comparing France and Germany, the option may be used in respect of all financial institutions (Germany) or be restricted to specified financial institutions (France). The option may apply to individual transactions (Germany) or to all transactions (France) and it may be exercised at any time (Germany) or it may be revocable (France). The option may be restricted to financial services supplied to taxable businesses (Germany) or it may apply to financial services supplied to registered as well as non-registered persons (France). If the concern is with cascading, the German approach is preferable. If the concern is with equal treatment of consumer services, the French approach scores better. Clearly, the German approach is simpler to administer and comply with. Poddar (2003, p. 368) opines that 'in its current form, [the financial services option] is thus only a modest and partial solution to the problem of taxation of business inputs, but it does move in the right direction'.

13.8 Accounts-Based Methods of Taxing Value Added

Can any of the other forms of broad-based consumption taxes discussed in Chapter 3 be used to tax financial services? The candidates that come to mind as alternatives to an invoice tax-credit VAT are two accounts-based versions of ascertaining value added: the addition method and a direct subtraction method tax.

Addition Method

Under the addition method, value added is computed as the sum of wages and business cash flow, i.e. capital income (including interest) net of the normal return on investment (see Chapter 3). Michigan's 'single business tax' (SBT) was based on the addition method, but banks were exempted. The Shoup Mission to Japan in 1949 (Sundelson, 1950) recommended the addition method as an alternative to the subtraction method, at the choice of the business, when proposing the introduction of a VAT in Japan in the early 1950s. However, the Japanese Government withdrew the proposal in 1954.

Current applications of the addition method are used as an adjunct to the VAT to compensate for the undertaxation of financial sector services on account of their exemption. Since inputs are presumptively subject to VAT, France applies the addition method partially, to payrolls. The Canadian province of Québec, on the other hand, used to zero-rate financial services, and hence applied the addition method to the sum of wages and business cash flow. Further, Israel ignores the presumptive taxation of inputs to the financial sector under its VAT and taxes financial institutions on the sum of payroll and profits, including the normal return to capital in violation of the requirement that the VAT should tax consumption and consumption only.

In France, financial institutions must pay the payroll tax if at least 90 per cent of their turnover is subject to VAT, which should be the case for most of them. The taxable base is equal to total turnover less that part of turnover that is either subject to VAT or zero-rated if exported. The *taxe sur les salaires* is levied at rates ranging from 4.25 per cent to 20 per cent. An argument in favour of the tax is that it taxes B2C financial services more fully in line with the VAT on other goods and services. At the same time, the cascading effects on B2B financial services become more severe.

Israel used the addition method, called wages and profits tax, as part of its tax-credit-type VAT, to tax deposit-taking institutions and insurers from 1976 (when the VAT was introduced) through 1979 (Goldman, 2017). In 1980, the tax on the financial sector was divorced from the regular VAT. It is now being administered separately. The taxable institutions cannot take credit for the VAT paid on inputs. As in France, B2C services are taxed more fully but, by the same token, B2B services are more overtaxed. Further, the inclusion of 'profits' rather than business cash flow is an alien element in the calculation of the base. Similar comments apply to the Québec compensatory tax, but, in addition, the combination of zero-rating of financial services and the application of the payroll tax creates a strong incentive for outsourcing of internal processing and administrative functions (Poddar, 2003), which saves on payroll tax while no additional non-creditable VAT is incurred. Denmark and Iceland also tax financial institutions on an addition basis.

There are several reasons why the general application of the addition method has not caught on as an alternative to taxing financial services. First, as noted, since the tax is not transactions-based, it cannot be invoiced to business users of financial services and hence cannot be taken by them as a credit. As a result, cumulative effects are probably greater than under the exemption approach of a tax-credit VAT. Presumably, some presumptive approach for allocating tax credits to business transactions could be used, but it would tend to be arbitrary. Second, there is no way of rebating the tax directly on the exportation of financial services. This rebate should comprise the tax levied under the addition method, as well as the input tax paid with respect to taxable purchases of the financial sector. In the absence of a rebate, the destination principle would be violated; exports of financial services would be discriminated against. Third, the base under the addition method cannot be derived directly from commercial accounts. Profits determined for commercial or income tax purposes must be adjusted for changes in the value of inventories and capital goods purchases must be fully expensed. In addition, reimbursements for employment-related expenses must be verified to ensure that they are not disguised wage income.[20]

Despite these drawbacks, the addition method has been revived in the form of a 'financial activities tax' (FAT), proposed by the International Monetary Fund (2010), in response to a request to review the existing tax treatment of the financial sector (including the VAT exemption and the corporate tax's debt bias) in the aftermath of the financial crisis (Keen, Krelove, and Norregaard, 2016).[21] While the FAT taxes B2C financial services more fully, it tends to overtax B2B services rendered to registered businesses subject to the credit-invoice VAT. This problem can be circumvented by confining the FAT to B2C services by apportioning wages and profits between B2B and B2C services, if possible. By extension, allowance could then be made to recover the input VAT attributable to B2B transactions.

[20] Under a variant of the addition method, net operating income (net interest income plus margins and fees from other activities) is used as the basis for calculating the VAT. Mexico uses this method for a small range of financial transactions (Schatan, 2003).

[21] At about the same time that the FAT was proposed, a 'financial transactions tax' (FTT) was recommended to curtail the size of the financial sector. Generally, FTT is an *ad valorem* tax on the value of the sale and/or purchase of securities, i.e. a turnover tax. For a cautious assessment, see Burman et al. (2016).

The European Commission (2010) has recommended the 'financial transactions tax' (FTT)—in other words, a turnover tax—to EU member states.

Subtraction Approach

Under the (direct) subtraction method, the value added of financial institutions would be calculated as the difference between interest received and interest paid or, more generally, the difference between lending revenues and borrowing costs. This basic idea inspired the Canada Department of Finance (1987) to propose a hybrid credit and subtraction method VAT for financial services. The credit method would apply to the sale of non-financial goods and services by financial institutions (and other entities) and to the sales of financial services for which an explicit fee or commission would be charged. The subtraction method would be used for the bulk of banks' activities, such as unpriced intermediation and cheque services.

As the White Paper made clear, calculating the taxable margin under the subtraction method would not be easy. First, in view of the great variety of transactions, computation of the taxable margin would only be possible on an overall (annual) basis and not separately for each transaction. Second, a deduction from the taxable amount would be required for bad and doubtful debts, because the margin includes a premium for default risk which should not be taxed. Third, rules would have to be drawn up for the timing of various inclusions and deductions, akin to those under the income tax. Fourth, adjustments would have to be made in respect of exports and transactions with related corporations. Fifth, a deduction would have to be allowed for the cost of equity funds (in addition to the deduction for the cost of borrowed funds) to ensure that the tax applies only to the margin earned on the investment of the equity funds rather than to the gross revenue therefrom. Finally, a credit would have to be allowed for any tax paid on purchases.

Clearly, the proposed computation of the taxable base for financial services would be complicated. Not surprisingly, the subtraction variant for dealing with financial services was dropped from the Canada Government's final proposal for a tax-credit-type VAT. Instead, it was proposed to exempt financial services. In addition to administrative considerations, the business community objected to the denial of an input tax credit for business depositors and borrowers. The White Paper had ruled out the credit because it would not be possible to specify it on a transaction-by-transaction basis. The Department of Finance believed that the cascade effects would be small, but its point of view was not shared by the business community.

Basically, the direct subtraction approach cannot be used for financial activities because it is not transactions-based so the VAT cannot be passed on to business users of financial services. However, this problem does not arise in the case of services rendered at retail to consumers or businesses. This exception to the credit method forms the basis for two special widely applied schemes, for the taxation of second-hand goods and travel agencies.[22] The registered dealer's margin on second-hand goods is taxed by permitting him to deduct the price of the purchase from a non-registered owner from his own selling price.[23] Accordingly, the trade in second-hand goods is not diverted from organized trading channels, because non-registered traders do not have an incentive to avoid those registered dealers. In short, neutrality is increased.

Another exceptional application of the direct subtraction method, which preserves neutrality, concerns travel agents. Applying VAT to the full consideration charged to travellers would involve double taxation if VAT would also be paid in respect of goods and services financed by the traveller's consideration. Doing so would violate the destination principle to the extent that part of the consideration would be spent abroad. To prevent this from happening, VAT is charged on the difference between the price charged to the traveller and the cost of purchases made by the agent for the direct benefit of the traveller. In short, the margin is taxed while the tax on inputs is not creditable, except on overheads. Again, this ensures that neutrality is preserved.

13.9 Out-of-the-Box Approaches: Cash-Flow Method and Modified Reverse-Charging

None of the tax-credit, addition, and subtraction approaches offers a satisfactory solution to the problems posed by the indistinguishability of the intermediation charge and the pure rate of interest plus the risk premium and by the need to allocate the aggregate measure of the value of financial services to individual transactions. Two approaches have been proposed in the tax literature to break this gridlock: the cash-flow method and modified reverse-charging.

Cash-Flow Method

Poddar and English (1997) have proposed a highly ingenious scheme of applying VAT to financial services, which essentially bypasses the problem of determining

[22] The particulars of the second-hand goods scheme can be found in articles 311 and 313–15 of the EU's Common VAT Directive (2006) and those of travel agents in articles 306–10.

[23] Note that this approach implies that inventories on second-hand goods include VAT, which violates the neutrality condition. This would not happen if registered dealers were able to credit the VAT presumptively included in the purchase price at the time the purchase is concluded rather than at the time the second-hand good is sold on. Obviously, the current treatment is less susceptible to abuse.

the pure rate of interest, yet fully taxes consumer use and only consumer use of financial services. In the proposal, financial services would be taxed on a cash-flow basis, which excludes the pure rate of interest without explicitly requiring it to be identified.

Under the cash-flow approach, cash inflows from financial transactions (deposits, interest, capital receipts) are treated as taxable sales, and cash outflows (loans, interest, capital payments) are treated as purchases of taxable inputs. The VAT on these inputs, along with the VAT on inputs of non-financial goods and services, would be creditable against the VAT on outputs. The VAT on outputs, in turn, would constitute input tax credits for other taxable persons involved in industry and trade (or, for that matter, banking). (At the same time, of course, these taxable persons would pay VAT on their inflows, i.e. loans extended by banks.) As a result, tax cascading, inherent to the exemption approach, would be avoided, while consumers would be taxed in full. Risks would be removed from the tax base by permitting an *ex post* deduction for losses.[24] Further, the cash-flow method can be made compatible with the destination principle, simply by ignoring the provision of financial services to or from non-residents.

A stylized, self-explanatory example of the cash-flow method is presented in Box 13.1. Note that the intermediation margin is divided automatically between the borrower and the lender by the rate of interest at which the government can borrow (and the depositor can invest).

However, as noted by Poddar (2003), the pure cash-flow method is not directly equipped to deal with transitional issues and tax rate changes. Also, borrowing requirements would increase, because taxable persons taking out loans would have to finance the VAT on the loans. To resolve these problems, a tax calculation account (TCA) could be introduced, to be administered by financial institutions (not by non-financial businesses). The TCA would permit the tax on cash outflows from financial institutions charged by non-financial businesses to be carried forward to the time when the loan is repaid. Thus, there would be no increase in borrowing requirements. The tax on cash inflows from financial institutions would similarly be postponed until deposits are withdrawn.

To account for differences in VAT liabilities due to differences in timing, the net balance in the TCA would be subject to an indexing adjustment at the short-term government borrowing rate (as a proxy for the pure rate of interest). The grossed-up balance would be payable or refundable (if negative) periodically, subject to a deduction of a notional amount equal to the tax rate times the amount of the loan outstanding at the end of the tax period. Tax rate changes, including the introduction of the VAT on financial transactions, would be handled by grossing up (down) the TCA balances when the VAT rate increased (decreased). Under

[24] Corrections to the tax base would also have to be made for transactions with owners and shareholders in the form of income or capital pay-outs or contributions, loans from private individuals, and changes in portfolio investments.

Box 13.1 Workings of the cash-flow method

Assumptions

- Bank pays 7 per cent on deposit of US$1,000 and lends it at 15 per cent in period 1; loan and deposit are paid back in period 2
- Gross margin is 8 per cent (15 per cent minus 7 per cent), but pure rate of interest and risk premium should not be taxed
- Assume that the sum of the pure rate of interest and the risk premium is 12 per cent (equivalent to, say, the interest on medium-term government bonds)
- Accordingly, the value of the intermediation charge is 3 per cent to the borrower and 5 per cent to the lender
- VAT rate is 10 per cent

✓ VAT that should be collected during the deposit and lending period is US$5 (10 per cent of (12 per cent minus 7 per cent) times US$1,000)

Period 1

- Depositor puts US$1,000 in bank and bank lends this to registered trader
- Bank is liable for US$100 output VAT on the deposit, but this is offset by the credit of US$100 on the transfer of the funds to the borrower
- Borrower pays US$100 VAT on the loan
- Depositor's VAT position is not affected whether or not he is registered: not liable to VAT or entitled to tax credit of US$100

✓ Total VAT payable in period 1 is US$100

Period 2

- Bank is liable to US$115 VAT on the interest and repayment of the principal and is entitled to a credit of US$107 on interest and repayment of the deposit
- Borrower is entitled to a credit of US$115 (10 per cent of (US$150 plus US$1,000))

✓ Total VAT payable in period 2 is *minus* US$107 (US$8 minus US$115)

Result

- Government can invest the period 1 revenue of US$100 at 12 per cent, so present value of revenue is US$5 (US$112 minus US$107), which should be collected (see above)
- Depositor, if registered, can invest period 1 tax credit of US$100 at 12 per cent, so no loss of liquidity
- Intuition: the only flows that do not cancel are the charge on initial borrowing and a credit on interest and principal to the depositor, which is positive in present-value terms to the extent that the government's discount rate exceeds the rate paid to the depositor

Conclusion

- ✓ Cash-flow approach allows credit-invoice VAT without cascading
- • Caveats: (1) pure rate of interest and risk premium (of relevance to government and depositor, if registered) have to be estimated and (2) administrative and compliance costs could be substantial
- ➢ Implementation can be simplified by the use of a 'tax calculation account' to defer VAT on cash flows in period 1; investigated in the EU, but not adopted

Source: Ernst & Young, 1996.

a variant of the cash-flow approach, B2B financial transactions would be zero-rated to simplify compliance, which would reduce the scope of the approach.

The cash-flow approach has been tested in an operational sense with ten large financial institutions in six EU member states. Apart from the fear of the unknown, complexity and compliance costs have been the central source of objection to the scheme (Kerrigan, 2010). As a result, it has not yet been implemented anywhere. Also, the choice of the appropriate lending rate, single or composite (reflecting different maturities of loans and deposits), and the frequency of the indexing adjustments appear to require further study. Administrative issues that need to be addressed concern the valuation of financial assets and liabilities required at the time of commencement of the cash-flow method, as well as the proper definition of financial institutions permitted to keep TCAs.

Modified Reverse-Charging

The basic version of the modified reverse-charging method, proposed by Zee (2005b), relies on the application of a reverse charge whereby a registered bank collects VAT on both the input and output sides of its business transactions. The registered bank self-assesses VAT on its interest payments to depositors and then takes credit for this input VAT against output VAT due on its supplies.

The main problem with the basic version of the modified reverse-charging method is that it overtaxes final consumers or non-registered persons who borrow. It therefore resembles the 'taxing gross interest' method in that case. The modified reverse-charging method can, in theory, solve this problem by relying on a 'franking mechanism' enabling borrowers to be granted VAT credits that are associated with deposits that have been reverse-charged. The necessary implementation details of the modified reverse-charging method have not been worked out and the method has not been tested anywhere. Its complexity and potential compliance costs appear similar to those of the cash-flow/TCA method (Gendron, 2008). Furthermore, it is unclear how the modified reverse-charging method would handle more complex—and quantitatively important—margin transactions, such as securities issuing and trading.

13.10 What to Do?

Financial services are difficult to tax under a tax-credit VAT, because the intermediation charge, which should be taxed, cannot be separated from the pure rate of interest and risk premium, which should not be taxed. Taxation of the combined amount is distortionary because it drives a wedge between the pure rate of interest paid to households and the pure rate of interest paid by businesses. Zero-rating of financial services would be a form of overkill. Table 13.4 summarizes the pros and cons of the various modifications of the tax credit method and the accounts-based approaches to determining value added discussed above. The various approaches are evaluated in terms of their distortion of producer decisions (self-supply bias, cascading, loss of international competitiveness) and consumer choices, administrative complexity, and revenue cost. The last column lists the countries that have (had) experience with the various approaches.

Approaches that narrow the application of the exemption are moves in the right direction. Taxing explicit fees and charges for financial services mitigates distortions, but may cost revenue if the services are mainly rendered to registered business users that can take credit for the tax. Zero-rating or partial input VAT recovery mitigates cascading effects, but does nothing to remove the distortion of consumer choices and may harm revenue. The effects of the option to tax B2B services should be similar to the taxation of fee-based services. Addition and subtraction methods greatly exacerbate cascade effects and cannot handle rate differentiation and exemptions, if desired. Taxation on a cash-flow basis seems to be the most promising approach, but, reportedly, its complexity is substantial.[25]

The foregoing review of the possible methods to enhance the VAT base for financial services suggests some lessons for African countries that consider reforming their VATs to capture more of the value added from the financial sector. First, methods that are very complex (e.g. the cash-flow VAT) should not be considered even if they can yield the correct result. Second, methods that do not arrive at the correct value added or amount of the intermediation charge on a transaction-by-transaction basis should be rejected. Based on the current state of knowledge and experience, it would seem that the most comprehensive but feasible approach to enlarge the VAT base as much as possible under the

[25] Recently, López-Laborda and Peña (2018) have proposed a new method for applying VAT to financial services, called the 'mobile-ratio method', which uses a periodically updated ratio to allocate the financial margin of businesses to each financial transaction. The authors claim to obtain near-complete taxation of the value added by financial services.

Table 13.4 Comparison of VAT methods for taxing financial services

Method	Distortion of registered producer decisions	Distortion of consumer choices	Administrative complexity	Revenue cost compared with comprehensive taxation	Examples of countries where found
Transactions-based					
Full exemption of margin and fee-based services	Self-supply bias, cascading, loss of international competitiveness	Undertaxation of B2C transactions	Great definitional and apportionment issues	Substantial if apportionment rules generous	EU member states; non-SACU African countries
Taxation of fee-based services and exemption of margin-based services	Reduces self-supply bias and cascading	Undertaxation less than under full exemption	Number of definitional and apportionment issues less than under full exemption	Less than under full exemption depending on division of fee-based services among producers and consumers	Botswana, Namibia, South Africa, Tanzania; to some extent: Australia, Singapore
Zero-rating of B2B services and exemption of B2C services	Distortions minimized	Undertaxation of B2C transactions	Definitional and apportionment issues mitigated	Greater than under full exemption	New Zealand
Partial input VAT recovery for B2B services and exemption of B2C services	Distortions mitigated but less than under zero-rating of B2B transactions	Undertaxation of B2C transactions	Definitional and apportionment issues mitigated	Less than under zero-rating of B2B transactions	Australia, Singapore

Continued

Table 13.4 *Continued*

Method	Distortion of registered producer decisions	Distortion of consumer choices	Administrative complexity	Revenue cost compared with comprehensive taxation	Examples of countries where found
Option to tax B2B services and exemption of B2C services	Distortions somewhat minimized	Undertaxation of B2C services	Definitional and apportionment issues mitigated depending on use of option	Somewhat larger than under full exemption	Austria, Belgium, Estonia, France, Germany, Lithuania
Cash-flow approach with TCA	No distortions if pure rate of interest correctly estimated	No distortions if pure rate of interest correctly estimated	Substantial	None	Not implemented
Modified reverse-charging	Allegedly, no distortions	Undertaxation of B2C services	Substantial	None	Not implemented
Accounts-based					
Addition method	Distortions maximized, because input VAT cannot be passed on	Distortions on account of producer distortions	Cannot handle rate differentiation and exemptions	Extra revenue on account of cascading	Iceland, Israel
Subtraction method	Value added taxed, but input VAT cannot be passed on	Distortions on account of producer distortions	Cannot handle rate differentiation and exemptions	Extra revenue on account of cascading	No general application, but applied to second-hand goods and travel agencies

typical constraints faced by African countries would involve the following steps (Poddar and Kalita, 2010; Gendron, 2016):

- tax all explicit fees and commissions;
- exempt margin services;
- allow for partial formula-based recovery of input VAT incurred to render exempt B2B margin services; and
- use direct attribution to allocate input credits and confine the allocation formula to residual mixed-use inputs.[26]

This chapter has shown that fully including financial services in the VAT base, however desirable, remains a somewhat elusive goal. As Tait (1988, p. 100) put it succinctly, 'trying to get to grips with banking...is akin to trying to get your hands around a piece of jelly'. Most economists and lawyers probably still share his conclusion that 'while unsatisfactory, the [modified] exemption of financial services from VAT, and the consequent cascade effect, looks to be the best solution for the time being'.

[26] As emphasized by Poddar (2003), the formula should measure revenues properly by excluding the principal value of financial instruments, including the net revenues from margin services, on a net rather than a gross basis and by segregating the revenue contributions of depositors and borrowers.

14
Insurance

Thus far, insurance services have been exempted under the VATs in African countries that are based on the EU's Common VAT Directive (2006). By contrast, the SACU countries, following the New Zealand example, tax all insurance except long-term insurance, such as health and life insurance.

This chapter starts by briefly reviewing the exemption of insurance under the EU's Common Directive, which has been adopted by most African countries. Instead, these countries, like most EU member states, impose various insurance (premium) taxes (francophone countries) or stamp duties (anglophone countries other than SACU countries). The form and implications of the VAT exemption are also discussed. It is argued that exemption and separate taxation are administratively complex and distortionary elements in the tax systems of African countries. As shown by the South African experience, inclusion in the VAT base of property and casualty insurance is feasible, and is simpler and more efficient than the current system. Full taxation would be more difficult for life and health insurance, which, if desired, can be taxed under the addition method. The last section summarizes the taxable status of insurance services under present arrangements and under the proposed approach, and provides some concluding thoughts.

14.1 Insurance and the EU's Common Directive

The EU exempts insurance because in the 1960s, when the VAT was introduced, lawmakers did not know how to tax it. At the level of the policyholder, the intermediation charge, which reflects the cost of the insurance service, cannot be separated from the capital transfer to the common pool from which indemnity and contingent pay-outs are made. Under a tax on consumption, such as the VAT, the consideration for the service provision should be taxed but not the capital transfer. Since value added could not be determined on a transaction-by-transaction basis, the lawmakers exempted insurance for lack of a better alternative. As is well known, this means that the services provided by insurers are not taxed, but also that insurers cannot credit the tax paid on purchases. Further, various EU member states introduced or continued to levy excise-type taxes or stamp duties on insurance premiums, as do African countries.[1]

[1] For a review of the EU situation and the best-practice approach, see Cnossen (2013a), on which this chapter draws.

Box 14.1 Definition of insurance services in the European Union

Article 135(1) of the EU's Common VAT Directive (2006) states that member states shall exempt the following transactions: 'insurance and reinsurance transactions, including related services performed by insurance brokers and insurance agents'. Article 137 does not allow a right of option for taxation in respect of insurance transactions.

The European Commission (2007c) provides the following definition of insurance services:

'Included in the definition of insurance services are:

- life policies including group life policies and policies covering longevity risks
- sickness, disability and unemployment insurance
- health insurance policies
- peril insurance policies
- liability insurance policies
- financial loss risk insurance policies
- reinsurance, retrocession and pooling of insurance policies
- financial loss and inconvenience risk insurance supplied with a block insurance policy

'Also included in the definition of insurance services are:

- product development for insurances
- underwriting of risk
- risk management
- investment management
- putting policyholders on risk
- claims handling
- issue, cession, renewal, prolongation and recision of contracts

'Excluded from the definition of insurance services are:

- identification of new insurance products/opportunities
- marketing
- insurance company administration
- policy administration
- motor vehicle damage assessment by an association whose members are insurance companies'

Box 14.1 shows the EU's definition of insurance services, which are exempt without a right of option for taxation. The definition of insurance services is rather broad, but does not include policymaking, marketing, and administrative activities, which involves potentially contentious delineation issues.

New Zealand and, following its example, Australia, Singapore, and South Africa—all of which introduced the VAT at a later date than the EU and could learn from the EU VAT's shortcomings—found a solution for the VAT problem in the field of insurance, which this book recommends for African countries. In particular, the designers of the New Zealand GST hit upon the idea of avoiding the problem of determining taxable value added on the basis of individual policies by shifting it to the level of the insurance company, where value added is the difference between premium receipts, on the one hand, and indemnity pay-outs and taxable purchases, on the other.[2] As is well known, this difference equals the sum of wages and above-normal returns (business cash flow), calculated on a cash-flow basis—in other words, the VAT base.

14.2 How Is Insurance Taxed in African Countries?

Starting with a brief taxonomy of insurance, this section surveys and evaluates the separate insurance premium taxes and stamp duties in African countries and then discusses the VAT treatment of insurance activities.

Insurance Premium Taxes

As shown in Table 14.1, the major forms of insurance can be distinguished into general or short-term insurance, long-term or life insurance, reinsurance, and export credit insurance. General insurance, purchased as a separate policy from an insurance company, basically takes two forms: (a) risk or hazard (property and casualty) insurance regarding material damage or financial loss of homes, properties, cars, and liability; and (b) personal insurance regarding health, injury, and disability—generally linked to medical care. General insurance involves indemnity payments (which make whole again or reinstate the previous position) for the loss incurred, as opposed to whole-life or term insurance, which takes the form of contingent payments (a claim arises on the occurrence of a specified event). Reinsurance does not involve individual policies, but is more a matter between insurance companies. Taxes and stamp duties on insurance premiums and contracts are not major sources of revenue. Generally, they contribute less than 1 per cent of total tax revenue.

[2] This clever idea was originally developed and discussed in the tax literature by Barham, Poddar, and Whalley (1987).

Table 14.1 Africa: types of insurance and taxes on insurance premiums, 2018

Country	General or short-term insurance		Long-term or life insurance and annuity policies	Reinsurance	Export credit insurance; risks outside country	Other
	Risk or hazard (property and casualty)	Health and personal injury				
Southern African Development Community (SADC)						
Madagascar	Fire: 20%, but 7% on movable property; transport: 4%	Exempt	3%; life annuities: 5%	Exempt	Exempt	4.5%
Mozambique	Car and transport: 2%	Personal accidents: 1%				5%; bail and credit: 3%
East African Community (EAC)						
Burundi	2%	2%	2%	2%	..	2%
Economic and Monetary Community of Central Africa (CEMAC)						
Chad	Fire: 25%; car: 15%; transport: 7%	..	1%	..	Exempt	20%
Congo	10%	10%	10%	Exempt	Exempt	10%
Gabon	Fire: 30%; transport: 5%	Exempt	8%		Exempt	8%
Economic Community of West African States (ECOWAS)						
UEMOA						
Benin	Fire: 20%; motor vehicles: 10%; transport: 5%	Exempt	Exempt	Exempt	0.25%	Miscellaneous: 10%
Burkina Faso	Fire: 20%; cars: 10%; commercial vehicles: 12%; transport: 8%	Exempt	8%; life annuities: 6%	Exempt	0.25%	12%
Côte d'Ivoire	Fire: 25%; cars: 14.5%; transport: 7%	8%, except if work-related	Exempt, but life annuities: 5%	Exempt	0.1%	14.5%

Continued

Table 14.1 *Continued*

Country	General or short-term insurance		Long-term or life insurance and annuity policies	Reinsurance	Export credit insurance; risks outside country	Other
	Risk or hazard (property and casualty)	Health and personal injury				
Guinea–Bissau	Transport: 5%; cars: 5%	4%	4%	Exempt	5%	5%
Mali	Transport: 5%	..	..	Exempt	..	20%
Niger	Fire: 20%; transport: 8%	..	9%, unless annuities deferred for more than 3 years	Exempt	1.2%	12%
Senegal	Fire: 5%; transport: 5%		Exempt, but life annuities: 6%		0.25%	10%; group: 3%
Togo	Fire: 25%; transport: 5%	..	3%	Exempt	0.2%	6%
WAMZ						
Cabo Verde	..	..	..	..	..	2%
Guinea	Transport: 8%; sport or sailing: 20%		5%, except non-residents	..	..	12%
Arab Maghreb Union (AMU)						
Algeria	Fire and general: 10%; transport: 4.5%		8%; annuities: 4%	5%	Exempt	Multiple risk: 20%
Mauritania	Fire: 10%; maritime: 5%; air and waterway: 10%		10%	Exempt	0.1%	10%
Morocco	Fire and air: 14%; maritime: 7%; death of cattle or hail: 14%	14%, except occupational accidents and illnesses	Exempt		Exempt	Third party: 14%; capital sum at birth or marriage: 3.5%

Tunisia	Air and maritime: 5%; agricultural or fishing risks: 5%		Exempt	Exempt	Exempt	10%
Intergovernmental Authority on Development (IGAD) and Egypt						
Djibouti	General: 20%	..	..	..	..	..
Egypt	Transport: 10%	1%	..	..	..	10%
Ethiopia	..	..	..	..	..	1%

Note: '..' means information not available and a blank means not taxed.

Source: IMF Tax Summaries and IBFD. Countries that impose stamp duties on insurance policies, but for which details are not available, are Cameroon, Central African Republic, Equatorial Guinea, Lesotho, Malawi, Namibia, Sierra Leone, Swaziland, Uganda, and Zimbabwe. Some information may be out of date or incomplete.

On the basis of this classification, Table 14.1 lists the crazy quilt of African taxes on insurance premiums and contracts, sometimes levied as stamp duties. The separate taxation of insurance is a typical francophone phenomenon. Countries with anglophone taxing traditions—more circumspect in taxing the financial sector—rarely tax insurance, although various newcomers to the VAT include property and casualty insurance in its base, as they should (see below).

Most countries define the type of insurance that is being taxed, while a few countries broadly tax general insurance but provide exemptions or reduced rates for, say, the transportation of goods, export-related activities, life insurance, and reinsurance. These activities would simply not be taxed under product-specific insurance taxes. Rates, generally *ad valorem*, vary widely across countries. Risk or hazard (property and casualty) insurance premiums with respect to fire, cars, and transportation are widely taxed. Health-related insurance is taxed less widely and, if taxed, rates tend to be lower than those for risk or hazard insurance. Quite a few countries tax life insurance and/or life annuities. Reinsurance is widely exempted, but export insurance is taxed more often, albeit at very low rates. Agriculture tends to be treated leniently, and Guinea-Bissau exempts insurance premiums altogether if the policies are taken out with domestic companies.

Taxes on insurance premiums and contracts are anachronistic levies, comparable with traditional stamp duties still found in many African countries, which are sometimes levied too on the same base. Unless insurance gives rise to negative externalities (because insured persons impose costs on other people—not very likely!), insurance taxes do not belong in a modern, rationally designed tax system based on the principles of equal treatment and economic neutrality. It is difficult to argue that insurance should be taxed differentially higher than other goods and services bought by consumers. Clearly, the insurance tax distorts consumer and producer choices: individuals and businesses will insure themselves less than they would do in the absence of the tax.

The only possible justification for the insurance tax is that it makes up for the less-than-full taxation of insurance services under the VAT, but this is an odd way of justifying the tax. Generally, discriminatory treatment is not neutralized through another form of discrimination. Another reason for the existence of a tax on insurance might be to prevent warranty agreements, whose cost is embedded in product prices taxable under the VAT, from being transformed into exempt insurance services,[3] but the insurance tax is not the appropriate response to this form of tax avoidance. Further, it may be assumed that collection and compliance costs are high relative to, say, the VAT, while the revenue raised through insurance taxes is generally negligible. Clearly, insurance services belong in the VAT base.

[3] As exemplified by the UK government's decision to increase the insurance premium tax to the level of the VAT, a decision whose legitimacy was sanctioned by the European Court of Justice (2004).

VAT Exemption

Under the EU's Common VAT Directive (2006), as in most African countries, all forms of insurance are exempt from tax.[4] In addition, there are various insurance activities not shown in Table 14.1 but relevant to the discussion. These activities involve, among others: (a) services of agents, brokers, and claim adjusters; (b) warranties provided through an insurance company or embedded in the selling price of a product; and (c) insurance that is not provided directly by an insurance company, such as credit card company protection of purchases against breakage, rental company protection against damage included in the rental fee, and insurance provided as part of a tour or travel package. The services of agents and brokers are exempt from VAT, but those of claim adjusters are taxed in some EU countries. Warranties provided through an insurance company are exempt, but the cost of warranties embedded in product prices is taxed. Insurance not provided directly through insurance companies is exempt.

The VAT exemption of insurance services violates the logic and functionality of the VAT. Since the value added by insurance companies (wages plus business cash flow) is not taxed, and disregarding the effect of insurance taxes, insurance services can be offered at lower prices to consumers than other fully taxed services. Other things being equal, consumers will then buy more insurance services than they would do if the services were fully taxed—an effect that does not, except by chance, cancel the opposite effect of insurance premium taxes. Further, exempt insurance companies cannot pass on the VAT on their purchases to VAT-liable businesses that buy insurance services. This causes a cascade effect, i.e. tax is levied on tax, which artificially stimulates vertical integration.

The non-creditable and non-refundable VAT also enters into the price of insurance services exported to other countries, which infringes on the efficient workings of international markets. In various countries, the tax on insurance services exported to third countries is refunded, but here contentious tax allocation issues arise because the VAT on purchases must be attributed to exempt services (non-creditable) and zero-rated export services (refundable), often in an arbitrary fashion. Further, exempt insurance companies will refrain from outsourcing various services, such as administrative services, because in-house provision saves the non-creditable VAT on the cost of labour included in purchase prices. Insurance companies will also be induced to avoid the VAT on purchases by setting up taxable subsidiaries from which they rent, say, computer services.

[4] In the EU, the exemption is also applicable to insurance agreed to without involving the services of insurance companies. However, actuarial services, repair contracts, *del credere* agreements, factoring contracts, damage assessment services, the recruitment of potential policyholders for an insurance company without actually concluding the insurance policy, and the commission that an insurance agent pays to a travel organization for passing on a customer do not fall under the VAT exemption. For a good review of the European situation, particularly the jurisprudence, see De la Feria (2007). For a broad legal treatment, reference is made to Schenk, Thuronyi, and Cui (2015, ch. 11).

In short, there is much to be said for making insurance services taxable under the VAT, as has been done in South Africa and other countries with modern VAT systems. South Africa makes a distinction between taxable short-term insurance and exempt long-term insurance. Typically, short-term insurance is for a period of one year and is renewable annually at the option of the insurer. Examples are policies related to homeowners, households (or all risks), fire, motor vehicles, and credit guarantees.[5] By contrast, long-term insurance policies usually have a specified term so there is no annual renewal involved. The most prominent example is life insurance or annuities, where the cover relates to death, disablement, or old age.[6] The following sections deal with the taxation of both short-term and long-term insurance under the VAT.[7]

14.3 Application of VAT to Insurance

Insurance Companies

To elucidate the application of the VAT to insurance services, Table 14.2 shows a stylized example of the cash-flow particulars of an insurance company (which can be found in the published annual accounts of most insurance companies). In the example, the insurance company collects US$100 million in premiums, which are subject to 20 per cent VAT. These premiums constitute the company's sales; after

Table 14.2 Cash-flow data of an insurance company in US$ million

Description	Amounts (excl. VAT)	20% VAT (incl. investment return)	20% VAT (excl. investment return)
1. Receipts	110		
a. Premiums	100	20	20
b. Investment return	10	2	
2. Expenses	105		
a. Wages	25		
b. Purchases	15	(3)	(3)
c. Pay-outs	65	(13)	(13)
3. Business cash flow (1 – 2)	5		
4. Net VAT payable		6	4

[5] Short-term property and casualty insurance is also taxed under the VAT in Botswana, Gambia, Ghana, and Tanzania.

[6] For an excellent treatment, see the brochure issued by the South African Revenue Service (2013).

[7] Admittedly, other forms of financial services, enumerated in article 135(1)b–g of the EU's Common VAT Directive (2006), for example, should also be taxed, but this is more complicated than the taxation of insurance services (see Chapter 13). Since insurance services can be taxed without taxing these other financial services, there is no reason not to proceed with bringing insurance services into the VAT base.

all, it 'sells' insurance policies. Part of the premiums are used to make pay-outs; another part flows into an equalization reserve to take care of fluctuations in pay-outs over time. The reserve's investments yield a return of US$10 million (in the example, this return can be viewed as the insurer's normal return), which can also be used to make pay-outs. To run its business, the insurer buys goods and services for which it pays US$15 million plus 20 per cent VAT. Further, the insurer pays the ongoing costs of its own organization (administrative personnel, canvassers, claim adjusters, etc.) of US$25 million, including the management cost of the equalization reserve. Indemnity pay-outs total US$65 million. Finally, the difference between receipts and expenses represents business cash flow (the above-normal return) of US$5 million.

Exemption of the insurance services—as under most current VAT regimes—means that the insurer only pays VAT on its purchases—i.e. US$3 million—although gross value added is US$35 million (calculated as the difference between premium receipts of US$100 million and pay-outs of US$65 million). Ignoring the treatment of the investment return (but see below), this involves a VAT revenue loss of US$4 million (US$7 million on the value added minus the input VAT of US$3 million). In the context of the VAT, this means that insurance services are grossly undertaxed. Taxing the premiums with 20 per cent insurance tax, without taking account of the input VAT, would generate a yield of US$20 million in the example. If we were to add the non-creditable VAT on inputs, then the total tax would be US$23 million, a sizable overtaxation of insurance services compared with other goods and services which are taxed only on the net value added.

For the correct computation of the VAT on insurance services, VAT should be attributed to pay-outs, which should be considered part of the 'purchases' of the insurer. After all, as capital transfers, these pay-outs do not belong in the VAT base. The VAT, which has been paid in respect of the pay-outs when the premiums were collected, can be washed out through a kind of reverse-charge procedure under which the insurer grants itself a VAT credit of 20 per cent of US$65 million, or US$13 million, which it credits against the VAT that has to be paid to the VAT office in respect of the premiums. Therefore, the VAT attributed to the pay-outs is not a cost to the insurer. Subsequently, the imputed VAT, along with the amount of the pay-out, is paid to claimants. If the claimant is a VAT-registered business, it has to include the indemnity payment (plus the imputed VAT) in sales on its VAT return. Earlier, the business received a credit for the VAT paid on the premium paid to the insurer, so, on balance, the VAT is not a cost to the business either. As a final consumer, an individual claimant cannot file a return for the VAT received along with the pay-out (earlier, he could not take a credit for the VAT on the premium). He can apply the pay-out plus the VAT to pay for the repair or replacement of the damaged or lost property. So, at that time, the VAT flows back into the treasury. And if he decides to keep the money, the VAT refund is appropriate since no consumption took place.

The pay-out on which VAT is reverse-charged includes an investment return of US$10 million which has not been subject to VAT. This return should also be taxed, to compensate for the VAT credit on the pay-out. Further, an adjustment should be made for the VAT paid in respect of taxable purchases. If all of these amounts are taken into account, the insurer should pay a net amount of VAT of US$6 million to the treasury (see Table 14.2). This equals the amount of VAT that would have been payable if the net value added of the insurer—calculated as the sum of wages of US$25 million and business cash flow of US$5 million—had been taxed.

Neither South Africa nor any of the other countries with a modern VAT taxes the investment returns of insurers. In consequence, a notional credit is provided for the VAT attributable to this return, although no VAT has earlier been paid in respect thereof. As shown in Table 14.2, the actual VAT payment then amounts to US$4 million, less than the full VAT, although more than the VAT on purchases.

Insured Individuals and Businesses

This ingenious approach deserves to be emulated by African countries. The result can be further elucidated with the aid of the following diagrams.[8] The top half of Figure 14.1 represents the VAT chain of a final consumer, generally an individual, who takes out an insurance policy. The insured pays US$100 for his policy plus 20 per cent VAT, which the insurer pays to the VAT office and for which the insured, being an exempt individual, cannot get a VAT credit. Next, the insured incurs a loss of US$30, which is paid out after the insurer has provided itself a VAT credit of US$6 (20 per cent of US$30). The pay-out is inclusive of the VAT of US$6, which after all would also have to be paid in case of repair or replacement of the insured object (and which, at that stage, would have to be paid to the VAT office). However, as the insurer has granted itself a VAT credit of US$6,[9] the net VAT received by the tax office is US$14. This is exactly the amount of VAT that should have been payable on the value added of US$70 (US$100 premium minus US$30 loss compensation).

If the insured is a VAT-liable business, the insurer's VAT payment would exactly compensate the VAT credit of the business (in both cases, US$20). And the same story applies in the case of a pay-out. The VAT of US$6 received by the business from the insurer has to be paid to the VAT office, but compensates the VAT credit of the same amount which the insurer grants itself. On balance, no VAT is payable, fully in accordance with the nature of the VAT as a tax on private

[8] The discussion in this section has benefitted from a bulletin issued by the Australian Tax Office (undated).

[9] This 'reverse credit' can be likened to the reverse credit that an importing business allows itself after imposing a reverse charge on out-of-state purchases under a deferred payment system.

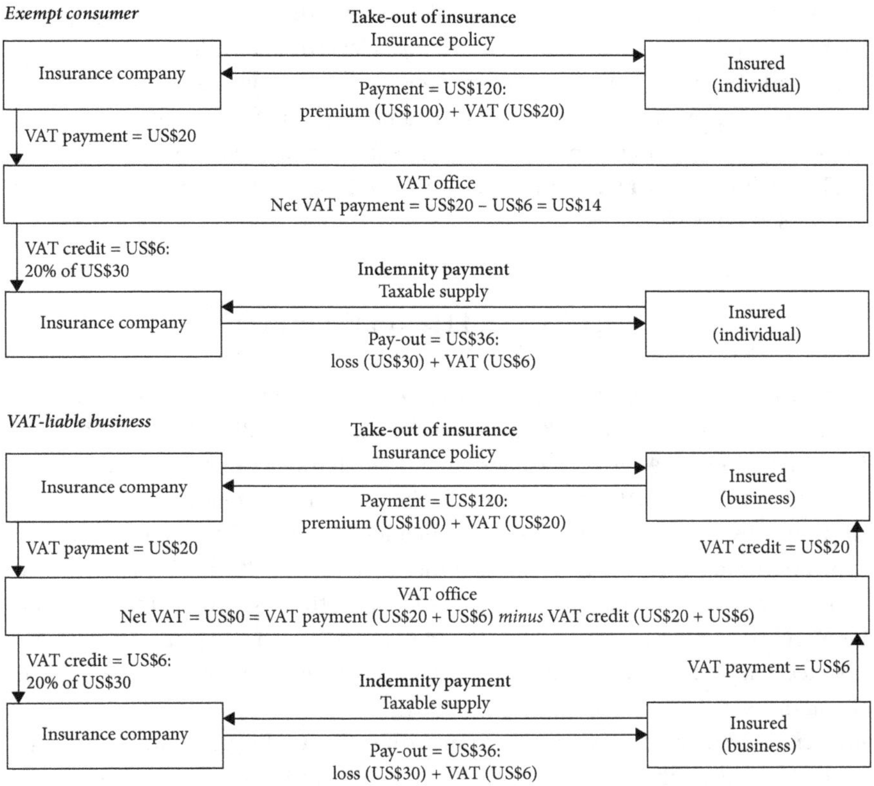

Figure 14.1 Explaining the treatment of property and casualty insurance under the VAT

consumption and not on business. The bottom half of Figure 14.1 shows the VAT chain for a VAT-liable business. Its workings are self-explanatory. Note that the insurer should make mention of the amount of the 'tax credit', which the insured business has to include in its VAT return, when it makes the indemnity payment.

Under the South African scheme, the insurer does not have to make a distinction between a VAT-liable and a VAT-exempt person. This has the disadvantage that a VAT-liable business has to pay the VAT received from the insurer to the VAT office. Australia, therefore, has simplified the scheme somewhat by permitting insurers to make a distinction between VAT-liable and VAT-exempt persons. VAT-liable persons receive the indemnity pay-out without the amount of the imputed VAT, while the insurer does not grant itself a credit for the same amount. Exempt persons, on the other hand, receive the VAT along with the pay-out, while the insurer gets a credit for the same amount. On balance, the result is the same therefore as under the South African approach.

The examples show that, even in hindsight, no distinction can be made at the level of the insured between the consideration that is paid for the service provided by the insurer and the capital transfer. The premiums and pay-outs, moreover, relate to different insured persons. Nevertheless, value added and only value added is taxed in line with the purport of the VAT, without causing administrative complexities or economic distortions. Perhaps there is an analogy here between the premium payment on a separate insurance policy, which is subject to VAT, and the payment in respect of a warranty embedded in product prices, which is also taxed.

14.4 Life and Health Insurance

The previous discussion focused solely on general or short-term insurance. With life insurance, there is the difficulty that, besides the pooling of risk, it involves intermediation between savers and investors. Barham, Poddar, and Whalley (1987) have shown that life insurance can be taxed in a similar fashion to general insurance by separating the charge for financial intermediation and the cost of protection from the gross premium in order to determine the non-taxable savings component. The charge for financial intermediation is simply the difference between the gross premium and the net premium shown on life insurance policies, while the cost of protection can be calculated using mortality tables. As the authors note, the major problem with this approach is that the charge for financial intermediation is not a constant proportion of the gross premium, while, in the later years of a policy, the actual cost of protection may greatly exceed the premium paid. Accordingly, the tax would rise in tandem and might actually exceed the annual premium. Policyholders would balk at this situation, although the result would be correct in present-value terms.

None of the countries that have adopted the New Zealand approach for taxing general insurance services has extended this treatment to life insurance. Life insurance and annuities resemble pension funds and annuity schemes, which would also have to be taxed on their intermediation services if equal treatment is to be provided. Further, there is the consideration that these forms of insurance target individuals rather than businesses; hence, cascading does not occur. This argument also applies to health insurance, which is a form of risk pooling, often universal, compulsory, and with redistributive elements—in other words, a quasi-tax that would hardly function better by imposing VAT on it.

14.5 Comparative Evaluation

Table 14.3 summarizes the tax situation for insurance services under current arrangements in Africa—i.e. the insurance tax and the VAT exemption—and the situation that would ensue if short-term insurance services were fully taxed as under the South African approach. Current arrangements are broadly summarized and may differ from one country to another. Under most insurance taxes, risk or hazard insurance is generally taxed. The treatment of health and life insurance is mixed: some countries tax them, others do not. Reinsurance is widely exempted but some countries tax export credit insurance. The exemption or non-taxation extends to various intermediation services and types of insurance not provided through an insurance company. All of these activities are currently exempted under VAT, although VAT has to be paid in respect of taxable purchases. However, warranties embedded in product prices are taxed, a reason why countries apply insurance taxes to warranties provided separately through insurance policies.

Table 14.3 Current and proposed taxation of insurance services in Africa

Type of insurance	Risks	General current taxable status		VAT proposal[a]
		Insurance tax	VAT	
a. Risk or hazard (property and casualty)	Car, household effects, home, liability, legal assistance, travel, cancellation	Taxed	Exempt	Taxed
	Transport of goods, aviation, seagoing vessels	Taxed	Exempt	Taxed
	Export credit	Taxed/ Exempt	Exempt	Taxed
b. Health	Sickness, disability	Taxed/ Exempt	Exempt	Exempt
c. Life		Taxed/ Exempt	Exempt	Exempt
d. Reinsurance		Exempt	Exempt	Taxed
e. Brokers and agents		Exempt	Exempt	Taxed
f. Loss adjusters		Exempt	Taxed	Taxed
g. Warranties				
- as insurance		Taxed	Exempt	Taxed
- in product price		Exempt	Taxed	Taxed
h. Insurance outside insurance companies	In credit card fee for loss or damage to purchased good	Exempt	Exempt	Taxed
	In lease fee for loss of damage to rented car or other object			
	As part of payment for travel			

[a] In the case of VAT-liable businesses, taxed means taxed with credit, including a refund of prior-stage tax if required.

Under the South African approach, all forms of short-term insurance (except health) and intermediation services would be taxed alike. It would not be necessary to make a distinction between taxable risk or hazard forms of insurance and non-taxable forms, such as goods transportation. Transport companies would simply be able to credit the VAT on insurance against the VAT on transport services. And upon shipment to other African countries or third countries, the full VAT on purchases and indemnity payments would be refundable. This would provide for a leveller playing field than is currently available. For similar reasons, reinsurance does not have to be exempted. However, an exemption from the VAT might be made for health-related and life insurance. For VAT purposes, health insurance would then be treated in the same way as other exempt health services, while life insurance, a long-term savings vehicle, would be exempted along with other B2C margin-based financial services. Both forms of insurance, moreover, are mostly taken out by individuals; hence, cascading effects do not occur. Importantly, correct treatment requires that insurers' investment returns, which are eligible for a reverse credit if paid out, should be taxed, although this is not done anywhere.

In conclusion, the insurance (premium) tax is an anachronistic levy for which there should be no place in a rational tax system. The same applies to the VAT exemption which violates the logic and functionality of the tax. No sensible argument can be made for why the VAT on insurance services should depend on the ratio between taxable inputs and exempt sales. This chapter has not touched upon the revenue consequences of the abolition of insurance taxes and the application of the standard VAT rate to insurance services. In most countries, the revenue from insurance premium taxes is negligible. Besides, the main argument is one of efficiency. Full taxation of general insurance services would improve the efficient workings of the market.

15
Lotteries and Gambling

This chapter reviews the issues regarding the VAT treatment of lotteries and gambling.[1] Following the introduction, a brief description is provided of the type of gaming activities that are being reviewed. Next, the approach commonly used to apply VAT to lotteries is discussed. The margin method, which is commonly used by countries that apply the VAT to the gaming industry, is also examined. South Africa's approach is given some prominence in view of the importance of its gambling industry and the fact that its treatment has been replicated by other SACU countries.

15.1 Introduction

The treatment of lotteries and gambling (collectively called gaming) under the VAT resembles that of insurance and second-hand goods. Lotteries can be taxed on ticket sales (output), while a reverse charge can be imputed to pay-outs (inputs), similar to property and casualty insurance. The value added of the lottery industry would thus be taxed after providing a credit for the VAT on inputs, against the gross tax liability. Gambling can be included in the VAT base under the margin method, where the margin is the difference between the sales of tokens and chips, on the one hand, and pay-outs, on the other. Again, a credit for VAT on other inputs should be allowed against the tax liability. Both approaches yield the same result. Under both approaches, too, lottery and gambling activities are implicitly viewed as consumer goods, which compete for leisure time and expenditure with alternative diversions such as cinema and golf, instead of as a financial investment where the asset procured offers a possible positive return but with a high risk, somewhat remotely akin to stock market speculation.

Within Africa, South Africa accounts for almost half of all legal gambling activities, followed by two island countries, Comoros and Mauritius, at about 10 per cent each (Vaillancourt and Ossa, 2011). All other countries each account for less than 1 per cent of continental gambling turnover. For 11 countries, no gambling is recorded. Although Africa is the smallest continental market for gambling in the world, lottery and gambling operations are one of the

[1] This chapter has greatly benefitted from Schenk (2010).

fastest-growing industries. Accordingly, their inclusion in the VAT base is of some importance.

A point worth noting at the outset is that gaming, like drinking and smoking, often is and certainly should be subject to excise duty to the extent that the activity gives rise to external costs.[2] Gaming can be a form of entertainment or an addiction. Addictive gamblers deprive their families of household monies or need medical attention at society's expense. This type of external cost is similar to that of the smoker who exposes his family to second-hand smoke. Gaming resembles drinking, too: like heavy drinkers, heavy gamblers should pay externality-correcting excises, but there is no need to impose this type of excise on moderate drinkers or entertainment gamblers. Like other forms of potential addiction, regulations concerning the age, place, hours, and other circumstances and conditions of gaming activities are important complementary measures to the imposition of the excises. Further, the VAT should be imposed on the excise-inclusive price of lottery tickets and gambling tokens and chips. This should apply to government-operated lottery and gambling establishments, too, even though their profits accrue to government.

15.2 Types of Lotteries and Gambling Activities

As indicated in Table 15.1, lotteries are the most widespread form of commercial gaming in Africa.[3] Lotteries differ in probability of winning, prize structure, frequency of drawings, and the sense of 'player participation'. General lotteries raise money by selling many tickets and choosing a few at random to win prizes. They may be exempted from VAT if the purpose is to finance a charity. Almost as popular are instant lotteries, which come in the form of scratch-off tickets with a thin covering that, once scratched off, reveal the prize. Somewhat less popular, lotto requires players to predict a set of winning numbers out of a larger set of possibilities. The outcome of sporting events is another opportunity for organizing a lottery. Owing to the nature of sport and the large number of independent matches, the outcome (if not rigged!) is effectively a random drawing.

Casinos are establishments where customers gamble by playing games such as roulette (a game in which a ball is dropped onto a revolving wheel with numbered compartments, the players betting on the number at which the ball comes to rest), craps (a dice game in which the players make wagers on the outcome of the roll, or a series of rolls, of a pair of dice), baccarat (a game of cards played by a banker and two or more punters who bet against the banker), blackjack (a comparing card game, also known as twenty-one, with one or more decks of 52 cards, usually

[2] For a comprehensive treatment, see Forrest (2008) who discusses policy in the EU, including the rise of the resort casino and remote gambling.

[3] Interestingly, the word 'lottery' derives from the Dutch word 'lot', which means fate.

Table 15.1 Lotteries and gambling

Type of lottery or gambling	Particulars	Number of African countries
1. Lotteries		
General	A drawing of lots in which prizes are distributed to the winners among persons buying a chance	22
Instant	Scratch-off tickets with thin covering that, once scratched off, reveal the prize	18
Lotto/Numbers	Players are to predict a set of winning numbers out of a larger set of possibilities	13
Toto/Football pools	Random drawing owing to nature of sport and number of independent matches	13
2. Casinos	Facilities in which customers gamble by playing games, such as craps, roulette, baccarat, blackjack, and video poker	27
3. Slot machines	Coin- or card-operated gambling machines that pay out according to the matching of symbols on wheels spun by a handle, including an electronic version	19
4. Racing		
Horse	Betting on the outcome of horse races	14
Greyhound	Betting on the outcome of greyhound races	0
Off-track betting	Sanctioned gambling outside race track	7
5. Bingo	Players mark off numbers on cards as the numbers are drawn randomly by a caller, the winner being the first person to mark off all the numbers	4
6. Cockfighting	Betting on a blood fight between two cocks, or gamecocks, held in a ring called a cockpit	0
7. Jai alai	Betting on a court game in which players use a long hand-shaped basket strapped to the wrist to propel a ball against a wall	0

Source: Clotfelter, 2005.

played between several players and a dealer, where each player in turn competes against the dealer but not against each other), or video poker (an arcade or casino game based on five-card draw poker, played on a computerized console similar in size to a slot machine). Blackjack is the most widely played casino banking game in Africa (and elsewhere in the world).

Slot machines, found in pubs, clubs, hotels, and amusement arcades as well as casinos, are coin- or card-operated gambling machines that pay out according to the matching of symbols on wheels spun by a handle. Electronic versions of poker, bingo, blackjack, keno, or reel games tend to be available, too. Slot machines are called the crack cocaine of gambling because of the immediacy of pay-offs and high pay-out rates, which have the potential to aggravate problem gambling. The addiction may be even worse under machines with less frequent but progressive pay-outs. Slot machines are often subject to licence-type excises, because of the difficulty of keeping track of amounts taken in and paid out.

Further, betting on horse or greyhound racing is found in various countries (e.g. Morocco). Usually, wagering takes the form of pari-mutuel betting, whereby the pay-off to a bet is determined by the distribution of wagers. In bingo, players mark off a number on cards as the numbers are drawn randomly by a caller, the winner being the first person to mark off all the numbers. Cockfighting is betting on the outcome of a blood fight between two cocks, or gamecocks, held in a ring called a cockpit. Finally, jai alai is a form of sports betting on a court game in which players use a long hand-shaped basket strapped to the wrist to propel a ball against a wall. Reportedly, there are no countries in Africa that engage in organized legal cockfighting or jai alai.

Following EU practice,[4] most African countries exempt games of chance from VAT. In contrast, countries with best-practice VATs, such as Australia, Canada, New Zealand, and Singapore, tax some or most games of chance.[5] Table 11.3 provides a broad picture of African practice, but does not list the countries that subject lotteries and gambling to an excise. Schenk (2010) cites legislation in naming Mozambique, Tanzania, Uganda, and Zambia as exempt countries and Botswana, Cameroon, Ethiopia, Ghana, and South Africa as countries that tax games of chance. PricewaterhouseCoopers (2015) surveys trends in Kenya, Nigeria, and South Africa. Sierra Leone exempts games of chance under its VAT, but imposes a separate tax (excise) on the activities. Obviously, this confuses the externality-correcting property of the excise with the revenue-raising efficiency role of the VAT. The following sections consider the implications of applying the VAT to lotteries and casinos.

15.3 Lotteries

The VAT treatment of lotteries is very much akin to that of property and casualty insurance. Effectively, betting transactions in, for instance, South Africa must comply with the country's Lotteries Act.[6] Under the country's VAT, the supply of

[4] Article 135(1)(i) of the EU's Common VAT Directive (2006) refers. It should be noted that inputs to the gaming industry other than winnings, such as the supply of gaming machines or admission fees, would be taxable under the EU's Common Directive and in African countries that exempt games of chance from VAT. For a report on gambling in the EU, see Swiss Institute of Comparative Law (2006). Of further interest is the European Commission's (2011) Green Paper on online gambling.

[5] Perhaps Singapore's GST has the widest coverage by taxing all forms of betting, fruit machines, games of changes, lotteries, and sweepstakes.

[6] In South Africa, all lotteries and sport pools are subject to the regulations of the National Lotteries Commission. See the useful description in National Lotteries Commission (undated). Incidentally, national lottery winnings are not subject to income or capital gains tax, but must be declared in the income tax return.

a betting transaction by a VAT-registered dealer is subject to tax at the rate of 15 per cent and output tax must be accounted for when payment is received. Since the payment is inclusive of VAT, output tax payable on a bet is calculated by applying the tax fraction (15/115) to the amount received. To arrive at the value added by the lottery dealer, the output tax should be reduced by the input tax, which equals an amount calculated by applying the tax fraction to any prize or winnings in relation to a supply of betting services (South African Revenue Service, 2012).

To illustrate, assume that a South African lottery operator, called a vendor, sells tickets for R10,000,000 (well above the VAT threshold of R1,000,000). The vendor's agents return R2,000,000 as unsold tickets. The lottery operator's taxable output from these sales is R8,000,000 × 100/115, or R6,956,522. Further assume that the lottery pays out winnings of R7,000,000, inclusive of VAT amounting to R913,043. The net VAT liability from the lottery is then R1,043,478 minus R913,043, or R130,435, which should be remitted to the VAT office. The same result is achieved by simply calculating the output tax on a net basis, i.e. as the difference between the net but VAT-inclusive proceeds of ticket sales and the VAT-inclusive winnings paid out, as is the practice in New Zealand. In the above example, the net proceeds inclusive of VAT are R8,000,000 minus R7,000,000, which equals R1,000,000. Applying the tax fraction of 15/115 to this amount yields the net VAT liability of R130,435.

Instead of issuing monetary prizes, a lottery operator may award, say, a motor car to the person submitting the lucky ticket. The operator would have bought the car and paid VAT on it. Would this VAT be deductible as an input VAT from the tax on the sale of the lottery tickets? Denying the credit would be tantamount to taxing the car twice: implicitly when the lottery tickets are sold and explicitly when the car is bought. One VAT payment would then be saved if the prize were awarded in cash and the winner used the cash to buy the car himself. To prevent this from happening, South Africa allows the operator to credit the input VAT actually incurred on the purchase of a car that is acquired for the purpose of awarding it as a prize. This form of preventing double taxation is also applicable to other non-monetary awards, such as free stays or meals in a hotel (South African Revenue Service, 2014).

In addition to the VAT imputed to winnings and the VAT actually incurred in respect of non-monetary prizes, lottery operators can deduct the VAT on inputs attributable to the taxable purchases of the lottery business, such as office furniture, computer facilities, utilities, printing, and promotional costs, if acquired for the purpose of conducting the business. A deduction would be denied if disallowed under the VAT legislation, such as for passenger cars. Finally, the usual input-VAT allocation rules apply for denying the input VAT on purchases relating to exempt supplies of, say, a lottery run by a non-profit organization, while the lottery operator also makes taxable supplies.

15.4 Casinos: Slot Machines and Table Games

The VAT treatment of casinos that operate slot machines and table games hardly differs from that of lotteries. Bets (output) placed in slot machines come in the form of tokens, cards, or cash. For table games, bets are placed with chips. A player purchases tokens, cards, or chips from a dealer or a cashier; these are subject to VAT even if not used immediately. Pay-outs of winnings are considered inputs of the casino eligible for a tax credit. The net taxable output (value added) can be measured by the difference (margin) between the cost of the tokens or chips bought, on the one hand, and those returned at the end of a gaming session for cash plus any winnings, on the other hand. This margin can be measured on a cash-flow basis or by the flow of tokens and chips. The cash-flow method may be most appropriate for table games, the flow of tokens approach for playing slot machines. Usually, the margin—i.e. the gambling business's gross value added—is calculated at the end of the day. As a result, commingled flows (playing with winnings) are implicitly netted out. If cash winnings exceed bets received, the margin is negative and must be carried over to the next period and included in that period's margin as cash winnings paid out.

A few other peculiarities of the VAT's application to gambling are worth noting. Receipts and payments for non-gambling transactions (e.g. admission fees or the purchase of furnishings) must be accounted for separately as part of the casino's output. This isolates the cash from gambling transactions from other transactions that fall under the regular VAT rules applicable to other businesses.[7] Promotional vouchers issued without charge and exchanged for tokens or chips should not affect the margin, but winnings with tokens or chips thus acquired do reduce the casino's margin. Tax credits for non-monetary prizes are handled in the same way as with lotteries. Bad debts and their recovery or write-off must be accounted for if gambling is allowed on credit, although some countries do not do so.

15.5 Some Answers

This chapter has argued that transactions involved in games of chance should be included in the VAT base, regardless of whether or not lotteries and gambling are subject to externality-correcting excises.[8] The charge should extend to all forms of gaming, except if feasibility considerations (e.g. village cockfights) preclude the

[7] The regular rules are also applied to transactions between bookmakers. To illustrate (Schenk, 2010, fn 49): 'If a gambling operator (such as a bookmaker referred to as the first bookmaker) receives bets and also places bets with a second bookmaker, the first bookmaker can claim an input tax deduction for the tax fraction of the bet (wager) placed with the second bookmaker, and must report as output tax the tax fraction of any winnings it receives from that wager'.

[8] This section attempts to answer the questions posed by Schenk (2010).

effective application of the VAT. The chapter has also shown that the reverse-charge approach and the margin method lead to identical outcomes in calculating the VAT liability. To prevent double taxation and diversion of transactions, the VAT paid for the acquisition of non-monetary prizes and awards should preferably be creditable against the VAT on sales of tickets, tokens, and chips. If a casino is part of a larger establishment operated by a registered business, the VAT on a non-monetary prize (say, a night's stay or meal at a hotel) should be denied to the casino in order to ensure that the prize's value is taxed once.

16
Small Businesses and Farmers

The design of the threshold level of turnover—also called the small-business exemption—above which businesses are required to register and charge VAT on their output and entitled to reclaim tax on their inputs invoiced by other registered businesses, is one of the most important issues under the VAT (Keen and Mintz, 2004). Too high a threshold may be costly in terms of revenue and unduly distort business organization around the threshold. Too low a threshold may involve high administration costs for the VAT department and disproportionately high compliance costs for small taxpayers. This chapter examines the issues, separately for small businesses and, partly overlapping, the agricultural sector.[1]

16.1 Small Businesses

Following a survey of the level of the thresholds in African countries, this section develops some thoughts on the estimation of an optimal or best-practice level and on whether or not small exempt businesses should pay some tax in lieu of VAT over and above the tax, if any, on inputs.

Threshold Levels

As shown in Table 16.1, thresholds in Africa vary widely, ranging from below US$20,000 in Algeria, Ethiopia, Malawi, and Mauritania to over US$150,000 in Chad, Djibouti, Equatorial Guinea, Mauritius, and Niger. Madagascar has an exceptionally high threshold equivalent to US$320,000, implying that its VAT is not a broad-based consumption tax and that, for revenue purposes, it continues to rely heavily on the turnover (and production) taxes levied prior to the introduction of the VAT.

In nearly 30 African countries, the VAT threshold (for goods) exceeds US$50,000, which should keep most small businesses out of the tax's ambit and enable VAT administrations to concentrate on large taxpayers. This stance is reinforced by some countries (e.g. Cameroon), which do not permit voluntary

[1] Unless otherwise indicated, agriculture is understood to include forestry and fishery.

Table 16.1 Africa: VAT registration thresholds, 2018

RECs and countries	National currency	Registration threshold (annual turnover)		Particulars (m = million, national currency)	Simplified regime (m = million, national currency)
		National	US$		
Southern African Development Community (SADC)					
SACU					
Botswana	BWP (pula)	1,000,000	105,000		
Lesotho	LSL (loti)	850,000	72,000		
Namibia	NAD (dollar)	500,000	42,000	No registration below 200,000	
South Africa	ZAR (rand)	1,000,000	84,000	No registration below 50,000 (120,000 for commercial accommodation)	
Swaziland	SZL (lilangeni)	500,000	42,000		
Other					
Congo, DR	CDF (franc)	80,000,000	50,000		
Madagascar	MGA (ariary)	200,000,000	320,000	8% in lieu of VAT + corporation tax on public procurement contracts	5% turnover tax if turnover <200m
Malawi	MWK (kwacha)	10,000,000	14,000		2% turnover tax if turnover <10m
Mauritius	MUR (rupee)	6,000,000	180,000	No threshold for professionals	
Mozambique	MZN (metical)	50,000,000	80,000		Simplified scheme if turnover <50m
Seychelles	SCR (rupee)	2,000,000	148,000		
Zambia	ZMW (kwacha)	800,000	80,000	No voluntary registration	Turnover tax if turnover <0.8m
Zimbabwe	ZWD (dollar)	60,000	60,000		

Continued

Table 16.1 *Continued*

RECs and countries	National currency	Registration threshold (annual turnover)		Particulars (m = million, national currency)	Simplified regime (m = million, national currency)
		National	US$		
East African Community (EAC)					
Burundi	BIF (franc)	100,000,000	57,000		
Kenya	KES (shilling)	5,000,000	50,000	6% withholding by designated agents	3% turnover tax if turnover <5m
Rwanda	RWF (franc)	20,000,000	24,000		
Tanzania	TZS (shilling)	100,000,000	44,000		0.3% local turnover tax
Uganda	UGS (shilling)	150,000,000	66,000	No threshold for professionals	
Economic and Monetary Community of Central Africa (CEMAC)					
Cameroon	XAF (CFA franc)	50,000,000	95,000	No voluntary registration	
Cent. Afr. Rep.	XAF (CFA franc)	30,000,000	57,000		Flat tax if turnover ≤30m
Chad	XAF (CFA franc)	100,000,000	190,000	Threshold 60m for services; no threshold for professionals	Simplified regime for goods if 20m<turnover<100m and for services if 10m<turnover<60m
Congo	XAF (CFA franc)	30,000,000	57,000		No VAT if lump-sum tax regime for business income tax
Equat. Guinea	XAF (CFA franc)	80,000,000	152,000		
Gabon	XAF (CFA franc)	60,000,000	114,000	Threshold 500m for forestry	Simplified regime
Economic Community of West African States (ECOWAS)					
UEMOA					
Benin	XOF (CFA franc)	50,000,000	95,000		Simplified regime
Burkina Faso	XOF (CFA franc)	15,000,000	28,000	Threshold 50m for unprocessed agricultural and fishery products	

Côte d'Ivoire	XOF (CFA franc)	50,000,000	95,000	Threshold 25m for services	
Guinea–Bissau	XOF (CFA franc)	..	..	No threshold for professionals	Simplified regime
Mali	XOF (CFA franc)	30,000,000	57,000	Threshold 1m for public works contractors	
Niger	XOF (CFA franc)	100,000,000	190,000		Simplified regime if 50m≤turnover<100m; licence duty if 5m<turnover<50m
Senegal	XOF (CFA franc)	50,000,000	95,000	Threshold 25m for services	Simplified regime
Togo	XOF (CFA franc)	50,000,000	95,000		
WAMZ					
Cabo Verde	CVE (escudo)	5,000,000	55,000		
Gambia	GMD (dalasi)	1,000,000	21,000	No registration below 500,000; no threshold for auctioneers and promoters of public entertainment	
Ghana	GHS (cedi)	200,000	46,000	No threshold for auctioneers, promoters of public entertainment, and governments	3% flat-rate scheme for businesses if turnover <200,000
Guinea	GNF (franc)	500,000,000	55,000	Withholding of 50% VAT by designated companies	3% minimum tax if 150m<turnover<500m
Sierra Leone	SLL (leone)	350,000,000	45,000	No threshold for promoters of public entertainment	
Arab Maghreb Union (AMU)					
Algeria	DZD (dinar)	130,000	1,000	Threshold 100,000 for services	
Mauritania	MRO (ouguiya)	6,000,000	17,000	Threshold 3m for services	Presumptive turnover tax if turnover <6m for goods and <3m for services

Continued

Table 16.1 *Continued*

RECs and countries	National currency	Registration threshold (annual turnover)		Particulars (m = million, national currency)	Simplified regime (m = million, national currency)
		National	US$		
Morocco	MAD (dirham)	500,000	55,000	Threshold 2m for wholesalers and retailers	
Tunisia	TND (dinar)	100,000 for retailers	42,000		
Intergovernmental Authority on Development (IGAD) and Egypt					
Djibouti	DJF (franc)	50,000,000	280,000	No threshold for law firms, notaries, and advisory and accounting firms	
Egypt	EGP (pound)	500,000	28,000		
Ethiopia	ETB (birr)	500,000	18,000	No threshold for vendors and producers of jewellery, electronics, flour, plastics, shoes, computers, and leather products	2% (10% on services) turnover tax if turnover <500,000
Sudan	SDG (pound)	100,000	55,000		

Note: The data are from secondary sources and may be out of date, incomplete, and, in some instances, perhaps even incorrect. Further, in determining the threshold, simplified regimes are not considered part of the VAT system, because they are generally applied to turnover rather than value added. The table therefore does not show countries 'without a registration threshold', in contrast to the summaries by the International Bureau of Fiscal Documentation (2018) and Ernst & Young (2018).

Source: Author's compilation from International Bureau of Fiscal Documentation (2018) and Ernst & Young (2018).

registration for businesses whose turnover is lower than the threshold. Other countries (e.g. Gambia, Namibia, and South Africa) have set a threshold, lower than the general threshold, below which voluntary registration is not possible. This saves on refunds to small operators selling zero-rated foodstuffs—hard to monitor anyway—and to hobby farmers whose refund position might otherwise tend to be more or less permanent.

Various countries have differentiated the threshold for activities whose value added tends to be higher on average as a proportion of sales. Thus, some UEMOA and AMU countries have lower thresholds for services. In their view, applying the same threshold as for goods would discriminate in favour of service providers. But an onerous distinction must be made between 'goods' and 'services'—not always easy. Presumably for similar reasons but probably easier to implement, Chad, Djibouti, Guinea-Bissau, Mauritius, and Uganda do not permit a threshold for the taxable activities of professionals, such as accountants and lawyers. And in the same vein, Gambia, Ghana, and Sierra Leone do not have thresholds for auctioneers and/or promoters of public entertainment. Ethiopia goes even further by denying the benefit of a threshold to vendors and producers of jewellery, electronics, flour, plastics, shoes, computers, and leather products. On the other hand, higher threshold levels are provided for forestry operations in Gabon and for unprocessed agricultural and fishery products in Burkina Faso. Morocco has a higher threshold for wholesalers and retail traders, even though various retailers, such as supermarkets, should be capable of complying with the requirements of the VAT. All of these differentiations involve potentially contentious delineation issues that have to be monitored by the VAT administration.

Regardless of the threshold, most countries require all legal persons to register for the VAT. Partnerships and associations of persons are considered as one entity for VAT, although each partner is obliged to register. Also, various countries have provisions preventing small businesses from splitting up their operations to benefit from the threshold. Proprietors of more than one business have to add up the sales of all their businesses to determine the eligibility for the threshold. Exempt supplies tend to be left out of account in determining the threshold, which is important in countries that do not charge VAT on various consumer goods, such as bread, dairy products, meat, vegetables, and fruit.

Small businesses that choose not to register for the VAT cannot take a credit for the tax on their purchases, which increases their costs of doing business. On the other hand, they do not have to charge VAT on their sales. Whether or not the exemption is advantageous to small businesses depends, among others, on the VAT status of their customers. If these customers are consumers, then small businesses should benefit from the exemption, assuming they operate under the same cost/price conditions as registered businesses. They would suffer financially, on the other hand, if their customers are registered VAT payers, because, in fully competitive markets, they would not be able to pass the VAT on their inputs on to these customers.

Accordingly, the option of registration is important for businesses situated between registered suppliers and registered customers. Optional registration may also be beneficial for small businesses incurring sizable capital expenditures or whose production is seasonal—enabling them to obtain a refund of any excess output VAT over input VAT. In no country can the tax on capital assets be refunded without registration for a minimum period. Optional registration is important, too, for small businesses exporting their output or being subject to a lower rate on sales than on purchases. Generally, a minimum registration period of 1–5 years applies to prevent small businesses that opt for registration from moving into and out of the system at will.

What Is the Optimal or Best-Practice Level for the Threshold?

The great variation in the level of thresholds among African countries begs the question of what the best-practice level of a threshold should be. Obviously, at least two competing considerations enter the equation: revenue and operational (administration and compliance) costs. The revenue gain (loss) of reducing (increasing) the threshold must be balanced against the higher (lower) administrative cost of applying the VAT to a larger (smaller) number of registrants. It should further be considered that compliance costs, as a percentage of turnover, tend to be much higher for small businesses than for large businesses.[2] Since compliance costs tend to be fixed costs, their incidence is likely to be regressive with respect to income, an aspect though which should be balanced against the competitive advantage that small exempt businesses may enjoy vis-à-vis their larger taxable competitors. In addition, the cost of the economic distortions that can be associated with behavioural changes of businesses just below or above the threshold should be taken into account.[3] Presumably, these costs increase as the threshold increases.

Apart from the cost of the economic distortions, the trade-off between revenue and operational costs is optimized, loosely speaking, at the point where the additional revenue from lowering the threshold equals the additional operational costs incurred. Keen and Mintz (2004) have formalized this trade-off in the following simple rule: $z^* = \{\delta A + \Gamma\} / \{(\delta - 1)\tau v(z)\}$, in which z^* is the threshold that maximizes revenue, A the administrative costs (assumed to be fixed), Γ the compliance costs (also fixed), δ the (constant) marginal cost of public funds, τ the VAT

[2] In the UK, for instance, the compliance costs of small businesses have been estimated to be on average 20 times the compliance costs of large businesses. See Sandford, Godwin, and Hardwick (1989).

[3] Liu and Lockwood (2015) show that there is bunching around the threshold, and the amount of bunching is negatively related to the intensity of input use and positively related to the share of B2C (business-to-consumer) transactions, consistent with the conceptual framework that they develop.

rate, and v the ratio of value added to sales. Based on Cnossen's (1994) estimate of operational costs for developed countries—US$100 for administrative costs and US$500 for compliance costs—a VAT rate of 15 per cent, a ratio of value added to sales of 35 per cent (typical for manufacturing in Canada), and a marginal cost of public funds of 1.3, Keen and Mintz compute an optimal threshold for developed countries of US$40,000.[4]

Informed estimates of administrative and compliance costs for developing countries are not available. Presumably, the optimal threshold should be higher for developing countries where most of the constants used above tend to be higher. Further, Keen and Mintz (2004) point out that the threshold would be lower if the ratio of value added to sales were higher, e.g. for services. On the other hand, given the level of revenue to be raised, the threshold can be higher if businesses below the threshold pay non-creditable VAT on inputs as, in practice, exempt businesses and entities do. A relatively high share of imports in the tax base should also permit a higher threshold. Further, the threshold should be set higher if the operational costs of the VAT are high relative to revenue, as they tend to be in African countries. Indeed, there are often sharply diminishing returns to adding smaller firms in terms of additional revenue collected.

Beyond that, there is the cost of the distortion of firm size to be considered. Based on Keen and Mintz's (2004) analysis, this cost can even dominate the more obvious revenue concern. All of this appears to suggest that there is a case for setting the optimal threshold in most African countries above the US$40,000 level. As indicated by Table 16.2, eight countries—roughly one in five of all countries surveyed—have a threshold that is lower than US$40,000.[5]

In addition to the optimal level of the threshold, there is a best-practice level. This level is understood as the threshold that allows for the collection of about 80 per cent of potential VAT revenues calculated on the basis of consumption expenditures in national accounts. In many countries, the observed concentration of taxable activities amongst a relatively small number of businesses—typically 20 per cent of all businesses—has led to the 80:20 rule, i.e. 80 per cent of the VAT revenue comes from 20 per cent of the businesses. This suggests that the VAT administration should be advised to focus its efforts on large taxpayers and not on exempt small businesses whose VAT would be limited to the tax on inputs, usually not a negligible amount, which they have to pay their registered suppliers.

To illustrate, assume that the size distribution of the business units by annual turnover in a country is as shown in Table 16.3.[6] Based on data on the number of

[4] For another approach to setting the optimal threshold, see Zee (2005a).

[5] Interestingly, there is no correlation between the level of the thresholds and the C-efficiency of the various VATs shown in Figure 6.1.

[6] Many tax administrations, particularly those with large taxpayer units, keep records of VAT collections matched to specific firms and turnover, so the analysis could also show the size distribution of firms by actual VAT collected.

Table 16.2 Africa: VAT registration thresholds by size in US$

0–20,000	20,000–40,000	40,000–60,000	60,000–80,000	Over 80,000
Algeria	Burkina Faso	Burundi	Lesotho	Benin
Ethiopia	Egypt	Cabo Verde	Mozambique	Botswana
Malawi	Gambia	Cent. Afr. Rep.	Uganda	Cameroon
Mauritania	Rwanda	Congo	Zambia	Chad
		Congo, DR		Côte d'Ivoire
		Ghana		Djibouti
		Guinea		Equatorial Guinea
		Kenya		Gabon
		Mali		Madagascar
		Morocco		Mauritius
		Namibia		Niger
		Sierra Leone		Senegal (goods)
		Sudan		Seychelles
		Swaziland		South Africa
		Tanzania		Togo
		Tunisia		
		Zimbabwe		

Source: Table 16.1.

establishments, turnover, and aggregate VAT collected, establishments with turnover of 250 million currency units and above represent merely 13.9 per cent of the total number of establishments. By contrast, they account for 87.0 per cent of aggregate turnover and 82.8 per cent of aggregate VAT paid. Conversely, many small establishments, again as measured by turnover, account for a small share of turnover and VAT paid. Specifically, establishments with turnover up to 250 million currency units account for 86.1 per cent of the total number of establishments, 13.0 per cent of turnover, and 17.2 per cent of aggregate (gross) VAT collected.[7]

Using the 80:20 rule mentioned above, these numbers suggest that a threshold of around 250 million currency units for the country under consideration would not be inappropriate. To be sure, each firm size distribution is country-specific and therefore the right threshold will differ from country to country. Many variables will influence local conditions and thus the best-practice threshold, including the industrial and trading structures, the effectiveness of the administration, the importance of exemptions and concessionary regimes, the size of the informal economy, and the openness of the economy. Each country's situation may also require flexibility in respect of changes in the threshold. For instance, the administration will want to increase the threshold periodically (e.g. every 6–12 months) in the presence of significant inflation to avoid unintended and revenue-unproductive growth in the registrant population.

[7] This example follows Gendron (2017).

Table 16.3 Size distribution of VAT registrants in a developing country

Taxable supplies range (000) (= lower bound, < upper bound)		Registrants			Taxable supplies			VAT paid			Effective VAT rate (%)[a]
		Count (units)	Share in total (%)	Cumulative share (%)	Amount (million currency units)	Share in total (%)	Cumulative share (%)	Amount (million currency units)	Share in total (%)	Cumulative share (%)	
= 0		554	21.1	21.1	0	0.00	0.00	2	0.01	0.01	-
> 0	500	39	1.5	22.6	7	0.00	0.00	1	0.00	0.01	9.01
500	1,000	26	1.0	23.6	21	0.00	0.00	1	0.01	0.01	5.02
1,000	5,000	171	6.5	30.1	463	0.07	0.07	22	0.14	0.17	4.77
5,000	10,000	167	6.4	36.5	1,250	0.18	0.25	45	0.28	0.45	3.59
10,000	15,000	145	5.5	42.0	1,751	0.25	0.51	62	0.39	0.84	3.52
15,000	20,000	135	5.1	47.2	2,348	0.34	0.85	97	0.62	1.46	4.13
20,000	50,000	420	16.0	63.2	13,865	2.01	2.86	522	3.31	4.77	3.76
50,000	100,000	299	11.4	74.6	21,014	3.05	5.90	735	4.67	9.44	3.50
100,000	250,000	302	11.5	86.1	49,069	7.11	13.02	1,217	7.73	17.16	2.48
250,000	500,000	162	6.2	92.3	57,242	8.30	21.31	1,570	9.97	27.13	2.74
500,000	1,000,000	80	3.0	95.3	57,305	8.31	29.62	1,200	7.62	34.75	2.09
1,000,000	5,000,000	95	3.6	98.9	185,434	26.88	56.50	2,885	18.32	53.07	1.56
5,000,000	10,000,000	17	0.6	99.6	122,107	17.70	74.20	1,911	12.13	65.20	1.56
10,000,000	and over	11	0.4	100.0	177,971	25.80	100.00	5,482	34.80	100.00	3.08
Total		2,623	100.0	100.0	689,849	100.00	100.00	15,751	100.00	100.00	2.28

[a] Average effective VAT paid rate; overall weighted average effective VAT rate appears in 'Total' row.

Source: Gendron, 2017.

Presumptive Taxation Schemes

In view of the high thresholds in most countries, generally African VAT regimes do not provide for administrative concessions in the form of longer filing and payment periods or simplified accounting methods to ease compliance. Generally, taxable output and creditable inputs have to be reported in the month following the month in which they occur, while the net VAT has to be paid within 2–4 weeks after the return should have been filed. Perhaps for the same reason, most African VAT legislations prescribe the 'invoice basis' of accounting and do not explicitly permit taxable persons to account for their transactions, and hence the VAT, on a 'payments or cash basis'. Specifically, no credit is allowed until such time as a 'tax invoice' is held by the taxable person as proof that that person is entitled to the tax credit. Obviously, an invoice basis of accounting is more difficult to maintain than a cash basis, because records have to be kept of cash received and paid, as well as of invoices issued and received.

Instead of administrative concessions, various African countries do apply presumptive taxation schemes to small exempt businesses, ostensibly to collect some revenue over and above the VAT on inputs.[8] The schemes, listed in Table 16.1 under 'Simplified regime', vary by country and are difficult to document. Generally, they are low-rate turnover taxes often levied on a presumptive basis. Child (2008) mentions the old small retailers VAT package in South Africa, which allowed small businesses to calculate the VAT payment as a flat percentage of turnover (depending on the nature of the trade sector of the business). In calculating the percentage, the VAT on inputs had been taken into consideration and hence was not creditable against the tax on turnover. South Africa abolished this simplified regime several years ago, because it was too cumbersome to administer. Further, Ghana introduced a flat-rate scheme in 2007, which requires the payment of 3 per cent of turnover. The French *régime forfaitaire* or *taxe unique* goes even further by imposing a legally binding amount of tax, supposedly agreed with the taxpayer, for the current year and the following two years.

A number of arguments have been advanced in favour of and against simplified schemes.[9] Arguments in favour include: reduction in compliance costs; encouragement of better record-keeping; minimization of number of contacts between taxpayers and administration (so fewer collusive practices); education of taxpayers prior to their graduation to regular regimes; reduction in administrative costs related to dealing with small businesses; and encouragement of formalization.

[8] As defined by Thuronyi (1996), 'Presumptive taxation involves the use of indirect means to ascertain tax liability, which differ from the usual rules based on the taxpayer's accounts. The term "presumptive" is used to indicate that there is a legal presumption that the taxpayer's income [turnover] is no less than the amount resulting from the application of the indirect method'. For an early analysis of the hard-to-tax, see Alm, Martinez-Vazquez, and Schneider (2005).

[9] Bird and Gendron (2007, chs 7, 9, and 10) provide an extensive review of the arguments on both sides on which these paragraphs draw. This section has benefitted from the input of Pierre-Pascal Gendron.

Arguments against simplified schemes include: low revenue yield; administrative costs from operating additional programmes; asymmetry of information in favour of invisible potential taxpayers; freezing of information flows and relegation of target taxpayers to forgotten status;[10] increase in the extent of exemptions and breaks in the VAT chain (and associated information chain); open door to negotiated tax burdens or coarse approximations thereof; penalty for graduation to regular regime if its statutory burden exceeds that of the simplified regime; and elimination of self-assessment as the first line of administration and retardation of the development of a self-assessment culture.

There are few field data on the effectiveness of simplified regimes. On the whole, the arguments against seem to outweigh those in favour, especially if one takes a long-term perspective of the development of the tax system. In the end, weak tax administrations cannot solve the information asymmetry that small but invisible potential taxpayers present to them. The costs of searching and finding those will usually exceed the pay-off in additional revenue. Besides, they will pay VAT on inputs and may eventually see the benefit in registering voluntarily or moving to the threshold and registering anyway. It is unlikely that there are compelling benefits from forcing this outcome.

To conclude, simplified regimes—created in response to the flood of taxpayers from a threshold set too low—are the wrong policy response. A properly set threshold under a single-rate VAT regime—aside, perhaps, from the opportunity for very small businesses to use cash accounting and reduced filing requirements—is likely to be the most effective way of dealing with small businesses (including farmers), especially if accompanied by taxpayer education campaigns that emphasize the benefits of being registered and the ability to claim input VAT credits (Cnossen, 1998b). While there are many conceptual problems with presumptive taxes (Thuronyi, 1996), the lack of revenue-raising capacity in relation to the administrative resources used to collect the tax is the fatal flaw of such schemes.[11]

16.2 Farmers

In many respects, the taxation of the agricultural sector is also a small-business or threshold issue. Small farmers will find it difficult to comply with the requirements of the VAT for a variety of reasons—e.g. illiteracy, no bookkeeping skills, great distance from the tax office, and lack of means of communication. But the effects of the threshold on farmers differ from the effects on, say, small exempt retailers that sell to non-registered consumers. Small retailers benefit from the exemption because their own value added (generally, the reward for their labour) is not

[10] This problem arises in many concessional tax regimes, including free zones.

[11] The hard-to-tax shade into the informal economy, which is quite sizable in Africa. Medina, Jonelis, and Cangul (2017) estimate that its size ranges from a low of 20–25% in Mauritius, South Africa, and Namibia to a high of 50–65% in Benin, Tanzania, and Nigeria.

taxed. This is also true with respect to farmers selling directly to consumers or exempt traders, but not to exempt farmers selling their products to taxable agro-processing firms. These farmers are stuck with the unrelieved VAT on inputs, which will likely have to be borne by them, because taxable farmers would be able to pass the VAT forward to other taxable stages of production and distribution. Accordingly, eliminating this unrelieved VAT in the agricultural sector is an important issue, particularly if voluntary registration is not a feasible option.

VAT and Agriculture

Basically, there are four practical ways, separate or in combination, in which VAT can be applied to the agricultural sector: (1) a taxation regime; (2) an exemption regime; (3) input VAT relief for exempt farmers; and, somewhat removed, (4) output VAT relief for farm products. Box 16.1 defines them. Equal treatment vis-à-vis other goods and services (neutrality), along with transparency, are important criteria in choosing between the alternatives. Neutrality implies that an effort should be made to eliminate the hidden input VAT of exempt farmers. Further, compliance costs, which, measured against income, tend to weigh more heavily on small taxable farms than on large farms, should be minimized.[12]

Under the *taxation regime*, as indicated in Box 16.1, the agricultural sector is treated the same as any other taxable sector. Producers whose turnover is below the threshold are exempted, but can register voluntarily. They would then incur compliance costs, whose burden is akin to that of a tax.

Under the *exemption regime*, regardless of the threshold, in principle no farmer would have to register for VAT purposes and all farmers would be assumed to be unable to pass the VAT on their inputs through to agro-processing firms. Again, optional registration could and generally should be made available, but this would increase compliance costs, particularly for small farmers. Agricultural processing firms, which would generally be large, would be registered. They would not be able to take a deduction for the VAT incurred by non-registered farmers on their inputs. Hence, this tax would cascade throughout the production–distribution process and would likely result in a higher VAT burden at the consumer level than if farmers and processing firms had been subject to a full taxation regime. Obviously, sales at the farm gate would not be subject to the tax-on-tax effect.

Input VAT relief can be made available to farmers under the taxation regime if their turnover falls below the threshold and they do not elect to register. With full

[12] In considering the options, it is assumed that, at every stage, the gross VAT on sales by taxable farmers is passed on in output prices and is deductible from the VAT on output of the taxable purchasers of their products. Further, farmers who are not liable to VAT on output are assumed not to be able to pass the unrelieved tax on inputs on to the taxable purchasers of their products, except perhaps with respect to sales to exempt purchasers, mainly consumers, who are confronted with VAT-inclusive prices of similar taxable products.

Box 16.1 Options for the VAT treatment of the agricultural sector (separate or in combination)

Taxation regime: Farmers are treated like other businesses subject to VAT—i.e. output is taxed and the tax on inputs is deductible from the tax on output. Small farmers whose output falls below the threshold are exempted but can elect to be registered.

Exemption regime: All or some categories of farmers are exempted from VAT regardless of turnover, but individual farmers can elect to be taxable.

Input VAT relief for exempt farmers under either regime:

a. Exemption of agricultural inputs.
b. Reduced or zero rate on agricultural inputs.
c. Flat-rate scheme:
   i. Farmers charge a presumptive tax on output at a rate that, on average, accounts for the VAT on their inputs; they keep the amount of the presumptive tax, while taxable purchasers of farm products deduct the amount of the tax from their VAT on output.
   ii. Equivalent in result, farmers do not charge tax on output, but purchasers of farm products are permitted a presumptive tax credit, which on average accounts for the VAT paid on inputs by farmers; they pay the amount of the credit to farmers.
d. Monetary compensation by the government of the VAT paid on agricultural inputs on the basis of individual refund claims or calculated as under the flat-rate scheme.

Output VAT relief for farm products: Farm products are exempted, zero-rated, or taxed at a lower-than-standard but positive rate at the retail level.

input VAT relief, the right of optional registration would not have to be exercised and the attendant compliance costs would not have to be incurred. Similarly, input VAT relief can be made available to any farmer under the exemption regime who does not elect to be registered.

Input VAT relief can take one of the following four forms:

- Specified inputs sold to farmers are exempted. This form of relief tends to be ill designed since farmers would still be stuck with the input VAT of suppliers. Also, the relief is ill targeted if users other than farmers would benefit from the exemption or be burdened by the unrelieved VAT on inputs of the exempt products if they are not registered for VAT. This can be prevented by so-called end-use exemptions, i.e. inputs would only be exempted if sold to farmers. However, end-use exemptions—redundant in the case of taxable farmers—are notoriously difficult to monitor.[13]

- Specified inputs, such as seed, feed, fertilizers, insecticides, and perhaps other inputs, such as agricultural machinery, can be taxed at a reduced rate or be zero-rated,[14] so that exempt farmers incur less or no VAT on their inputs of these goods and, hence, there is less or no hidden tax in the price of their output. The problem with this approach is that dual-use goods, such as building materials and means of transportation, which can be used for business as well as private purposes, in as well as outside the agricultural sector, should not be zero-rated if revenue leakage is to be prevented. Accordingly, it is advisable to confine the reduced or zero rate to goods and services that can only be used for agricultural purposes.
- Agricultural inputs are taxed, but farmers are compensated for the VAT included in the price of these inputs through a *flat-rate scheme*—i.e. they charge a presumptive VAT on their sales to agro-processing firms (which would be able to take a credit for this VAT), but would not have to register and file returns themselves and would be able to keep the VAT on sales as compensation for the VAT on purchases. Alternatively, but equivalently, farmers would not charge VAT on their sales but agro-processing firms would still be able to credit the presumptive VAT on farmers' inputs and presumably pass the benefit back to farmers. Importantly, the flat rate should approximate the average tax on inputs. Flat-rate schemes are a unique European phenomenon.[15]
- The VAT on specified inputs, collected from suppliers by the government, can be paid out to farmers proportionate to their purchases of these inputs. Either farmers would have to file refund claims for the input VAT or the average pay-outs would be calculated in the same way as the rate under the flat-rate scheme. This form of input VAT relief is not found in many countries.

Output VAT relief means that (un)processed farm products sold to consumers are exempted, zero-rated, or taxed at a positive but lower-than-standard rate. Of course, the benefit of this form of relief accrues primarily to consumers, but some of the benefit may be passed back to farmers, depending on demand and supply elasticities. This form of relief is found in many countries, although newcomers to

[13] In practice, various Latin American and African countries exempt principal agricultural inputs from VAT. See Tait (1988, ch. 7) and Cnossen (2015).

[14] Zero-rating has been recommended by Tait (1988) and Due (1990).

[15] Note that the presumptive agricultural flat-rate scheme is different from the equally presumptive flat-rate schemes used to tax small traders. While the latter schemes are meant to extract some tax from small traders (in lieu of VAT on their value added, which is difficult to ascertain), agricultural flat-rate schemes are meant to compensate exempt farmers for the VAT incurred on inputs, which they cannot recoup otherwise. Presumably, the two presumptive approaches are also different in the direction in which VAT policy designers would wish to err.

the VAT have tended to stay away from output relief. The pros and cons of lower or zero rates on foodstuffs are discussed in Chapter 7.

VAT Treatment of Agriculture in African Countries

Table 16.4 shows the approaches to the agricultural sector and its products which African countries have adopted, as well as the VAT treatment of agricultural

Table 16.4 Africa: VAT treatment of farmers, agricultural inputs, and foodstuffs, 2018

RECs and countries	Basic approach to taxing farmers and foodstuffs	Agricultural inputs		
		Feed, seed	Fertilizer, insecticides, pesticides	Implements, machinery
Southern African Development Community (SADC)				
SACU				
Botswana	Sector taxed; specific products zero-rated if not served as a meal or as cooked or prepared food	T	Z	Z
Lesotho	Sector taxed; specific products zero-rated	Z/T	Z	T
Namibia	Sector taxed; specific products zero-rated if not served as a meal or as cooked or prepared food	T	T	T
South Africa	Sector taxed; specific products zero-rated	Z	Z	T
Swaziland	Sector taxed; specific products zero-rated	Z	Z	T
Other				
Congo, DR	Sector exempt; wheat, maize, flour, bread, and fish exempt	E	E	E
Madagascar	Sector exempt; paddy, rice, and corn exempt	E	E	E
Malawi	Sector exempt; meat, fish, eggs, dairy products, and honey exempt; salt zero-rated	Z	Z/E	Z
Mauritius	Unprocessed products exempt; specific products zero-rated	E	Z	E/T
Mozambique	Sector exempt; specific products zero-rated	E	E	E
Seychelles	Specific products exempt	T	T	T
Zambia	Unprocessed products exempt; bread and wheat zero-rated	E	E	Z
Zimbabwe	Specific products exempt or zero-rated if not served as a meal or as cooked or prepared food	Z	Z	Z/T

Continued

Table 16.4 *Continued*

RECs and countries	Basic approach to taxing farmers and foodstuffs	Agricultural inputs		
		Feed, seed	Fertilizer, insecticides, pesticides	Implements, machinery
East African Community (EAC)				
Burundi	Unfinished products sold by producer exempt; lower rate on imports	E	T	T
Kenya	Unprocessed products and maize exempt	E	E	E/T
Rwanda	Unprocessed products exempt (except milk)	E	E	E
Tanzania	Basic agricultural products exempt, except if supplied by restaurants	E	E	E
Uganda	Unprocessed foodstuffs exempt; cereals of local origin zero-rated	Z	Z	E
Economic and Monetary Community of Central Africa (CEMAC)				
Cameroon	Sector exempt; bread, milk, and fish exempt	E	E	E
Central African Republic	Basic, locally produced foodstuffs exempt; lower rate on imported milk, meat, and sugar	E	T	T
Chad	Unprocessed products sold directly to consumers exempt; bread, milk, poultry, and meat exempt	E	T	E
Congo	Products of local origin and basic foodstuffs exempt; lower rate on sugar, salt, and tomatoes	E	E	E
Equatorial Guinea	Raw products supplied by farmers directly to consumers exempt; lower rate on bread, rice, dairy products, meat, and infant foods	E	E	E
Gabon	Unprocessed products of local origin exempt; lower rate on chicken and sugar	E	E	E
Economic Community of West African States (ECOWAS)				
UEMOA				
Benin	Sector exempt; milk exempt	E	T	E
Burkina Faso	Unprocessed foods (fresh or frozen) exempt, including fish and meat	E	T	T
Côte d'Ivoire	Foodstuffs exempt; lower rate on milk and pasta	E	T	E

Guinea-Bissau	Foodstuffs exempt; lower rate on cereals, rice, flour, bread, and milk	E	T	T
Mali	Products exempt if basic nature not altered	E	E	E
Niger	Farmers exempt; rice, flour, poultry, meat, vegetable oil, fruit, and vegetables exempt	E	E	E
Senegal	Sector exempt; basic unprocessed products exempt	E	T	T
Togo	Sector exempt	E	T	T
WAMZ				
Cabo Verde	Specific basic foods exempt	E	E	T
Gambia	Unprocessed products supplied by producer exempt; basic foodstuffs exempt	E	E	E
Ghana	Products in their raw state exempt; specific basic foodstuffs exempt	E	E	E
Guinea	Sector exempt; rice, flour, wheat, bread, palm oil, and fish exempt	E	E/T	T
Sierra Leone	Rice in its raw state exempt; fish, birds, fruit, and vegetables exempt	E	E	E
Arab Maghreb Union (AMU)				
Algeria	Sector exempt; bread and milk exempt; lower rate on basic foodstuffs	L	L	T
Mauritania	Basic foodstuffs exempt	E	T	T
Morocco	Bread, cereals, milk, sugar, and edible oil exempt; lower rates on basic foodstuffs	Z	Z	Z
Tunisia	Sector exempt; retail sales of basic foodstuffs exempt	E	L	T
Intergovernmental Authority on Development (IGAD) and Egypt				
Djibouti	Sector exempt	T	T	T
Egypt	Sector exempt; infant food, sugar, tea, and coffee exempt; lower rate on some others	E	L	T
Ethiopia	Sector exempt; injera, bread, grain, wheat, maize, sorghum, cereals, palm oil, and milk exempt	E	E	T
Sudan	Products supplied in raw condition exempt; poultry, meat, fish, dairy products, and locally produced bread exempt	E	E	T

Note: The letters have the following meaning: T = taxed at the standard rate; E = exempt; Z = taxed at the zero rate; L = taxed at a lower-than-standard rate.

Source: Appendix A.

inputs. In view of the European background of the various VATs, it is not surprising that most countries have chosen to exempt the agricultural sector in full from the VAT requirements, although optional registration is generally available. Often, the exemption takes the form of not taxing 'unprocessed agricultural products' or 'agricultural products in their raw state or condition'. In other instances, specified farm products are exempted and sometimes the qualification is added that they must be sold directly to consumers by the producer. By contrast, countries that have followed the New Zealand approach—notably the SACU countries—have opted for taxing the agricultural sector[16] (subject to a fairly high threshold and the possibility of registration), although little tax is levied because various foodstuffs and agricultural inputs are zero-rated.

The treatment of farm inputs—taxed at the standard rate, exempted, zero-rated, or taxed at a lower-than-standard rate—is important under the exemption regime but also for small exempt farmers under the taxation regime. Table 16.4 indicates that treatment varies widely. Feed and seed are widely exempted, but some SADC countries and Morocco apply a zero rate and Algeria a lower rate. Much the same picture emerges with respect to the treatment of fertilizer, insecticides, and pesticides, although taxation is more prevalent than for feed and seed. This is understandable because the products are more likely to be imported or provided by large producers than feed and seed, which may often be obtained from within the domestic agricultural sector itself.

It should be noted that chemical fertilizer, insecticides, and pesticides tend to be environmentally unfriendly products whose external cost should be accounted for in price. Obviously, the *ad valorem* VAT cannot be seen as a proxy for the environmental tax that should be levied, because it is creditable by registered farmers. The appropriate instrument would be a non-creditable specific excise, which can be directly linked to the size of the environmental damage. This excise should apply to imported as well as domestically produced chemical fertilizers, insecticides, and pesticides, while the VAT should be applied to the excise-inclusive value of the products. No African country levies an excise on these products and only a limited number tax them under the VAT.[17]

Fertilizers, insecticides, and pesticides have little alternative use outside the agricultural sector. It is difficult, therefore, to divert their use to purposes not covered by the VAT. This means that exemption or zero-rating does what it is

[16] The two regimes meet, of course, if as many farmers would opt for registration under the exemption regime as would be required to register under taxation. But this is unlikely, since the option of registration entails compliance costs, which can be avoided under the exemption regime but not under the taxation regime for farmers whose turnover exceeds the threshold.

[17] Currently, excises on fertilizers and/or pesticides are levied in Belgium, British Columbia (Canada), Denmark, Finland, France, Italy, Louisiana (USA), the Netherlands, and Norway. The rationale of these excises is to reduce the volume of toxic pesticides and fertilizer and to promote the transition to low-toxicity alternatives. The World Health Organization has estimated that 3 million cases of pesticide poisoning occur every year, resulting in over 250,000 deaths. See the overview in United Nations Development Programme (2017) and the in-depth analysis on the form, use, and effect of these products in Denmark, France, Norway, and Sweden in Böcker and Finger (2016).

supposed to do, i.e. relieve farmers of input tax which cannot be passed on to other registered businesses. This is not necessarily true of farming implements and machinery, which, unless clearly delineated, can also be used for non-taxable ends. Exemption (at import, for instance) or zero-rating has the advantage that input tax does not get stuck because farmers cannot opt for registration.

Preferred Choice

When choosing among the alternative approaches to providing VAT relief for agricultural inputs, it should be pointed out that the flat-rate scheme is highly arbitrary. The choice of the compensation rate is politically charged and the scheme may be used to subsidize agriculture indirectly, which has happened in the EU (Cnossen, 2018a). Its application also brings its own complexities in train if farmers also carry on other activities that are subject to the normal VAT. The EU is dissatisfied with the scheme and most new member countries have not adopted it. Similarly, monetary compensation of farmers for the VAT incurred on inputs should not be considered by African countries.

Best practice would be to provide relief for the VAT on inputs by zero-rating various major inputs, such as feed, seed, chemical fertilizers, pesticides, and perhaps agricultural machinery—in short, inputs that do not or hardly have alternative uses. The following arguments can be put forward in support of this solution:

- In contrast to the flat-rate scheme, the zero-rating of major inputs is relatively easy to administer. Generally, the zero-rated inputs would be sold by large manufacturing or trading units with good accounts and capable of accounting for VAT refund claims. Obviously, zero-rating would not involve the farmers themselves in issuing invoices or keeping accounts.
- Zero-rating would involve a current benefit, whereas under the flat-rate scheme the time that elapses between the date of purchase of the inputs and the date the invoice is issued for the output, and when compensation would become available, would imply that farmers would incur an interest cost on the VAT that is to be compensated. This cost can be high in times of high inflation.
- The same argument applies if processing firms pay farmers for their output and the VAT attributable thereto some time after farmers have invoiced the presumptive VAT on inputs. Again, the farmer would incur an onerous interest cost.
- In contrast to the flat-rate scheme, zero-rating would also work if exempt livestock farmers buy, say, grain or corn from exempt crop farmers, since the latter would not have paid VAT on inputs either.

Perhaps there is no reason why farmers farming for their own consumption and for the local market should also benefit from the zero rate on agricultural inputs. In their case, the unrelieved VAT can be viewed as a tax on their own consumption and on the consumption of customers not paying taxes either. This tax can be made to stick by stipulating that the zero rate applies only if the zero-rated inputs are sold by manufacturers or wholesalers directly to farmers in quantities of at least, say, 10 kilograms, as is done in Ireland (Cnossen, 2018a). But this means that farmers would have to show a certificate to suppliers stating that they are genuine farmers, a rather awkward administrative complication.

This review suggests that first-best VAT practice is to treat the agricultural sector the same as any other sector, as is done under the VATs in SACU countries. Large farmers are not really different from other businesses (Ebrill et al., 2001, ch. 9). They can register for VAT purposes and pass the tax on inputs on to agro-processing firms if they want to get credit for the VAT. Farmers who sell at the farm gate can choose to remain exempt, a status that would be beneficial to them and, presumably, to their customers. In addition, major inputs, such as fertilizers, that have no alternative use outside the agricultural sector could be zero-rated. This should relieve small farmers of most of the VAT on inputs. To prevent revenue leakage, building materials and general farm implements should not be zero-rated.

16.3 A Generous Threshold

In conclusion, the single most important measure the authorities can take to 'assist' small businesses and farmers is to set a fairly high and single registration threshold with an option to register voluntarily. If the rule of thumb that 80 per cent of VAT is collected from 20 per cent of all businesses is correct, as it seems to be, then most countries should be advised to have a threshold equivalent to US$50,000 or higher. Perhaps South Africa's threshold is a good lodestar.

A high undifferentiated threshold implies that the VAT administration can concentrate its efforts on large taxpayers and that small businesses are not bothered by the taxman. Although voluntary registration is an important safety valve to limit economic distortions, a minimum threshold, as in South Africa, below which registration is not possible, is also to be recommended. On the other hand, threshold differentiation for services, professions, and trading channels increases administrative complexity and should not be contemplated. That applies also to presumptive taxation schemes, which yield little revenue, involve undue discretion, and are a nuisance for small businesses.

A generous threshold without further ado would also be appropriate for the agricultural sector, except that small exempt farmers would have to cope with the cascading effects of the input VAT on feed, seed, fertilizers, pesticides, insecticides, and farm implements and machinery. Voluntary registration would not work in view of low literacy levels, the absence of basic accounts, and the lack of communication. The solution appears to lie in a combination of a reasonably high threshold (the same as for other small businesses) and the zero-rating of major agricultural inputs, which have no alternative use outside the agricultural sector.

17
Basic Administrative Processes

In most African countries, improving the quality of VAT administration is critical to the long-term success of VAT as a revenue instrument.[1] 'Success' in the present context refers to the performance of the tax, as measured by an array of indicators, such as compliance and administrative costs per unit of revenue raised, revenue yield, VAT productivity, C-efficiency, and so on (see Chapter 6). Naturally, the quality of VAT design itself—the subject of this book—should have a major influence on the tax administration's ability to operate the VAT, at a given administrative capacity.

This chapter reviews various related but separable core administrative functions associated with the VAT: registration, filing, payment/collection, enforcement, and audit. It concludes with a brief note on fraud. The discussion focuses on the administration of an existing VAT. A separate literature exists that discusses planning for the introduction of a VAT and actually launching one.[2] Every process is important and is related to every other process. A defect anywhere in the administrative system can bring down even the best-designed VAT. It is worth looking at this rather dry topic in a little more detail. As noted earlier, how well the above functions are performed will determine the VAT's economic effects, its burden distribution, and its administrative efficacy (in terms of collection and compliance costs per unit of revenue). The discussion that follows highlights the key issues and outlines some best practices.

17.1 Registration

Registration is one of the most basic administrative requirements to operate a VAT. Its primary purpose is to build the sample of businesses (out of the total population of businesses) that will be relied on to collect the VAT on behalf of

[1] This chapter has been contributed by Pierre-Pascal Gendron. For a useful account of experience with the interaction between VAT design and administration, see Gendron (2017). The discussion in this chapter relies heavily on Bird and Gendron (2007, ch. 9) and also on several chapters in Tait (1991) and Ebrill et al. (2001). For a highly useful concise review and evaluation of VAT administration in anglophone Africa, see Kloeden (2011).

[2] See Holland (1991) and Bird and Gendron (2007); for a summary treatment, see Cnossen (1992). In addition, experiences with VAT launches have been discussed in various specialized journal articles.

the government. Registration and the important related process of taxpayer identification are fundamental to the efficient and equitable operation of the VAT. Administering these processes involves several decisions and sub-processes: determining the range of persons to be registered; implementing measures to promote registration; assigning VAT numbers or taxpayer identification numbers (the latter are preferable and could be published online); and setting up contingency plans to handle typical registration and numbering problems. Challenges include changing taxpayer characteristics and the existence of multiple taxpayer identification numbers.

Subject to the registration threshold, every person, sole proprietor, corporation, partnership, or other legal entity that engages in an activity that is taxable under VAT should be required to register. Registration creates the legal obligation for the registrant to maintain proper identification, issue invoices, keep books of account, collect VAT, and file returns. A good registration process is central to a good VAT. The VAT registration threshold is an important parameter in this process. Other key related variables include the time needed to register and the quality of service to new registrants. Typically, those two areas require improvement in many African countries. The economic reality of applications for new registration must be verified to prevent the creation of 'shell' companies or other fictitious traders that can be used as the basis for fraudulent credit claims. Persons engaging in fraudulent practices at the registration stage or any later stage must be promptly investigated and prosecuted, if necessary.

In many countries, a fairly large number of businesses registered for VAT purposes are dormant taxpayers, i.e. they do not pay VAT on a regular basis. Dormant registration numbers can be used to siphon off revenues through fraudulent refund claims. It is important, therefore, to remove these taxpayers from the VAT register by withdrawing their registration number. In case of doubt, proof of existence should be required in the form of ownership papers, utility bills, etc. Verification by chambers of commerce, law offices, accountants' offices, and tax consultants could also be required. Voluntary registrations, past and present, should be scrutinized with particular care, and a threshold should be introduced below which businesses cannot register for VAT.

In view of the relatively small total number of active VAT payers in many countries (e.g. see Kloeden (2011)), it could be worthwhile to recanvass all VAT registrants on the basis of a carefully designed instruction manual. Registrants could be classified into three groups: (1) active registrants, meaning that VAT returns and payments have been made in the last two calendar quarters; (2) suspended registrants, who have not filed a VAT return and/or made a payment in the last two quarters; and (3) non-active registrants, who have not filed returns and/or paid VAT in the last year. The registration number of non-active registrants should be removed without further ado. Suspended registrants should be sent a letter asking them to explain why they do not file returns. If the suspension is temporary, these registrants should be scrutinized regarding their address, business establishment, bank affiliation, etc. on the basis of a full risk-based analysis of the registrant's profile using all the information available in the tax and customs administration. In countries with a high threshold, registered VAT payers might be required to appoint a representative from a reputable accounting, law, or tax consultancy firm (not having an interest in the business of the registrant) to act as point of contact for the VAT administration. This should ensure professional representation.

At the same time, it is essential not to make the already slow and complex process of establishing a new business in many countries more burdensome than it already is. Generally, new businesses need better service and support from government than they now receive in most countries and this is also true of tax services. The ideal service model is the one-stop shop with complete and accurate forms and records, clear explanations, and quick processing. Those familiar with the way tax administrations actually function in African countries may find such advice too far removed from reality to be practicable. Nonetheless, unless tax administrations and other 'interfaces' between the government and the private sector encourage rather than discourage the development of the formal economy, many countries are likely to remain underdeveloped.

Registrants should be required to keep at least minimal books, essentially records of sales and purchases. Where possible, keeping complete accounts—or, better, audited financial statements—should be encouraged. In a well-designed and adequately administered VAT, the incentive to register for most traders (in the form of the creditable VAT on purchases) should be sufficiently great that it should not be necessary to undertake an extensive (and expensive) 'outreach' registration process. That being said, the benefits of registration should be publicized using information campaigns through traditional media as well as the internet. If a VAT is properly designed and administratively credible, potential registrants who sell to businesses already in the VAT system will enter that system voluntarily since it will clearly be in their interest to do so.[3]

17.2 Filing

Registrants must file regular VAT returns to discharge their obligations, and the administration should identify those registrants that are candidates for collection action: those that fail to produce a return and those that produce a return but do not pay the sum due. In order to facilitate taxpayer compliance, several practices are helpful. First, VAT return forms and instructions should be easily accessible to registrants. Many countries have made good on this by posting tax forms and instructions on the tax administration's website. Some even allow the use of

[3] For further discussion of registration, see Tait (1988) and Casanegra de Jantscher and Silvani (1991).

internet forms to enter information directly into the tax administration's server. Second, the amount of information requested should be proportionate to its intended use by the administration. Information that is collected but not used is not only useless but also costly.

Registrants are usually required to file returns on a monthly basis if their annual taxable sales exceed some specified limit. Exceptionally (e.g. in Botswana, Mauritius, and South Africa), smaller taxpayers are allowed to file every two months or quarterly. Most African countries allow a registrant between 10 and 31 days to file a VAT return after the tax period ends, with an average lag of about 20 days. Some countries have different types of returns for different taxpayers, especially when some file on a 'simplified' or 'quick' basis. Field experiences suggest two important observations: first, there is usually room for simplification and improvement of the forms; and second, registrants greatly benefit from having internet access to forms and instructions on how to fill in and submit those forms. Of course, there are other benefits to this as it minimizes physical (in-person) interactions between registrants and the tax administration.

If a registered taxpayer fails to file a return on time, a failure-to-file notification should be issued automatically and the delinquent filer charged an appropriate penalty (e.g. a fixed amount or a percentage of the tax due, whichever is greater). All countries levy at least interest or penalties on delinquent accounts, with a majority levying both. For those who continue to be delinquent, an official assessment needs to be issued promptly. Such a pro forma assessment can be made, for example, by calculating the estimated tax payment as the average of recent returns or perhaps as a pro-rata share of estimated annual gross receipts. In many countries, pro forma assessments outnumber voluntary returns, an indication of the gap in taxpayer education and cooperation.

Tax authorities create trouble for themselves if they set up assessment procedures incorrectly. A worrying feature of some estimated assessment programmes is that once a payment is made—even a negligible one—the account is cleared. With such rules, taxpayers who are assessed an amount (taking into account any penalty applied for non-filing) that comes to less than what they would have owed had they filed an accurate return have a strong incentive not to file a return at all.[4]

17.3 Payment

The payment of the tax due, sometimes referred to as the 'remittance' of tax, discharges the obligation of most registrants. For others, filing and payment communicate useful information to the VAT administration so that it can take additional steps such as audit and enforcement, discussed below.

[4] For an extended discussion of filing and return forms, see Silvani and Vehorn (1991).

All payments, including those on estimated assessments, should be accompanied by returns. A reverse paper trail between the taxpayer and the administration is necessary to protect taxpayer rights and the administration whenever money changes hands. 'Stacking rules', which specify the order in which payments are applied, are important. If payments are made without an associated return, either the taxpayer must indicate to which assessments the payments apply or some stacking rule (e.g. delinquent principal first, then penalties, then interest, and then surcharges) should be invoked and applied. If an overpayment is made with a return for a particular period, a similar stacking rule may be used after the current tax due is covered. Alternatively, a taxpayer who overpays may receive either a credit (to be carried forward against future liabilities) or a refund. Even if the government pays interest on such credits (as it should but rarely does in African countries), most such taxpayers will probably request refunds. Most countries allow refunds under conditions of varying stringency. Some countries allow refunds only in the case of capital goods, while others allow refunds for tax on any inputs. It is important to note that the conditions to obtain a refund are stringent in most countries, so registrants must pass a number of administrative tests.[5]

Tax payments may be made at recognized financial institutions such as banks, the revenue department itself, or both. Different countries have different systems. Countries that do not already make use of financial institutions both to receive payments and perhaps to do some initial processing of simple returns (e.g. those accompanied by full payment) should explore this possibility further. As a matter of good policy, it seems best to keep the function of actually collecting and processing money out of the hands of the tax administration. Revenue officials should be more concerned with ensuring that the right people pay the right amount than spending their time adding up the day's proceeds. Obviously, keeping the cash out of the tax office reduces the opportunity for theft and corruption. Using the banking sector to perform this function thickens the paper trail.

17.4 Enforcement

Of course, if tax due is not paid or is paid only in part, appropriate penalties and interest must be promptly assessed and enforced. If payment is not made in a timely fashion, then there must be an immediate and credible sanction, such as the interception of cash flows or seizure of property. If the penalties set in the law are considered too high to be properly enforced—a belief that seems to be widely held in many countries, given the surprisingly high number of waivers of penalties and interest for delinquent taxpayers—then they should be reduced to levels that fit the transgression and are administrable. After all, the primary purpose of the penalty is to bring delinquent registrants back into the system rather than to

[5] For the seminal paper on refunds, see Harrison and Krelove (2005).

drive them further underground. But if reasonable, the penalties should be enforced without exception. If that is not done, no tax—VAT or otherwise—can long withstand the constant erosion of the tax system as 'bad' taxpayers crowd out 'good' taxpayers.

VAT differs from other taxes in that delinquency is not simply a matter of tax collection but in effect the embezzlement of public funds. Firms liable for VAT have collected revenues from others on behalf of the government. If they do not remit the funds to the treasury in the prescribed fashion, they defraud the government. Rigorous penalties for such an offence seem appropriate. At the very least, interest should be charged immediately once a payment becomes delinquent. Moreover, taxpayers should not have the option of objecting to assessments and hence delaying payment as they sometimes do. If they object, they can do so after reaching a satisfactory arrangement about payment.

Given the relatively strong incentives for taxpayers in many developing countries not to file and pay in a timely fashion, it is not surprising that in practice some VAT liabilities are inevitably based on estimated rather than self-assessed assessments (Kloeden, 2011). Nor is it surprising that many of these 'official' assessments are not paid on time. The result is often that interest and penalties accumulate rapidly and soon exceed the initial (and usually low) assessment. In such circumstances, taxpayers almost invariably appeal to have interest and penalties waived. Such appeals have no merit. Indeed, waiver and relief programmes should be eliminated except in extenuating circumstances (e.g. through 'hardship' or 'fairness' provisions in the VAT law).

When countries build up a considerable stock of accrued interest and penalty liabilities—after efforts have been made to collect the most recent and largest accounts in arrears—it may perhaps be worth considering a one-time amnesty of accrued interest and penalties to clear the books of what are likely to be uncollectable debts. However, it is important that any such tax amnesty should be accompanied and preferably preceded by a clear and credible tightening of payment, audit, and enforcement procedures to preclude signalling future clemency. There is a 'moral hazard' that taxpayers will repeat non-compliant behaviour if they expect tax amnesties in the future as well. Amnesties are a tricky business and cannot be recommended as a first-line solution.[6]

17.5 Audit

Conceptually, audit is the first significant step in enforcement. 'If VAT auditing is not reasonably effective, VAT administration will be ineffective' (Casanegra de Jantscher, Silvani, and Holland, 1991, p. 67). The purpose of VAT audit

[6] Le Borgne and Baer (2008) weigh the advantages and disadvantages of tax amnesties, drawing on the results from the theoretical literature, econometric evidence, and selected case studies. The authors conclude that the costs of tax amnesty programmes often exceed the programmes' benefits.

(sometimes referred to as verification or inspection) is to uncover three types of non-compliance: tax fraud, under-reporting, and tax avoidance. Fraud is the most serious type of non-compliance as it often involves sophisticated methods such as the forgery or falsification of documents. Under-reporting of tax liabilities is generally not committed with the intention of committing fraud (unless expressly accompanied by fraud). The level of under-reporting tends to be sensitive to the probability of detection and the severity of penalties. Finally, avoidance is a vague concept by which taxpayers exploit loopholes in the tax law in ways that were not intended by the legislator.

Different types of audits serve different purposes. The ostensible purpose of a mere advisory visit to the registrant's premises may be to communicate with and educate the registrant. However, that may provide valuable information to decide whether one or more further steps (desk audit, full VAT audit in the field, or fraud investigation) are warranted. Audits involve three important decision variables: selection, frequency, and scope. The first concerns the identity of the registrants selected for audit, whatever the criteria. The second concerns the time intervals that elapse between audits. The last concerns the breadth and depth of the audit. Correct choices are important because audits can consume significant administrative resources.

Audits can rely on a very broad range of information. Many types of data are useful, and it is always possible to collect more data with larger budgets to do so. The most typical types should include: financial records and invoices; external information held by customers and suppliers (e.g. invoices) and customs; physical records on production, inventory, warehousing, and materials use; and tax returns, amended returns, and tax files. While audit methodologies have become more sophisticated over time, the basic steps remain essentially the same: review, matching, reconciliation, cross-checking of information, and financial ratio analysis. Those methodologies now coexist with more sophisticated ones that owe a conceptual debt to models from the economics literature on game theory and asymmetric information (e.g. Rasmusen, 1991, part II). In addition, more advanced methodologies are made possible by cheap computing power and data-mining techniques. In all cases, increased data-processing costs must be factored into the tax administration's budget.

It is difficult to identify an African country where auditing procedures do not need modernizing or strengthening. Auditing is the core of the tax system and especially so for self-assessed taxes such as VAT. In many countries, the primary data (signals) needed to design sound audit policies exist on completed tax forms. In principle, audits should be done both on a random basis and on a selective (or 'risk-assessment') basis, taking account of the risk profile of different types of taxpayers. Since VAT is applied in effect to the difference between sales and purchases (or the 'gross margin', as it is often called), a critical factor is the reported mark-up coefficient—the ratio of supplies (output) to inputs. When this ratio is less than 1.0, the taxpayer is, in effect, reporting that his sales are less than purchases. In other words, the taxpayer is claiming that the gross margin (or value added) on such sales is negative. Taxpayers who persistently realize very low mark-ups (e.g. less than 0.5) may sometimes have reasonable explanations, but these are evidently not sustainable in the medium or long run. Firms in particular lines of industry that persistently report lower mark-ups than their competitors would seem to require close and automatic examination by tax auditors.

Auditing is also the main way in which taxable activities hidden within the large informal sector found in many developing countries can be included in the tax net. Much better use can be made of the information available in most countries, not only to cross-check selected transactions within the sample of VAT registrants but also to follow the audit trail out into the unknown pool of those who are not in the system but should be. To do so effectively, however, officials need training in a range of accounting, investigative, and information technology (IT) skills, as well as clear direction and encouragement from above.

A key tool in enforcing VAT compliance is to cross-check purchases of one taxpayer against sales recorded by others. Few countries, however, seem to systematically use this tool to detect under-reporting, let alone outright fraud. Some early attempts at comprehensive 'matching' of VAT invoices suggest that the results are not worth the effort. More recent attempts using modern IT to match invoices of buyers and sellers seem to have been more successful and less costly. Nevertheless, the widespread adoption of this approach cannot be recommended to the overburdened tax administrations found in most developing countries. If such countries are to administer VAT at a satisfactory level, higher priority must be given to the implementation of standard methods for improving audit practices, such as exchanging information with business income tax audits (or, preferably, auditing the two taxes at the same time) and customs and excise tax audits. Without such backup, even the fanciest computer-assisted techniques are unlikely to produce significant and lasting gains.

In practice, returns and taxpayer accounts might initially be scanned to determine whether their mark-up ratios (or other parameters such as wage bills) fall within normal ranges for comparable firms in a given industry. Those that fall outside those parameter values (or a confidence interval thereon) should then be subjected to additional desk investigation (e.g. cross-checking information with income tax and customs for the period in question). Although it is not good practice to focus audits solely on refund cases or to audit all cases involving refunds, initial refund claims by new businesses should have a high probability of being audited. When these or other 'issue' audits of any particular tax period uncover potential problems, comprehensive audits of all taxpayers involved—preferably encompassing all taxes—should be undertaken for a period of several years. A quick 'pre-payment' audit may be useful with respect to refund applicants judged risky. Much more critical, however, are selective 'post-payment' audits on a partially random selection of all VAT registrants, large or small, claiming refunds or not.

Developing and implementing a good tax audit system is not easy, but such a system is essential to the achievement of good and sustainable tax administration. Achieving a satisfactory level of tax administration is not a once-and-for-all task: every tax administration must continually strive to maintain performance at a satisfactory level and adapt to the changing world in which the tax system operates.

17.6 Fraud

As a transactions-based but accounts-controlled tax, VAT is as susceptible to fraud as are other accounts-controlled taxes, such as income taxes. Under either form of taxation, the verification of the reported turnover figure is the most difficult but also the most important element in the compliance control process. Both taxes, too, have to cope with taxpayer failure to register, file returns, and pay tax, with the misclassification of products (VAT) or expenses (income tax), and with private spending 'through the business' involving a fraudulent VAT credit or income deduction (Harrison and Krelove, 2005; Keen and Smith, 2006). Frauds distinct to the VAT are false claims for credit or refund, and credit claimed for VAT on purchases that are not creditable, although essentially similar phenomena can be found under the income taxes, given the direct relationship between credits and underlying transactions in determining the respective tax liabilities. This emphasizes the need to put the VAT under the same organizational umbrella as the business income tax, particularly for audit purposes (Kloeden, 2011).

VAT fraud comes in various guises, but the following main types can be distinguished:

- *Bogus or fictitious traders*—where fraudsters register for VAT, make false claims for repayments (paid out by the VAT office!), and then abscond.
- *Suppression fraud*—genuine businesses that understate their sales or falsely inflate their claims for VAT on purchases through fictitious invoices. Credit claimed for taxable supplies used in exempt activities, on private purchases, and regarding invoices from unregistered suppliers would also fall under this category. Obviously, this type of fraud can only be dealt with through comprehensive audits.
- *Insolvency fraud*—genuine businesses that purchase taxable goods, which they sell on at inflated prices, providing (high) tax credits to (related) purchasers, and that subsequently go insolvent without paying their VAT liabilities. In a cross-border context, this is referred to as carousel fraud. In the event, fraudsters register for VAT, import goods VAT-free from another country, sell them on at VAT-inclusive prices, and then disappear without paying the VAT due. In either case, obtaining a VAT registration number—validly or fraudulently—is crucial for this type of fraud.

- *Shadow economy fraud*—genuine individuals and businesses with a turnover above the registration threshold that deliberately do not register for VAT. Car garages and construction companies with turnovers in excess of the threshold might engage in offering their services 'VAT-free' against payment in cash.[7]

Attempts to estimate the size of VAT fraud can be distinguished in top-down or national accounts approaches and bottom-up or operational and intelligence analyses. Under the top-down approach, the full-compliance VAT is calculated from national accounts data on taxable consumption and intermediate inputs of exempt sectors, corrected for VAT revenue forgone on account of the threshold. This full-compliance VAT is then compared with actual collections and the difference, expressed as a percentage of full-compliance collections, is called the VAT gap. Operational or intelligence analyses, on the other hand, project country-wide VAT evasion from the results of individual or sector-wide investigations. It would be advisable for African countries to attempt to calculate the VAT gap from national accounts using the approach developed for South Africa by the International Monetary Fund (2015). A detailed estimate of the size and composition of the VAT gap could serve as a starting point for stepping up measures aimed at prevention, detection, and enforcement.

17.7 Balancing Enforcement and Assisting Taxpayers

To conclude, if someone is caught cheating on VAT, the tax administration must first act quickly to stop the practice and then impose civil penalties as appropriate. Such penalties might include measures such as intercepting income flows to delinquent taxpayers, seizing assets, and perhaps even temporarily closing businesses, a method that has proven effective in some jurisdictions. Finally, but only in very serious cases, the administration must be ready to proceed to the always lengthy and difficult level of criminal prosecution. A simple way to build credibility for a penalty system without going to the extreme of launching criminal procedures may sometimes be to publicize the names of the individuals or organizations on whom penalties have been imposed.

Last but not least, measures aimed at uncovering and prosecuting VAT fraud should be balanced by measures aimed at assisting honest taxpayers to meet their tax obligations and by fast-tracking refunds to taxpayers with a good compliance record. Importantly, interest at commercial rates should be paid on late refunds.

[7] For estimates of the size of the shadow economy in various countries, see Schneider and Klinglmair (2004). For reviews of approaches used by tax policymakers and administrators to achieve better control of cash transactions, see Awasthi and Engelschalk (2018).

18
Agenda for VAT Modernization

This treatise started by showing that many African countries need to increase their tax revenues. The most important instrument for achieving this is the VAT. But current VATs are riddled with exemptions, exclusions, and zero rates on domestically consumed goods and services. Accordingly, base-broadening rather than rate-increasing is the recipe to enhance yields. This requires a thorough review of the standard and, especially, non-standard exemptions and zero rates. Not only do these concessions depress tax collections, they also distort consumer and producer choices, discriminate against exports, favour imports, greatly increase administrative complexity, and promote tax avoidance. Moreover, they do not or hardly affect the VAT burden distribution in favour of the poor.

18.1 Need for VAT Base-Broadening

In 28 out of 45 African countries with a VAT, total tax revenue as a percentage of GDP (called the tax ratio) is around 15 per cent or less. In 17 countries, the tax effort may be called low, i.e. the tax ratio divided by tax capacity (the tax revenue as a share of GDP that a country can raise given its economic and institutional environment) is 0.67 or less. Another 20 countries exhibit a medium tax effort in the range 0.68–0.80. In half of these 37 countries, the tax ratio does not exceed 17 per cent. Merely eight countries exhibit a high tax effort, of 0.81 or more. In most African countries, therefore, the tax intake falls short of what is feasible and necessary to finance basic human and economic development. In this connection, the International Monetary Fund (2017) has called for an increase in tax collections of at least 1 per cent of GDP per annum over the next five years or so. A broad-based consumption tax, such as the VAT, appears the best instrument to achieve this since it is less detrimental to economic growth than an income tax is.

Most current African VATs are not revenue-raising instruments, because they are riddled with concessions. In three out of four countries, the tax collected by 1 percentage point of the standard rate, called the VAT's C-efficiency, is 0.50 or less, meaning that less than half of consumption expenditure is subject to the full VAT. In 19 countries, the C-efficiency is less than 0.35. For the continent as a whole, the C-efficiency is 0.37, on average—distinctly lower than the global average of 0.47. This may be attributable to economic factors (such as the degree

Table 18.1 Converting African VATs into best-practice VATs

Goods, services, and sectors	African VATs		Best-practice VAT		Transitional measures
	Treatment	Original argument	Treatment	Reason	
A. Non-standard exemptions and zero rates					
1. Basic foodstuffs, medical supplies	Exemption or zero rate	Mitigates VAT burden on lower-income groups	Tax at uniform rate	Exemption or zero rate is ill-targeted instrument	Confine exemption to few, enumerated unprocessed foodstuffs
2. Public utilities, petroleum products	Exemption or social tranche	Mitigates regressivity and accommodates positive externalities	Tax at uniform rate	Not different from other goods and services	Continue to exempt public transportation, but abolish social tranches for water and electricity; tax petroleum products
3. Newspapers, printed materials	Exemption or zero rate	Positive externalities	Tax at uniform rate	Exemption or zero rate is ill-targeted instrument	Provide free school books, for instance
4. Services	Enumerated if taxable	Some services too difficult to tax	Comprehensive inclusion in base	Not different from goods; generally, income-elastic items of consumption	None
5. Agricultural inputs	Exemption or zero rate	Tax relief for farmers and mitigation of cascading	Tax at uniform rate	Adequate threshold should suffice	Perhaps zero-rate main agricultural inputs that have no alternative use
6. Industrial machinery and equipment	Exemption or zero rate	Promotes investment and reduces need for refunds	Tax at uniform rate	Keeps VAT's integrity intact	Reverse-charge at import to reduce cash-flow problems
7. Economic free zones	Zero rate	Reduces need for refunds at export	Tax at uniform rate	Not different from domestic exporting firms	Keep account of zero-rated items and check against refund claims at export

B. Standard exemptions and exclusions					
1. Governments and their agencies	Out-of-scope	Act as governments with public authority; taxation would be pay-out/claw-back arrangement	Full taxation or refund of tax on inputs	Eliminates self-supply bias and investment disincentive and, if fully taxed, competitive distortion	Keep exclusion, but tighten VAT rules on activities that can also be performed by private sector
2. Healthcare, education, social services	Exemption	Positive internal and external effects	Full taxation or refund of tax on inputs	Exemption is ill-targeted instrument	Keep exemption, but refund tax on inputs
3. Immovable property	Exemption, except if newly created	Rental values and rents difficult to tax	Full taxation, except rental values, rents, and sales of used dwellings	Greater neutrality and fairer	Eliminate transfer and stamp duties, except on transfers between non-taxable persons
4. Financial services, insurance (and gambling)	Exemption	Value added difficult to determine on a transaction-by-transaction basis	Tax fee-based financial services and zero-rate B2B services; tax insurance premiums and impute tax credit to indemnities	Greater neutrality and fairer	Eliminate separate taxes on banking activities and insurance
5. Agriculture	Exemption	Difficult to tax	Full taxation, subject to adequate threshold	Greater neutrality	Perhaps zero rate on fertilizers and pesticides
6. Small businesses	Exemption; sometimes subject to presumptive tax	Difficult to tax	Turnover exemption of at least US$50,000; no presumptive tax	Reduction of administration and compliance costs	Reconsider presumptive taxes

of monetization), the size of the agricultural sector (often perforce exempted), lack of administrative effectiveness, low taxpayer morale, or, more likely, a combination of these factors. No doubt, however, the low C-efficiencies in Africa should also be attributed to the tax policy gap, i.e. the myriad exemptions, exclusions, and zero rates on domestic goods and services.

Accordingly, base-broadening rather than rate-increasing reforms are called for if revenue is the goal. Base-broadening involves a review of the standard exemptions and exclusions (so-called because they are also found elsewhere) and the non-standard exemptions and exclusions and zero rates (which are more of an African phenomenon). A welcome side effect of base-broadening would be that it should make the VATs easier to monitor and enable the tax administration to concentrate its efforts on compliance control and audit rather than on contentious legal issues relating to, say, definitional boundaries. Better VAT design should make VAT administration more effective.

Table 18.1 provides a bird's-eye view of the base-broadening proposals discussed at length in this book. The present treatment of various goods, services, entities, and sectors in most African countries is compared with the best-practice treatment. The table also indicates the transitional measures, if any, that can be contemplated to soften the impact of the base-broadening changes. It is advisable to abolish most non-standard exemptions and zero rates, which are not found in countries with best-practice VATs. For the time being, some of the standard exemptions can be left in place, but immovable property, financial services, insurance, and gambling should be taxed more widely. South Africa's VAT could be the lodestar to follow for most other African countries considering a second-round reform of their VATs.

18.2 Abolishing Non-Standard Exemptions and Exclusions

Non-standard exemptions and zero rates have proliferated in Africa. The most important are the following: basic foodstuffs and medical supplies; public utilities and petroleum products; newspapers and printed materials; services not enumerated in the law as being taxable; agricultural inputs; industrial machinery and equipment; and extraterritorial exemptions for activities in economic free zones.

As discussed above, the non-standard exemptions and zero rates on domestically consumed goods and services do not or hardly mitigate the VAT's impact on the poor or facilitate the imposition of the VAT, and are especially detrimental to revenue. The exemptions and zero rates have turned most VATs into what may be called extended excise tax systems. After all, in practice, it should not make much difference whether goods are specifically enumerated as being taxable (the excise tax approach) or whether a large number of specifically enumerated goods are exempted or zero-rated (the African VAT approach). Economically, the non-standard exemptions give rise to indeterminate variations in effective VAT rates depending on the ratio of VAT on taxable inputs to tax-exclusive consumer prices, while the zero rates (other than on exports) greatly complicate VAT administration. Last but not least, the exemption or zero-rating of many widely consumed goods effectively turns the standard rate into a tax on luxury goods and services.

Foodstuffs and Medical Supplies

Basic foodstuffs are widely exempted in francophone African countries, while anglophone countries tend to zero-rate them. Sometimes, the favourably treated items are enumerated, particularly in SADC countries. Like most continental European countries, various CEMAC and AMU countries impose a positive reduced rate on processed foodstuffs.

The favourable VAT treatment of foodstuffs is based on the belief that they are disproportionately consumed by the poor; hence, the VAT on foodstuffs is thought to be especially regressive. While this is true in relative terms, in absolute monetary amounts higher-income groups benefit more, much more. The South African Katz Commission (1994), for instance, found that the rich benefitted six times as much from the zero-rating of 19 basic foodstuffs and kerosene than the poor, findings that were confirmed by Go et al. (2005). More recently, the South African National Treasury (2011) found that, with the exception of maize (meal), bread flour, and maize rice, the share of VAT savings attributable to zero-rated foodstuffs rose sharply as expenditures on them increased across expenditure groups. This was also true for expenditures on cooking oil and paraffin (kerosene), which tend to be major expenditure items in most household budgets.[1]

More generally, most incidence studies provide evidence that zero rates (or exemptions) for foodstuffs hardly affect the VAT burden distribution in favour of low-income groups. A practical consideration is that in developing countries, most poor people buy their foodstuffs in local markets supplied directly from farms. In view of the high thresholds, it is unlikely that these foodstuffs would bear much VAT, except to the extent exempt farmers and traders use taxable inputs. More importantly perhaps, low-income households are best helped through compulsory health and education programmes. The revenue from taxing foodstuffs at the standard rate could be used to help finance these programmes.

Nonetheless, the social case for not applying the VAT to basic foodstuffs remains strong. Two issues arise if concessionary treatment is considered: which foodstuffs should receive favourable treatment and how should that treatment

[1] The tax treatment of kerosene is of particular interest since its use generates negative externalities in the form of CO_2 emissions, which makes zero-rating difficult to justify.

be effected. As regards the kind of foodstuffs, there is much to be said for confining the concessionary treatment to a small number of specifically enumerated unprocessed items not supplied as a cooked meal. This is what Botswana, Namibia, and some other countries do. The choice of method mainly involves administrative and compliance considerations rather than tax burden distribution issues since most basic foodstuffs are not sold through taxable distribution channels. Zero and/or lower rates increase the number of registrants and require refunds of prior-stage tax.[2] Exemption should be preferred, therefore, since it protects the VAT administration from hard-to-verify refund claims of domestic suppliers. As economic development proceeds, the exemptions should be replaced by the standard rate or, second-best, a lower-than-standard rate, as applied in the EU and the AMU countries.[3]

The arguments for not zero-rating foodstuffs and limiting their exemption apply also to most medical supplies, particularly over-the-counter pharmaceutical products.

Public Utilities and Petroleum Products

Similar to foodstuffs, not taxing water and electricity disproportionately benefits higher-expenditure groups, as documented by South Africa's National Treasury (2011). Further, a social exemption (tranche) for water and electricity, as found in various francophone countries, is hard to administer properly and is not favoured. In South Africa, the same regressively distributed VAT benefit pattern is found for exempt public transport, regardless of the mode of transport. According to the National Treasury (2011), the blanket exemption of public transport may even have increased the VAT's regressivity.

Many public utilities tend to be provided by (local) governments. If so, it may be argued that they pay their net profits into the treasury anyway and, therefore, might as well be exempted. This argument is wrong. The nature and form of imposition of a transactions-based consumption tax differ from those of an accounts-based income tax. One way to avoid arguments about the nature of public utilities is to

[2] South Africa counters this by prescribing a minimum threshold below which registration is not possible, although this defeats the purpose of the zero rate.

[3] In addition to trying to mitigate the regressivity of the VAT, nearly all African countries attempt to promote the progressivity of the tax system, not by imposing higher-than-standard VAT rates on products regarded as luxury items of consumption, but, equivalently, by levying excise duties on them. However, little can be said in favour of progressivity-enhancing taxes on luxuries. Aggregate expenditures on the usual luxury products tend to comprise little more than 1–2% of consumption expenditures. Hence, the effect on progressivity or revenue is negligible. Moreover, many luxury products can easily be purchased abroad, particularly by higher-income groups. Subsequently, their importation could be concealed, would fall within the limits of the personal exemption, or would not be noticed at all. In short, a fairly strong case can be made for abolishing the excises on luxury products. They tend to be wasteful of the use of scarce administrative resources. However, passenger cars (and luxury housing) are a notable exception to this verdict.

give the Minister of Finance the authority to designate the economic activities of public entities (as well as welfare organizations and public–private partnerships) as 'enterprise' activities for supplies in competition with private sector supplies. This is what South Africa (and Canada) does: public utilities have to register for VAT purposes and are deemed to supply a taxable service for grants or subsidies received from public authorities, which are taxed at the standard rate. The use of the enterprise concept bypasses the difficulty of determining whether or not supplies are made in actual or potential competition with the private sector.

It is difficult to find a justification for not applying the standard VAT rate to petroleum products, which are zero-rated in SACU countries and exempted in some other SADC and most EAC countries. In these countries, the reasoning is that since an excise is levied on these products, applying the VAT would be tantamount to double taxation. But this confuses objectives and instruments. The objective of the excise is to account for the (substantial) external costs that attend the use or consumption of petroleum products. These costs should be internalized in price; they are not different from, say, production or distribution costs. As a revenue instrument, the VAT should then be imposed on the excise-inclusive price of petroleum products so that relative prices vis-à-vis other taxable goods and services do not change.

Newspapers and Printed Materials

Reading materials are widely exempted or zero-rated across Africa, although they are income-elastic items of consumption. Moreover, they compete with taxable forms of information dissemination. It is often argued that the taxation of books amounts to a tax on knowledge, but, according to South Africa's National Treasury (2011), the relatively low book penetration in the country has its origins primarily in low levels of literacy and generally poor reading skills—in other words, in the failures of the education system. Additional VAT revenue collected by taxing newspapers and printed materials could be used to upgrade learning levels.

Services: Why Enumerate?

In imposing VAT, many African countries specifically enumerate the services that are included in the tax base. The implication is that services not listed as taxable do not attract VAT. This is at odds with VATs in best-practice countries, which define the performance of services as any economic activity that does not involve goods. The inclusion of all services in the VAT base furthers equity (services tend to be income-elastic items of consumption) and efficiency (elimination of potential cascading).

VAT has greatly increased the feasibility of taxing services (and goods) that have extensive mixed use. The reason is that a best-practice VAT is in little need of conditional exemptions by reference to the use that is made of the services or the status of the purchaser, whether a producer or a consumer. Compliance and administration are greatly eased if both goods and services are taxed at the same rate and subject to the same threshold. The much-preferred approach, therefore, is to tax services comprehensively, rather than selectively. This obviates the need for fine legal distinctions, which add to administrative complexity. Services should only be exempted if there are weighty social considerations (healthcare, education, social services) or decisive administrative reasons (margin-based financial services, rents and rental values, small businesses and farmers) for doing so. The bottom line is that a VAT functions best if all goods and services are taxed equally and if, subject to the threshold, all persons selling such goods or services are liable to VAT.

Agricultural Inputs

The exemption of basic unprocessed foodstuffs eases the administrative problems of imposing zero rates on them, but leaves an indeterminate amount of VAT paid on taxable inputs in output prices even if the foodstuffs are traded through non-taxable distribution channels. The effect of the input taxes on prices can be nearly fully eliminated by combining the exemption for basic foodstuffs with the application of a zero rate on major farm inputs, such as seed, feed, fertilizers, pesticides, equipment, and implements. This form of zero-rating is easier to administer than the zero-rating of basic foodstuffs since the suppliers of these farm inputs tend to be large firms with adequate accounts.

There are two arguments against adopting this approach. First, as Keen (2008) argues, agricultural inputs should be taxed as a way to secure some revenue from the sector, which tends not to be subject to the income tax either. Moreover, zero-rating, if applied, should be confined to inputs that have no alternative use outside the agricultural sector, which is true of fertilizers, pesticides, and well-defined equipment and implements, but not to, say, drainage and building materials. Second, fertilizers and pesticides tend to be environmentally harmful products. A specific excise can be used to internalize the external cost of their use, but in its absence the VAT can be viewed as a second-best proxy for the excise that should have been levied. Perhaps these arguments tip the balance in favour of taxing agricultural inputs.

Industrial Machinery and Equipment

It is common in African countries—Malawi is a particularly striking example—to exempt or zero-rate industrial machinery and equipment from VAT, often at the import stage. Of course, this violates the integrity of the VAT since end-use exemptions have to be monitored. Also, the machinery may be sold on to an exempt user who, as a result, would not pay VAT on inputs and would have no incentive to become registered. However, exemption has the advantage that refund problems do not arise in the case of businesses that are in excess-credit situations, because they start up operations, are seasonal, or export their output. Taxation without a full credit or involving a delay in refunding the input VAT is tantamount to a tax on investment. A better alternative would be to apply a reverse charge on capital goods imports. This would eliminate the cash-flow problem of the purchaser having to pay the VAT up front but ensure taxation in subsequent exempt stages of production and distribution.

Economic Free Zones

Nearly all African countries give VAT concessions granted through investment codes in connection with industrial free zones, tax holidays, or individualized tax rulings. These regimes establish extraterritorial VAT jurisdictions, which are difficult to police properly. In essence, they should not be necessary if the VAT credit and refund mechanism works as it should, since no business, producing for the domestic or the foreign market, would prepay or bear any VAT whatsoever on inputs. There is much to be said, therefore, for abolishing the extraterritorial exemptions. In any case, they should be administered much more tightly than is the case at present.

18.3 Reviewing Standard Exemptions and Exclusions

Following the example of the EU's Common VAT Directive (2006), most African countries exclude or exempt governments, activities in the public interest, services that are difficult to tax conceptually, and, for administrative reasons, small businesses and the agricultural sector. Generally, the exemptions and exclusions are more generous than is needed. In particular, immovable property, financial services, insurance, and gambling could be taxed more widely.

Governments and Their Agencies

Governments and their agencies, collectively called public bodies, are considered out-of-scope of the VAT in all African countries, subject to some potentially tortuous provisos that they should be governed by public law, that they should be operated under public authority, and that their activities should not involve significant distortions of competition. Although their taxation would largely be in the nature of a pay-out and claw-back arrangement, the VAT on their inputs causes the same non-neutralities and complexities as other exemptions: distortion of input choice, self-supply bias, unfair competition, and tax avoidance. The taxation of as many supplies by public bodies as possible promotes simplicity, accountability, transparency, and the workings of the VAT. Delineation issues regarding taxable versus non-taxable activities become redundant and the VAT chain remains intact through to the consumer level. Distortions of input and outsourcing choices are reduced and so are administrative costs because the VAT on taxable purchases does not have to be allocated between taxable and exempt supplies. Although public bodies do not pursue profit maximization, cost minimization should be their aim and this goal is promoted by applying the VAT as widely as possible.

But this advice comes with an important caveat. While developed countries would do well to consider seriously the full taxation of the public sector, this conclusion should not be extended to African countries that do not have well-developed and sophisticated tax administrations. One of the reasons is that such a reform would require important (and most likely prior) reforms on the expenditure side of the budget. Depending on circumstances, however, more limited but still substantial reforms could be undertaken. Various activities could be taxed more fully, such as public broadcasting, public postal services, admissions to museums, parks, and nature reserves, the sale of licences and permits, waste disposal, and rentals of public facilities for conferences, concerts, and sporting events.

Healthcare, Education, and Social Services

Healthcare, education, and social services are often called 'merit goods', whose consumption should not be constrained by the imposition of VAT. But even if the merit-good argument is acknowledged, full taxation (inclusive of subsidies, if any) in combination with increased subsidies could leave the total net amount of the (VAT-inclusive) charge for the service unaffected without distorting the exempt entity's input choices and outsourcing policies and without discriminating against similar taxable services provided by the private sector (which should then also be subsidized). Best-practice VATs therefore tax most of these services, albeit sometimes at a zero rate, which alleviates the distortions, except the competitive edge vis-à-vis the private sector which may be aggravated.

But, as in the case of governments, the best may again be the enemy of the good. Since, in many developing countries, health and education are politically sensitive areas whose taxation would be difficult to explain to the public, it probably makes sense to maintain the exemption on supplies in these sectors. Even in this context, though, various exemption-narrowing measures could be considered—e.g. regarding over-the-counter pharmaceuticals. In most countries, the poor derive limited benefits from preferential VAT treatment of medical products, because most are largely unaffordable or of a low priority to them, and exemption or zero-rating would not save the poor the VAT if they can access medical services and medicines free through the public health system.

Higher-expenditure groups benefit disproportionately from the exemption for education. The exemption, moreover, causes administrative complications when exempt institutions of higher learning are engaged in taxable activities, such as research and the sale of books, whose taxation requires the apportionment of input tax. At present, however, full taxation or zero-rating (involving refunds of input tax) seems a bridge too far. Also, it does not seem to make much sense to tax the administrative costs of social services.

Immovable Property

Obviously, it is not possible, administratively and politically, to tax the rental value or sale of owner-occupied dwellings. For this reason, most African countries (along with other countries) exempt immovable property but, with some exceptions, tax new buildings as a proxy for the VAT on the services that the buildings will render over their lifetime. In addition, there is usually an option to be taxed with regard to non-residential buildings, obviously with a credit for the tax on new buildings. By contrast, SACU countries always tax the sale and leasing of non-residential buildings, which provides for a fuller inclusion of immovable property in the VAT base, because future increases in values will also be taxed. Accordingly, this approach is preferred.

In many countries, sales of immovable property are also subject to registration, transfer, or stamp duties, which tend to give way if VAT applies. It would be best if these duties were confined to transfers of immovable property between non-taxable persons, while the VAT would apply to sales of all non-residential property. Sales of building materials (exempted or zero-rated in various countries) and repair and maintenance services should always be fully taxable (subject to the registration threshold). So should social housing, although the higher tax could be compensated by a replacing subsidy. This would separate tax policy from social policy. Taxing immovable property more fully would most likely mitigate the regressive impact of the VAT, since housing is an income-elastic item of consumption.

Financial Services

Most African countries exempt all financial services (as does the EU), whether fee- or margin-based. Margin-based services are difficult to tax under a tax credit method VAT, because the value of the intermediation charge (which should be taxed) is embedded in interest rates, returns, or rewards (which should not be taxed), and hence cannot be attributed to customers on a transaction-by-transaction basis—necessary if VAT-liable customers are to credit the tax against their VAT on output.

By contrast, fee-based services can be taxed without further ado, as is done in Botswana, Mauritius, Namibia, South Africa, Tanzania, and Zambia. It is strongly recommended that other African countries consider taxing all explicit financial fees and commissions, too, and confining the exemption to margin-based services. Revenue would benefit, particularly since most financial services are fee-based and because disintermediation has made it less likely that substitution by margin-based services will occur. In due course, consideration could be given to allowing partial formula-based recovery of input VAT incurred in rendering B2B margin services, which would alleviate cascading problems.

Property and Casualty Insurance

Like banking services, all insurance is exempted from VAT in most African countries, again because the taxable intermediation charge cannot be separated from the non-taxable capital contribution to the common pool. Instead, most countries subject insurance premiums to anachronistic, cascading insurance taxes (francophone countries) or stamp duties (anglophone countries). In New Zealand's footsteps, the SACU countries have pioneered a solution under which the value added of property and casualty insurance is taxed in a roundabout fashion by imposing VAT on insurance premiums (and, of course, permitting a credit for the VAT on insurance companies' taxable inputs), which is creditable by VAT-liable clients, and imputing a tax credit to indemnity payments. The VAT-liable entity receiving the payment is obliged to include in its VAT return the tax credit that is included in the indemnity payment, while an individual recipient will pay VAT on the replacement asset (or keep his capital intact).

While property and casualty insurance can thus be taxed, health and life insurance should probably remain exempt. For VAT purposes, health insurance would then be treated in the same way as other exempt health services, while life insurance—a long-term savings vehicle—would be exempted along with other financial B2C margin-based services. Both forms of insurance, moreover, are mostly taken out by individuals; hence, cascading effects are unlikely to occur.

Lotteries and Gambling

Following EU practice, most African countries exempt games of chance from VAT. In contrast, countries with a best-practice VAT, such as New Zealand, Singapore, and South Africa, tax most games of chance. Lotteries can be taxed on ticket sales (output), while a reverse charge can be imputed to pay-outs (inputs), similar to the best-practice VAT treatment of property and casualty insurance. The value added of the lottery industry would thus be taxed after providing a credit for the VAT on inputs and in respect of pay-outs, against the gross tax liability. Gambling can be included in the VAT base under the margin method, where the margin is the difference between the sales of tokens and chips, on the one hand, and pay-outs, on the other. Again, a credit for VAT on other inputs should be allowed against the tax liability. Both approaches yield the same result. VAT should be applied to transactions involving games of chance, regardless of whether or not lotteries and gambling are subject to externality-correcting excises.

Small Businesses and Agriculture

The single most important measure the authorities can take to 'assist' small businesses for VAT purposes is to set a fairly high, single registration threshold with an option to register voluntarily. If the rule of thumb that 80 per cent of VAT is collected from 20 per cent of all businesses is correct, as it seems to be, then most countries should be advised to have a threshold equivalent to US$50,000 or higher. They should also be aware that there are often sharply diminishing returns to adding smaller firms in terms of additional revenue collected over and above the VAT on taxable inputs of exempt small businesses and farmers.

A high undifferentiated threshold implies that the VAT administration can concentrate its efforts on large taxpayers and that small businesses are not bothered by the taxman. Although voluntary registration is an important safety valve to limit economic distortions, a minimum threshold, as in South Africa, below which registration is not possible, is recommended if the VAT administration is not to be bogged down in dealing with too many small businesses requesting refunds, etc. Further, threshold differentiation for services, which increases administrative complexity, is not recommended. This applies also to presumptive taxation schemes, which yield little revenue, involve undue discretion, and are a nuisance for small businesses (which, being exempted, pay VAT on taxable inputs anyway).

A generous threshold without further ado would also be the most appropriate approach for the agricultural sector. The problem is, however, that small exempt farmers would still have to cope with the cascading effects of the input VAT on feed, seed, fertilizers, pesticides, insecticides, and farm implements and machinery. Voluntary registration would not work in view of low literacy levels, the absence of basic accounts, and the lack of communication. A solution could lie in the zero-rating of various major agricultural inputs that have no alternative use outside the agricultural sector, such as feed, seed, fertilizers, and pesticides, unless the VAT is viewed as a substitute for the externality-correcting excise that should be levied (Cnossen, 2018a) or as some form of taxation on a sector that hardly pays any other tax (Keen, 2008).

18.4 The Reason for Modernization

Most African countries need to raise more tax revenue to finance human and economic development. The VAT is the best instrument to do so, but current VATs are riddled with exemptions, zero rates, and exclusions, which depress revenue, are highly distortionary, and greatly complicate the VAT's administration. This book has argued for a thorough review of the exemptions and exclusions with a view to abolishing most of them.

It has done so in the widely shared belief that VAT's role in the tax system primarily is to raise revenue, predictably and efficiently. The VAT differs from the excise taxes in that it is not intended to internalize external costs or change people's behaviour; it differs from the import duties in that it should not be used to support trade policy; and it differs from the income tax in that it is not the instrument of first choice to influence the tax burden distribution or to stimulate industry through investment incentives. The expenditure system is a much better instrument to mitigate the plight of the poor through targeted health and education programmes. Investment incentives, if considered desirable, should be incorporated in taxes on profits, because they purport to raise the net return on investment.

In short, under the VAT, the primary goal should be revenue and revenue alone. The major design principle that follows from this view on the role of the VAT is that it should tax all goods and services used or consumed in the country equally at a uniform rate. A broad base and a single rate are indicated since they distort the efficient allocation of resources brought about by the market as little as possible. Exemptions should be restricted to those strictly necessary on administrative grounds. An adequate threshold should keep small businesses and farmers, who face high compliance costs, out of the VAT net.

The case for VAT base-broadening is greatly strengthened by the finding that the benefit of exemptions and zero rates mainly accrues to higher-income groups and that the favourable treatment of foodstuffs does little, if anything, to mitigate the VAT burden of low-income households. Even more persuasive are incidence studies that show that the net result of fiscal systems can be equalizing if the revenue from broad-based VATs is used to finance in-kind transfers, such as healthcare and education.

The emphasis on VAT policy in this book should not detract from the centrality of VAT administration in shaping desirable outcomes. It is well known that African administrations are hamstrung by, among others: (a) their technical inability to track value chains for enforcement purposes; (b) the lack of data sharing within the tax administration and across government; (c) the frequent absence of automation, including limited use of POS (point of sale) machines, which have been shown to be quite effective in improving outcomes; and (d) the politicization of tax collection, likely hampering collection from larger and better-connected firms, including at border posts.

But the old dictum that 'tax administration is tax policy' is by no means absolute. VAT administration is at best misdirected and becomes at worst dysfunctional if, as a result of VAT policy, scarce administrative resources are diverted to settling refunds (of input VAT on zero-rated domestically consumed goods and services), monitoring lower rates (on 'deserving' products), imposing turnover taxes on small firms (whose inputs are already subject to VAT), or spending time in court (because of litigation), rather than being directed towards basic taxpayer education and compliance control processes, such as audit.

Finally, modernizing VAT systems requires a change in mindsets. At present, the attention of most bodies politic is very much focused on changes in the tax system that are perceived to be pro-poor (VAT exemptions and zero rates, for instance) and pro-growth (tax holidays and other such concessions under the income taxes) rather than on changes in the expenditure system that are really pro-poor (healthcare and basic education) and pro-growth (intellectual and physical infrastructure; legal certainty and protection). In developing countries elsewhere that have successfully taken off economically, it is the latter mindset that has been central to government policymaking. Clearly, fiscal modernization, the VAT included, is also a political question.

APPENDICES A, B, AND C

AFRICA: VATs, EXCISE TAXES, AND SALES TAXES, 2018

Appendix A lists the goods and services that are accorded favourable treatment under the VATs in Africa on a country-by-country basis. It shows the standard rate, the non-standard exemptions, and the goods and services that are subject to lower-than-standard rates, including zero rates, other than on exports. Under exemptions, no refund or credit is available for input tax paid in respect of goods and services that go into or are used in the production of the exempt goods and services. As a result, the effective VAT rate at the consumer level will be unknown, but will differ from and usually be lower than the statutory rate. When a zero rate is applied, all input tax will either be creditable against the VAT on other goods and services, or be refunded. Hence, no VAT is incurred on zero-rated items of consumption.

Non-standard exemptions are all exemptions that, in OECD terminology, cannot be regarded as standard exemptions. Standard exemptions consist of hospital and medical care (including ambulance services), dental care, education, charitable work, non-commercial activities of non-profit organizations (e.g. amateur sporting clubs), the rental, occupation, and sale of used residential property, cultural services (except radio and television broadcasting), financial services, insurance, and reinsurance. Since standard exemptions tend to be common across Africa, they are not shown in the tables.

The VATs in most African countries list a large number of non-standard exemptions. The exempt goods and services, usually taxable in developed countries, often consist of the following goods and services:

- processed and unprocessed foods, cereals, eggs, dairy products, vegetables, fruit;
- agricultural inputs, i.e. seed, fertilizer, pesticides, farm implements;
- water, electricity, kerosene;
- pharmaceuticals, medical equipment, funeral services;
- newspapers, periodicals, books;
- public passenger transportation; and
- public postal services.

In addition, many VATs in Africa apply a zero rate to various domestically consumed or used goods and services, and some VATs a lower-than-standard rate. If a zero rate is applicable, its coverage resembles the goods and services that may be exempted in other countries. Some countries, notably the member states of the Arab Maghreb Union, tax some or most of the items listed above at a lower-than-standard rate. The non-standard exemptions and the lower-than-standard rates generally cover goods and services that are disproportionately consumed by lower-income groups. Accordingly, the exemptions and lower rates purport to mitigate the regressivity of the VAT.

Zero-rating of exports in line with the destination principle, applied by all countries, is not shown in the appendices. This applies also to the zero-rating of export-associated services, including services provided in relation to goods in transit, goods and services connected with fishing or activities carried out on the high seas, and goods and services connected to international aviation.

The progressivity of VATs may be promoted by applying higher-than-standard rates to goods and services disproportionately consumed by higher-income groups. However, hardly any country levies higher VAT rates (Egypt is a notable exception). Instead, most countries impose excise taxes on goods and services regarded as items of luxury consumption.

Appendix B shows the higher-than-standard VAT rates found in some countries and the excise taxes (other than on traditional excise goods, such as tobacco, alcohol, petroleum, and motor vehicles, which are taxed everywhere) levied for revenue purposes (e.g. on soft drinks, sugar, coffee, and tea) or to enhance the progressivity of the tax system by taxing luxury goods. The following items are examples of luxury goods:

- toiletries, cosmetics, perfumes;
- jewellery, precious stones and metals;
- leather and fur products;
- watches, clocks;
- cameras, binoculars;
- radios, TVs, recorders, videos;
- motor vehicles;
- pleasure boats; and
- firearms, ammunition.

Appendix C lists the African countries that have not yet converted to the VAT, but still impose production and turnover taxes.

Source: International Bureau of Fiscal Documentation, online collection of tax systems, last accessed in April 2018; Ernst & Young (2018); and International Monetary Fund, tax summaries in country reports, various years. Although every effort has been made to collect accurate information, it should be emphasized that most data are from secondary sources. Some data may be out of date, incomplete, or incorrect. In various instances, moreover, the taxable status of particular goods and services had to be determined by inference. If, for instance, a particular good or service is not mentioned as exempt, it is assumed to be taxable.

APPENDIX A

Africa: VAT Treatment of Essential Goods and Services, 2018

RECs and countries	Standard rate	Non-standard exemptions	Lower rates
Southern African Development Community (SADC)			
A. Southern African Customs Union (SACU)			
Botswana	12%	Prescription drugs, condoms Passenger transportation by road or rail (other than for tourists) Goods for welfare or charitable purposes	*0%* Millet grain, millet meal, wheat grain, flour, sugar maize cobs, sorghum, and maize meal, except when furnished or served as a meal or as cooked or prepared food Samp, rice, brown bread, fresh milk Vegetables, fruits Water for household consumption up to 5,000 litres or 25 drums of 200 litres per month Fertilizers, pesticides, farm tractors, and a broad range of tools, including ploughs, harrows, cultivators, forage harvesters, weeders, and hoes Kerosene, petrol, diesel fuel Goods or services for the president and his family
Lesotho	14%	Water Passenger transportation Public postal services Low-income housing Unimproved land; lease or letting of commercial immovable property	*0%* Beans, bread, lentils, maize, peas, sorghum, wheat, flour, samp Milk, eggs, livestock Poultry feed, seed, fertilizers, pesticides Kerosene used for cooking, illuminating, or heating Goods supplied for repairing or renovating a commercial building used for taxable supplies and transportation for commercial enterprises *5%* Electricity Telecommunications

Continued

RECs and countries	Standard rate	Non-standard exemptions	Lower rates
Namibia	15%	Public transportation (excluding tour operators) Unprocessed imports of fish, crustaceans, molluscs, and other aquatic invertebrates Imported goods solely for use in prospecting for or mining of natural oil or gas	*0%* Mahango, maize, fresh and dried beans (excluding canned and frozen beans), bread, cake flour, sunflower cooking oil, milk, and sugar, except when served as a meal or as cooked or prepared food Livestock on the hoof Water, electricity Medical services by nurses, midwives, or paramedics; aids and devices for the physically handicapped; funeral services Creation, extension, or improvement of a building Land and buildings Telecommunications Illuminating or heating kerosene, gas oil, petrol, diesel fuel Refuse removal, sewerage Supplies to the head of state
South Africa	15%	Passenger transportation by road or rail	*0%* Brown bread, maize, samp, mealies, dried beans, lentils, rice, milk, milk powder, eggs, cooking oil (excluding olive oil) Vegetables, fruit, vegetable oil, edible legumes, pulses of leguminous plants, pilchards/sardinella in tins Animal feed, fertilizers, pesticides, plants and seeds for use in cultivation Illuminating kerosene for use as fuel or heating, petrol, diesel fuel Housing subsidies Municipal property rates
Swaziland	14%	Tap water Electricity Passenger transportation (excluding tour operators) Postage stamps Lotteries, gambling Burial and cremation services Sewage	*0%* Maize meal, samp, beans, brown bread, rice Milk, eggs, vegetable oil (except olive oil) Fresh fruit, vegetables Feed, seed, fertilizers, pesticides Prescription drugs, medicines School textbooks Kerosene intended for cooking, illuminating, and heating, petrol, diesel fuel

B. Other SADC countries			
Congo, DR	16%	Wheat, maize, flour, bread, fish Agricultural inputs, fishing boats and nets Pharmaceutical products (and inputs), medical equipment and materials, prostheses, mosquito nets, funeral services Newspapers, books, journals, and magazines (except advertisements), magnetic drives with scientific, cultural, or educational information Postage stamps and pre-stamped paper Admissions to monuments, museums, national parks, zoos, and culture, leisure, and sporting events Equipment, supplies, and chemicals for use in the mining and petroleum industry Works of art, handicraft	None
Madagascar	20%	Paddy, rice Corn, potato seed, breeding stock Water up to $10m^3$, electricity up to 100kWh Agricultural inputs, farming equipment Medicines, pharmaceuticals, medical equipment, corrective lenses, impregnated mosquito nets and coils Kerosene, butane Newspapers and periodicals (excluding advertisements), books, educational materials, paper manufacturing machinery Materials and sports facilities for public use Postage stamps Narrow fabric items, labels, kits Admissions to amateur sports clubs Solar panels, renewable energy materials, refrigeration compressors	None
Malawi	16.5%	Agriculture, meat, fish, birds' eggs, dairy products (including fresh milk and infant's milk), natural honey Live animals, animal or vegetable fats, waxes, and oils Vegetables, fruits, nuts, cereals, malt, starch, oil seeds, roots, tubers, oleaginous fruits, food waste and residues Coffee, tea	*0%* Salt Feed, fertilizers, agricultural, horticultural, forestry, poultry-keeping, and bee-keeping machinery Pharmaceuticals, cycle ambulances, condoms, mosquito nets Goods needed for water and electricity generation

Continued

RECs and countries	Standard rate	Non-standard exemptions	Lower rates
		Insecticides, fungicides, pesticides, hessian sacks Medical equipment, ambulances, funeral services Newspapers, printed matter Postal services (except couriers) Lotteries, gambling Personal transportation, tractors, heavy trucks Kerosene, petrol, diesel fuel Raw materials for the manufacture of fertilizers, medicines, and pharmaceuticals Raw tobacco, sawdust, wood waste, scrap	Exercise books Goods vehicles, trailers Machinery for electricity generation, printing, telecommunications, water utility, metal, mining, and dairy industries, textile production (excluding household and laundry-type washing machines), cleaning, sorting, and grading, fishing equipment Machinery used in manufacturing and construction Building materials for factories and adjoining warehouses Large buses Goods for the tourist sector Supplies for the president and the vice-president
Mauritius	15%	Bread, baby food, breakfast cereals, milk, unprocessed agricultural products Feed, bio-pesticides, water for irrigation Materials and equipment used for bio-farming Fishing vessels, aircraft Pharmaceutical products, coco peat, medical equipment, funeral services Public passenger transport, semi-low-floor buses Journals, periodicals Admissions to cinemas, concerts, shows; films Stamps and postal services Works of art, antiques Renting of telephone lines Gambling Plates, sheets, and strips for mobile phones Plant, machinery, and equipment used in petroleum exploration and production	*0%* Rice, wheat flour, sugar (cane), butter, milk, cream, whey, yogurt, cheese, curd, edible oil, margarine, live poultry Agricultural irrigation, fertilizer Pharmaceuticals Water and electricity supplied by government Kerosene, chilled deep-sea water for air conditioning Books, printed matter, music, educational material Passenger transportation by air and sea
Mozambique	17%	Seed, fertilizers, agricultural and fishing equipment Soap, medicines, pharmaceutical products, wheelchairs for the disabled, prosthetic materials, burial and cremation supplies Newspapers, journals, books, copyrights, art objects Stamps and stamped paper	*0%* Rice, maize flour, wheat, bread, salt, sugar, tomatoes, mackerel, infant milk powder, edible oils Mosquito nets, bicycles, condoms Jet fuel

		Cultural guides Garbage removal Gambling	*7.2%* Services related to public works on construction and rehabilitation of roads, bridges, and infrastructure for water supply and rural electricity (lower rate applied in the form of 60% reduction of the taxable amount)
Seychelles	15%	Fresh bread; rice, meat, fish, edible oil, milk powder, vegetables, fruit, flour, lentils, edible oil, margarine, salt, sugar, infant food, malt extract food preparations Animal feed Water, electricity Public transportation Sanitary towels, napkins, tampons Pharmaceutical products, antibiotics, vaccines Newspapers, printed books, musical instruments, postcards, calendars Postage stamps Fuel Construction of residential buildings Leasing or renting of residential dwellings Energy-saving electric bulbs Retreaded tyres	
Zambia	16%	Unprocessed agricultural, animal, and dairy products, fish, infant foods, livestock Fertilizers, pesticides, insecticides Water, sewerage services Kerosene Articles for the blind and disabled Newspapers, journals, books, maps, charts Transport services Funeral services Gambling Supplies for the president	*0%* Bread, wheat Fresh vegetables, agricultural products predominantly sold in export markets Agricultural equipment Drugs, medicines, medical equipment Energy-saving appliances Boat cruises, walking safaris Hotel accommodation in the Livingstone district Tourism for local tourists
Zimbabwe	15%	Eggs, vegetables, fruits, rice, margarine, lactose, mahewu Live animals Water for household use, sewerage Passenger transportation Protective farm clothing	*0%* Bread, mealie, maize, flour, cereals, eggs, meat, butter, milk, cream, cooking oil, infant foods—except when supplied in the course of furnishing or serving a meal, refreshment, or cooked or prepared food or drink for immediate consumption

Continued

RECs and countries	Standard rate	Non-standard exemptions	Lower rates
		Petrol, diesel, kerosene Tourism-related services (other than accommodation)	Vegetables, fruit, potatoes Sugar (cane), salt Feed, seed, plants, fertilizers, pesticides, tractors, animal remedy Electricity Prescription medicines, invalid carriages, orthopaedic appliances Electronic cash registers Building bricks
East African Community (EAC)			
Burundi	18%	Unfinished agricultural products (including from animal husbandry and fishing) sold by producer Water and electricity for personal use Pharmaceutical products, medical equipment Domestic passenger transportation Postage stamps, fiscal stamps	*10%* Imports of food, agricultural products, and livestock
Kenya	16%	Unprocessed agricultural products, maize, live animals Bread, milk and food specially prepared for infants Water supplied by the government (except if bottled) Feed, seed, fertilizers, pesticides, tractors, agricultural services Specified medicines, sanitary towels, contraceptives Public passenger transportation Lotteries, gambling Materials for solar equipment producers Taxable supplies for construction and infrastructural works in parks of 100 acres or more Taxable supplies for power-generating plants and for geothermal, oil, or mining prospecting Biogas, biogas digesters, leasing of biogas-producing equipment	*0%* Unprocessed maize, flour, bread, milk, cream Specified medicaments and pharmaceuticals Pesticides

Rwanda	18%	Agricultural and livestock products, except if processed (except milk) Agricultural inputs, fishing equipment Clean water Kerosene Specified medicines, medical equipment, equipment for the disabled, burial and cremation services, hearses Newspapers, books, journals, educational material, trade union subscriptions Mobile telephones, SIM cards Gaming activities Transportation Environmental services, except sewage treatment Imported building and finishing materials Imported equipment for the tourist and hotel industry, ambulances, fire engines, refrigeration Information, communication, and technology equipment Imported industrial machinery, raw materials, and energy supply equipment	*0%* Minerals sold in the domestic market
Tanzania (separate VAT in Zanzibar)	18%	Food, basic agricultural products and livestock supplies for human consumption (unless provided by restaurants and hotels) Oil and cotton cake, maize, wheat and rice bran Water (not canned or bottled), sewerage Agricultural, fishing, bee-keeping, and dairy equipment Animal feed, fertilizers, pesticides, insecticides, veterinary supplies Approved medicines and pharmaceutical products (excluding vitamins or food supplements), medical equipment and aids for the handicapped, sanitary pads, funeral services Newspapers, books, educational materials, children's colouring and drawing books, examination question papers and answer booklets Passenger transport (except taxis, rental cars, boats, and air charters) and tourist services Gaming supplies Petrol, diesel, kerosene, natural gas, butane gas, bitumen Importation of equipment Mining, drilling, solar, and firefighting equipment	None

Continued

RECs and countries	Standard rate	Non-standard exemptions	Lower rates
Uganda	18%	Unprocessed foodstuffs and agricultural products (except wheat grain), livestock Agricultural machinery, tools, and implements Insecticides, veterinary services Medical equipment, cotton wool, nappies, contraceptives, sanitary towels and tampons, mosquito nets, life jackets, maternity kits, examination gloves, funeral services Passenger transportation (other than tour and travel operators), ambulances Postage stamps Lotteries, gambling Petroleum products, LPG, solar power and equipment Equipment for hydroelectric power projects Photosensitive semiconductor devices	*0%* Cereals grown and milled in Uganda Medicines and pharmaceuticals Seed, fertilizers, pesticides, hoes Educational materials
Economic and Monetary Community of Central Africa (CEMAC)			
Cameroon	19.25%, including 10% surcharge	Bread, milk, fish Fertilizers, pesticides, seeds, and other agricultural, livestock, and fishery inputs Production of agricultural machinery and tools, leasing of farm equipment Pharmaceutical inputs, medical goods to fight AIDS Water up to $10m^3$ and electricity up to 110kWh per month Newspapers, periodicals (except advertisements) Postal stamps, fiscal stamps Two-fifths of lottery and entertainment receipts Wood sawing, modelling, and assembling Sale of crude oil, petroleum products used by fishing companies Solar and wind energy equipment Mining products	None
Central African Republic	19%	Locally produced bread, milk, meat, fruit, infant food Local fruit and vegetables Locally produced pharmaceutical products, antibiotics, insulin, quinine, dental wax, materials for X-rays, hygiene and pharmaceutical rubber products, condoms, surgical gloves, medical equipment	*5%* Imported milk, meat, sugar

		Water up to $10m^3$ per month Electricity up to 110kWh per month Newspapers (except advertisements), books Postal stamps, fiscal stamps, stamped documents Gold, diamonds	
Chad	18%	Unprocessed agricultural and fishing products sold directly to consumers Bread, milk, poultry, meat Agricultural and fishing equipment Drinking water up to $14m^3$ per month Electricity, including equipment used for production and distribution Medicines, glasses Newspapers, periodicals (excluding advertisements) Postal stamps, fiscal stamps, stamped paper Admissions to amateur sporting events, shows Entertainment Gambling Painters, sculptors (up to CFA 20 million) Locally produced building materials Equipment for cotton production and exploratory and mining activities Rental of non-building land and unfurnished premises	None
Congo	18%	Agricultural, stock-breeding, fishing, and hunting products of local origin (excluding industrial fishing), livestock Enumerated basic products Fertilizers, agricultural, horticultural, forestry, and fishery machinery and equipment Water and electricity up to a maximum Selected medicines Newspapers (excluding advertisements), periodicals, books Entertainment, cultural services, sports Postal stamps Philatelic items, artworks (up to CFA 20 million) Rental of unfurnished houses and undeveloped land Goods for research, production, transport, and marketing of crude oil Petroleum products subject to excise tax	*0%* Local wood sales *5%* Sugar, salt, tomatoes Cement Petroleum products

Continued

RECs and countries	Standard rate	Non-standard exemptions	Lower rates
Equatorial Guinea	15%	Raw products supplied by farmers, fishermen, and hunters directly to consumers Fertilizers, insecticides, agricultural inputs Pharmaceutical products, insulin, quinine, X-ray films, dental chairs, antibiotics, surgical gloves Newspapers (except advertisements), periodicals, educational books Culture, sports Imported capital equipment, turbines, machinery Mining	*6%* Bread, rice, dairy products, meat, infant foods
Gabon	18%	Unprocessed agricultural, fishing, and hunting products of local origin Bread, flour, gluten, rice, dairy products, eggs, canned sardines, pilchards, pasta, sugar Fertilizers, agricultural machinery and equipment (excluding forestry and fishing) Medicines Newspapers (except advertisements), periodicals, textbooks Low-rent housing Postal stamps, fiscal stamps, stamped paper Renting of undeveloped land and unfurnished premises Artists up to CFA 200 million Butane Capital goods imports and raw materials used by mining and cement industry Utilities, chemicals, equipment used by wood industry, timber transport by rail Mineral products	*5%* Cement *10%* Chicken, sugar, mineral water, computers
Economic Community of West African States (ECOWAS)			
A. West African Economic and Monetary Union (UEMOA)			
Benin	18%	Bread, maize, milk, potatoes, peas, beans, millet, sorghum, cereals (except rice), vegetables, fruits, tubers, horticultural products, fish offal Animals, agricultural activities and inputs (except veterinary services)	None

		Feed, seed, cocoa beans, machinery and equipment for agriculture, animal husbandry, and fisheries, products for livestock breeding, poultry, and aquaculture Inputs for small businesses processing and storing agricultural products, phytosanitary instruments Pharmaceutical products, condoms, invalid carriages, dental work Public passenger transportation, (mini)buses Newspapers, periodicals (except advertising), books, teaching materials Postage stamps Computer equipment Gas, equipment for oil service stations, tanker trucks Artists' original works	
Burkina Faso	18%	Unprocessed foods (fresh or frozen), including fish and meat Pharmaceutical products, medicines Newspapers, books, brochures Mobile and land phones Rental of unfurnished houses Construction materials for social housing Artists' sales (except jewellery and industrial art) Solar energy equipment Goods and services for immovable property of taxpayers subject to simplified regime Software and IT materials for specified institutions and projects New cars for use as taxis, transport vehicles Sales by public bodies of an industrial or commercial nature	None
Côte d'Ivoire	18%	Foodstuffs for domestic consumption Newspapers, periodicals, books, records, magazines Agricultural equipment and spare parts Transportation (also if involving tourism) Low-cost housing, construction activities by companies Activities related to tourism and transport Inputs for research and exploration activities Heavy oil, fuel oil	*9%* Milk, pasta Petroleum products Solar energy equipment

Continued

RECs and countries	Standard rate	Non-standard exemptions	Lower rates
Guinea–Bissau	17%	Foodstuffs Independent professional services	*0%* Medicines *10%* Cereals, rice, flour, bread, milk, agricultural products Newspapers, magazines Hotels, restaurants Natural gas, materials and equipment for solar energy production Consulting
Mali	18%	Agriculture and fishery products without their basic nature having been altered, grain, livestock, raw meat Agricultural equipment and inputs Medicines Original works by artists Unprocessed metals and minerals extracted by traditional methods	*5%* Computer hardware, solar energy equipment
Niger	19%	Farmers, stockbreeders, fishermen Rice, flour, poultry, meat, vegetable oil Fruit, vegetables Agricultural inputs Water, electricity Pharmaceuticals Stamps and stamped paper Newspapers, periodicals (except advertisements) Cultural centres, museums Lease of unfurnished buildings Passenger and goods transportation by road Gambling Uranium	None
Senegal	18%	Unprocessed food products listed as basic necessities Agriculture, fisheries, livestock Medicines and pharmaceutical products Water, electricity (up to specified maximums) Public transportation	*10%* Tourism (hotels and catering)

		Newspapers and periodicals (except advertisements), books, printing paper Rental of unfurnished residential property Authors' original work Investment goods	
Togo	18%	Agricultural and fishing activities Passenger transportation Entertainment Petroleum products	None
B. West African Monetary Zone (WAMZ)			
Cabo Verde	15%	Specified basic foods, such as meat, fish, eggs, milk, fruit, vegetables Goods used in agriculture, stockbreeding, forestry, and fisheries, such as seed, fertilizers, and fishing tools Pharmaceutical products, funeral services Postal stamps and stamped paper Cultural and recreational services Garbage removal Original works of art and copyrights	None
Gambia	15%	Basic foods, including rice, flour, sugar, meat, fish, fresh vegetables, salt, cooking oil, bread, infant food Unprocessed agriculture and aquaculture products supplied by the producer Seeds, fertilizer, fishing nets, machinery exclusively used in agriculture and aquaculture Prescription drugs Water and electricity supplied to households Domestic passenger transport (except for tourists)	None
Ghana	17.5%, including 2.5% National Health Insurance Levy	Animal, agricultural, and aquatic food in its raw state Animals, livestock, poultry raised in Ghana Rice, millet, maize, sorghum, cassava, yam, guinea corn, plantains, shea butter, meat, salt Agricultural and fishing inputs, including fertilizers, insecticides, drugs, seeds, bulbs, rootings, nuts, and vegetables; locally manufactured agricultural machinery and implements	5% Immovable property sold by real-estate developer

Continued

RECs and countries	Standard rate	Non-standard exemptions	Lower rates
		Essential drugs, mosquito nets, goods for the disabled Water (except if bottled or distilled) Electricity (up to a maximum) Newspapers, books, printed matter (except if imported) Transportation by bus, train, boat, and air Postage stamps Industrial and mining machinery Petroleum products Supplies to the president of Ghana Exports of non-traditional products, such as cocoa beans, lumber, logs, electricity, and minerals	
Guinea	18%	Rice, flour (including alimentary oils), wheat, bread, palm oil, fish Manure Pharmaceutical products Newspapers (except advertising), books, educational supplies Postage stamps Second-hand goods	None
Sierra Leone	15%	Rice in its raw state, animals, fish, birds Edible fruits, nuts, vegetables Seeds, bulbs, roots Feed, fertilizer, pesticides, agricultural machinery Pharmaceutical products, condoms, mosquito nets, goods for the disabled, funeral services, coffins Water Newspapers, books, printed matter Transportation of passengers Industrial and mining machinery Petroleum products	None

Arab Maghreb Union (AMU)			
Algeria	19%	Bread, milk Specified pharmaceutical products, vehicles for the handicapped Newspapers, periodicals, books Sports materials and equipment produced in Algeria and acquired by the National Sports Federation Plant and machinery for SONOTRACH (state oil company) Machinery, equipment, and services for new entrepreneurs Individual insurance contracts, bank loans for personal dwellings, reinsurance	*9%* Basic foodstuffs, olive oil Cattle feed, fertilizers, pesticides Pharmaceutical products Natural gas less than 2,500 therms and electricity less than 250kWh per quarter Albums and drawing books for children, e-books Fuel oil, diesel oil, propane and butane gas Inputs for concentrated vitamins Concerts, entertainment Subscriptions to an internet provider Personal computers and laptops LPG, air conditioners using LPG Construction work and sale of housing Mortgage loans to individuals Agents and brokers Assembly of knocked-down cars Traditional handicraft and silver work Transactions by EPIC/SONELGAZ (natural gas company) Zinc and steel sheets
Mauritania	16%	Bread, meat, fish, vegetables, other basic foodstuffs Newspapers, periodicals (except advertisements)	None
Morocco	20%	Bread, cereals, milk, sugar, edible oil Public baths, traditional ovens Newspapers (except advertisements), books, sheet music, documentaries and educational films, artistic shows Self-supplies for personal dwellings not exceeding 300m^2 Loans for social housing Local hand-made carpets Driving schools	*0%* Agricultural inputs Sale of social housing *7%* Canned sardines, milk powder, water Pharmaceuticals School supplies Economic cars

Continued

RECs and countries	Standard rate	Non-standard exemptions	Lower rates
		Input tax not deductible for various professions	*10%* Rice, pasta, salt, edible oils Catering, restaurants Hotel accommodation Housing and hotel loans Liberal professions *14%* Tea, butter Electricity, solar water heaters Transportation, light-duty vehicles, mopeds
Tunisia	19%	Retail sales of milk, flour, edible oils, sugar, other foodstuffs Magazines, periodicals, books (except if bound in leather), brochures Retail sales of medicines and goods for pharmaceutical industry Solar water heaters Drilling equipment and spare parts Raw materials and semi-finished products used in the production of plant and machinery Services related to cruise tourism	*7%* Animal feed, fertilizers, transport of agricultural products Pharmaceutical products Electricity, gas Passenger transportation Local crafts *13%* School books Hotels, restaurants Internet subscriptions Professional services, training services Wildlife parks, golf courses, spas, fairgrounds Computers, radios, TVs, audiovisual equipment Imports of European plant and machinery
Intergovernmental Authority on Development (IGAD) and Egypt			
Djibouti	10%	Newspapers (except advertisements) Cultural services	*0%* Import of goods for the construction of hotels, immovable property, and industries
Egypt	14%	Infant food, sugar, tea, coffee Medicines Electricity Advertising Crude oil and natural gas	*5%* Processed potatoes, crackers, flour products, vegetable and animal oils, tallow Soap, detergents Fertilizers, pesticides Air-conditioned means of transportation

			Construction work Petroleum products Machinery and equipment, gypsum Professional and consultancy services Media and programme production
Ethiopia	15%	Injera, bread, grain, wheat, maize, sorghum, cereals, palm oil, milk Water (except if bottled) Medicines, medical supplies, mosquito nets Electricity Books, printed materials Postal services Transportation Seeds, fertilizer, insecticides Kerosene, fuel gas Pickle, wet blue, and crests for leather Skin and hides for shoe factories Workshops for the disabled Government imports	None
Sudan	17%	Agricultural products supplied in raw condition Cattle, meat, poultry, fish, dairy products Bread, locally produced flour Medicines for humans and animals Seeds, fertilizers, pesticides	None

APPENDIX B

Africa: VAT and Excise Tax Treatment of Selected Goods and Services, 2018

RECs and countries	Standard VAT rate	Higher-than-standard VAT rates	Excises (other than on tobacco products, alcoholic beverages, petroleum products, and motor vehicles)
Southern African Development Community (SADC)			
A. Southern African Customs Union (SACU)			
Botswana	12%	None	*5%*: toiletries, TV sets, office machines; *7%*: essential oils, perfumery, apparel and fur skin, glasses, clocks, binoculars, cameras, projectors, film, microphones, cell phones, dishwashers, air conditioners, video and hi-fi equipment, optical lenses, photographic and cinematographic equipment, firearms
Lesotho	14%	None	*5%*: toiletries, TV sets, office machines; *7%*: essential oils, perfumery, apparel and fur skin, glasses, clocks, binoculars, cameras, projectors, film, microphones, cell phones, dishwashers, air conditioners, video and hi-fi equipment, optical lenses, photographic and cinematographic equipment, firearms
Namibia	15%	None	*5%*: toiletries, TV sets, office machines; *7%*: essential oils, perfumery, apparel and fur skin, glasses, clocks, binoculars, cameras, projectors, film, microphones, cell phones, dishwashers, air conditioners, video and hi-fi equipment, optical lenses, photographic and cinematographic equipment, firearms
South Africa	15%	None	*4%*: plastic bags; *5%*: toiletries, TV sets, office machines; *7%*: essential oils, perfumery, apparel and fur skin, glasses, clocks, binoculars, cameras, projectors, film, microphones, cell phones, dishwashers, air conditioners, video and hi-fi equipment, optical lenses, photographic and cinematographic equipment, firearms
Swaziland	14%	25% Tobacco, alcohol	*5%*: toiletries, TV sets, office machines; *7%*: essential oils, perfumery, apparel and fur skin, glasses, clocks, binoculars, cameras, projectors, film, microphones, cell phones, dishwashers, air conditioners, video and hi-fi equipment, optical lenses, photographic and cinematographic equipment, firearms
B. Other SADC countries			
Congo, DR	16%	None	*10%*: soft drinks, carbonated mineral water, fruit juices, soap, shoe polish; *20%*: plastic and rubber products; *10%, 15%, 20%*: perfumery, toiletries, cosmetics
Madagascar	20%	None	Fruit, vegetables; soft drinks, carbonated water; vanilla; cosmetics, perfumes; audiovisual equipment; telecommunications (10%), mobile telephone use, paid satellite TV; pylons, antennas, relays, or masts installed by telecommunication companies; diamonds, gold

Malawi	16.5%	None	*8%*: tea, sugar; *10%*: airtime, electronic goods, television subscriptions; *30%*: perfumes, cosmetics
Mauritius	15%	None	*Specific*: plastic bags, soft drink containers; many others
Mozambique	17%	None	*15–30%*: toiletries, cosmetics, perfumes, firearms, ammunition; *40–55%*: animal skins, furs, jewellery, precious stones and metals, sail and motor boats; *65–75%*: paintings, sculptures, antiques, engravings, aircraft devices
Seychelles	15%	None	Various
Zambia	16%	None	*7%*: electricity; *10%*: soft drinks, mobile phone airtime
Zimbabwe	15%	None	Soft drinks (5%); second-hand motor vehicles
East African Community (EAC)			
Burundi	18%	None	*6,600 franc/kg*: sugar; *30,000 franc/hl*: soft drinks, lemonades, sodas; *13%*: mineral, carbonated, or flavoured water; *12%*: GSM calls, subscriptions and purchases of audiovisual recharge cards
Kenya	16%	None	*5 shilling/l*: mineral water; *10 shilling/l*: fruit and vegetable juices; food supplements; *120 shilling/kg*: plastic shopping bags; *2%*: catering and tourism; *7%*: sugar; *10%*: food supplements, perfumes, cosmetics, and beauty products; mobile wireless phone and airtime; fees charged by financial institutions, including commissions to insurance brokers; *15%*: telecommunications
Rwanda	18%	None	*5%*: fruit juices; *10%*: powdered milk, mineral water, telephone communications; *13%*: gaming activities; *39%*: soft drinks, lemonade
Tanzania	18%	None	*3%*: dairy industry levy; soft drinks, mobile phone airtime; *14.5%*: electronic communication services; plastic bags
Uganda	18%	None	*25 shilling/kg*: sugar; matches; *10%*: telecommunication services
Economic and Monetary Community of Central Africa (CEMAC)			
Cameroon	19.25%	None	*25%*: Pacific salmon, foie gras, caviar, natural juices; soft drinks, imported mineral water; pearls, precious stones and metals; mobile phone communications and internet services. *Special ad valorem levies*: precious stones and metals and building materials
Central African Republic	19%	None	Phone calls (plus 2% on turnover of companies); *10%*: imported soft drinks; *25%*: salmon, foie gras, caviar; perfumes, cosmetics; jewellery, precious stones; firearms, ammunition; industrial waste, air/boat tickets, radioactive materials, waste water, imported bags and lockers
Chad	18%	None	Sale of livestock; internet and mobile telephone consumption, foreign incoming calls, prepaid phone cards; *5%*: mineral and carbonated water; *30%*: cosmetics, jewels, precious stones; electrical and electronic materials

Continued

RECs and countries	Standard VAT rate	Higher-than-standard VAT rates	Excises (other than on tobacco products, alcoholic beverages, petroleum products, and motor vehicles)
Congo	18%	None	Telecommunication services, pollution; *25%* (but 10% if locally manufactured): perfumery, jewellery, worked gold; camcorders, consumer electronics
Equatorial Guinea	15%	None	*25%*: photo/video/TV cameras, film projectors; non-military firearms, accessories and ammunition; *32%*: soft drinks, toiletries, cosmetics, perfumes, jewellery, pearls, precious metals and stones
Gabon	18%	None	*25%*: cameras, firearms, ammunition; *30%*: foie gras, caviar, salmon; *32%*: perfumes, cosmetics
Economic Community of West African States (ECOWAS)			
A. West African Economic and Monetary Union (UEMOA)			
Benin	18%	None	*1%*: wheat flour, cooking oils, fats; *3%*: non-carbonated water, soft drinks; *5%*: coffee; *7%*: soft drinks, perfumes, cosmetics
Burkina Faso	18%	None	*10%*: energy drinks, coffee, tea, cola nuts
Côte d'Ivoire	18%	21.31% Tobacco sold at wholesale	*7%*: soft drinks (except water)
Guinea–Bissau	17%	20%	*5%*: basic necessity products, mineral water; *10%*: soft drinks; *15%*: perfumes, cosmetics; *15%, 20%, 40%*: fireworks, ammunition, firearms, gunpowder, explosives
Mali	18%	None	*3%*: gold; *10%*: perfumes, cosmetics; *25%*: cola nuts; *45%*: ammunition
Niger	19%	None	*12%*: tea, coffee; *15%*: cola, fruit juice, edible oils, fats, cosmetics, perfumes
Senegal	18%	None	*2%*: telecommunications; *2.75%*: soft drinks; *3.8%*: coffee, tea; *5%*: fats (15% if refined); *10%*: perfumes; *30%*: cola nuts
Togo	18%	None	*1%*: wheat or rye flour, groats, meal, mixed wheat and rye semolina, oils, fats; *2%*: soft drinks; *10%*: coffee; *15%*: perfumery, cosmetics
B. West African Monetary Zone (WAMZ)			
Cabo Verde	15%	None	*10%*: general
Gambia	15%	None	Soft drinks, fruit juice, precious metals and articles thereof, nails, soap, mobile phone services
Ghana	17.5%	None	*5%*: plastic products; *6%*: communication services; *20%*: mineral water, soft drinks

Guinea	18%	None	Soft drinks (specific); *5%*: perfumes, toilet waters, beauty, shaving and hair care products; *10%*: wheat flour, soft drinks; soap, paints, varnishes; dinnerware, other household items, iron and aluminium products; *15%*: fruit and vegetable juices; candles, plastic bags, plastic chairs and other furniture; jewellery, silverware, precious metals, pearls, wigs; telecommunications
Sierra Leone	15%	None	Telecommunications
Arab Maghreb Union (AMU)			
Algeria	19%	None	Salmon, caviar, bananas, matches, gold and silver artefacts
Mauritania	16%	18% Telecommunication, fuel	*15%*: processed milk; *30%*: plastics; *50%*: mineral water
Morocco	20%	None	Soft drinks, mineral water
Tunisia	19%	None	Certain foodstuffs; soft drinks; cloth and clothes; jewellery; electrical and mechanical equipment and spare parts
Intergovernmental Authority on Development (IGAD) and Egypt			
Djibouti	10%	None	Soft drinks
Egypt	14%	22% Soda water, soft drinks, toiletries, large TVs and refrigerators, air-conditioning units, golf carts, mobile telephones, telecommunication	None
Ethiopia	15%	None	*10%*: textiles, TV receivers; *20%*: leather, clocks, watches, dolls, toys, personal adornments, goods made of plastic and asbestos; *30%*: salt, bottled water, washing machines, carpets, light cars, petroleum products; *33%*: sugar; *40%*: mineral water, soft drinks (except fruit juices), audio and video equipment; *50%*: furs, jeeps; *60%*: personal adornments; *80%*: dishwashers; *100%*: perfumes, toilet water
Sudan	17%	30% Telecommunication	Mineral water, soft drinks, sugar, paints, varnishes, cement

APPENDIX C

Africa: Sales Taxes and Excise Systems in Non-VAT Countries, 2018

Countries (year of introduction)	Type of sales tax	Standard rate	Exemptions (other than standard exemptions)	Lower-than-standard rates	Higher-than-standard rates	Excisable products[a]
Angola (2010)	Consumption tax on domestic producers and imports plus tax on a wide range of services (water, energy, hotels, telecommunications, public auction sales, rental of space for conferences, parking, exhibits, advertising, etc., rental of machines or equipment, consultancy, photography, security, tourism, real-estate management, admissions to cultural, artistic, or sports events, vehicle rentals) Also, 1% stamp duty on all business transactions	10%	Unprocessed products from agriculture, livestock breeding, fisheries, and forestry Certified raw materials and equipment used in domestic production Homemade handicrafts Minerals Specified services rendered to oil investment companies	*2%* Bread, wheat, rye, corn, rice, flour (except if packed for retail sale), beans Milk, cream, edible fats, oils, and pulps Fresh or frozen meat, edible offal of bovine animals and poultry Sugar, saccharine Medicines, pharmaceutical products, soap Medical goods, invalid carriages Books, brochures, albums Photographic films Telecommunication services Machinery for food and drink industry Floating structures Unworked gold, stainless steel Antiques Firearms, ammunition Aircraft, space vehicles	*20%* Soft drinks Watches, clocks Shawls, scarves, neckties, bow ties Bags, suitcases Imitation pearls, jewellery Ornamental pottery Cameras, radios, televisions, recorders *30%* Toiletries, beauty products, wigs Leather clothes, skins, furs Cameras, projectors Crystal objects, precious stones and metals	Subsumed by production tax

				5% Water, electricity, transportation, telecommunications, rental of space for parking or conferences, consultancy, photographic services, private security agencies, port and airport services, canteens, sleeping places, sport and cultural events, tourism, vehicle rental		
Comoros (2010)	Consumption tax on local producers, imports, and various services	10%; 15% on imports	Agricultural and fishery products Doctors and midwives Newspapers, periodicals (except advertising) Leasing of buildings and agricultural land Retail sales of petrol and diesel Legal services Stamps Imported inputs by priority businesses	*1%* Private education, including meals *3%* Water, electricity, inter-island airfares *5%* Telecommunication, hotels, restaurants, banking services, international airfares	*25%* Casinos	Rice Insurance
Eritrea (2002)	Sales tax on domestic producers (with refund of tax on raw materials used in production) and imports plus tax on selected services	5% on goods; 10% on services	Cereals, legumes, injera, rice, bread, vegetables, animals for food Fish nets, beehives Water, ice preparation, electricity Medical equipment and services Admissions Banking, insurance Trucks, buses, trains, boats, transport services	*3%* Some goods *5% on services* Contractors, hairdressing and beauty salons, tailoring, repair and maintenance, gymnasiums and swimming pools, billiards and bowling, carpentry, grain milling, printing, internet	*12%* Soft drinks, textiles, furniture	*15%* Mineral water, soft drinks *Various* Cosmetics, perfumery, artificial hair

Continued

Countries (year of introduction)	Type of sales tax	Standard rate	Exemptions (other than standard exemptions)	Lower-than-standard rates	Higher-than-standard rates	Excisable products[a]
			Machinery for agriculture, industry, and construction, tiles, bricks for furnaces, firefighting equipment, belts Wood hives and barrels, incubators Kerosene, furnace oils, aviation fuel, solar energy			
Liberia (2000)	Sales tax on domestically produced goods and imports, supplemented by a service tax Taxable services include the provision of water, electricity, telecommunications, hotels, restaurants, gambling, travel agencies, tickets for international transport, sports, vehicle rental, car repairs, and professional services	7%	Foodstuffs served in educational and philanthropic institutions Medicines, pharmaceutical products, medical aids and appliances Textbooks Raw materials and machinery	None	*10%* Water, electricity, restaurants, hotels, telecommunications (+8% surtax), travel agencies, tickets for international transport, sports, gambling	*5%* Sugar, scrap metal *10%* Imported jewellery and soft drinks *20%* Preserved fruits, jams, jewellery, diamonds, precious metals, leather products, electric household appliances, cameras, latex *30%* Gambling equipment, monosodium glutamate *35%* Stone, asbestos, roofing, building materials, imported water *50%* Revolvers, pistols

Nigeria (1993)	Turnover tax (called value-added tax) with credit for tax on raw materials and intermediate goods that become ingredients of taxable output, but no credit for tax on capital goods and services Taxable services include most professional services, assembling, (re-)packing, telecommunications, entertainment	5%	Beans, yam tubers, cassava, maize, millet, rice, milk, meat, fish, infant food Fertilizers (if locally produced), farming machinery and implements, veterinary medicines Medical goods and pharmaceutical products Books and educational materials Newspapers, magazines Baby products Commercial vehicles and spare parts Industrial machinery	None	None	Food Blankets, household goods Medicaments Perfumes, cosmetics Steel products
Sao Tomé & Principe (1976)	Consumption tax on domestic producers, imports, and service providers	2%–20%	Raw materials and equipment for use in domestic industry Medical services Immovable property transfers subject to real-estate transfer duty	5% Services	In the form of excises incorporated in the consumption tax	Wide range of excises incorporated in the consumption tax at rates up to 149%
Somalia (1990)	Sales tax on producers and wholesalers and on hotel services	10%	Foodstuffs (except canned items), water Local agricultural products, livestock Medicines Electricity, petroleum products	5% Hotel services	None, but see excise taxes	Wide range with rates ranging from 5% for some basic foodstuffs, textiles, furniture, and spare parts, to 100% on tobacco, alcohol, and petroleum products

Continued

Countries (year of introduction)	Type of sales tax	Standard rate	Exemptions (other than standard exemptions)	Lower-than-standard rates	Higher-than-standard rates	Excisable products[a]
South Sudan (2010)	Sales tax on domestic producers, imports, and hotel, restaurant, and bar services	18%	..	*5%* Outside austerity period *15%* Small businesses	None	Soft drinks, mineral water Cars, motorcycles Transport vehicles, air transport Insurance, telecommunications, charters

[a] Other than tobacco products, alcoholic beverages, petroleum products, and motor vehicles.

Note: Dots (..) mean that information is not available.

APPENDIX D

Africa: Basic Economic and Institutional Indicators in VAT Countries, 2016

RECs and countries	GNI per capita, PPP (current US$)	Agricultural value added (% of GDP)	Imports of goods and services (% of GDP)	Exports of goods and services (% of GDP)	Non-standard exemptions	Threshold (US$, 2016)[a]	Primary completion rate (% of age group)	Ease of doing business (1–190)	Governance (–2.50 to +2.50)		C-efficiency (2015)	Standard VAT rate
									Government effectiveness	Control of corruption		
Southern African Development Community (SADC)												
SACU												
Botswana	16,380	2	54	52	Few	107,206	100	81	0.35	0.85	0.50	12
Lesotho	3,390	6	88	40	Some	78,381	77	104	–0.58	0.19	0.48	14
Namibia	10,550	7	68	44	Few	18,707	86	106	0.11	0.29	0.74	15
South Africa	12,860	2	30	30	Few	92,213	86	82	0.34	–0.06	0.63	15
Swaziland	7,980	10	49	48	Some	46,106	79	112	–0.56	–0.43	0.34	14
Other												
Congo, DR	730	21	29	25	Many	86,486	67	182	–1.56	–1.30	0.27	16
Madagascar	1,440	24	36	33	Many	82,822	69	162	–1.30	–0.84	0.25	20
Malawi	1,140	28	45	33	Many	23,564	79	110	–0.63	–0.75	0.31	16.5
Mauritius	20,980	4	59	49	Various	130,430	101	25	1.04	0.35	0.56	15
Mozambique	1,190	25	77	35	Various	84,000	48	138	–0.72	–0.67	0.52	17
Seychelles	28,390	3	98	83	Many	156,912	109	95	0.36	0.44	1.00	15
Zambia	3,790	5	47	37	Many	130,022	81	85	–0.50	–0.34	0.45	16
Zimbabwe	1,920	11	38	22	Some	60,000	90	159	–1.21	–1.39	0.30	15
East African Community (EAC)												
Burundi	770	40	32	6	Some	64,655	62	164	–1.13	–1.26	..	18
Kenya	3,130	36	23	15	Some	56,868	105	80	–0.33	–0.93	0.29	16
Rwanda	1,870	32	33	15	Many	29,307	61	41	–0.03	0.76	0.31	18

Continued

RECs and countries	GNI per capita, PPP (current US$)	Agricultural value added (% of GDP)	Imports of goods and services (% of GDP)	Exports of goods and services (% of GDP)	Non-standard exemptions	Threshold (US$, 2016)[a]	Primary completion rate (% of age group)	Ease of doing business (1–190)	Governance (−2.50 to +2.50)		C-efficiency (2015)	Standard VAT rate
									Government effectiveness	Control of corruption		
Tanzania	2,740	31	19	18	Many	24,213	74	137	−0.66	−0.75	0.21	18
Uganda	1,820	24	28	18	Many	19,232	53	122	−0.50	−1.09	0.13	18
Economic and Monetary Community of Central Africa (CEMAC)												
Cameroon	3,250	23	29	23	Many	101,290	74	163	−0.79	−1.16	..	19.25
Cent. Afr. Rep.	700	43	30	13	Many	60,774	40	184	−1.85	−1.16	..	19
Chad	1,950	50	38	30	Many	60,774	38	180	−1.50	−1.32	..	18
Congo	5,380	9	79	57	Many	81,000	71	179	−1.11	−1.18	..	18
Equat. Guinea	17,020	3	44	55	Many	162,000	50	173	−1.50	−1.77	0.07	15
Gabon	16,720	5	27	41	Many	121,548	74	167	−0.64	−0.69	..	18
Economic Community of West African States (ECOWAS)												
UEMOA												
Benin	2,170	26	40	31	Various	89,907	78	151	−0.46	−0.67	0.37	18
Burkina Faso	1,680	33	37	25	Various	101,000	62	148	−0.58	−0.46	0.28	18
Côte d'Ivoire	3,610	21	30	33	Various	50,645	63	139	−0.83	−0.42	0.11	18
Guinea–Bissau	1,580	44	36	30	Various	..	62	176	−1.58	−1.54	0.27	17
Mali	2,040	41	27	20	Various	101,290	51	143	−1.10	−0.75	0.32	18
Niger	970	..	39	17	Many	6,077	69	144	−0.70	−0.69	0.45	19
Senegal	2,480	18	45	29	Various	101,000	57	140	−0.40	0.06	0.51	18
Togo	1,370	41	63	43	Various	101,290	84	156	−1.25	−0.89	..	18
WAMZ												
Cabo Verde	6,220	10	61	40	Various	2,000	102	127	0.07	0.94	0.66	15
Gambia	1,640	18	42	24	Various	45,660	71	146	−0.67	−0.69	0.14	15

Ghana	4,150	20	48	41	Many	30,663	101	120	−0.28	−0.19	0.26	17.5
Guinea	1,200	20	46	24	Various	70,257	62	153	−1.23	−1.06	0.07	18
Sierra Leone	1,320	61	54	24	Many	54,541	66	160	−1.24	−0.94	0.18	15
Arab Maghreb Union (AMU)												
Algeria	14,720	13	34	24	Some	1,241	106	166	−0.48	−0.60	0.46	19
Mauritania	3,760	27	65	37	Various	20,000	68	150	−0.99	−0.93	..	16
Morocco	7,700	13	45	35	Various	237,916	103	69	−0.07	−0.27	0.55	20
Tunisia	11,150	10	51	40	Various	58,904	100	88	−0.12	−0.04	0.40	20
Intergovernmental Authority on Development (IGAD) and Egypt												
Djibouti	..	4	77	57	Few	281,340	64	154	−0.97	0.60	..	10
Egypt	11,110	12	20	10	Various	7,743	104	128	−0.82	−0.62	0.29	14
Ethiopia	1,730	37	28	8	Various	26,165	54	161	−0.42	−0.44	0.39	15
Sudan	4,290	39	13	10	Various	17,509	57	170	−1.53	−1.45	..	17

[a] Various countries subject small businesses to simplified regimes based on turnover, which are not considered part of VATs in this book; hence their upper limit is the threshold for the VAT. The thresholds for Burkina Faso, Cabo Verde, Congo, Equatorial Guinea, Mauritania, Mozambique, and Senegal are estimates based on information for the simplified regimes.

Source: World Bank, *Development Indicators*, country profiles; non-standard exemptions: Table 4.1; thresholds: Fiscal Affairs Department, IMF; ease of doing business: World Bank (2017a); governance indicators: World Bank (2017b). Some data relate to previous years. Dots (..) mean that information is not available.

References

Adams, T.S. (1921), Fundamental Problems of Federal Income Taxation, 35 *Quarterly Journal of Economics* 4, 527–56.

Agha, A., and J. Haughton (1996), Designing VAT Systems: Some Efficiency Considerations, 78 *Review of Economics and Statistics* 2, 303–8.

Agreement (2015), Agreement between the Government of the Republic of South Africa and the Government of the Kingdom of Lesotho on Mutual Assistance and Co-operation and the Prevention of Fiscal Evasion with respect to Value-Added Tax, *Government Gazette* (South Africa), no. 38747.

Ahlerup, P., T. Baskaran, and A. Bigsten (2015), Tax Innovations and Public Revenues in Sub-Saharan Africa, 51 *Journal of Development Studies* 6, 689–706.

Aizenman, J., and Y. Jinjarak (2008), The Collection Efficiency of the Value Added Tax: Theory and International Evidence, 17 *Journal of International Trade & Economic Development* 3, 391–410.

Alarie, B., and P-P. Gendron (2011), The VAT Treatment of Real and Immovable Property in Canada, 83–121 in: R.F. van Brederode (ed.), *Immovable Property under VAT: A Comparative Global Analysis*, Alphen aan de Rijn, Netherlands: Kluwer Law International.

Alderman, H., and C. del Ninno (1999), Poverty Issues for Zero Rating Value-Added Tax (VAT) in South Africa, *Informal Discussion Papers*, Washington D.C.: World Bank, Country Department I, Africa Region.

Alm, J., J. Martinez-Vazquez, and F. Schneider (2005), 'Sizing' the Problem of the Hard-to-Tax, 11–75 in: J. Alm, J. Martinez-Vazquez, and S. Wallace (eds), *Taxing the Hard-to-Tax*, Amsterdam, Netherlands: Elsevier.

Andrews, W.D. (1974), A Consumption-Type or Cash Flow Personal Income Tax, 88 *Harvard Law Review* 6, 1113–88.

Arnold, J.M., B. Brys, C. Heady, Å. Johansson, C. Schwellnus, and L. Vartia (2011), Tax Policy for Economic Recovery and Growth, 121 *The Economic Journal* (February), F59–F80.

Auerbach, A.J. (2008), The Choice between Income and Consumption Taxes: A Primer, 13–46 in: A.J. Auerbach and D.N. Shaviro (eds), *Institutional Foundations of Public Finance: Economic and Legal Perspectives*, Cambridge, MA: Harvard University Press.

Auerbach, A.J., and R.H. Gordon (2002), Taxation of Financial Services under a VAT, 92 *American Economic Review* 2, 411–16.

Aujean, M. (2010a), Le Système de TVA et le Marché Unique Européen, 49 *Reflets & Perspectives de la Vie Économique* 2, 91–104.

Aujean, M. (2010b), Commentary, 63 *Tax Law Review* 2, 509–16.

Aujean, M., P. Jenkins, and S. Poddar (1999), A New Approach to Public Sector Bodies, 10 *International VAT Monitor* 4, 144–9.

Australian Society of CPAs (1998), Tax Reform in New Zealand—The Shape of Things to Come in Australia? *Discussion Paper*.

Australian Tax Office (undated), *GST and General Insurance*, available on the internet.

Awasthi, R., and M. Engelschalk (2018), Taxation and the Shadow Economy, *Policy Research Working Paper* 8391, Washington D.C.: World Bank Group.

Bakker, C., and P. Chronican (1985), *Financial Services and the GST: A Discussion Paper*, Wellington, New Zealand: Victoria University Press for the Institute of Policy Studies.

Barbone, L., R.M. Bird, and J. Vazquez-Caro (2012), The Cost of VAT: A Review of the Literature, *Working Paper* 12-22, Atlanta, GA: International Center for Public Policy, Andrew Young School of Policy Studies, Georgia State University.

Barham, V., S.N. Poddar, and J. Whalley (1987), The Tax Treatment of Insurance under a Consumption Type, Destination Basis VAT, 40 *National Tax Journal* 2, 171–82.

Barlow, R., and W. Snyder (1994), The Tax that Failed: The VAT in Niger, 14 *Public Budgeting & Finance* 3, 77–89.

Baunsgaard, T., and M. Keen (2010), Tax Revenue and (or?) Trade Liberalization, 94 *Journal of Public Economics* 9–10, 563–77.

Benedek, D., R. de Mooij, M. Keen, and P. Wingender (2015), Estimating VAT Pass Through, *Working Paper* WP/15/214, Washington D.C.: International Monetary Fund.

Bettendorf, L., and S. Cnossen (2015), The Long Shadow of the European VAT, Exemplified by the Dutch Experience, 71 *FinanzArchiv* 1, 118–39.

Bird, R.M. (1989), Tax Harmonization in Federations and Common Markets, 139–51 in: M. Neumann (ed.), *Public Finance and Performance of Enterprises*, Detroit, MI: Wayne State University Press.

Bird, R.M. (1995), Indirect Tax in Belarus: VAT by Subtraction, 10 *Tax Notes International* 9, 589–99.

Bird, R.M., and P-P. Gendron (2000), CVAT, VIVAT and Dual VAT: Vertical 'Sharing' and Interstate Trade, 7 *International Tax and Public Finance* 6, 753–61.

Bird, R.M., and P-P. Gendron (2001), VATs in Federal Countries: International Experience and Emerging Possibilities, 55 *Bulletin for International Fiscal Documentation* 7, 293–309.

Bird, R.M., and P-P. Gendron (2007), *The VAT in Developing and Transitional Countries*, Cambridge: Cambridge University Press.

Bird, R.M., and S. Wallace (2010), Taxing Alcohol in Africa: Reflections and Updates, *Working Paper* 10-31, Atlanta, GA: International Studies Program, Andrew Young School of Policy Studies, Georgia State University.

Bird, R.M., and E. Zolt (2005), Redistribution through Taxation: The Limited Role of the Personal Income Tax in Developing Countries, 62 *UCLA Law Review* 6, 1627–96.

Böcker, T., and R. Finger (2016), European Pesticide Schemes in Comparison: An Analysis of Experiences and Developments, 8 *Sustainability* 4, 378–99.

Botes, M. (2001), Regressivity of VAT—The First Decade's Experience in South Africa, 12 *International VAT Monitor* 5, 237–44.

Buettner, T., and K. Erbe (2014), Revenue and Welfare Effects of Financial Sector VAT Exemption, 21 *International Tax and Public Finance* 6, 1028–50.

Burman, L.E., W.G. Gale, S. Gault, B. Kim, J. Nunns, and S. Rosenthal (2016), Financial Transactions Taxes in Theory and Practice, 69 *National Tax Journal* 1, 171–216.

Canada Department of Finance (1987), *The White Paper: Tax Reform* 1987, Ottawa.

Casanegra de Jantscher, M., and C. Silvani (1991), Guidelines for Administering a VAT, chapter III in: A.A. Tait (ed.), *Value-Added Tax: Administrative and Policy Issues*, Occasional Paper 88, Washington D.C.: International Monetary Fund.

Casanegra de Jantscher, M., C. Silvani, and G. Holland (1991), The Audit of VAT, chapter VII in: A.A. Tait (ed.), *Value-Added Tax: Administrative and Policy Issues*, Occasional Paper 88, Washington D.C.: International Monetary Fund.

Central Statistical Service (1992), *Survey of Household Expenditure* 1990, Pretoria, South Africa.

Chambas, G. (2005), Foreign Financed Projects in Developing Countries and VAT Exemptions, paper presented at the VAT Conference, *International Tax Dialogue*, Rome, Italy.

Child, D. (2008), VAT Administration: Addressing Private Sector Concerns, 129–41 in: R. Krever (ed.), *VAT in Africa*, Pretoria, South Africa: Pretoria University Law Press (PULP).

Clotfelter, C.T. (2005), Gambling Taxes, 84–119 in: S. Cnossen (ed.), *Theory and Practice of Excise Taxation: Smoking, Drinking, Gambling, Polluting, and Driving*, Oxford: Oxford University Press.

Cnossen, S. (1983), Harmonization of Indirect Taxes in the EEC, 150–68 in: C.E. McLure, Jr (ed.), *Tax Assignment in Federal Countries*, Canberra, Australia: ANU Press.

Cnossen, S. (1987), VAT and RST: A Comparison, 35 *Canadian Tax Journal* 3, 559–615.

Cnossen, S. (1992), Key Questions in Considering a Value-Added Tax for Central and Eastern European Countries, 39 *IMF Staff Papers* 2, 211–55; reprinted as 73–107 in: C. Sandford (ed.) (1993), *Key Issues in Tax Reform*, Bath: Fiscal Publications.

Cnossen, S. (1994), Administrative and Compliance Costs of the VAT: A Review of the Evidence, 8 *Tax Notes International* 25, 1649–68.

Cnossen, S. (1998a), Global Trends and Issues in Value Added Taxation, 5 *International Tax and Public Finance* 3, 399–428.

Cnossen, S. (1998b), *Value-Added Taxes in Central and Eastern European Countries: A Comparative Survey and Evaluation*, Paris, France: European Commission and OECD.

Cnossen, S. (1999a), VAT Treatment of Financial Services, 91–104 in: G. Lindencrona, S-O. Lodin, and B. Wiman (eds), *International Studies in Taxation: Law and Economics—Liber Amicorum Mutén*, Deventer, Netherlands: Kluwer.

Cnossen, S. (1999b), What Rate Structure for Australia's GST? The OECD Experience, 18 *Tax Notes International* 21, 2137–50.

Cnossen, S. (2002), Evaluating the National Retail Sales Tax from a VAT Perspective, 215–44 in: G.R. Zodrow and P. Mieszkowski (eds), *United States Tax Reform in the 21st Century*, Cambridge: Cambridge University Press.

Cnossen, S. (2003), Is the VAT's Sixth Directive Becoming an Anachronism? 43 *European Taxation* 12, 434–42.

Cnossen, S. (2004), VAT in South Africa: What Kind of Rate Structure? 15 *International VAT Monitor* 1, 19–24.

Cnossen, S. (ed.) (2005), *Theory and Practice of Excise Taxation: Smoking, Drinking, Gambling, Polluting, and Driving*, Oxford: Oxford University Press.

Cnossen, S. (2006a), IRAP—A Crypto VAT? 15 *EC Tax Review* 1, 4–5.

Cnossen, S. (ed.) (2006b), *Excise Tax Policy and Administration*, Pretoria, South Africa: UNISA Press.

Cnossen, S. (2010a), *Commentary* on I. Crawford, M. Keen, and S. Smith, Value Added Tax and Excises, 376–92 in: J. Mirrlees, S. Adam, T. Besley, R. Blundell, S. Bond, R. Chote, M. Gammie, P. Johnson, G. Myles, and J. Poterba (eds), *Dimensions of Tax Design: The Mirrlees Review*, Oxford: Oxford University Press for the Institute for Fiscal Studies.

Cnossen, S. (2010b), Excise Taxation in Australia, chapter 10 in: *Australia's Future Tax and Transfer Policy Conference*, Melbourne, Australia: Melbourne Institute of Applied Economic and Social Research, University of Melbourne.

Cnossen, S. (2011a), A VAT Primer for Lawyers, Economists, and Accountants, 23–51 in: *The VAT Reader: What a Federal Consumption Tax Would Mean for America*, Falls Church, VA: Tax Analysts.

Cnossen, S. (2011b), Coordination of Indirect Taxes in the Southern African Development Community, 61 *Tax Notes International* (March), 943–69.

Cnossen, S. (2011c), A Proposal to Improve the VAT Treatment of Housing in the European Union, 32 *Fiscal Studies* 4, 455–81; reprinted as chapter 7 in: R. de la Feria (ed.), *VAT Exemptions: Consequences and Design Alternatives*, Alphen aan de Rijn, Netherlands: Wolters Kluwer.

Cnossen, S. (2013a), A Proposal to Apply the Kiwi-VAT to Insurance Services in the European Union, 20 *International Tax and Public Finance* 5, 867–83.

Cnossen, S. (2013b), Reform and Coordination of Indirect Taxes in the ASEAN Free Trade Area, 63 *Tax Notes International* (February), 589–612.

Cnossen, S. (2015), Mobilizing VAT Revenues in African Countries, 22 *International Tax and Public Finance* 6, 1077–108.

Cnossen, S. (2017a), African Countries without VAT, 28 *International VAT Monitor* 5, IBFD online.

Cnossen, S. (2017b), VAT, RST, or a Reverse Charge Mechanism: Which Is Best? 86 *Tax Notes International* 5, 453–9.

Cnossen, S. (2018a), VAT and Agriculture: Lessons from Europe, 25 *International Tax and Public Finance* 2, 519–51.

Cnossen, S. (2018b), Corporation Taxes in the European Union: Slowly Moving toward Comprehensive Business Income Taxation? 25 *International Tax and Public Finance* 3, 808–40.

Cnossen, S. and G. Badenhorst (2008), *South Africa: VAT, Transfer Duty, and Stamp Duty on Fixed Property*, report prepared for the Tax Policy Unit, National Treasury of South Africa, and the South African Revenue Service.

Commission on Taxation (1984), *Third Report: Indirect Taxation*, Dublin: Stationery Office.

Common VAT Directive (2006), Council Directive 2006/112/EC of 28 November 2006 on the Common System of Value Added Tax, OJ L347/1 recasting Sixth Council Directive 77/388/EEC of 12 May 1977 on the Harmonisation of the Laws of the Member States relating to Turnover Taxes—Common System of VAT: Uniform Basis of Assessment, (1977) OJ L145/01.

Conrad, R. and A. Grozav (2008), Real Property and VAT, 81–112 in: R. Krever (ed.), *VAT in Africa*, Pretoria, South Africa: Pretoria University Law Press (PULP).

Copenhagen Economics (2013), *VAT in the Public Sector and Exemptions in the Public Interest*, Final Report for TAXUD/2011/DE/334, Brussels, Belgium: European Commission.

Crawford, I., M. Keen, and S. Smith (2010), Value Added Tax and Excises, chapter 4 in: J. Mirrlees, S. Adam, T. Besley, R. Blundell, S. Bond, R. Chote, M. Gammie, P. Johnson, G. Myles, and J. Poterba (eds), *Dimensions of Tax Design: The Mirrlees Review*, Oxford: Oxford University Press for the Institute for Fiscal Studies.

Davis, E.H., and J.A. Kay (1985), Extending the VAT Base: Problems and Possibilities, 6 *Fiscal Studies* 1, 1–16.

De la Feria, R. (2007), The EU VAT Treatment of Insurance and Financial Services (Again) under Review, 16 *EC Tax Review* 2, 74–89.

De la Feria, R. (2009), The EU VAT Treatment of Public Sector Bodies: Slowly Moving in the Wrong Direction, 37 *Intertax* 3, 148–65.

De la Feria, R. (2010), Partial-Exemption Policy in the United Kingdom, 21 *International VAT Monitor* 2, 119–23.

De la Feria, R., and R. Krever (2013), Ending VAT Exemptions: Learning from Experience, towards a Post-Modern VAT, chapter 1 in: R. de la Feria (ed.), *VAT Exemptions: Consequences and Design Alternatives*, Alphen aan de Rijn, Netherlands: Wolters Kluwer.

De la Feria, R., and B. Lockwood (2010), Opting for Opting-In? An Evaluation of the European Commission's Proposals for Reforming VAT on Financial Services, 31 *Fiscal Studies* 2, 171–202.

De la Feria, R., and M. Walpole (2009), Options for Taxing Financial Supplies in Value Added Tax: EU VAT and Australian GST Models Compared, 58 *International and Comparative Law Quarterly* 4, 897–932.

De Mooij, R., and M. Keen (2015), 'Fiscal Devaluation' and Fiscal Consolidation: The VAT in Troubled Times, 443–85 in: A. Alesina and F. Giavazzi (eds), *Fiscal Policy after the Financial Crisis*, Chicago, IL: University of Chicago Press.

Diamond, P.A., and J.A. Mirrlees (1971), Optimal Taxation and Public Production I: Production Efficiency, 61 *American Economic Review* 1, 8–27.

Dixon, J. (1991), Option to Tax Financial Services—Part I and Part 2, 2 *VAT Monitor* (July/August and September), 2–8 and 2–9.

Due, J.F. (1990), VAT Treatment of Farmers and Small Firms, 58–69 in: M. Gillis, C.S. Shoup, and G. Sicat (eds), *Value-Added Taxation in Developing Countries*, Washington D.C.: World Bank.

Ebeke, C., M. Mansour, and G. Rota-Graziosi (2016), The Power to Tax in Sub-Saharan Africa: LTUs, VATs, and SARAs, *Working Paper* 154, Clermont-Ferrand, France: Fondation pour les Etudes et Recherches sur le Développement International (FERDI).

Ebrill, L., M. Keen, J-P. Bodin, and V. Summers (2001), *The Modern VAT*, Washington D.C.: International Monetary Fund.

Ebrill, L., J. Stotsky, and R. Gropp (1999), *Revenue Aspects of Trade Liberalization*, Occasional Paper 180, Washington D.C.: International Monetary Fund.

Edgar, T. (2001), Exempt Treatment of Financial Intermediation Services under a Value-Added Tax: An Assessment of Alternatives, 49 *Canadian Tax Journal* 5, 1133–219.

Emran, M.S., and J.E. Stiglitz (2005), On Selective Indirect Tax Reform in Developing Countries, 89 *Journal of Public Economics* 4, 599–623.

Engel, E. (1857), Die Productions- und Consumptionsverhältnisse des Königreichs Sachsen, *Zeitschrift des Statistischen Bureaus des Königlich Sächsischen Ministerium des Inneren* 8–9, 28–9.

Ernst & Young (1996), *Value Added Tax: A Study of Methods of Taxing Financial and Insurance Services*, Taxation Studies 0002, Brussels, Belgium: Directorate General Taxation and Customs Union, European Commission.

Ernst & Young (2017), *Managing Indirect Tax Refunds*, available on the internet.

Ernst & Young (2018), *Worldwide VAT, GST and Sales Tax Guide*, London: Ernst & Young, Global Ltd.

EU's Common VAT Directive (2006), Council Directive 2006/112/EC of 28 Nov. 2006 on the Common System of VAT, OJ L347/1 recasting Sixth Council Directive 77/388/EEC of 12 May 1977 on the Harmonisation of the Laws of the Member States relating to Turnover Taxes—Common System of VAT: Uniform Basis of Assessment, (1977) OJ L145/01.

European Commission (2007a), Proposal for a Council Regulation Laying Down Implementing Measures for Directive 2006/112/EC on the Common System of Value Added Tax, as regards the Treatment of Insurance and Financial Services, COM(2007) 746 final (28 November), Brussels, Belgium.

European Commission (2007b), Proposal for a Council Regulation Amending Directive 2006/112/EC on the Common System of Value Added Tax, as regards the Treatment of Insurance and Financial Services, SEC(2007) 1555 (28 November), Brussels, Belgium.

European Commission (2007c), Draft Regulation: Financial and Insurance Services of Working Party No 1: Harmonisation of Turnover Taxes, TAXUD/2146/07 (13 July), Brussels, Belgium.

European Commission (2008), Financial and Insurance Services, *Background Paper Requested by the Council Presidency*, Directorate General Taxation and Customs Union, TAXUD/2414/08 (March), Brussels, Belgium.

European Commission (2010), *Financial Sector Taxation*, SEC(2010) 1166/3, Brussels, Belgium.

European Commission (2011), *Green Paper on On-Line Gambling in the Internal Market*, SEC(2011) 321 final, Brussels, Belgium.

European Council (1967), Second Council Directive of 11 April 1967 on the Harmonisation of the Legislation of Member States Concerning Turnover Taxes: Structure and Procedure for Application of the Common System of Value Added Tax, 67/228/EEC, Brussels, Belgium.

European Court of Justice (1989), *Carpareto Piacentino and Rivergaro*, Joint Cases C-231/87 and C-129/88, ECR I-3233.

European Court of Justice (1990), *Commune di Carpaneto Piacentino and Others*, Case C-4/89, ECR I-1869.

European Court of Justice (1991), *Ayuntaniento de Sevilla*, Case C-202/90, ECR I-4247.

European Court of Justice (2000), *Commission vs. Greece*, Case C-260/98, ECR I-6537.

European Court of Justice (2004), *GIL Insurance Ltd and Others v Commissioners of Customs & Excise*, Case C-308/01, ECR I-04777.

European Court of Justice (2008), *Isle of Wight and Others*, Case C-288/07, ECR I-7203.

European Court of Justice (2009), *Salix*, Case 102/08, ECR I-4629.

Evans, C. (2008), Taxation Compliance and Administrative Costs: An Overview, 447–68 in: M. Lang, C. Obermaier, J. Schuch, C. Staringer, and P. Weninger (eds), *Tax Compliance Costs for Companies in an Enlarged European Community*, London: Kluwer Law International.

Fenochietto, R., and C. Pessino (2013), Understanding Countries' Tax Effort, *Working Paper* WP/13/244, Washington D.C.: International Monetary Fund.

Forrest, D. (2008), Gambling Policy in the European Union: Too Many Losers? 540–69 in: S. Cnossen and B. Genser (eds), Fiscal Policy in Action, 64 *FinanzArchiv* 4.

Fourie, F.C.V.N., and A. Owen (1993), Value-Added Tax and Regressivity in South Africa, 61 *South African Journal of Economics* 4, 308–19.

Galbraith, J.K. (1984), *The Affluent Society*, 4th edition, New York: Houghton Mifflin Co.

Gale, W.G. (1998), *The Flat Tax: Simple, Fair, Efficient? Or Is It?* Washington D.C.: Brookings Institution.

Gendron, P-P. (2008), VAT Treatment of Financial Services: Assessment and Policy Proposals for Developing Countries, 62 *Bulletin for International Fiscal Documentation* 11, 494–507.

Gendron, P-P. (2013), VAT Treatment of Public Sector Bodies: The Canadian Model, chapter 3 in: R. de la Feria (ed.), *VAT Exemptions: Consequences and Design Alternatives*, Alphen aan de Rijn, Netherlands: Wolters Kluwer.

Gendron, P-P. (2016), Policy Forum: Canada's GST and Financial Services—Where Are We Now and Where Could We Be? 64 *Canadian Tax Journal* 2, 401–16.

Gendron, P-P. (2017), Real VATs vs the Good VAT: Reflections from a Decade of Technical Assistance, 32 *Australian Tax Forum* 2, 257–82.

Gillis, M. (1985), Federal Sales Taxation: A Survey of Six Decades of Experience, Critiques, and Reform Proposals, 33 *Canadian Tax Journal* 1, 68–98.

Glenday, G., and D. Hollinrake (2005), *Assessment of the Current State of VAT Implementation in SADC Member States*, report prepared for the SADC Trade, Industry, Finance and Investment Directorate, Gaborone, Botswana.

Go, D.S., M. Kearney, S. Robinson and K. Thierfelder (2005), An Analysis of South Africa's Value Added Tax, *Policy Research Paper* 3671, Washington D.C.: World Bank.

Godbout, L., and S. St-Cerny (2011), Are Consumption Taxes Regressive in Quebec? 59 *Canadian Tax Journal* 3, 463–93.

Goldman, D. (2017), Loan Intermediary Services: Israel, chapter 9 in: R.E. van Brederode and R. Krever (eds), *VAT and Financial Services: Comparative Law and Economic Perspectives*, Singapore: Springer Nature.

Goretti, M., and H. Weisfeld (2008), Trade in the WAEMU: Developments and Reform Opportunities, *Working Paper* WP/08/68, Washington D.C.: International Monetary Fund.

Grubert, H., and R. Krever (2013), VAT and Financial Services: Competing Perspectives on What Should Be Taxed, chapter 9 in: R. de la Feria (ed.), *VAT Exemptions: Consequences and Design Alternatives*, Alphen aan den Rijn, Netherlands: Wolters Kluwer.

Grubert, H., and J. Mackie (2000), Must Financial Services Be Taxed under a Consumption Tax? 53 *National Tax Journal* 1, 23–40.

Gulde-Wolf, A-M., C. Tsangarides, and J.K. Martijn (2006), Central African Economic and Monetary Community (CEMAC): Selected Issues, *Country Report* 06/309, Washington D.C.: International Monetary Fund.

Hall, R., and A. Rabushka (1985, 1995), *The Flat Tax*, 1st and 2nd editions, Stanford, CA: Hoover Institution Press.

Harrison, G., and R. Krelove (2005), VAT Refunds: A Review of Country Experience, *Working Paper* WP05/218, Washington D.C.: International Monetary Fund.

Hasseldine, J. (2005), Measuring and Reducing Administrative Costs and Tax Compliance Costs, paper presented to Global VAT Conference, Rome.

Hemming, R., and J.A. Kay (1981), The United Kingdom, 70–82 in: H.A. Aaron (ed.), *The Value Added Tax: Lessons from Europe*, Washington D.C.: Brookings Institution.

Henderson, Y.K. (1988), Financial Intermediaries under Value-Added Taxation, *New England Economic Review* (July/August), 37–49.

Henkow, O. (2008), *Financial Activities in European VAT: A Theoretical and Legal Research of the European VAT System and the Actual and Preferred Treatment of Financial Activities*, Deventer, Netherlands: Wolters Kluwer.

Henkow, O. (2013), *The VAT/GST Treatment of Public Bodies*, Deventer, Netherlands: Wolters Kluwer.

Hoffman, L.A., S.N. Poddar, and J. Whalley (1987), Taxation of Banking Services under a Consumption Type, Destination Basis VAT, 40 *National Tax Journal* 3, 547–54.

Holland, G. (1991), Planning for VAT, 17–29 in: A.A. Tait (ed.), *Value-Added Tax: Administrative and Policy Issues*, Occasional Paper 88, Washington D.C.: International Monetary Fund.

Huizinga, H. (2002), A European VAT on Financial Services? 17 *Economic Policy* 35, 497–534.

IHS (2010), The Effect of VAT on Price-Setting Behaviour, in: Institute for Fiscal Studies, CPB, CAPP, CASE, CEPII, ETLA, IFO, and IHS, *A Retrospective Evaluation of Elements of the EU VAT System*, report prepared for the European Commission, TAXUD/2010/DE/328.

Inchauste, G., N. Lustig, M. Maboshe, C. Purfield, and I. Woolard (2015), The Distributional Impact of Fiscal Policy in South Africa, *Commitment to Equity (CEQ) Working Paper* 29, New Orleans, LA: Tulane University.

Institute for Fiscal Studies (1991), *Equity for Companies: A Corporation Tax for the* 1990s, IFS Commentary 26, London.

Institute for Fiscal Studies (2011), Quantitative Analysis of VAT Rate Structures, in: Institute for Fiscal Studies, CPB, CAPP, CASE, CEPII, ETLA, IFO, and IHS, *A Retrospective Evaluation of Elements of the EU VAT System*, report prepared for the European Commission, TAXUD/2010/DE/328.

International Bureau of Fiscal Documentation (2018), Corporate Taxation—Country Surveys—8, Value Added Tax, available on the internet.

International Monetary Fund (2005), Uganda: Fifth Review under the Three-Year Arrangement under the Poverty Reduction and Growth Facility—Request for Waiver of Performance Criterion and Extension of Arrangement, *Country Report* 05/306, Washington D.C.

International Monetary Fund (2010), *Financial Sector Taxation: The IMF's Report to the G-20*, edited by S. Claessens, M. Keen, and C. Pazarbasioglu, Washington D.C..

International Monetary Fund (2015), South Africa Technical Assistance Report—Revenue Administration GAP Analysis Program—*The Value-Added Tax GAP*, Washington D.C.

International Monetary Fund (2017), Blog, 5 December: *Taxes, Debt and Development: A One-Percent Rule to Raise Revenues in Africa* by V. Gaspar and A.A. Selassie.

Ishi, H. (2001), *The Japanese Tax System*, 3rd edition, Oxford: Oxford University Press.

Jack, W. (2000), The Treatment of Financial Services under a Broad-Based Consumption Tax, 53 *National Tax Journal* 4, 841–51.

James, K. (2015), *The Rise of the Value-Added Tax*, Cambridge: Cambridge University Press.

Jenkins, G.P., and R. Khadka (1998), Value Added Tax Policy and Implementation in Singapore, 9 *International VAT Monitor* 2, 35–47.

Jenkins, G.P., C-Y. Kuo, and K-N. Sun (2003), *Taxation and Economic Development in Taiwan*, Cambridge, MA: John F. Kennedy School of Government.

Katz Commission (1994), *Interim Report* of the Commission of Inquiry into Certain Aspects of the Tax Structure of South Africa, Pretoria, South Africa: Government Printer.

Kaufmann, D., A. Kraay, and M. Mastruzzi (2010), *The Worldwide Governance Indicators: Methodology and Analytical Issues*, Washington D.C.: Brookings Institution.

Kay, J.A., and E.H. Davis (1990), The VAT and Services, 70–82 in: M. Gillis, C.S. Shoup, and G.P. Sicat (eds), *Value Added Taxation in Developing Countries*, Washington D.C.: World Bank.

Keen, M. (2000), VIVAT, CVAT and All That: New Forms of Value-Added Tax for Federal Systems, 48 *Canadian Tax Journal* 2, 409–24.

Keen, M. (2008), VAT, Tariffs and Withholding: Border Taxes and Informality in Developing Countries, 92 *Journal of Public Economics* 10–11, 1892–906.

Keen, M. (2009), What Do (and Don't) We Know about the Value Added Tax? A Review of Richard M. Bird and Pierre-Pascal Gendron's The VAT in Developing and Transitional Countries, 47 *Journal of Economic Literature* 1, 159–70.

Keen, M. (2013), The Anatomy of the VAT, 66 *National Tax Journal* 2, 423–46.

Keen, M., R. Krelove, and J. Norregaard (2016), Policy Forum: The Financial Activities Tax, 64 *Canadian Tax Journal* 2, 389–400.

Keen, M., and J.E. Ligthart (2001), Coordinating Tariff Reductions and Domestic Tax Reform, 56 *Journal of International Economics* 2, 407–25.

Keen, M., and J.E. Ligthart (2005), Coordinating Tariff Reduction and Domestic Tax Reform under Imperfect Competition, 13 *Review of International Economics* 2, 385–90.

Keen, M., and M. Mansour (2010), Revenue Mobilisation in Sub-Saharan Africa: Challenges from Globalisation I—Trade Reform, 28 *Development Policy Review* 5, 553–71.

Keen, M., and Mintz, J. (2004), The Optimal Threshold for a Value-Added Tax, 88 *Journal of Public Economics* 3–4, 559–76.

Keen, M., and S. Smith (1996), The Future of Value Added Tax in the European Union, 11 *Economic Policy* 23, 375–411 and 419–20.

Keen, M., and S. Smith (2000), Viva VIVAT, 7 *International Tax and Public Finance* 6, 741–51.

Keen, M., and S. Smith (2006), VAT Fraud and Evasion: What Do We Know and What Can Be Done? 59 *National Tax Journal* 4, 861–87.

Kenyon, D.A. (1996), A New State VAT? Lessons from New Hampshire, 49 *National Tax Journal* 3, 381–99.

Kerrigan, A. (2010), The Elusiveness of Neutrality—Why Is It So Difficult to Apply VAT to Financial Services? 21 *International VAT Monitor* 2, 103–12.

Khandewal, R. (2004), COMESA and SADC: Prospects and Challenges for Regional Trade Integration, *Working Paper* WP/04/227, Washington D.C.: International Monetary Fund.

Kloeden, D. (2011), Revenue Administration Reforms in Anglophone Africa since the Early 1990s, *Working Paper* WP/11/162, Washington D.C.: International Monetary Fund.

Kosonen, T. (2015), More and Cheaper Haircuts after VAT Cut? On the Efficiency and Incidence of Service Sector Consumption Taxes, 131 *Journal of Public Economics*, 87–100.

Krever, R. (2008a), Designing and Drafting VAT Laws for Africa, 19–28 in: R. Krever (ed.), *VAT in Africa*, Pretoria, South Africa: Pretoria University Law Press.

Krever, R. (ed.) (2008b), *VAT in Africa*, Pretoria, South Africa: Pretoria University Law Press.

Lauré, M. (1953), *La Taxe à la Valeur Adjoutée*, 2nd edition, Paris, France: Librairie du Receuil Sirey.

Lauré, M. (1957), *Au Secours de la TVA*, Paris, France: Presses Universitaires de France.

Le Borgne, L., and K. Baer (2008), Tax Amnesties: Theory, Trends and Some Alternatives, *Special Studies*, Washington D.C.: International Monetary Fund.

Liu, L., and B. Lockwood (2015), VAT Notches, *Working Paper* WP15/06, Oxford: Oxford University Centre for Business Taxation.

Lockwood, B., D. de Meza, and G. Myles (1994), When Are Origin and Destination Regimes Equivalent? 1 *International Tax and Public Finance* 1, 5–24.

López-Laborda, J., and G. Peña (2018), A New Method for Applying VAT to Financial Services, 71 *National Tax Journal* 1, 155–82.

Lustig, N. (2017), Fiscal Policy, Inequality, and the Poor in the Developing World, *WIDER Working Paper* 2016/164, revised version August 2017, Helsinki, Finland: United Nations University World Institute for Development Economics Research (UNU-WIDER).

Mansour, M. (2015), Tax Policy in MENA Countries: Looking Back and Forward, *Working Paper* WP/15/98, Washington D.C.: International Monetary Fund.

Mansour, M., and G. Rota-Graziosi (2013), Tax Coordination, Tax Competition, and Revenue Mobilization in the West African Economic and Monetary Union, *Working Paper* WP/13/163, Washington D.C.: International Monetary Fund.

Martinez-Vazquez, J., and R.M. Bird (2011), Value-Added Tax: Onward and Upward? chapter 6 in: E. Albi and J. Martinez-Vazquez (eds), *The Elgar Guide to Tax Systems*, Cheltenham: Edward Elgar.

McLure, C.E., Jr (1989), Alternative Tax Policies for the Future in Light of the Current Economic and Budget Outlook, 4 *Journal of Accounting, Auditing and Finance* 3, 388–96.

McLure, C.E., Jr (1990), Income Distribution and Tax Incidence under the VAT, chapter 3 in: M. Gillis, C.S. Shoup, and G.P. Sicat (eds), *Value-Added Taxation in Developing Countries*, Washington D.C.: World Bank.

McLure, C.E., Jr (2000), Implementing Subnational VATs on Internal Trade: The Compensating VAT (CVAT), 7 *International Tax and Public Finance* 6, 723–40.

McLure, C.E., Jr, and M.A. Bloomfield (1987), *The Value-Added Tax: Key to Deficit Reduction?* Washington D.C.: American Enterprise Institute.

Meade, J.E. (1978), *The Structure and Reform of Direct Taxation*, London: Allen & Unwin for the Institute for Fiscal Studies.

Medina, L., A. Jonelis, and M. Cangul (2017), The Informal Economy in Sub-Saharan Africa: Size and Determinants, *Working Paper* WP/17/156, Washington D.C.: International Monetary Fund.

Millar, R. (2010), VAT Treatment of Immovable Property Revisited, chapter 9 in: R. de la Feria (ed.), *VAT Exemptions: Consequences and Design Alternatives*, Alphen aan de Rijn, Netherlands: Wolters Kluwer.

Mugoya, P.K.D. (1998), Equity and VAT in Tanzania, 7 *African Journal of Finance and Management* 1, 22–32.

Muñoz, S., and S.S. Cho (2003), Social Impact of a Tax Reform: The Case of Ethiopia, *Working Paper* WP03/232, Washington D.C.: International Monetary Fund.

Musgrave, R.A. (1969), *Fiscal Systems*, New Haven, CT: Yale University Press.

Nathoeni, S., and T. Braakman (2010), Option for Taxation of Financial Services—Is It an Option? 21 *International VAT Monitor* 2, 113–20.

National Lotteries Commission (undated), Lotteries and the Law, available on the internet.

National Treasury (2011), *The VAT Treatment of Merit Goods and Services*, Document T16/05, Pretoria, South Africa.

Organization for Economic Cooperation and Development (1988), *Taxing Consumption*, Paris, France: OECD Publishing.

Organization for Economic Cooperation and Development (2012), *Consumption Tax Trends* 2011: *VAT/GST and Excise Rates, Trends and Administration Issues*, Paris, France: OECD Publishing.

Organization for Economic Cooperation and Development (2014), *The Distributional Effects of Consumption Taxes in OECD Countries*, Paris, France: OECD Publishing.

Organization for Economic Cooperation and Development (2015), *Taxing Consumption* 2014, Paris, France: OECD Publishing.

Organization for Economic Cooperation and Development (2017), *International VAT/GST Guidelines*, Paris, France: OECD Publishing.

Organization for Economic Cooperation and Development/Korea Institute of Public Finance (2014), The Distributional Effects of Consumption Taxes in OECD Countries, *OECD Tax Policy Studies* 22, Paris, France: OECD Publishing.

Pallot, M. (2011), Financial Services under New Zealand's GST, 22 *International VAT Monitor* 5, 310–15.

Poddar, S. (2003), Consumption Taxes: The Role of the Value-Added Tax, 345–80 in: P. Honohan (ed.), *Taxation of Financial Intermediation: Theory and Practice for Emerging Economies*, New York: Oxford University Press for the World Bank.

Poddar, S. (2010), Taxation of Housing under a VAT, 63 *Tax Law Review* 2, 443–70.

Poddar, S., and M. English (1997), Taxation of Financial Services under a Value-Added Tax: Applying the Cash Flow Approach, 50 *National Tax Journal* 1, 89–111.

Poddar, S., and J. Kalita (2010), Treatment of Financial Services under a UAE VAT, Ernst & Young.

Pohmer, D. (1983), Allgemeine Umsatzsteuer, part 4 in: N. Andel and J. Haller (eds), *Handbuch der Finanzwissenschaft*, Band II, Tübingen, Germany: Mohr.

Pommeranz, D. (2015), No Taxation without Information: Deterrence and Self-Enforcement in the Value Added Tax, 105 *American Economic Review* 8, 2539–69.

Pons, T. (2006), Option for Taxation of Financial Services in France, 17 *International VAT Monitor* 5, 182–5.

PricewaterhouseCoopers (2006), *Final Report for the European Commission*, TAXUD/2005/AO-006, Brussels, Belgium: European Commission.

PricewaterhouseCoopers (2015), *Taking the Odds*, Gambling Outlook: 2015–2019, South Africa—Nigeria—Kenya, 4th annual edition.

Rasmusen, E. (1991), *Games and Information*, Oxford: Blackwell.

Rodrik, D. (2014), An African Growth Miracle? *Working Paper* 20188, National Bureau of Economic Research (NBER).

Sahn, D.E., and S.D. Younger (1999), Dominance Testing of Social Sector Expenditures and Taxes in Africa, *Working Paper* WP/99/172, Washington D.C.: International Monetary Fund.

Sandford, C., M. Godwin, and P. Hardwick (1989), *Administrative and Compliance Costs of Taxation*, Bath: Fiscal Publications.

Sandford, C., M. Godwin, P. Hardwick, and I. Butterworth (1981), *Costs and Benefits of VAT*, London: Heinemann Educational Books.

Schatan, R. (2003), VAT on Banking Services: Mexico's Experience, 14 *International VAT Monitor* 4, 287–94.

Schenk, A. (2010), Gambling and Lotteries, 47–70 in: R. Krever (ed.), *VAT in Africa*, Pretoria, South Africa: Pretoria University Law Press (PULP).

Schenk, A., V. Thuronyi, and W. Cui (2015), *Value Added Tax: A Comparative Approach*, 2nd edition, Cambridge Tax Law Series, Cambridge: Cambridge University Press.

Schenk, A., and H.H. Zee (2004), Financial Services and the Value-Added Tax, 60–74 in: H.H. Zee (ed.), *Taxing the Financial Sector: Concepts, Issues, and Practices*, Washington D.C.: International Monetary Fund.

Schiff, M., and L.A. Winters (2003), *Regional Integration and Development*, Washington D.C.: World Bank and Oxford University Press.

Schneider, F. and R. Klinglmair (2004), Shadow Economies around the World: What Do We Know? *IZA Discussion Paper* 1043, Bonn, Germany.

Seidman, L.S. (1997), *The USA Tax: A Progressive Consumption Tax*, Cambridge, MA: MIT Press.

Shoup, C.S. (1990), Choosing among Types of VATs, 3–16 in: M. Gillis, C.S. Shoup, and G.P. Sicat (eds), *Value Added Taxation in Developing Countries*, Washington D.C.: World Bank.

Siemens, W. von (1920), *Veredelte Umsatzsteuer*, Siemensstadt, Germany.

Silvani, C., and C.L. Vehorn (1991), Invoices, Books of Account, and Tax Return Forms for VAT, chapter IV in: A.A. Tait (ed.), *Value-Added Tax: Administrative and Policy Issues*, Occasional Paper 88, Washington D.C.: International Monetary Fund.

Slemrod, J. (1997), Deconstructing the Income Tax, 87 *AEA Papers and Proceedings* 2, 151–5.

South African Revenue Service (SARS) (2012), Interpretation Note: No. 84 on the Value-Added Tax, Treatment of Bets, available on the internet.

South African Revenue Service (SARS) (2013), VAT 421: *Value-Added Tax, Guide for Short-Term Insurance*, available on the internet.

South African Revenue Service (SARS) (2014), Interpretation Note: No. 41 (issue 3) of 31 March, available on the internet.

South African Revenue Service (SARS) (2017), Government, available on the internet.

Southern African Development Community (SADC) (2016a), *Guidelines for Co-operation in Value Added Taxes in the SADC Region*, available on the internet.

Southern African Development Community (SADC) (2016b), *Guidelines for Co-operation in Excise Taxes in the SADC Region*, available on the internet.

Sullivan, C.K. (1965), *Tax on Value Added*, New York: Columbia University Press.
Summers, V.P., and E.M. Sunley (1995), An Analysis of Value Added Taxes in Russia and Other Countries of the Former Soviet Union, 10 *Tax Notes International* 2, 117–19.
Sundelson, J.W. (1950), Report on Japanese Taxation by the Shoup Mission, 3 *National Tax Journal* 2, 104–20.
Swiss Institute of Comparative Law (2006), *Study of Gambling Services in the Internal Market of the European Union: Final Report*, Lausanne, Switzerland.
Tait, A.A. (1988), *Value Added Tax: International Practice and Problems*, Washington D.C.: International Monetary Fund.
Tait, A.A. (ed.) (1991), *Value-Added Tax: Administrative and Policy Issues*, Occasional Paper 88, Washington D.C.: International Monetary Fund.
Terkper, S.E. (1996), VAT in Ghana: Why It Failed, 11 *Tax Notes International* 23, 1801–16.
Terkper, S.E. (2000), Ghana Reintroduces VAT—Lessons Learned and Progress after a Year, 20 *Tax Notes International* 11, 1253–68.
Terra, B., and J. Kajus (2007), *Introduction to European VAT* 2007, A Guide to the European VAT Directives, vol. 1, Amsterdam, Netherlands: International Bureau for Fiscal Documentation.
Terra, B., and J. Kajus (2015), *Commentary—A Guide to the Recast VAT Directive*, Deventer, Netherlands: Kluwer Publishers.
Thuronyi, V. (1996), Presumptive Taxation, chapter 12 in: V. Thuronyi (ed.), *Tax Law Design and Drafting*, Washington D.C.: International Monetary Fund.
Ueda, J. (2017), The Evolution of Potential VAT Revenues and C-Efficiency in Advanced Economies, *Working Paper* WP/17/158, Washington D.C.: International Monetary Fund.
United Nations Development Programme (2017), *Taxes on Pesticides and Chemical Fertilizers*, available on the internet.
US Congressional Budget Office (1992), *Effects of Adopting a Value-Added Tax*, Washington D.C.
US Department of State (2002), West African Economic and Monetary Union (WAEMU), Fact Sheet, Bureau of African Affairs, 18 November, Washington D.C.
US Department of the Treasury (1977), *Blueprints for Basic Tax Reform*, Washington D.C.: Government Printing Office.
Vaillancourt, F., and R. Ossa (2011), The Taxation of Gambling in Africa, *Working Paper* 11-10, Atlanta, GA: Georgia State University, Andrew Young School of Policy Studies.
Van Brederode, R.F. (ed.) (2010), *Immovable Property under VAT: A Comparative Global Analysis*, Series in International Taxation, Deventer, Netherlands: Wolters Kluwer.
Van Oordt, M. (2016), *A Quantitative Measurement of Policy Options to Inform Value-Added Tax Reform in South Africa*, doctoral thesis, Pretoria, South Africa: University of Pretoria.
Vermeulen, R., G. Schellmann, and C. Amand (2005), Immovable Property and VAT—Lessons from Past Experience, 16 *International VAT Monitor* 5, 325–38.
Waerzeggers, C. (2007), Value Added Tax in Francophone Africa: Design Features and Considerations, 217–45 in: R. Krever (ed.), *VAT in Africa*, Pretoria, South Africa: Pretoria University Law Press (PULP).
Warren, N. (2008), A Review of Studies on the Distributional Impact of Consumption Taxes in OECD Countries, *OECD Social, Employment and Migration Working Paper* 64, Paris, France: OECD Publishing.
Wassenaar, M.C., and R.H.J.M. Gradus (2004), Contracting Out: The Importance of a Solution to the VAT Distortion, 50 *CESifo Economic Studies* 2, 377–96.
Williams, D. (1996), Value-Added Tax, chapter 6 in: V. Thuronyi (ed.), *Tax Law Design and Drafting*, Washington D.C.: International Monetary Fund.

Williams, D., and B. Guthleben (1990), Problems with the Present Wholesale Consumption Tax, 7 *Australian Tax Forum* 4, 465–503.

World Bank (2012), *Defragmenting Africa: Deepening Regional Trade Integration in Goods and Services*, Washington D.C.

World Bank (2016), 2016 *World Development Indicators*, Washington D.C.

World Bank (2017a), *Doing Business: Economy Rankings*, Washington D.C.

World Bank (2017b), *Worldwide Governance Indicators*, 2017 Update, Washington D.C.

World Health Organization (undated), Tobacco Free Initiative: Poverty, available on the internet.

Yang, Y., and S. Gupta (2005), Regional Trade Arrangements in Africa: Past Performance and the Way Forward, *Working Paper* WP/05/36, Washington D.C.: International Monetary Fund.

Younger, S.D., D.E. Sahn, S. Haggblade, and P.A. Dorosh (1999), An Analysis Using Household Data, 13 *World Bank Economic Review* 2, 303–31.

Zee, H.H. (2005a), Simple Analytics of Setting the Optimal VAT Exemption Threshold, 153 *De Economist* 4, 464–71.

Zee, H.H. (2005b), A New Approach to Taxing Financial Intermediation Services under a Value-Added Tax, 58 *National Tax Journal* 1, 77–92.

Index

Note: Tables, boxes, and figures are indicated by an italic *t*, *b*, and *f*, respectively, following the page number.

The manufacturer's authorised representative in the EU for product safety is Oxford University Press España S.A. of el Parque Empresarial San Fernando de Henares, Avenida de Castilla, 2 – 28830 Madrid (www.oup.es/en or product.safety@oup.com). OUP España S.A. also acts as importer into Spain of products made by the manufacturer.

www.ingramcontent.com/pod-product-compliance
Lightning Source LLC
LaVergne TN
LVHW020925031026
849429LV00003B/19

* 9 7 8 0 1 9 8 8 4 4 0 7 5 *